Distinguished Discord

Distinguished Discord

Discontinuity and Pattern
in the Critical Tradition of
The Turn of the Screw

Robin P. Hoople

Lewisburg
Bucknell University Press
London: Associated University Presses

Associated University Presses
440 Forsgate Drive
Cranbury, NJ 08512

Associated University Presses
16 Barter Street
London WC1A 2AH, England

Associated University Presses
P.O. Box 338, Port Credit
Mississauga, Ontario
Canada L5G 4L8

The paper used in this publication meets the requirements of the American National Standard for Permanence of Paper for Printed Library Materials Z39.48–1984.

Library of Congress Cataloging-in-Publication Data

Hoople, Robin P., 1930–
    Distinguished discord : discontinuity and pattern in the critical tradition of The turn of the screw / Robin P. Hoople.
        p.   cm.
    Includes bibliographical references (p.) and index.
    ISBN 0-8387-5326-4 (alk. paper)
    1. James, Henry, 1843–1916. Turn of the screw. 2. James, Henry, 1843–1916—Criticism and interpretation—History. 3. Ghost stories, American—History and criticism—Theory, etc. 4. Criticism—United States—History—20th century. 5. Governesses in literature. 6. Children in literature. I. Title.
PS2116.T83H66 1996
813'.4—dc20   96-34807
                                                                                  CIP

PRINTED IN THE UNITED STATES OF AMERICA

for my children

Carolyn, Suzanne, Ross
Jill, Felicity, Christopher

Just in proportion as he reacts and reciprocates and penetrates, is the critic a valuable instrument.

—Henry James

In general effect, moreover, Sainte-Beuve's work is itself markedly synthetic. What a complete picture it presents, at the same time continually illustrating the truth that the wiser business of criticism is to occupy itself with examples and the ideas they evoke, not with theories and systems they threaten!

—W. C. Brownell

We swing from general to particular and back again, each swing making the interpretive hypothesis more complex and more inclusive. Evidently, such a procedure is not uncontrolled, and is not mere judgment without some sort of objective check, for it is the same procedure of the most 'objective' sciences. But neither does it produce absolute certainty or dispense with the need for imagination, guesswork, and hunches.

—John M. Ellis

Contents

Acknowledgments

I am happy to have so many to thank for help with this book. The University of Manitoba awarded me a grant in 1988 to begin this project. the Social Sciences and Humanities Research Council of Canada awarded me a grant from 1989 to 1990 to continue the work. That grant included the services of a graduate student assistance, Peter Wilman, who assisted me with the technical aspects of computers when I was new to their use; Peter was nimble at hunting down elusive materials. Several of my colleagues read portions of the manuscript and offered suggestions. James Keller, Edward Dyck and Joseph Donatelli gave me valuable advice and insight and sometimes offered useful challenges to my ideas. Judith Weil helped me weed out some extravagances.

The staffs of several libraries assisted me: those of The New York Public Library; The Bobst Library of New York University; the Boston Public Library. My principal debt is to the staffs of the Harvard University Library system; and to my home Library at The University of Manitoba. At Hard, I was one of the early users of a computer in the stacks. Charles Montalbano, chief of stacks at the Widener library helped to smooth the way for this was not always an easy innovation. Mary Smith and Marion Schoon in Reference at the Widener helped me to find a number of obscure words. Barbara Bennell of the Interlibrary Loan Desk at the University of Manitoba was indefatigable in her search for hard-to-find items. The support staff of the Department of English at the University of Manitoba helped materially. Ann King and Erica Walker helped with interpretations of the Reference Manuals of the computer systems that I was using. Lucia Flynn helped with formatting, printing, the arcana of computer use and other technical matters. Michael Koy, Managing Editor; Evelyn Apgar, Production Editor; and Julien Yoseloff, Director of Associated University Presses, shepherded the manuscript through the stages of production.

Friends and family assisted me in many ways, some intangible and some quite practical. My daughter Suzanne Bonnell showed me how to make my computer operate when it was dismayingly new. My brother and sister-in-law, Donald and Sally Hoople visited, encouraged, discussed, sent clippings. My friend Janice Thalin gave me a "first reading" of *The Turn of the Screw* when I needed to confirm my sense that first readings usually returned a verdict in favor of the governess. Fred and Jane Fiumara provided a serene environment. Others of my children helped with moral support and believe in the project.

The Henry James/W. C. Brownell correspondence 1901–1908 comes from the Archives of Charles Scribner's Sons, Box 81, Subfolder 3, passim, Manuscripts Division, Department of Rare Books and Special Collections, Princeton University Libraries. Published with permission of the Princeton University Libraries.

The Demuth paintings are published with the permission of the Philadelphia Museum of Art:

'66-68-8   Demuth, Charles

    ◆ Miles and the Governess, 1918, from "The Turn of the Screw"
Philadelphia Museum of Art: Given by Frank and Alice Osborn

'66-68-9   Demuth, Charles

    ◆ The Governess First Sees the Ghost of Peter Quint
Philadelphia Museum of Art: Given by Frank and Alice Osborn

'66-68-10   Demuth, Charles

    ◆ The Governess, Mrs. Grose and Children
Philadelphia Museum of Art: Given by Frank and Alice Osborn

'66-68-11   Demuth, Charles

    ◆ Flora and the Governess
Philadelphia Museum of Art: Given by Frank and Alice Osborn

List of Abbreviations

k   Robert Kimbrough, Norton Critical Edition of
       The Turn of the Screw (1966).
w   Gerald Willen, *A Casebook on **The Turn of the
       Screw*** (1960).
an   *The Art of the Novel*, the collected prefaces to
       the New York Edition of James's works,
       ed. R. P. Blackmur, 1934.
SPR   Society for Psychic Research.
PSPR   Publications of the Society for Psychic Research

Distinguished Discord

Introduction

A PROBLEM TEXT

The Turn of the Screw has generated a very special critical tradition, unlikely to be duplicated by that of any other single work, and filled with idiosyncrasies. It has provoked readings from many able minds, and it has enticed readers to try by critical coup to attach the novella to their sides, as James himself might say, like a deer park to a mansion house. More than one critic risked losing any claim to critical dispassion in the heat of the ensuing quarrels. James seems to have written so that the mere attempt to explicate automatically promotes the clash of arms. The desire to answer all the questions, clear up all the mysteries, silence all the oppositions, explicate the tale definitively has proved an irresistible temptation to a multitude of critics. The eccentric critical tradition makes *Screw* unique, and in spite of sharing the spotlight with a number of other noted problem tales—Conrad's *Heart of Darkness*, for example, or James's own tale "The Figure in the Carpet"—its criticism develops along lines applicable mainly to itself. James complicates the reading of the tale by inviting the reader, in his New York preface (1908), to regard it as a trap. Edna Kenton exploits James's invitation and provokes an outburst of controversy with her article "James to the Ruminant Reader" (1924), which claims to prove that James's trap springs because the governess in the tale has hallucinated the ghosts. Edmund Wilson in his "Ambiguity" (1934) avails himself of Kenton's argument, taking her idea to its Freudian limit. But even as these curiosities create an eccentric pattern, the *Screw*'s critical tradition shows that the elucidation of the text evolves over time. And however eccentric, its critical tradition uncovers accidents that might affect the critical tradition of any work.

The Turn of the Screw has been used as a locus text to condemn the very exercise of criticism.[1] While there is evidence of slackness in the practice of some—even many—critics over the ninety-odd years of the tale's existence, the advances in insight have been startling, since we know more about the inner workings of the tale than did its first readers. We know more about the implications of the psychology of its characters than did the first readers to alight on the idea of the governess's hysteria. Its later critics have taken the tale more seriously than did its first readers and have lavished greater care on the explication of its details. On the other hand, the tale's first readers— whose responses we must infer largely from the journalists who reviewed the tale when it first appeared—often observed striking things. It is a vagary of the process of critical accumulation that the reviews form only a slight part of the acknowledged common body of critical insight into the tale. The submergence of this initial reading is by itself a sufficient ground for reappraising the critical tradition and reassessing the value of its development. If we are to assert that there have been advances in our understanding of the tale since the first stages of critical response, we need to know quite exactly what the first public readers knew. We need to ally this knowledge to later events. One such event is James's invitation to consider the tale as a trap. Another such event is the critical clash over the character of the governess, beginning a quarter of a century after the reviews. Thus, in the early stages, at least three important distorting or distending movements shape the asymmetry of the composite reading of *The Turn of the Screw*: the neglected first readings; James's invitation to reconsider the basis of the story; the sudden explosion of controversy over the tale's meaning, which exploited James's invitation.

Questions about the nature of criticism tend to evoke questions about the relation of the reader to the critic. James tells us in his prefaces that the reader's job of work is to assist in the creation of the artifact. Wolfgang Iser, the reader-response theorist, echoes James in declaring that the reader's task is to fill in the blanks left by the text. Iser's abstract "reader" sets out in quest of aesthetic experience and may find an infinite number of blanks in the text; but the critic in search of elucidation is likely to be concerned with the blanks that preceding criticism has failed to account for, or with reassessing problems of meaning through recombining the blanks already illuminated. In part, the controversy over the character of the governess reflects Kenton's contention that prior critics had failed to note that the governess is the only character in the text ever reported as seeing the ghosts. The resulting extended battle over the governess's psychology between the advocates of hysteria and the advocates of monsters—hallucinationists and apparitionists—featured charges of defective New Critical close reading by each armed camp against the other. Meanwhile, though more and more textual blanks yielded to exposition, others remained as uncharted as they had been for the earliest readers in 1898. The first careful exposition of the role of Douglas, the intermediate narrator of the frame tale, came only in 1959, when the tale was over sixty years in print (Jones 1959). The significance of the fireplace setting in the frame tale received adequate primary exposition only in 1977 (Felman 1977), or over three-quarters of a century into the development of the critical tradition. The pivotal importance of the external narrator, who claims ownership of the title in the frame tale (and thus claims to have written at least "The Turn of the Screw") still awaits definitive exposition some ninety-five years after first publication of the tale.

Any study that includes consideration of a great majority of the published statements in criticism about the work since its first appearance—or even those statements falling within some definable period of study within the larger history—might well provide the groundwork for answering questions about the relation of criticism at one stage of its development to another. For example, the Freudian dimension of the earlier critical development of *The Turn of the Screw* made a great deal of noise in its time; but its critical triumph of the moment lost caste even with those sympathetic to its Freudian basis because of later critical reassessments and advances in critical theory. Mark Spilka, for example, chided Wilson for not being Freudian enough (1963); and Shoshana Felman, noting Spilka's objection, declares that Wilson's reading answers neither *for* James's text nor *through* Freud's (1977). But we may ask whether Spilka and Felman have advanced critical insight beyond Wilson or whether they have merely adjusted the language of criticism to their own times and styles, as Roland Barthes describes the progress of criticism (1976, 258 original publication 1963).[2] The problem for the study of the critical tradition of a work is to distinguish between mere casual changes in critical method or its vocabulary on the one hand—changes that make no difference to the substance of the collective reading of the tale—and the development of important critical insights that give solid evidence of an advance of knowledge on the other. Readers have been looking closely at *The Turn of the Screw* for nearly a century without being able to resolve its critical issues into a consensus on meaning or on the status of its various narrators. On this finding, the inquiry into the tale's critical tradition might be expected to confirm the tenets of critical theory that challenge absolute meaning or the absolute critical hegemony of a particular authority. The challenge arises because experience shows that the text refuses to yield unassailable, absolute meaning even to fanatically close readers, as one discovers on looking at the prototype of close reading in the *Screw* tradition, Cranfill and Clark's *Anatomy of The Turn of the Screw* (1965a).

The very asymmetry of this critical development tends to confuse the relation between its earlier and later stages. But there can be no doubt that, at least to some extent, there is a cultural lag in the development. Critical interest in character, or in the idea of personality that accompanies Hypolite Taine's focus on time, place, and milieu, prevailed in popular criticism and reviewing when *Screw* was first published; it tended to emphasize the character of the governess, especially in her conventional role of destitute gentlewoman, and to deflect critical interest from matters like formal narrative structure. On the other hand, the sudden urgent ripening of psychoanalytic criticism a generation later focused critical attention on the depth psychology of a fictional character who confesses an association with ghosts, especially when the ghosts savor of illicit sexual practices. The development in the last thirty years of theoretical interest in narrative inevitably propels discussion toward the story and discourse of the tale. This interest supports inquiry about the linguistic means used by the author to create parallels among the tale's narrative levels, with the title phrase being the most persistent and ineluctable of the signs of those parallels. That is, the subject involving the elements of the turned screw occurs in the title, in the frame tale, and in the governess's narrative. Admittedly some of the differences in critical emphasis are simply matters of prevailing cultural preoccupations. Yet there are important textual blanks in the tale whose exposition depends on these shifts in critical emphasis to make them a convincing part of the collective elucidation of the tale. The critical and cultural lag in the development of the criticism are the essence of the asymmetry of the critical tradition of this tale and focus one area in which the eccentric *Screw* tradition reflects the sort of accident that could happen in the critical tradition of any work.

It was James himself who first signaled the problem of blanks in his tale. In his preface (1908) he declared quite categorically, "my values are positively all blanks." The context features James's declaration that "from beginning to end of the matter [there is] not one inch of expatiation" (k 123, preface). He qualifies by explaining that his technique invites the reader to "read into them [his blanks] more or less fantastic figures" (k 123). In the preface he plumes himself, by the time of writing, on his success in inducing audiences to read fantasticalities into the tale. In what I have said above, I have emphasized the process of elucidation of the story and discourse of *The Turn of the Screw*. But the specialness of its critical tradition reflects in various ways the problem of the indeterminacy, the insolubility of some of its systems. I have leaned toward the suggestion that time and critical ingenuity will ultimately "solve" the mysteries of the tale. But that is not necessarily so. It is sometimes the imperfections of a work, the things that cannot be solved, that make it enduring. To the extent that literature entertains the mysteries of existence and offers alternative ways of wrestling with them, it proposes to illuminate our struggles rather than to explain their causes. There is no critical resolution for the grim figure of Oedipus leaning on the arm of his daughter and feeling his blind way down the road to Colonus. If he has outraged the gods, it is at least possible to say of him that his greatest sin was to forge ahead on imperfect knowledge. He doesn't say, but we might be tempted to say for him, that he has been more sinned against than sinning. In any case, we must be prepared to settle for the image without expecting any neat moral for the story. In *The Turn of the Screw* the undetermined matters weave in and out of the relationship between the governess and the ghosts, and provoke questions about which party gives sovereignty to the other, a confusion of dreams like that between Alice and the Red King. To learn more about the tale and its implications than we knew before by reading the developing criticism is not automatically to know everything nor to solve every elusive cause. The text still maintains its hold on some of its blanks.

Perhaps it is this defect of criticism, if it is a defect, that gives force to Wolfgang Iser's decided opposition to practical criticism. Recurrently in his studies of the aesthetics of reader-response he tells his reader that "if texts actually possessed only the meaning brought to light by interpretation, then there would remain very little else for the reader" (1971, 6; 1989, 3). I decline to think that practical critics, at least at their best, declare that the only meaning of a work is that brought to light by interpretation. As I have suggested above, the "reader" and the "critic" have somewhat different goals in the reading process, the reader to find delight in the experience of the work and the critic to find light in the explication of the work. Though the one goal does not exclude the other in either case, the two goals are substantially different from each other in what they are designed to achieve. It is perilous to the literary soul, however, if the figure designated as "the critic" never occupies the role of the "reader"—never enjoys the pleasure of naive experience in the act of reading. This naive experience of reading is the place where the creation of response begins. And in this area of study, Iser and other reader-response specialists make important contributions to the theory of reading.

For Iser himself, the reader is an autonomous meaning-maker, seen by tendency, as a naive reader, that is, as engaging in an act of direct creation of the text by filling in the textual blanks through acts of the imagination. He says that the process of reading attempts to create a balance between the self and the other, between that which is knowable and that which can at best only be inferred: "Balance can be attained only if the gaps are filled, and so the constitutive blank is continually bombarded with projections. The interaction fails if the mutual projections of the social partners do not change, or if the reader's projections superimpose themselves unimpeded upon the text. Failure, then, means filling the blank exclusively with one's own projections" (1978, 167). The establishment of a sense of the text occurs through a readjustment of the reader's projections upon the textual blanks. But the text must nonetheless exert a control over the reading process. Portions of the subject of the writing are deliberately concealed, and the reader exercises creative force in supplying these concealed subjects. Iser says that while this process certainly goes forward with all reading, the blanks nonetheless do not contain absolute meanings and therefore the reading process—or that of projecting appropriate phenomena for the deliberate gaps—is continuous.

But Iser goes further; the reading process is transformatory, and through the "repertoire" of the fiction—its rootedness in the codes of time and place as well as in the author's own set of prescripts for the world created—the ultimate resulting text is infinitely various, dependent on the reader's combination of imposed projections or "protensions" and responses in kind to the identifiable codes of the text. Iser says, "The process of serial transformation therefore has a catalytic function: it regulates the interaction between text and reader neither through a given code nor through the discovery of a hidden code, but through a history which is actually produced in the act of reading. This is the history of changing standpoints, and as a history it is a condition for the production of new codes" (212). Since the production of the text by the reader involves so many shifts that no reader can ever keep the entire fiction in view, the reader is reduced to perspectives visible from the vantage point of some present of the novel, a perspective that Iser calls "a horizon" (97). The text produces neither an ideal nor a real reader, but rather implies its reader (27–30). The role of the implied reader is "prestructured by three basic components: the different perspectives represented in the text, the vantage point from which he joins them together, and the meeting place where they converge" (36).

And this implied reader differs from the reader designated by the text, the "faithful reader" addressed by the author. Thus for Iser, the whole process of reading is represented in the mechanics of reception, a process that includes the areas of knowledge of any specific reader, in considering, for example, literary allusions fabricated by the author in the text.

Hans Robert Jauß, Iser's colleague and collaborator, applies a different and more abstract focus to his treatment of the aesthetics of reception. Jauß, in "Literary History as a Challenge to Literary Theory,"[3] concerns himself with the modes of reception and places special emphasis on the varieties of demands a text is likely to make of its readers. For this purpose, he uses the word *horizon* differently from Iser. Where Iser had established the horizon as the prospect visible from any nexus in the text, Jauß establishes the horizon by summarizing the possible varieties of reader expectations from a text. Thus, any text that develops according to an accepted formula fulfills the reader's expectations and does not press against the reader's horizon of expectations. Jauß refers to a work that fits this category as a literary lollipop. However, the books that are likely to attract critical attention are those which press in varying degrees against the horizon of expectations and, instead of being simple culinary delights, turn out to be more or less challenging fare (LHaC, 1970, 15). Jauß sees acutely that "the first reception of a work by the reader includes a test of its aesthetic value in comparison with works which he has already read" (LHaC, 1970, 8). Further, he tells us that the synthesis between the canons of an art and the forward process of reading is a continuing relationship in the enrichment of the comprehension of the literary work through the development of its "history of reception" (LHaC, 1970, 8–9). The center of Jauß's argument proposes a close consideration of this integration of aesthetics with the reading process. As Jauß says, the argument demands that "in opposition to the objectivism of positivist literary history...a conscious attempt to establish canons, which, on the other hand—in opposition to the classicism of the study of traditions—presupposes a critical review if not destruction of the traditional literary canon" (LHaC, 9).[4]

Jauß and Iser both see that first readers are crucial to the process of understanding how artistic works are received, and that first readers supply an important link in the development of the tradition of a particular work. Furthermore, Iser sees that our access to the minds of first readers reading is limited by the inaccessibility of these minds, especially prior to the vast extension of public printing attendant on the development of journalism in the eighteenth century. Reviewing is a development of this journalism occupying a spectrum of importance in particular journals all the way from space filler to central purpose. Since the development of reviewing, as a subcategory of criticism, depends on the existence of journalism,[5] the fiction that breaks the mold, like any revolutionary art, arouses immediate hostility and can lead to violent reactions. One thinks of a sequence of occasions in the earlier part of the twentieth century reflecting responses to three artistic revolutions— the premiere of Stravinsky's *Rite of Spring* (1913), where the audience booed, shouted, and in large numbers walked out; the New York Armory show (1913), where the mass of modern painting (the show displayed 1,600 pieces) was regarded with indignation and outrage and where Marcel DuChamps's *Nude Descending a Staircase* enjoyed a succès de scandale; and James Joyce's *Ulysses* (Paris, 1922) which raised a howl of protest over its obscenity and required a court trial in the 1920s before receiving American public sanction. Each of these revolutions pressed against the horizons of expectation, as Jauß would say, well beyond the levels of comfort, and well beyond any conceivable conventions; they produced responses to match. The important point is, however, that each of the revolutions produced works that have become a landmark in the development of their respective arts.

While James's *Turn of the Screw* did not by any means cause its first audience to break the furniture or to raise placards boycotting the author, it went well beyond the established conventions for the ordinary tale, for ghost narrative, or for confessional fiction. Its first public readers gave it a wide spectrum of responses ranging from damnation to praise and from sensations of defilement to convictions of great aesthetic achievement. A description of the critical tradition of the tale thus calls for both a resuscitation of its submerged first reading and an assessment of the aesthetics of response by this very special section of readers who, if not representative of first readers in general, offer at least a range of response suggestive of the horizon of expectations of the general group of first readers. Moreover, a majority of the reviewers published anonymously.[6] Where we can check on the responses of first readers whose reactions were not publicized at the time of the reviews, we usually find the responses less pointed and less well articulated than those of the reviewers and thus useful only in establishing the basic emotional responses of first readers.[7] The reviewers discovered a fair amount of the geography of the text and some of its deeper implications, but left a good deal of explication to further and more intensive reading.

ANOMALIES

The asymmetry of the *Screw*'s critical tradition remains a signal feature through most of the years of its development. For example, Edna Kenton surely deserves credit for the first published challenge to a "traditional" reading of the tale; however, many years later (1957), Leon Edel unearthed Harold Goddard's essay claiming that since 1920 he had been challenging the "tradition" by pressing his Swarthmore students to regard the governess as hysterical and as hallucinating the ghosts. Who, then, deserves the accolade for initiating the challenge? Again, as an accent to Kenton's article in *Arts*, the editor included a reproduction in black and white of four *Screw* illustrations executed by Charles Demuth in 1917. It is unclear whether Kenton knew of the paintings before they appeared with her article (and thus whether they formed any part of the aesthetic apprehension of the tale featured in her essay). But it is clear that at least to some extent these illustrations formed part of the aesthetic property of Edmund Wilson in his formulation of the Freudian reading of the tale, since he mentions not only the influential Kenton article in the opening of his "Ambiguity of Henry James" (1934) but also the Demuth paintings (the paintings are mentioned prominently in this first appearance of the article but decline in importance in later versions).

Wilson's conclusion that James was depicting a conventional sexually deprived Victorian old maid in the governess may well have derived some force from the character given to her by Demuth's paintings. The paintings form some possible influence on the development of the *Screw*'s critical tradition, but the very indefiniteness of Kenton's and Wilson's responses to them leaves the amount of that influence unsettled. Furthermore, once the reproductions of the paintings appear with Kenton's article and then ascend to Wilson's notice in the first appearance of his article, they submerge into obscurity and resurface only by oblique reference (for example, by John Sweeney in 1943) or by reference through Wilson's article (Allara, 1970; Haskell, 1987). The critical belief in the disordered psychology of the governess persists in a stream of the criticism of the tale, but at least one powerful aesthetic force that might have shaped the early appearances of that critical postulate has submerged. The earnest question about exactly what Demuth saw in the governess—what his paintings mean, or tell us about what Demuth thought of James's artifact—remains unresolved in the history of responses to the tale. But the subsidiary question of who holds primacy in the "discovery" of the abnormal psychology of the governess is all the more tormented by the Demuth exponent in the larger equation.

Anomalies remain a part of the *Screw* critical tradition until the present. The strife for hegemony between the parties warring over the governess's psychology continued unabated for almost forty years of the tradition, from Wilson's first skirmishes in 1934 until the mid-1970s. Then a group of theorists, unknown to each other, simultaneously exploited Tzvetan Todorov's postulate of a new genre—the Fantastic—to suggest that both readings are provisionally embedded in the tale and that there can be no hegemony.[8] Again, apparently unknown to each other, a group of critics suddenly in 1968 and 1969 seized on the force of the image of "the long glasses," the full-length mirrors of Bly, in which the governess sees herself at full length for the first time in her life and begins to elongate her own concept of "the full image of a repetition" (k, 21). While the interest in this configuration reflects to some extent the concept of the mirror-stage of human psychological development featured in Jacques Lacan's *Ecrits*, the simultaneous appearance of the three or four pieces suggests at least to some extent an accident and an anomaly in the history of responses to the tale. Again, one of the most brilliant of the tale's expositors nonetheless makes an extraordinary assumption about so commonplace a matter as the meaning of the title of the tale. Shoshana Felman, who gives such exemplary illumination to the psychology of the fireplace setting of the *Screw* frame tale, assumes that the title is limited to a reference to a wood screw. True, she argues from the text and from the image of Flora's screwing a straight stick into a board to make a mast for a ship, giving significance to the image of the wood screw. But she misses entirely the rich implications of the turned thumbscrew as a device of exorcism, a matter that seems to have an inevitable place in the tale, since the governess sets out to exorcise the ghosts on the assumption that they have possessed the children. It does not matter that the thumbscrew image does not extinguish the wood-screw image. In a sense, the anomalies reach a peak of oddity when in the late 1980s, in all apparent innocence, two writers solemnly summoning the paradigm of existing criticism to aid, though without benefit of citation, publish essays that are almost pristine examples of the two sides in the first clash in the wars over the governess's psychology, as though there had been no fifty years of controversy, as though these two critics had invented the critical positions. These essays appear in the wake of a flood of some of the tradition's most distinguished and illuminating entries, which in isolation from those extraordinary insights might seem to justify Freundlieb's (1984) use of the critical tradition to condemn the practice of criticism.

THE PLEASURES OF THE TRAP

From what I have read in the panorama of responses to the tale, it seems to me that we do not know enough about the critical tradition of *The Turn of the Screw*. If we have some rather splendid recapitulations of the earlier criticism in works such as Cranfill and Clark's *Anatomy* (1965a) and Kimbrough's Norton Critical Edition (1966), a scrutiny of the criticism itself shows that the histories of response are likely to leave gaps in the collective process of reading, just as the experiential reading of the text is likely to create as many gaps as it fills. The asymmetry of the critical tradition sketched here emphasizes the sense of accident in the cumulative process of establishing meaning. I am proposing that we have not made sufficient scrutiny of the implications of the reviews as an index of the condition of first public reading of the texts. But I am going further to suggest that prior criticism has tended to consider the reviews as superficial comments and therefore as important only for flavor. As a start to my project I propose to go back to the reviews to study with some care the ways in which first readers establish their own horizons of aesthetic experience with respect to a problem fiction and the ways in which the representation of this horizon indicates the character of its challenge to the generic convention and to the first readers' own aesthetic assessments. I am proposing to go the step beyond Iser and Jauß to translate their general theories into the language of actual readers reading the text.

One very specific result of this inquiry will be to show that the first public readers exhibited a broad range of experience with the text. A second result will be to show that the responses tended to be pronounced whether positive or negative and that the sense of awe and mystery that survives the most sophisticated of these readings tends to show both that this work was artistically successful and that it engaged in breaking new ground, constituting a challenge of some intensity to the readers. A third result of this scrutiny will be to show that the new calculus in the presentation of the tale qua ghost story qua confessional fiction inevitably confronts these readers with aesthetic, structural and thematic problems that they have not, by the time of this first reading, had the capacity to solve and distribute among the literary conventions as they understood them. In one sense the student of the history of responses will conclude that the story never adjusts itself to any easy sense of literary convention. Stravinsky's *Rite of Spring* provides a useful parallel. Musicologists tend to agree that the piece not only defied all formal conventions in its time but has exerted its influence on the tonalities of later music rather than on its actual structures, as the more neoclassical of Stravinsky's work has tended to do. The *Screw* has also tended to stand alone as an artifact without progeny except in the sense of the liberation from the conventions of the tale and in the introduction of new standards in thematic treatment of the child in the tale. *The Turn of the Screw* applied special pressures and produced special responses in its first readers because it was unique in its composition and subsequently remained unique in the development of the subgenre of the tale.

The study will proceed beyond the reviews to show the growth of the critical tradition in its relation to the first readings. The study will use this relationship to construct a hypothesis that the critical understanding develops incrementally over the course of the years in spite of unhelpful repetitions and the failure of some critics to keep up with the advances; and will contend that such advances amount to something more substantial than casual changes in critical and theoretical styles and critical vocabularies. The study will consider both the orderly and the asymmetrical relations between one stage of criticism and another—the rootedness of so much of it in the wars of the 1930s and 1940s, for example, or the phenomenon of the submergence of the Demuth illustrations in the literary criticism only to see them resurface in the artistic criticism of Demuth's work. The study will apply pressure to reader-response theory by exploring some aspects of readers reading the text and readers reading the work of critics. The study will discuss at some length the several very significant pools of time when major new insights were added to the collective reading and splendid essays appeared to brighten previously dark corners of the tale and of the aesthetic apprehension of it. The study will try to assess the nature of the compositional blanks according to the theories of Iser and other reader-response theorists on the one hand against the blank values trumpeted by James in his preface on the other.

James disavows any attempt to supply accent in the tale. He virtually swears that he has given a value-free account in the tale as a whole; that he does not expatiate on the psychology of the governess or on the malignity of the ghosts; that he does not go beyond report on such subjects as the behavior of the servants "dead in the employ of the house" (k 118, preface). No hidden agendae lie behind the assertions of the narrators; no authorial guile hides, falsifies, distorts or manipulates.

As Iser might say, James seems to suggest that the tale is without codes to direct the reader's response to it. When James qualifies, however, by saying that some mysterious force might have "excited horror, promoted pity ... created expertness" and that these reader responses have "read into [the blanks] more or less fantastic figures," he permits us to complain that his disclaimers are disingenuous and that he has been cutting the long rope on the balloon of romance when we were not looking. If he plumes himself on having trapped us on our early acquaintance with the tale, we can plume ourselves in our turn in catching him—on a second look—cutting the balloon free. In this lovely combination of the ingenuous and the disingenuous regarding the value blanks of his tale, James has told us some important things about the arduous and rewarding job of reading.

1

Naive Public Reading

Henry James was far from pleased with the reviewing of his fiction in the public press. His displeasure prompted him to declare that "The critical sense is so far from frequent that it is absolutely rare, and the possession of the qualities that minister to it is one of the highest distinctions" (James, [1893] 1986). He was lamenting the journalistic urge to rush into print, to review everything that was published, to comment on works of art offhand. Criticism, he suggested, had come to seem like a river that had overflowed its banks; it was the filler that reduced the quantity of mere blank space in any given journalistic signature.[1] James wanted a criticism that reflected his notion that the reader's job was to assist the artist in the creation of the work. But James refused to allow for the pressures that his very sophisticated work applied to his readers. He took himself as the exemplary reader he sought for his work (as he suggests later in the New York preface to *The Golden Bowl*); he seems to have discounted the difficulties with which his groundbreaking work might confront even sophisticated initial readers. The first flood of print about *The Turn of the Screw* was a small and unruly river of its own, which rushed and tumbled over itself and might be said to have burst its banks. Linda Taylor in her bibliography (1982) shows, for instance, that newspapers as widely separated from each other as the *Springfield (Massachusetts) Republican*, the *Detroit Free Press*, the *St. Paul Daily Pioneer Press* and the *Portland Morning Oregonian* all felt called upon for judgment of *The Two Magics*, in which *The Turn of the Screw* first appeared in book form.

The first state of public response to James's novella was thus reviewerly; as James's brief comment on criticism might have predicted, it was uneven. Yet from our perspective, this first state of response was interestingly symptomatic of the energetic critical quarrels to come. It originated an extensive paradigm of critical insights against which to assess any developments in the later critical investigation of the tale. The reviews taken collectively supplied an example of shaped published response to a complex work, where the reviewers fairly uniformly intimated that the work reordered or dislodged some part of their definition of the genre to which they assigned it. This is a useful instance of the genesis of criticism at its very foundations, at the moment of issue of the work. The reviews reinforce the idea that the earliest response to a new work is at base emotional rather than intellectual and that the horizon-shifting power of a work that reforms the genre will generate strong emotions on either side of the receptive divide.

REVIEWS AS NAIVE PUBLIC READING

If one wishes to study the horizons of expectation of first readers of a literary work there is a special virtue to consulting the early printed reviews in response to it. The potential horizons of readers are many, including the horizon of sophistication, the horizon of skill, learning, or intelligence, the horizon of aesthetic response, the horizon of technical information, and so on. But the one that will come under notice here is the reader's horizon of expectations, since this concept is most central to the question of how readers respond upon first reading of a text; and for purposes of studying the response to James's *Turn of the Screw*, how readers responded to a work that seemed to fit a familiar genre, but challenged expectations about what a work in that genre looked like. Hans Robert Jauß, for example, has put us in his debt by pointing out the impact on the expectations of readers of a variety of types of new works. But he is content merely to posit the existence of such an horizon among readers in his *Toward an Aesthetic of Reception* (1982b), without showing us its practical dimensions or its necessary limitations.

One might look in many places for first readers on whose readings to judge the character of primary response—among the author's circle, among the best cultured readers of the day, among academics, among literary theorists, among, say, the students in a class who encounter a work of literature for the first time. Each of these groups might offer valuable insights into the initial reading process; moreover, each group might have a particular value for such a reading. For better or worse, however, none of these groups can be counted on reliably to give readings that conform to the three principles of naive reading: that they be first, consistently available; second, coeval; and third, credibly naive or uninfluenced by the views of other readers. The readings of those who do not review the work are not reliably consistent because they are usually not published and thus are unavailable to a critical community. Such readings are unlikely to be coeval with publication because any response is likely to be sequestered by its recipient and can come at any time after publication. Such readings are unlikely to be credibly naive because the admixture of other opinions, such as reviewers' comments, is likely to influence the judgments. Moreover, such readings are likely to generate gut reactions rather than shaped criticisms of even the weight of reviews.

Oscar Wilde's comment on *The Turn of the Screw* appeared in a letter to a friend around the time of publication, for instance, and amounted only to the offhand remark that "it was a most wonderful, lurid, poisonous little tale, like an Elizabethan tragedy" (Gard, 1968, 227). We might hear volubly from one or another group or from an individual reader on the occasion of the first appearance of a particular artifact, but it is more likely that one or another of the principles given above—especially coevality—will be breached in the surfacing of first comments, increasing the risk that the judgment has been modified by the views of others in its formulation—"this little book everybody has been talking about." By and large, the early reviews—say, within the first six months of publication of the work—avoid the risk of breaching the principles of naive reading and therefore make a useful test of at least one sort of reader's horizon of expectations with respect to a given artifact. It will be one of the purposes of the present chapter to demonstrate that the initial reading of *The Turn of the Screw* disclosed that the work defied the expectations of readers familiar with the genre of the ghost tale, and that though the emotional response was strong enough to expose a number of the areas of the geography of the tale, the dimensions of the tale that caught the eyes of the critic-reviewers tended to be restricted by the enormous power of the governess's narrative, which almost obliterated the subtleties of the frame tale for these first readers. This restrictive power of the ghostly presence in her narrative likewise tended to obscure the prologue for the majority of the tale's public readers in its first quarter century of existence.

We might ask what happens in a review in general. Coleridge outlined a simple sequence of critical questions: What was the author trying to do; was it worth doing; how well did he succeed? An old freshman textbook varied by suggesting that the three pertinent questions inquired: "What is the author trying to do? What are his materials? How well does he succeed?" (Shaw, 1955). It is certainly worth the labor to inquire into the materials, as Shaw suggests, as well as to question whether the undertaking was worthwhile with Coleridge. The answers to the questions will inevitably address the worth of the project. Because reviews tend to be written while the work is either still in press or just released, they are too new to reflect the views of other readers of this particular artifact. The absence of shared experience of the work does not mean that reviewers will have no opinions of the writer, especially one who is well known; any existing position will influence the reading. In addition, reviewers tend to reflect two constraints—the urgent need to be original and a correlative desire to earn credit for a definitive judgment about the work, preferably in advance of all other commentators. Reviews are by nature prone to express strong and direct emotions about the work, since emotional response is a shortcut to definitive statement. If as a reviewer I like the work, my response will immediately propose that the work is likable, is likely to attract other readers. If I dislike the work, I will make this the cornerstone of my review in the expectation that it will have a like effect for other readers. If I am strongly moved by the work without warming to it, I may well say that it is significant and challenging. I am likely to expect this judgment to be ratified by other readers.

As Coleridge suggests, reviews attempt to judge the literary work— to ask how well it succeeds. The reviewer's desire to produce a definitive judgment of the work means one is prepared to compare it to other works and to look at its own particulars, or, as one tends to do in all defining gestures, its genus and differentiae. The comparison to other texts ranks the work under review according to the appropriate criteria—subgenre, the local standard of work of the same character, or to the monuments of its type if the work challenges comparison on such a scale. The consideration of parts allows the reviewer to judge craft, style, technique. Part of the reviewer's success in approximating the definitive judgment will depend on the success of dissecting out those particles most responsible for the work's impact, a chore demanding a profound skill in reading. It is easy to respond to characterization in fiction, for example, but if structure happens to be the particle that contains the writer's own most intensely wrought effect and the reviewer misses it, then the review will fall short of the intention of defining the artifact. Since what follows will reflect on the criticism of *The Turn of the Screw,* I can offer an example from its reviews. The reviewers uniformly felt and responded to the horror of the tale, and to the characters beyond the living record—the ghosts, Peter Quint, and Miss Jessel. These same reviewers missed, almost completely, however, the fact that the story was structured to be narrated on three levels. They spotted the governess's narrative, and a few could find Douglas or at least the figure who spoke of "dreadfullness," but they could neither see nor speak intelligently of the external narrator, the one who gives the total narrative its title, so that the phrase "the turn of the screw" exists at all three levels of narrative. That device, that gnomon, does indeed point to the defining term of the tale, and if all reviewers neglected it, then none succeeded in defining the tale.

That or something like it is what Jauß is talking about when he speaks of the aesthetic distance of a challenging new literary work at its first perception: "If one characterizes as aesthetic distance the disparity between the given horizon of expectations and the appearance of a new work, whose reception can result in a 'change of horizons' through negation of familiar experiences or through raising newly articulated experiences to the level of consciousness, then this aesthetic distance can be objectified historically along the spectrum of the audience's reactions and criticism's judgment (spontaneous success, rejection or shock, scattered approval, gradual or belated understanding)" (LHaC, 1970, 25). This relative distance helps to distinguish between the "culinary" work—the literary lollipop—and the more serious and demanding work of the sort that produces "horizonal change." The most important contribution of reviews to the larger process of determining the status of a new work is their disclosure of expectations. While Jauß might be content with a general and perhaps ideal figure such as "the reflective reader" (24) in designating the process of first response, the actual effect of early journalistic response to a work of literature (supposing a wide enough comparison group) is to produce a grid of reader expectations with respect to the work. This grid, though uneven in both quality and insight, expresses a universe of discourse at least to the extent that it lays bare the underlying critical assumptions of the reviewers as the bases of judgment and thus makes a step toward sketching the cultural environment in which the judgments take place. The distinctions between the American and British journalistic first reactions to James's late work are striking in some respects, for example, with regard to James's treatment in *The Turn of the Screw* of Miles's expulsion from his school and rejection from further enrollment. That is a serious matter for British readers, who give the governess full marks for her assumption that something is seriously wrong; American readers tend to see it as an evidence of the governess's tendency to react hysterically to minor stimuli. British readers are appalled that the children are left with mere servants to be corrupted; American readers are likely to see the practice as an inoculation of democracy for youngsters otherwise liable to indoctrination by snobs.[2]

However lax we might find the standards underlying any given review, all reviews tend rather surprisingly toward a degree of uniformity in their implicit canons of judgment. If the author is well known, the tendency of the reviews is to assess the new work in relation to the author's acknowledged greatest or most popular work; to the generality of his work; to his most recent work; to the scale of his work in general; to his contemporaries' work; to some larger axiological framework like the genre or the national environment from which it comes or to the major thematic paradigm apparent in its attempt or achievement. If the author is less well known, then the canons of judgment reflect the author's recent work; a projection for the career as indicated by this production; its relation to other contemporary work in the same genre, both among aspiring and established artists; and its relation to the development of the genre. If the work is by an unknown author, then the initial concern is with the quality of this work; the grounds it supplies for predicting a future course for the author's career; its relation to the work of others in the vein; its evidences of craft; its contribution to the development of the genre. The cultural environments together with the canons of judgment—given a sufficient sampling— suggest very powerfully a grid of expectations on the route to establishing a generic horizon of expectations.

The summary of the reviews of a new work offers a ground for judging the initial scope of reader expectations for the work and should give some indication of the paradigm of possible perceptions of its rating on the scale of challenge to the reader. The synthesis of the reviews will provide a responsible assessment of the work to the extent that the reviewers must respect the values of the readership of the publication so far as these values can be reproduced, assumed, or projected by the reviewer. The values of the readership are the ultimate test of any of the possible horizons that might be projected for the study of responses by readers in any particular reader collective or cultural unit. What will become quickly apparent to the historian looking back is that a substantial portion of reader expectations will be based on assumptions that are clearly out of date for the period in which the attempt to render responsible judgment takes place. These anachronistic expectations will lead readers to condemn a major writer who has been breaking new ground and to accuse the writer of having lost touch with the earlier, more familiar, and therefore more popular personality of his work. A further substantial proportion of the reviewers will be struggling with what is new, recognizing the differences and either launching complaints about what is changed or announcing the first insights into what will become the standard conceptual statement of the later critical perception. A very small proportion of the reviewers will also be critically sophisticated and will not only recognize the changes but will applaud them and begin to assess where they are taking the author. This paradigm very clearly applies to George Meredith in virtually the same moment as it does to Henry James, and, since the earliest responses to Conrad's *Lord Jim* will come in the same journal issues as the earliest responses to *The Soft Side* (1900), we can see the beginnings of the pattern with respect to Conrad. That pattern will be notorious only slightly later with figures such as Joyce, Pound, Eliot, Yeats, and Lawrence. Thus, troubled, James's later readers in the new century will look back fondly to the safe titles of a quarter of a century before, lamenting the lost lucidity of *Roderick Hudson*, *Daisy Miller*, *The Portrait of a Lady*, and perhaps only slightly less often of *The American*. It is important to consider that even the most sophisticated and discerning readers among the reviewers will miss some major points in the problem fiction, as one can see in the responses, for example, to "The Figure in the Carpet," *What Maisie Knew*, *The Turn of the Screw*, and *The Sacred Fount*.

The distribution of subjects undertaken by the reviewers of *The Turn of the Screw* makes summary difficult. But some categories of commentary recurred with sufficient frequency to admit of labels, and it is these categories, by and large, that I shall discuss below. The reviewers wanted to judge James's achievement, frequently in both *The Turn of the Screw* and in *Covering End*, the two tales included in the first book publication of the ghost tale, but uniformly in *The Turn of the Screw*. Along with his achievement, they wanted to talk about his treatment of technical matters in the tale; about style, which was a heated issue in James criticism generally; and about the quality of horror and terror in this ghost tale. They wanted to talk about the story or the theme or the idea. They wanted to talk about the characters in the tale and about how they saw these characters in relation to one another. A few wanted to talk about the various literary matrices implicit in the publication of a ghost tale: about its relationship to other writers of ghost tales; about its relationship to other works in James's portfolio; about *Covering End*. A few reviewers made assumptions about the cultural or intellectual background of the author—the grounds for a ghost tale that lay in the author's personal rather than his occupational past.[3] Only one or two spotted the prologue to the tale; virtually none attempted to explain its title. In these broader categories we find the ancestors to some of the later critical conclusions about the nature and purport of the tale.

The reviews carry the first state of public response from early October 1898 to the middle of 1899. Together with other early sources they make up the prelude to James's own criticism of the tale in the preface to volume 12 of the New York Edition. In this period, mid-1899 to 1907–8, the particular criticism of this tale merges with the growing number of assessments of James's corpus in his late life. Though the criticism of *The Turn of the Screw* is a relatively minor issue in this broader assessment, the tale has the distinction of being for some of the critics the benchmark for the late work and the late style.

THE FIRST STATE OF PUBLIC READING

Achievement

In assessing James's achievement in *The Turn of the Screw*, the reviewers show a fair sense of the range of expectations that will form the horizon for this book. Explicitly these reviews collectively show the dimensions of the horizon of expectation and the corresponding general response to a book by James in the late 1890s, in which he employs the ghostly, the occult, and the malign. It would be likely, the reviewers generally agreed, that this work would be successful in its depiction of characters, in its representation of the occult, in its grasp of the psychology of the human sufferers, in its sense of the evil ambiance and, subtly, in its ability to move the reader. The collective mood registered superlatives, setting aside for the moment the disposition of the reviewer to applaud or deplore. The reviewers' imagery tended to reproduce, even unconsciously, the imagery of the tale.

Reviewers said such things as "The very breath of hell seems to pervade some of its chapters"; "it is indeed a deliberate, powerful, and horribly successful study of the magic of evil"; "one of the most appalling ghost stories ever told"; "one of the most thrilling stories that we have ever read" (*New York Times*; Huneker; Mabie; *Chautauquan*). Chilling, appalling, hell breathing the tale may be, but the reviewers declare that it is likewise deliberate and successful. A number of them praise its execution as "appropriate": "an original and fascinating idea in appropriate form"; "in absolutely appropriate form"; "he shocks his readers but his skill and subtlety keep a horrible subject within bounds" (*New York Tribune*; *Portland Morning Oregonian*; *Dixie*).[4] If the reviewers show a prepossession here, it is that the novella fits James's métier and that James the master has done full justice to it.

That view is not contradicted by the tale's disfavoring reviewers; it is merely inverted. All the skills at James's command serve merely to make the repulsive aspects of the tale powerfully repulsive. "We have never read a more sickening, a more gratuitously melancholy tale"; "James is by no means a safe author to give for Christmas"; "the most hopelessly evil story that we have ever read in any literature, ancient or modern" (*Bookman*; *Ainslee's Monthly Magazine*; *Outlook*). The reviewers who dislike the tale echo those who approve because the shuddering reaction to its evil power is shared by both responses. The reviewer for *Independent* unites these alternate forms of response, the praise along with the objection: "literary art could not be used with more refined subtlety of spiritual defilement." Thus for this reviewer, the art, the skill, the genius behind the tale receives notice, but the disapproval of the artist's questionable leaning ("spiritual defilement") receives accent. The dark vision attributed to the author recurrently invokes magic, undoubtedly suggested by the book title enclosing the two tales, but subtly confirmed in the character of reader responses. The mention of horror couples with the language of thrill to expose the pleasure of horror. "The reader is bound to the end by the spell," says the writer for *Critic*, echoed by the writer for *Chautauquan*: "the intangible is here painted with a skill little short of the supernatural." There is even some threat to the reader's independence of will in James's magnetic power: "however we may depreciate the art which does not permit happiness in its enjoyment, however strong may be our wish that the 'society with the long name'[5] should protect children from abuse in fiction as well as in life, we can nonetheless feel only admiration for the touch with which this and in an earlier instance [*What Maisie Knew*] Mr. James has depicted the child mind" (*Literary World*).

James's grasp of the child mind exhibits even more deeply the issues of psychology, magic, and artistic skill. The complex *Bookman* review conceded James's skill but damned *The Turn of the Screw*. The reviewer accuses James of misunderstanding child nature in spite of "unmistakeable signs of a close watchfulness and a living admiration of children of the more distinguished order." But James has allowed a theory to run away with him and has used "a few dark facts" to "give a brilliant setting to his theory." The reviewer does not dispute that James's subtlety has "given his examination of the situation an air of scientific precision." But for all the art, "the clever result is cruel and untrue." In saying this, the *Bookman* critic has taken a stand on child nature that antedates Hawthorne[6]: has apparently presumed innocence as a fact of nature and for all intents has posited that corruption can only come with experience that belongs to a later stage of life than Miles and Flora have reached. But James is not simply in error: he is also cruel. In some sense the writer proposes that James's purpose is not to uncover some vital human truth but rather to torment and to falsify nature along the way. The writer for *Bookman*, like the writer for *Literary World*, wishes to prevent fictional cruelty to children, an issue that still remains vexed and largely unsolved today.

There is thus a restless undercurrent in the reviewers' attempts to appraise James's achievement in *The Turn of the Screw*. They saw power in the work and, as first readers, shuddered under it.[7] Their assessments reflect an appreciation of James's skill, conceding it if they intended to malign the tale; celebrating it if they wished to applaud its artistry. The later student of the reviews can sympathize with James's dislike of this periodical mode of judgment without quite joining him in condemning its unsalvageable futility. James devoutly wished for a readership that would perform a part of the artistic labor of the creation of the artifact. The groping quality of the reviews suggests a readership that could discern surfaces while only barely sensing depths—and even then often rendered scarcely more than an evocative outburst either praising or denouncing the work. But these readers nonetheless struggled to give an account, however imperfect, of the artifact and in the process showed something of the paradigm of the work's challenge to the reader in the light of common expectations: its place on the spectrum of invited responses, which range from the lollipop to the horizon shifter—for what was offered was not criticism in any rigorous sense of that term, but rather a tangible sequence of reactions. The reviewer operates in the unclosed synapse between the unknown text and the carefully adjudicated artifact.

The comment of a practicing critic of the same time illustrates the difference. In one of the earliest attempts to summarize James's career as a writer of fiction, Cornelia Atwood Pratt (1899) put James's entire corpus under scrutiny. She wrote without the reviewer's pressure to comment simultaneously with the publication of a particular work. She could thus consider works together in patterns, exploring the developments from one stage to the next, assessing the consolidation of the work as these developments moved the works collectively from corpus to canon. Her essay is called "The Evolution of Henry James," and thus contains a working premise and a thesis. While the reviewers of *The Turn of the Screw* were caught in the whorls of a problem fiction intractable to easy solution—so that they could not see that this is the reading-problem—Pratt could quickly find containing terms for such intractability by reference to the dimension of the problematic in

James's work at large. When she discusses "The Altar of the Dead," for example, she discovers that "while recognizing how untrue it is to the outer existence, we are aware in every fiber of its deep realism as toward the soul's life." The issue is realism, as the reviewers of the age in general were inclined to argue. But Pratt shows us that in the work of James, what is imperfectly real on the surface of an artifact may be real in its depths, as she speaks of "the soul's life." What she says here of "The Altar of the Dead" is a useful expression of the problem of *The Turn of the Screw*: it summarizes what the reviewers on both sides of the magnetic field were struggling to say about the ghost tale. Pratt's observation does not solve either *The Turn of the Screw* or "The Altar of the Dead"; it merely solves the difficulty of how to state the problem. Pratt goes on to praise James's work of the 1890s as "feats of execution." She compares James to a mythical figure much like Thoreau's Artist of Kouroo.[8] She concludes that James has surpassed the limit that Kant set upon the reason, at least as far as execution is concerned, for she declares that James, like La Farge's architect, "has set forth the 'Thing Itself' which he has sought to express" (342). The ghost tale is one of those feats of execution; for this critic, the horizon of expectations has been of a high order. But her horizon has been expanded by a recent and enthusiastic consideration of James's work. For Pratt the critic the horizon of literature has altered less than it has for the reviewers. She is responding to her current developed sense of James's work by pursuing an evolutionary premise; the reviewers, on the other hand tend to be responding to a more generalized and perhaps hazy sense of James's work—its variety and cultivated complexity—tyrannized by a growing whisper that the convolutions of the late style were no added grace.[9]

The reviewers, though in conflict over the morality of the tale, joined in believing the tale unique to James and a triumph of his especial artistry. The reviewer for *Literary World*, who disapproved the fictional abuse of children, squeezed out some praise: "we find our great enjoyment in Mr. James's book, and a genuine one, more in the fashion of telling than in the story told." A number join in their belief that only James could have kept the tale from falling off the rails: into the lugubrious on one side; into the ludicrous on the other. Lanier (1898) praises the tale's ability to produce "a living, vivid, indelible impression on the mind." His summary is the most laudatory of the first state of response: "To my mind it is the finest work he has ever done." The writer for *Outlook* holds that "the tale has nothing in common with the ordinary; it is altogether on a higher plane both of conception and art." The *Athenaeum* writer appreciates that James succeeds with "only

a touch where a coarser hand would write a full page description."
Droch[10] says that the tale is the product of the very highest literary art
and that James succeeds "in a way to raise goose-flesh." *Ainslee's
Magazine* distinguishes between possible readers: "For people who read
stories for mere amusement the tale would hold no attraction; but for
those who enjoy Mr. James in his most elusive and artistic vein it could
not fail to be interesting." The *New York Times* reviewer elaborates this
idea: "But to the contention that this seemingly frail story—with a
theme which would surely fail of effect and might become simply
ludicrous in the hands of almost anyone of its author's
contemporaries—is one of the most moving and in its implied moral,
most remarkable works of fiction published in many years, we
steadfastly cling." The tale prompted James Gibbons Huneker—like
Pratt, a careful reader of James—to say that "the great American
novelist is in existence." Henry Harland, James's London novelist
friend, simply asked "who else could have told the story of 'The Turn
of the Screw.'"

Technical Skills

Though the reviewers performed the first public reading of *The
Turn* of the Screw, their patterns of response as a reflex of horizon of
expectations incorporated a broad range of concerns about the technical
skills of the telling. The reviewers could not discuss James's
achievements without touching on some of the techniques—narrative
skill in managing plot, for example, or stylistic skill in evocation of the
evil ambience. Since what is being written is not exacting criticism, the
treatment of skills is superficial. But its range is broad with glances at
point of view, the technique of indirection, style, characterization, the
problem of credibility of report, with comments on the generic
implications of the tale, on psychology and its relation to the
supernatural. In other words, this treatment goes about as far as the
criticism of the time in identifying the issues of fictional technique. Of
course the coverage is uneven, and some reviewers identify, label, and
analyze elements of technique while others merely describe what
happens and point incidentally to technical features in the process.

Narrative perspective receives some notice. The reviewer for
Literature, after noting the activities of the former governess (Miss
Jessel, here not named), tells the reader that "the tale is told by the new
governess, a girl of twenty"; this reviewer notes that the governess has
no name. The reviewer for the *Critic* adds that the governess "recounts
her slow recognition of the situation and her efforts to shield and save

her charges." The *Tribune* sees the narrative as the governess's inner response to compulsion. The writer suspects her ghost sighting of the taint of "feminine intuitions" and impugns her conclusions: "the heroine ... has nothing substantial upon which to base her deep and startling cognitions." *Chautauquan* sees the narrative arising from a governess "keenly sensitive to psychic impulses." Cornelia Pratt speaks in general of "the high-mindedness of the young girl" in her essay on James and perhaps summarizes the reviewers' grasp of the character of the narrator and of the narrative. For the recognition of the crucial issue of the governess's character as the center of tale's moral portent remains the enduring issue of the criticism. At least one reviewer sees flaws in the perfect monolith of the governess's self-representation.

The reviewers appreciate James's sophisticated use of narratorial indirection. *Literature* takes it in snuff, complaining that James "leaves everything unexplained"—that he may be among the most interesting of writers, but "he is not among the most lucid." But *Athenaeum* applauds the skill in his making "triumphant use of his subtlety." Droch, more acutely, sees that James is working by "elimination" of detail, by a reduction of what is actually depicted, so that when he "seems to be vague he is by elimination creating an effect of terror, of unimaginable horrors." *Bookman* had not liked the tale, but the reviewer acknowledges James's power in indirection: the setting "is a sink of corruption, never uncovered, but darkly, potently hinted." *Independent* adopts the governess's version of the events at Bly, concluding that "the ghosts defile [the children's] souls." But this reviewer also proposes that the process happens offstage "in a way and by means darkly and subtly hinted rather than portrayed by Mr. James." The *Bookman* reviewer of *The Awkward Age* (1899) summarizes the reviewers' grasp of the technique of indirection by saying that in the ghost tale James has "cast off all restraint and revealed depths of horror lurking under the fairest surface." While no detailed account of James's practice with innuendo surfaces in the reviews, there is a fairly widespread awareness of James's skill in its use.

James's style had already become a critical toy by the time of *The Turn of the Screw*. Nonetheless, the consensus on style here inclines toward praise. It is typically Jamesian (*Times, Outlook,* Pratt). Style is part of the interest of the tale (*Athenaeum, Literary World, Overland Monthly*). Pratt addresses the issue of James's late style by concurring with the reviewers that it lacks the grace and ease of the earlier James, but demurs from the general howl in contending that it "succeeds in carrying to the reader's mind the exact impression that the writer means to convey, as smoother sentences could not do" (1898, 342). Once again, Pratt as critic identifies the deeper issue, recognizing that James is specifically in pursuit of "the exact impression" and an accurate exhibition of the psychology of perception. *Literary World* sees the ghost tale written "with a beauty of style that can bring unquestioned into close comparison and one judgment pictures that are as far separated as the powers of light and the powers of darkness." The writer for *Tribune* proposes that "not a word could be spared." This writer complains about James's style and indirection in general but makes an exception for this tale: "The art of suggestion that Mr. James has employed before so fantastically that it has been more irritating than a flood of words could be here plays its part with consummate effect." Enthusiastically the writer denies that we are seeing a fiction with a plot (or a style), claiming that "instead of watching a drama, one becomes part of it and passes with the supposititious narrator and her two young charges through unprecedented spiritual adventures." The astute reviewer for *Springfield Republican* decides that the governess "seems to have been a close student of Mr. James, for she in turn gives her tale by hints, by fragments of conversation, in which a nod or a trick of the eye expresses more than words." *Bookman* remains a dissenter from the whole production, and the reviewer claims that James has used "symbolism to help him with his theme"—that is, with the ghosts as the origin of evil; such symbolism is "clumsy," the writer declares, "but only there in the story has James failed." The writer declines to exemplify the offending symbolism. The writer for *Literature* hesitates as well, complaining of James's want of lucidity in the central problem of the tale because "the subject does not admit of any plain statement of it." Droch is the most analytical of the reviewers and searches vigorously on his own part for the right words to give an exact sense of the impression that James is after: "He creates the atmosphere of the tale with those slow deliberate phrases which seem fitted only to differentiate the odors of rare flowers. Seldom does he make a direct assertion, but qualifies and negatives and double negatives, and then throws in a handful of adverbs, until the image floats away upon a verbal smoke. But while the image lasts, it is artistically, a thing of beauty." The writers see James in the style but it is too early in the critical history for them to try to assess the possible stylistic distance between James and his narrator.

Genre makes an appearance among these technical interests. The ghost story, the reviewers suggest, has undergone an evolution in the past century with some notable texts. But the advance of science has tended to thin out the more imaginative ghost hypotheses, both in the form of categorical denials of phenomena so profoundly contrary to the ordinary experience and in the practice of scientizing the study of apparitions in forms approved by the Society for Psychic Research (hereafter referred to as the SPR).[11] In one form or another, the reviewers suggest, the genre of the ghost story has fallen into disrepute; James is here reviving it with extraordinary skill. The writers are concerned to decide on the validity, the probability, the psychological accuracy of the tale, a concern not unfamiliar to the later critical tradition. There is some consensus on the view that the tale is psychologically conceived, that is, that it does indeed reflect the recent studies of the SPR. One reviewer tells us that it is merely an update of the old-fashioned ghost story. Another allows that it is full of apparitions, but denies that it is a ghost story, complaining that the ghosts are part of the "impossible circumstances of the tale." H. W. Lanier in the *Review of Reviews* declares that it is "an entirely new vein for Mr. James and one in which his delicate, subtle psychology shows to its best advantage." The writer for *Literature* is rather baffled: "we cannot enter," the writer says, "into the morbid psychology of such a work. The question is whether, given the impossible circumstances, the action and reaction of good and evil in childhood ... is well described." The writer proposes circumstances "impossible" to the new empiricism, or in other words denies that there can be ghosts in the common notion of the term and then goes on merely to question the psychology of the children in relation to the imaginary spirits. The writer for *Critic* says that the governess "perceives what is beyond all perception."

James's superior character development comes in for repeated commendation. *Sewanee Review* declares that "his character analysis ... deserves not a little praise." *Overland* tells us that James's characters, in "both ways and speech have grown more intricate since Daisy Miller's time." Droch, who never settles into an easy posture in his critical relation to James, begins an essay in which he praises the writer's achievement by damning his usual practice: James, he tells us, "has frequently given his readers shivers by the coldness with which he treats intense emotions." But here, according to Droch, James takes a new tack, makes the reader sting with the reality of the pain in the story. Regardless of the other fiction, however, the characters of this tale have a clear sense of urgent life for him.

Closely related to the study of character in the novella is the association of horror with character creation. The writer for *Literature* is appalled at the particular horror of the possession of the children by the ghosts, at the obscene cooperation between the ghosts and the children. Harland sees the children victims of "two particularly hideous and evil ghosts." Lanier sniffs the "foul breath of the pit itself, [which] strikes the reader full in the face as he follows the plot." *Bookman*, faithful to its dissent over the tale, is alive to every inch of the picture, which "seems an outrage in our first heat." But worse still, "if we admit the fact of infant depravity, if we own that children are supreme actors, and can bar doors on their elders most effectually, we must deny the continuity and the extent of the corruption as suggested here." And *Literary World* is chilled by the children, with a sense that the corruption that we must fear is in the children themselves: "the subtle crowning horror is the joy with which the two children, supernaturally trained in deceit and hypocrisy, welcome their evil spirits, a joy so depraved in its suggestiveness as to be more gruesome than the most vividly imagined physical fear." *Bookman*, too, declares that the ghosts' "horrible invitations are joyfully responded to." The ghosts are, then, the "horror and the ingenuity that lie behind this simple outline" (*Literature*).

Through superior technical skills, James has succeeded in creating a thing of beauty according to the majority of reviewers. There is more a sense that this achievement has materialized through the writer's technical skill than the reviewers' skill in analyzing it; the enthusiasts are better capable of affirming the creative miracle than in saying how it has come about. The writer for *Sewanee Review* declares, rather helplessly, that "his manner of dealing with the supernatural is quite unique." Harland marvels about his parting sense of the tale: it is full of horrors, he says, and yet James contrives "not to make the story ugly, not to make it horrible, sinister, repulsive, not to make it ridiculous either, but to make it beautiful, simply and entirely beautiful." Huneker approves in like sentiments: "yet the treatment is never morbid; it is uplifting, almost comforting, and comfort the reader needs in the terrifying flashes of an evil beyond that the writer gives us." Since Huneker is among the most sophisticated of the known first readers of *The Turn of the Screw*, his comment here serves well to focus the technical achievement of the tale. Without being able to reach through the machinery of technique to say why the story has so profound an effect, he isolates the effect acutely. We emerge from the tale with a sense of affliction and in need of comfort. Without doubt he has specified for this tale what Pratt had seen of James's achievement in general: his extraordinary ability to reproduce the feelings, the impressions, associated with deep emotional crises. This Huneker finds beautiful as well as moving. The evil is irrepressibly there—in the story, in the beautiful children, in the vision of the governess—just as it is dissolved into the texture of the world of which they are uncanny representations. The beauty is the art of reproducing so faithfully these things true of human experience but fugitive to the aesthetic grasp. Perhaps it is exactly to the extent that Huneker can feel these things without being able to state them in absolute terms that he can achieve this strong aesthetic response to the tale. He is a superior example of a good reader of the text and a good reader of James, however far he remains from solving its riddles or however unstable the text itself might be. He gives us some insight into the integrity of the text in an enlightened aesthetic response.[12]

Character Relations

The reviewers' final response depends heavily on how they see the characters in relation to one another: whether they see the governess as good and wholesome or as tending to replicate Bram Stoker's recent creation (*Dracula* appeared in 1896). The reviewers of *The Turn of the Screw* seem to have reached a general agreement on tret and tare: the governess is almost uniformly judged good, reliable, and self-sacrificing; the children parallel the governess in apparent sweetness, but are horribly corrupted; the ghosts and their living antecedents are unquestionably depraved. Here and there a reviewer varied this pattern by questioning the more obvious interpretation, but the pattern holds. The reviewers, in short, seem to have adhered to James's wishes in this respect and by and large recorded their impression that the governess as narrator is sufficiently reliable to transmit the events at Bly; sufficiently mature to be honestly self-sacrificing in her efforts for the children. The reviewers may waver on the perfection of the governess's ability to see what she reports, or upon whether it is consistent with the nature of children to suffer the corruption attributed to Miles and Flora, but they are confident in condemning the ghosts and their living originals.

The machinery of haunting generated powerful emotional reactions in the reviewers: reviling the ghosts seems to have been a satisfactory purge. *Outlook* proclaims "the possession of two lovely children by two evil spirits." Huneker recoils from "the soul-poisoning of two lovely children by two depraved people." *Chautauquan* shudders over the "influence on two children of a disreputable governess and her accomplice after their disappearance." *Ainslee's Magazine* (1899) speaks of "how two beautiful and innocent children were haunted by the ghosts of two wicked retainers in their family." *Literature* is even more lurid: the ghosts are "an infamous former valet of their father's [*sic*], an infamous former governess of their own." *Tribune*, suggesting that the children's beauty makes the spirits "trebly awful," emphasizes the "sharp contrast between the mortals and the evil spirits." For *Bookman* the ghosts are "a rascally valet" and "an iniquitous governess": "the origins of the evil [to the children] in their lifetime, who haunt the children after their death." *Literary World* offers the fullest interpretation among the reviews of the role of the ghosts in the tale : "the spirit of the man who attacks the boy as that of the woman who visits the little sister is evil undiluted; in life they were in guilty association, guilty in their relation with each other and in their damnable and successful efforts to pervert in ways inexpressible the child minds intrusted to their care, and after their tragic deaths they were still united in their hellish endeavor to maintain their vile influence and to add to their own damnation that of the two child souls." *Springfield Republican* is also without hesitation in taking the ghosts for full value and the children for depraved: "the conception of the two little children acting like angels in the presence of the governess, and stealing away at every opportunity to meet their familiar spirits from the infernal jail, is most sinister, and the tragedy at the end gives the extra turn of the screw which justifies the title."

The reviewer for *Literary World*, then, summarizes the responses of the reviewers to the ghosts. An acute later observer of the perversities of criticism like Christine Brooke-Rose would be likely to accuse the reviewer of extratextual interpretation in this series of observations: there is no textual mandate for much of what the reviewer says. We are free to accept the governess's speculation that there is a pairing of the sexes in any process of corruption. Though we are invited to see successful efforts to pervert the children, we do not see it happen onstage with what James would later call "weak specification." If the corruption proceeds "in ways inexpressible," the assumption is that decency forbids the reviewer to name such horrors. But unless we are prepared to join Mrs. Grose in her submission that Flora's sudden access of vulgarity compels belief in the corruptive powers of the ghosts, the quality of the perversion remains unspecified. And though the governess may preen her feathers on her moral supremacy over the ghosts, her narrative fails to show us explicitly how the ghosts "endeavor to maintain their vile influence" or how they "add to their own damnation that of the two child souls." The need to supply the details, what James would happily identify as the reader specifying for himself, tells us of the strenuous demands of the tale upon the imagination, and perhaps justifies the later speculation that James created the tale for revenge on his readers after the demise of his theatrical career.[13]

If the ghosts are depraved, the children are victims. Opinion divides on whether they are passive—the mere sleeping prey of the malignant spirits—or whether they court their corruption. Droch calls them "two supremely beautiful children" but does not find their plight "awe-inspiring." The *Times* speaks of "daily, almost hourly, communication with lost souls" and assures the reader that the children possess the imagination of evil. *Tribune* speaks of "the two powers of evil who have half entered into Miles and Flora." *Literary World* speaks of "two orphaned children with outward show of more than human perfection who are in communication with two apparitions or rather familiar spirits." Lanier winces over the portrayal: "there is something particularly against nature, something indescribably hellish in the thought of the beautiful children holding unholy communion with the wraiths of two vile servants who, when alive, had corrupted them." But the *Independent* cries out against the very depiction of the children who "when they are but helpless babes, fall under the influence of a governess and her lover who poison the very core of their conscience and character and defile their souls." These comments extend the purport of *Literary World*'s claim that the children welcome the malign intentions of the spirits with joy.

The agonizing consciousness of the corruption of the children is sufficient excuse for the reviewers to take the governess for granted and to award her rather limited space. They incline toward reserve rather than emotion in their references to her. From what James says in the later preface, it seems that this response is more or less what he had hoped for, since the narration of the events at Bly is to be seen as "crystalline." The reviewers mainly take the governess as a function character, as the vehicle of the narrative and as a pointed contrast to her predecessor. Part of that function is recognized (though only by a few) to be the intermediate victim of the neglect of the uncle in Harley Street. The reviewer for *Literature* is among these few in seeing that the governess is "employed by the children's uncle who lives in London, taking no interest in them whatever." *Independent* manages to see that "the guardian leaves [the children] in a lonely country house"; the governess is employed "to supervise [the children] and manage the large old house in Essex in which they live." *Literary World* lists the governess among the cast of characters merely as "a devoted governess." *Literature* tells us that the governess "finds both children charming: but haunted and possessed." *Tribune* sees the governess and "an old family servant" fight the ghosts. Even though the reviewer for *Critic* had observed that the governess bases her suspicions of the children on "nothing in the least substantial," with a hint that she is manufacturing the ghosts out of her own morbidity, the review ends by conceding the governess's view: "the reader who begins by questioning whether she is supposed to be sane ends by accepting her conclusions and thrilling over the horrors they involve." The reviewer is anticipating the later controversy over the governess's state of mind; but this controversy will lie dormant for some time before it germinates into the flower of literary warfare. The reviewer for *Bookman*, despite displeasure for the immorality of the story, praised the craft of its narration, perhaps a bit ominously referring to "the plottings of the good governess and the faithful Mrs. Grose to combat the evil." Aside from this reference and her inclusion in *Literary World*'s cast of characters as "a homely, dear, old, English nurse," Mrs. Grose is ignored in the early reviewing.

The other characters tended to go unnoticed. Quint and Jessel are rarely named. Douglas is only dimly seen. Griffin, whose tale leads to the disclosure of the governess's narrative, is invisible in this stage of the published response to the tale. The uncle in London is merely mentioned with a single dissenting voice impeaching his character. The external narrator who takes credit for the transmission of the tale to the reader fails to register. The various figures around the house at Bly, the servants and the bailiff, secure no notice. The governess, except for a momentary cavil, marches forward to the strains of martial and commendatory verse.

Literary Matrices

The reviewers used comparison as a tool to assess the appropriate literary place of *The Turn of the Screw*. Inevitably, they compared it to its companion tale in *The Two Magics*; and they held it up to others of James's works, especially the most recent forebears. The tale invited comparison to the work of other writers, especially those who wrote ghost stories. In the comparison with *Covering End*, the reviewers ranged from indifference—"the other [tale] hardly counts"; "the other [tale] is almost hackneyed" —to lyrical enthusiasm— "a delightful story of the magic of love"; "the other 'magic' ... is in James's happiest manner." *Ainslee's Magazine* snubbed *Covering End*: "Mr. Henry James has been much talked about on account of his new book ... or rather on account of the first of two long stories that make up the volume." The reviewers recurrently experimented with two speculations about James's intentions for the juxtaposition: one, his exploitation of the idea of magic; the other, his use of the second tale in the volume as an antidote to the first.

James was dealing in magic. The ghost tale, the reviewers thought, was the magic of evil, or perhaps the magic of the supernatural or even more darkly, the magic of hidden guilt; the comedy was, if a magic at all, a charming one, compellingly natural, an exercise in the magic of love, the ebullience of a fascinating woman's influence. But not all reviewers were prepared to play the game. The writer for *Literature* resisted the idea of companion magics: "we cannot say with any confidence why the volume, which contains in one cover two generically dissimilar stories, should be called as a whole, 'The Two Magics,' or why one half of it should be entitled 'The Turn of the Screw.' Nor are we sure whether these two stories are thus associated fortuitously or from design." *Literary World* likewise emphasized the difference: "it is seldom that one finds within the same covers two stories so widely different." *Tribune* goes farther, finding *Covering End* "forced and infelicitous," and decrying the fall "from the masterpiece to the experiment." The writer declares that the pairing provokes both joy and resentment, the resentment being for the notable imperfections of the second tale. The writer for The *Nation* was more complacent and approved of the contrast between the two stories: "the gaiety and grace of the second tale make an effective contrast. Never has a finer tribute been paid to the surprising charm of the American woman who unaffectedly smacks of her native land." *Springfield Republican* finds *Covering End* trifling except for James's touches of wit. In the process, this reviewer applauds James's treatment of Americans, a view hardly shared by the majority of contemporary American readers of James. *Overland* went so far as to suggest, though without disclosing the grounds, that "the second story...is a faint reminder of 'Daisy Miller,'" with a glance, perhaps, at a rather fugitive American innocence. However, many of the reviewers knew of Maisie's revelation that everything had something hidden behind it. Taking Maisie's discovery as a Jamesian parti, they were undoubtedly trying to find what James had hidden behind the juxtaposition of the two tales. There is no reason why their deductions should have been in error. But by chance, the critical development of *The Turn of the Screw* has diminished the alliance between the two magics, and has vacated any remedial power the magic of love might have had for its gloomier companion by the disjunction of *The Turn of the Screw* from *Covering End* in the New York Edition and by the extinguishing power of its very much greater critical significance.

The reviewers' most frequent comparative use of James's other work is with concurrent publications: *In the Cage* and *Maisie*. The reviewers had not liked *In the Cage*. They felt the subject slight and they complained of the style. Huneker comes to *The Two Magics* in relief after the "crabbed polyphony" of "In the Cage." *Critic* compares

In The Cage with *The Turn of the Screw*, suggesting to us that the former "deals...with thoughts before thinking," while the latter "pushes the same audacity to more surprising lengths." Nonetheless, says the reviewer, the heroine of the former had human things on which to base her speculations, while the heroine of the latter lacked a sound empirical basis. Lanier scoffed at *Cage* and suggested that if any one else had written the work it would have been regarded as "stupid, strained and overdrawn," but that because the work was James's it became, perhaps legitimately, complex psychology. The writer for *Ainslee's* merely reports that the style of *Cage* is "equally involved" as the style of his "second autumn book *The Two Magics*."

The reviewers, however, liked and praised *Maisie* and appeared to be pleased with the ghost tale for its similar high achievement. They tended to put this novel and *Screw* on a positive continuum. Thus, Huneker—"immensely moral it is as is 'What Maisie Knew.'" *Bookman* might have been expected to dissent: "nearly all [James's] later stories have been tending to the horrible, have been stories of evil, beneath the surface mostly, and of corruption." But the writer concedes that even in these late "studies of human putrescence" James shows us "perfect manners" and if *What Maisie Knew* stunk of humanity, "it was a triumph of beauty in the end." The *Bookman* review of *The Awkward Age* (1899) goes back over the territory of these late studies of wickedness: "In *What Maisie Knew* [James] suggested the tragic circumstances surrounding a young life with a delicacy and a restrained pathos that were admirable." It was in *Screw* that he cast off such restraint. The reviewer for the *Boston Sunday Post* was comprehensive for the later work: in *The Awkward Age*, he says, we find the psychological qualities that made *Maisie* fascinating, 'In the Cage' depressing, and [*The Turn of the Screw*] maddening." *Literary World* says "if we can call 'What Maisie Knew' a picture of purity in the midst of pollution, so we might call this story of Little Miles and his sister Flora a picture of corruption in the midst of rare loveliness." Huneker, perhaps, makes the definitive comparison in conceiving Maisie sitting in judgment of Miles and Flora: "Maisie herself would be aghast at the subterrene depths revealed in the nature of little Miles and Flora." The writer for the *Tribune* is a dissenter who praises the ghost tale at the expense of its immediate predecessors: "At one leap the author of 'What Maisie Knew' and 'In the Cage' and a dozen other fatuities takes his place among the creators of literature." Indeed, says the writer, if the ghost tale had "appeared at the beginning instead of toward the end of Mr. James's career, his critics would have prophesied for him, we think, a bright immortality." It stands out from his other works, then, as a notable success.

The generic comparisons with ghost tales by other hands favor *The Turn of the Screw*. *Screw* is most frequently compared to Stevenson, but especially to *Dr. Jekyll and Mr. Hyde*. The *Detroit Free Press* declares that it "equals but is wholly unlike 'Jekyll and Hyde' in dreadfulness." *The Times* tells us that *Screw* is as powerful a description of evil as literature has produced "since Stevenson wrote his 'Jekyll and Hyde tale.'" Huneker insists on its superiority in a sweeping judgment: "Hawthorne would have envied it; it makes the allegory of 'Dr. Jekyll and Mr. Hyde,' and the magic lantern slide of Kipling's East Indian bogies ... coarse by comparison[;] Maupassant's 'Horla' is the merest fringe by its side." The *Nation* sees Kipling as the model democrat and James as the model aristocrat with the difference in the thrust of the ghostly a further representation of these ironic differences. *Athenaeum* also hindsees Hawthorne's envy: the tale has "a way which would have made Hawthorne envious on its own ground." *Tribune* declares that it might have "descended from Hawthorne in a fortunate moment." And certainly a comparison to Poe would be irresistible in such a context. Droch tells us that James "has written a story of the Poe sort—and he does it extremely well." Lanier, again, is quite categorical: the tale "puts to shame by its penetrating force and quiet ghostliness the commonplace, unreal 'horrors' of the ordinary ghost story."

But of course these associations with James's own work and with the works of others—his placement, then, in the context of the cultural world from which he derives—naturally evokes the sense of place for at least some of the reviewers. Though James is a native New Yorker, and though the bulk of the reviewing is done in that newly triumphant American cultural capital, the reviewers, if they reflect at all on the cultural antecedents, fix James in the context of New England under the aegis of the Puritans. Huneker, for example, tells his readers that "Mr. James's magnificent New England conscience and his equally magnificent art are the factors in the creation of a dread imagining." For Huneker, the force of place and the power of the moral past are preeminent with the author of the ghost tale. The writer for *Outlook* similarly designates the tale as the product of New England. This writer speaks of "the problem of evil from which men of Puritan ancestry seem never to detach themselves." Mabie in the *Book Buyer* assumes that the reader knows that New England Puritanism is behind the tale in remarking that "men of his intellectual ancestry" have a compelling interest "in the problem of evil."

Peripherals

The important peripherals of *The Turn of the Screw* are its title and its prologue. For this tale these features are crucial to an ample reading. Today, almost a hundred years after first publication, these areas still remain imperfectly read, with aspects still uninterpreted and unassimilated in the struggle to render a satisfactory account of *The Turn of the Screw*. It is not surprising that busy reviewers should find relatively little to say about these matters; but it is a fact that they pay only passing attention to them. Even the exceptions barely touch the implications of the tale. With respect to the prologue, for instance, Lanier, who must be remembered as the reviewer who believes that the ghost tale is the best of James's works, discards the "introduction to 'The Turn of the Screw' [as] a needlessly awkward method of starting the story." The writer for the *Times* shows an awareness of the prologue as a statement about setting and appropriateness: "The introduction to this tale is conventional, but one decides, in looking back, that it serves better than another would. A Christmas house party, with ghost stories told around the fire-place, develops the 'Turn of the Screw' in a tale of a ghost first seen by an innocent child and this leads to the production of this ghost story read from the faded manuscript (supposedly) of a gentlewoman who had had experience with these possessed children. The style of the manuscript, in spite of the insistence upon the woman's penmanship, is obviously the style of Mr. Henry James. But one appreciates not the less the characteristic touch in the statement that it was read 'with a fine clearness that was like a rendering to the ear of the beauty of the author's hand.'" Droch has an ear keen enough to catch Douglas's own characterization of the governess's narrative and quotes his key line in the process of telling us about the "semblance of terror" in the first of the two stories in the latest volume—"a genuine story of 'uncanny ugliness and horror and pain.'" The writer for the *Springfield Republican* shows promise of grappling with the frame, but finally leaves real penetration for the future: "the subject is brought up in a country house, and one of the guests matches a ghost story with this, beginning it himself and continuing it from the manuscript of the governess of the poor little children."

As to the title of the tale, critics still tend to assume that we all understand the same thing by it, most frequently without bothering to say what the understanding comprehends. *Ainslee's* calls the title of the ghost tale "weird." Lanier is no more at ease with the book title nor yet with the story title for *The Turn of the Screw* than he is with the awkward introduction. The general title, he tells us, "is not felicitous" under any conception he can cudgel out of his brain for putting the two tales together. But he does see that the very redoubtable power of the tale "gives an extra 'turn of the screw' beyond anything of the sort that fiction has yet provided." The reader for *Literature* "cannot say ... why one half of [the volume] should be called 'The Turn of the Screw.'" The writer for the *Times* is likewise uncertain: "the title, used to express a stronger shade of horror and mental anguish than the ordinary ghost story represents, does not seem quite as apposite as some of Mr. James's titles." But Droch understands perfectly well: "he calls the story 'The Turn of the Screw,' and he does not hesitate to give it that extra twist that makes the reader writhe under it." He does, that is, seem to understand that at least one apposite sense of the title is that it intimates torture and at least allows for the hypothesis of exorcism. With respect to the title *The Two Magics*, the writer for *Literary World* approves fully: "one reading proves the suggestion [in the title] excellent and the 'Two Magics' are indeed two with a world between them." The writer for the *Springfield Republican* agrees with Lanier that the cover title is not a perfect fit, but agrees with Droch that "the title, 'The Turn of the Screw,' is explained clearly enough in the very first chapter, though its full significance is not brought out till the very last page of the book."

The Theme and Impact

Henry Harland was sufficiently perplexed by the tale to serve quite satisfactorily as a reader of the late-twentieth rather than the late-nineteenth century: very simply, he says that he understands the tale; and very simply, he shows that he does not. His assertion that he grasps the tale has, as well, just the right sense about it of the intuitive: "When the story was first revealed to Mr. James, he saw the beauty in it ... because he saw the story not as an episode, separated from life, but as an instance, illustrative of the rest of life; and he presents it to us not as an anecdote, but, tacitly, as an illustration. He presents it to us as a moment in a continuity, related to the life that had gone before it, that went on about it, that came after it. And so he succeeds in making us see it as beautiful too—as all saturated and suffused with beauty." We have seen enough already to know that the positiveness of these sentiments is not universally shared among those first readers of the tale who put themselves on public record. And thus, by virtue of hindsight, we can contradict his statement in its sense as a mere statistic of the force that James succeeds in making us, readers in general, apprehend his tale as beautiful. But the interest of Harland's statement is not restricted by its mere, though only partial, historical inaccuracy. He also contends that he has told us something about the provenience of that beauty, though in practice he declares the thematic value of the tale as illustration without the slightest attempt to show what it illustrates. I do not mean this as a reproach against Harland, only as an illustration of that quality of the tale that has continued to sustain its readers in the certainty that they have mastered it while their comments indicate that something of importance has eluded them.

What Harland says elaborately here, others say rather more helplessly. *Outlook* assures its readers that the tale illustrates "a profound moral law." It does not trouble to cite the chapter. Mabie has the same certainty without a bit more capacity to show how he has settled on this value for the tale: "It is conceived from a higher point of view; it is a projection of the working of moral law in another sphere." No more skilled in reading this riddle is the *Detroit Free Press*, which tells us that the tale "holds a deep and moving moral." The writer is no more explicit about what this moral is than is Harland. Huneker is more candid: "Just what is the lesson of the master in this powerful allegory I cannot pretend to say." Nonetheless, "immensely moral it is." *Tribune* says that the tale is a "picture of spiritual states so subtly and yet so poignantly observed that all the usual paraphernalia of ghostliness recede into the background as irrelevant." *Springfield Republican* tells its readers that "'The Turn of the Screw' is grewsome [*sic*],and would seem out of character, did one not recollect the carefully suppressed vein of the supernatural which has broken out in his work from time to time," and proceeds to recall "The Ghostly Rental" and "The Altar of the Dead." *Literature* informs its audience of its hope that the subject of *The Turn of the Screw* will not become a common motive with novelists, for it is nothing less than "the demoniac possession of two young and otherwise delightful children." But the writer declines all blame "if we fail to understand Mr. James's book" because "he leaves everything unexplained."

The writer for *Overland* seems to be delighted with the thrill of the tale: "The reader's hair will rise at the beginning of this remarkable tale, and it will not settle down comfortably even when the end is reached." *Literary World* offers the tentative view that "the story is simple enough when you state the plot," following this with the cast of characters. *Critic* says as simply that "the story concerns itself with the hideous fate of two beautiful and charming children" who have been subjected to evil forces. Mabie concludes that "it is less shocking to the senses than many more grossly handled tales, but it is full of horror for the imagination." But *Bookman* and *Independent* are more anguished about the theme or the impact, agreeing on the implication of the reader in the vile rites of the tale: "You cannot help but assist at their interviews, and throb with their anxiety" (*Bookman*); "The feeling after the perusal of the horrible story is that one has been assisting in an outrage upon the holiest and sweetest fountain of human innocence, and helping to debauch—at least by hopelessly standing by—the pure and trusting nature of children" (*Independent*). Even the stiff-necked *Times* shudders that the ghost tale is "the strongest and most affecting argument against sin we have lately encountered in literature." The writer parenthesizes that James, though effective, is not didactic and does not force the moral on the reader.

But what, according to the reviewers, is the outcome of the tale? By and large, they are as cautious on deciding the plot outcome as they are on disclosing the "moral." As the *Nation* had told us, "one sups full of horrors." And as more or less all reviewers agree, "the story concerns itself with the problem of evil" (*Outlook*). Again, there is a general agreement that "you are amply convinced of the extraordinary charm of the children" (*Bookman*). *Critic* has the temerity to tell us that the ghosts complete the ruin that their living originals had begun. *Tribune* assures us that "a lofty flight of imaginative art is never unreal and fruitless." But few go as far as the writer for *Literature*, who tells us that so far as there is a story, it concerns "the trials of the new governess." This writer concludes of the story: "its end seems as regards the boy, tragical; and, as regards the girl, inconclusive. The boy dies, after a striking scene in which the new governess rids him of the demon; the girl is merely taken away in a carriage by the housekeeper, and it is uncertain whether her end, logically, is peace." The writer goes on to raise the question of the validity of James's observation and recording of the nature of childhood and the issues of good and evil in relation to it.[14]

The Resulting Paradigm

The question is, as *Literary World* emphasizes, after one reading, what did the public readers know about the tale? And how did they know it? The issue of the value of a single reading as opposed to careful study of the tale will resurface endlessly in the critical experience with the tale. The refrain might well be summarized in the form: "after a single reading of the tale, I thought it meant this; but when I looked again I discovered my first reading to be in error." Goddard, for example, exulted in "explaining it ... [and then finding] the majority of fellow readers ready to prefer [my explanation] to their own" (k, 184).

A succession of later readers (Tzvetan Todorov [1973]; in his wake, Shoshana Felman [1977]; Shlomith Rimmon [1977]; Christine Brooke-Rose [1976–77; 1981], for example) will decide that there are two stories, and though these students do not venture to reconsider the preliminary grid of newspaper reviews—which expresses whatever we can recover of a collective "naive" public reading—they will fundamentally divide the two stories into a literal and an intensely interpretive reading.[15] However, a probe shows that this collective naive reading is anything but simple, literal or singular. The original paradigm of this reading, whose primary virtue is that it avoids the risk of intrusion from entrenched and perhaps inflexible ideological positions, seems to me irreplaceable if we are to understand the critical tradition of the tale. In order to establish that there is a paradigm in this early writing, we will have to say that it emerges from the collective act of the reviewing—that even if only one of the reviewers spots an idea or describes a perspective, it is part of this grid. This paradigm will have to accommodate disagreements, even diametrical oppositions.

Two related questions concern us about this first reading: We need to know what these readers know and we need to know how they know it. The reviews suggest that they know a good deal about the text, both about its words and its workings, about its sources and backgrounds. The same reviews suggest, however, that the writers take little time or exert little effort to show how they know what they report. They sense, for example, something about the oddity of the title, that it may in fact work its engines on the reader—make this participant "writhe under it" (Droch). They catch, then, the hint that there is anguish associated with it, and perhaps anguish means that they know that there is torture associated with it and only perhaps torture means that there is or may be an act of exorcism involved in the tale. Only a few look at the title, and some puzzle over it, with at least one declaring that it is not as "appropriate as some of Mr. James's other titles" (*Times*).

They sense the existence of the prologue to the tale, again with a ripple of discomfort about it. It is an awkward beginning, possibly a cliché. On the other hand, it might also be appropriate, might successfully collocate Christmas, an old country house, and ghost tales; might find a use for a warm fire and a gathering of friends. There is a bare register of the prior ghost tale and its presenting a ghost to a child. There is the hint that the second ghost tale, the one that we hear, is somehow in competition with the first. There is a suspicion as well that style is a problem, but that the problem of style is to adjust the complex language of the prologue to the possible claimants for possession of the central narrative, with the palm awarded to James. There is the sense that the prologue might identify an important problem in the equation made between the beautiful hand of the gentlewoman who is credited with the writing of the narrative and the mellifluous voice of the gentleman, her proxy as reader of the tale. And this early reading spots Douglas's own critique of the tale "[that it is quite too horrible] for ugliness and horror and pain." The prologue emerges in this composite reading, if only in the barest of outlines.

They see that the implications of the tale are moral, that the moral complexity of the tale is intense, that moral laws are involved and that these moral laws have something to do with the Puritan ethos that so pervades James's work, according to the reviewers who trouble to look into backgrounds. They see an affinity between *The Turn of the Screw* and Hawthorne's work—that James's novella works with the sort of material recognizably Hawthorne's own, but the reviewers' comments are limited to generic similarity and not to the sort of sharing that exists between them from the first, and that supersedes James's rather caustic snubbing of Hawthorne for his provincialism in the English Men of Letters biography (1879). The reviewers thus register the power of the moral implications of the tale without being able to analyze its mechanisms or to account for their sense of its urgency, and they perhaps see the occasion for their juxtaposition of Hawthorne with James without quite seeing its implications. In the same vein, these reviewers sense the analogy between James's ghost tale and Stevenson's allegory of the division of selves in his good doctor without quite being able to specify its function: *Screw* is analogous to *Jekyll and Hyde* in its dramatizing of psychological states by the use of occult narrative. The difference lies perhaps in Stevenson's focusing on the division between the benign and the maleficent within the human being and James's focusing on the terrible question of the locus of evil— within, beside, beyond, outside, remote from the self. One way of talking about the struggle of the governess's narrative is to see her attempting to locate the evil outside herself. The Hawthorne analogy suggests itself everywhere in the corpus of his work but perhaps nowhere more powerfully than in "Ethan Brand," where the first step Brand takes in his journey in quest of the Unpardonable Sin has already consummated the quest in his own person. Emerson had told the Brands of the world not to seek outside themselves.

If these early readers pride themselves on any aspect of their collective reading over any other, it is on their knowledge of the ghosts and the interaction of these horrors with the children. The ghosts are "real" for the overwhelming majority of the readers in the tale's own generic space—that is, problematically real within the limits of conventions that the readers tended to regard as perfectly respectable. There were some murmurs of dissent—the sense recorded that the ghosts represented a view of existence no longer tenable to the reading community in which the story occurs. This dissent acknowledges the invasion of the empirical into the environment of the reading act; but there is dissent from the dissent—the notion that the rejection of the convention of the ghost tale is itself a gratuitous limitation of the range of the imagination. The ghosts, then, are "real," and their assault on the children is tangible, categorical, annihilating. The perfection of this corruption involves an unwavering purpose on the part of the revenants and a joyous reciprocity on the part of the children: these angels savor "daily, even hourly communication" with their corrupters; and the corrupters in turn function with a sort of mad delight in their machinations. These violators are perfectly malignant as they are apprehended by the reviewers. Robert Heilman, so violently cudgeled for his Edenic vision of Bly in the *Screw* wars half a century later, has, in another context, adroitly suggested the sense of what the reviewers struggle to grasp about the ghosts of *The Turn of the Screw*: the same motiveless malignity that he attributes to Iago in this villain's machinations against the heroic Othello. Heilman contends that Iago works his evils for the same reason as the ghosts, or so the reviewers seem to glimpse: in support of the *invidia*, the distinguishing mark of the satanic in relation to the unbearable beauty of purity.

These reviewers know a bit about the governess. They know her age, her employment and its responsibilities, the nature of her charge, the nature of her response to what she finds at the old country house. They know about the dear old housekeeper, but they carefully shield their readers from hearing her name, as though to protect the innocent. They know about the ghosts—about the former valet and about the former (sometimes iniquitous) governess, though if it is an act of altruism that keeps them from naming the housekeeper, it cannot be the same motive that keeps them from naming the ghosts and/or the former valet and governess. They are barely aware of the uncle in London; they know something of what Douglas says, though they do not name him either; they know nothing of Griffin, though they do refer to his tale, which precedes the introduction of Douglas's reading of the governess's narrative. Again, what they declare they know seems to come from intuition rather than from any demonstration of what is in the text.

They know something about the power of the tale, about its capacity to touch and to wound. This power is seen as a beauty by some and as a horror or an ugliness by others. Lanier, for example, goes so far as to say of the tale that "one instinctively compares it to a beautiful pearl: something perfect, rounded, calm, unforgettable" (733). *Independent* flinches over how "Mr. James could, or how any man or woman could, choose to make such a study of infernal human debauchery." There is thus a sense of beauty, even perhaps a suffusion, but at the same time, it derives from the ugliness of evil. The impulse that discovers an indissoluble bond here between beauty and the ugliness of evil tends to discover in the artistry of the tale the intense craft that compels the reader regardless of the reader's moral stand. This recognition of the bond between evil and good is in divers forms a virtual collective acknowledgment of James's success in what he had set out to achieve in writing the tale. It was, after all, only some ten years later in the preface to *Maisie* that James made clear his appreciation of the "close connection between bliss and bale." And again, if we listen to the language of the New York preface to the tale, we find that James first disavows any expatiation in the tale and then declares that he wishes to make the reader "think the evil for himself" so that he, the author, can be "released from weak specification" (k 123). More than one reader after the groping first attempt of the reviewers has come to grief attaching to James inescapable impressions about the tale that, for all their splendid inevitability, belong to the reader rather than to a strict evidential mustering of the text. But these first public readers know the tale's power and its beauty, and perhaps they nourish a suspicion of its dangerous technique of playing with the reader's own depth psychology in making the reader think the evil for himself.

The reviewers know something of the tale's style. They know something of its mechanisms for producing powerful images in the minds of readers. They know something of the vulnerability of children. They can see the implications of guilty knowledge in the tale, and especially of guilty sexual knowledge. They do not tell us how they know of the sexual guilt of Quint and Miss Jessel; and if they believe that it is this sexual knowledge that the ghosts have passed on to the children, they do not show us the textual evidence for it, or the process of its transmission, or the irresistible reflection of its force in the specific actions of the children. There is a conviction among the reviewers that there is abuse in the tale—perhaps of the gift of life by the ghosts before their deaths, perhaps of the children, perhaps of the reader who is by virtue of the story subjected to the sexual or other truths or affirmations that the story either constrains or allows the reader to infer. And indeed, they know a great deal overall. I have suggested a few of the things that might expose deficiencies of comprehensive knowledge in this collective first reading; it remains to be seen how extensive the comprehensive understanding might become through later critical investigation.

The question remains how these first readers know. I have suggested the power of James's craft in promoting the readers' responses. His craft is the key to the first readers' knowledge (and of course to their reading errors). Norman Hapgood (mentioned above in n. 1), writing at the time of composition of *The Turn of the Screw*, makes a provocative statement about James's descriptive technique: "The author is not to a large degree a man for whom the visible world exists, in the sense of Gautier's famous phrase. Its interest is adjective mostly: the interest of its effect on persons first, and, second, an interest of suggestion" (1898, 198). Hapgood is talking about James's craft and discounting to some extent the force of the physical as a part of it. At the same time he is emphasizing James's very great gift for suggestion, or as he says, James "has a rare, distinguished genius, and it is the genius of an artist, but the artist is a psychologist" (199). The passage quoted above begins with a statement about clothing and physical appearance.

When Hapgood says, therefore, that the interest of the visual world for James is "adjective mostly," and when he asserts that the interest lies in the effects on people, he is offering penetrating comments about James's method. The context of clothing incorporates color by dyeing, and in dyeing, the *adjective* is a substance required to fix dyes and to prevent colors running. What Hapgood recognizes about James's psychological technique is no less than an affirmation of the reality of impressions: that James's descriptive technique involves the apposition of color to his world, made as colorfast as the psychology of impressions can make it. It is this technique that so organizes the responses of readers to his fiction, especially the fiction that explores psychic states; the first public readers were especially susceptible to it. This technique—that is, the deployment of the epistemology of impressions—discloses to us how the reviewers come to know the features of James's world. It is this technique in *Screw* that allows James to delight in being accused of imposing his demons and dark voids upon his readers when in fact these monsters are generated from the readers themselves. The "adjective" in James's descriptive technique is the psychological fixative that moors the readers' response in lieu of James's own expatiation.

It is worth asking as well what this study shows about reviewing. In the critical history of James's work as a whole, the ghost tale is a pivotal point. For those who hearkened back to the purity of "Daisy Miller" and considered everything that James wrote afterward to be a decline from that high point of his career—and there are many—this tale represents a return to clarity and to power. The ghost tale is thus a benchmark of the achievement before the movement into the final phase of his work, with five completed novels to come. At least one of the reviewers declared this work to be James's greatest achievement and speculated that if it had come at the beginning, it would automatically have led to predictions of a great career. The tale thus turns on the reviewers and smokes out their own naive process of reading James and prompts disclosure of long-term dissatisfaction with James, especially over the matter of style. It is clear that either James has lost his initial power and therefore has squandered his promise, or that he is applying a creative pressure to the community of readers of which the reviewers supply the first form of the public component for which no reading experience has prepared them.

H. R. Jauß quite legitimately objects to careless literary historicizing. But he does not go far enough or take sufficient notice of the first state of public reading when he comments that "there are works that at the moment of their appearance are not yet directed at any specific audience, but that break through the familiar horizon of literary expectations so completely that an audience can only gradually develop for them. When, then, the new horizon of expectations has achieved more general currency, the power of the altered aesthetic norm can be demonstrated in that the audience experiences formerly successful works as outmoded" (1970, 26–27). It is quite true, for instance, of the critical tradition of *The Turn of the Screw* that the tale outstripped any number of contemporary best-sellers in lasting public interest. But the reviewers' grid of responses to the work, analyzed above, suggests that the process was nowhere near as uniform as Jauß's representation proposes. The tale was applauded and condemned. It was undoubtedly condemned for the wrong reasons, as one sees in the reviewer for *Bookman* who objected to it as immoral and cruel. It is also possible to say that it was applauded for the wrong reasons, or at least for insufficient reasons, in some of the reviews. The reviewers' incapacity to state even the vaguest terms of the tale's moral in the wake of pronouncing it most intensely moral signals the area of possible challenge.

The reviewers who applauded the tale also seemed satisfied that it suited the horizon of expectations for a work in its genre. If we look at the ghost stories of M. R. James, written at about the same time as *The Turn of the Screw*, we find that they fulfill nicely the demands of the normal horizon of expectations: some violation has taken place; the guilty party is now to pay for it. In "A Warning to the Curious," Paxton hears of the buried crowns sacred to ancient England, unearths one according to local directions, feels unseen pursuit and, though he restores the crown to its earthly vault, he dies, apparently at the hands of his pursuers. Paxton has been represented as a pure philosophical empiricist who does not believe in any aspect of the occult. That transaction is typical of M. R. James's ghost stories: there is sin, especially the sin of doubting the force of the spirit world; and there is retribution, sometimes with our sense that the sufferer is more sinned against than sinning. In Henry James's tale, on the other hand, regardless of whether the first readers see it, arises a very distinct problem in the assignment of the sin if indeed the wages of sin is death. Quint dies; Jessel dies; little Miles dies. Flora, so far as the narrative goes, does not. But it is difficult to see what value to assign sin in the moral economy of James's tale. What does death mean—is it physical and accompanied by the agony of spiritual torture, or is it spiritual only and accompanied by the pains of hell? One or two of the reviewers sense that the governess might be impeached on her record of events. Is she, as so many of the psychological critics suggest, the real perpetrator of evil in the tale? And if so, what are the wages of her sin? We know her, after all, in the toils of the fiction because she has risen to a place of high preferment, notwithstanding her perils at Bly. And we have Douglas's word for it that she is highly distinguished in her preferment. Is the governess sublime in attempting to shield her charges, or is she a sublimator who re-creates reality with mendacious narrative to serve the ends of concealing her own guilt? But James does not say, as a critic of a later work might have observed.[16] What he does show his reader is not the simple morality tale of sin and retribution, not merely the seductive odors of the flowers of evil, but the labyrinth of human motive and human consciousness, the intense impressions of a mind under great stress and the imperfect system of the mind in coping with the contending states of reality that seem to be available for selection in a cosmos that does not determine right and wrong according to absolute standards.

It is worth remarking, almost 175 years after the event, that Croker's review of Keats's *Endymion*, of which wound, according to Shelley's furious riposte, Keats died, was nonetheless a perfectly sound review if indeed what Croker were reviewing had been a bad book. Without trying to decide that question definitively, one can at least see Croker's point. Without the brilliance of Keats's vision, it might be difficult indeed to see the connection between the rhymes and the sense of the poem.[17] *Endymion* might easily be regarded as the fulminations of a gifted mind that had not yet discovered its discipline. Or put in perhaps less controversial terms, even in his towering anger, Byron does not try to defend himself against Jeffrey's criticisms of *Hours of Idleness*. He merely says that two can play at the slashing game—and he does so with a very satisfying vengeance. But surely nobody who cares about poetry is prepared to defend a poem that drops on every wave a tear. Keats's work was epoch making; Byron's was mere kindling for a very amusing round of logomachy. The reviewer is always in the difficult position of not being equipped to distinguish the great new work, the work with what Jauß calls horizonal implications, from the merest jejune offering; it is safer, statistically, to condemn than to praise.

In what James next publishes, two problem novels in a row—*The Awkward Age* and *The Sacred Fount*—there will be solid grounds for the less skilled readers among the periodical reviewers to cavil and declare that the aging James has lost or surrendered his creative powers. What is interesting is that this tendency to cavil over the problem novels carries over into the reviewing of all three of the final completed novels. The results are interesting for both the reviewers and for the student of James's major novels. The thin line between bafflement at groundbreaking work and legitimate grousing about reading difficulty and gratuitous involution of style is appropriate matter for an extensive exploration of the reviewer's job of work. Much of what James finally does with his themes and supports with his style has begun to appear in the tortuosities of *The Turn of the Screw*. The tale is adept in the imagination of disaster; it is intense in its appreciation of the uncanny. It provides a last foothold for journalists who would prefer to celebrate Marie Corelli and her *Master Christian* than to struggle through the fields of tormented souls who inhabit James's fictional landscape. James does not hesitate to collocate beauty with the most intense sense of the presence of evil. There are students of James's late novels who would be prepared to swear that this collocation was James's most enduring recognition about the life of the spirit in his time.

2

The Genesis of a Critique

THE AMERICAN SCENE

Though we might say that the years between the publication of *The Turn of the Screw* and the New York Edition were characterized by what we now know as James's major phase, the principal Jamesian event to his countrymen was his return to the United States after a long expatriation, from the summer of 1904 to the summer of 1905.[1] He returned to a mixed response: his countrymen showed some enthusiasm for the late novels at their publication, but also a good deal of bafflement and confusion, and the overall result fell short of a contemporary perception that their author was enjoying a major renaissance. This mixed response surfaces in the variety of the critical attitudes to James's work, best illustrated, perhaps in articles by William Crary Brownell (1905), in a kind of fascinated hostility, and H. G. Dwight (1907), in a kind of helpless praise.

James seems to have accepted Brownell as his major critic of the time,[2] despite the latter's hostility toward the late fiction; there is no evidence that James knew of Dwight's more favorable overview. Brownell, born a decade later than James, had, like James, gotten his literary start as a reviewer for the *Nation*, also a decade later than James. The latter had begun with Godkin's then new periodical by reviewing what would be for both James and Brownell a central critical and cultural text, Matthew Arnold's *Essays in Criticism*, in 1865.[3] Brownell himself was soon reviewing James for the *Nation*, and his review of the *Hawthorne* (1879) is now generally known. Brownell, however, had remained a man of letters—a critic, a student of prose mastery, a theorist of criticism, of style, and ultimately of their relation to the culture of a democratic society—and had become a senior literary editor with Scribner's by the 1890s so that he was in place when James was planning the New York Edition with the firm. Roger Gard says that it was Brownell who guided the New York Edition through the press (1968. 395). Logically, Brownell was Scribner's agent in the arrangements for the New York Edition. This probable collaboration between two very similar and simultaneously very dissimilar Arnoldians expresses some of the oddness of events for a student of the criticism of *The Turn of the Screw*. When James's editor ventures a rather unfavorable critical evaluation of James's career—as he does in the *Atlantic* article of 1905—and simultaneously takes responsibility for giving the work its permanent form, we can judge some of the pressures under which the novelist is working. If Brownell is James's nomination for his most perceptive critic, we can perhaps pardon James for his antipathy to literary journalism.[4]

The time between the publication of the ghost tale in 1898 and the authorized edition of the works a decade later was in any case a time of low density in the criticism of the tale. As I have suggested above, it was a time when those concerned with such matters were moving toward a general assessment of James's work, under the assumption that the bulk of it was completed. Indeed, Dwight in 1907 was very much concerned about the character of these journalistic acts of summation. He expresses his dismay that "among a considerable number of reviews formal and informal, and of those letters from readers which are so interesting to a student of manners, [I] happened to encounter only four notices which were completely favorable to the subject of this paper" (Gard 1968, 434). He cites numbers of public commentators who disparaged and caviled, often without so much as the pretense of trying to understand the work. Dwight constituted himself James's defender by summarizing the journalistic judgments of James's work and ultimately by offering his own insights into the values of the work that the journalists often missed.

The most dramatic event in the criticism of the tale is that for its sins *The Turn of the Screw* was banned in Boston. Mark Twain had enjoyed a good laugh at the expense of Cambridge, Massachusetts when the library association banned *Huckleberry Finn*. He wrote gleefully to an admirer in Cambridge that he could thank that enlightened town for seriously boosting the sales of the book. No record I can find shows that James even knew that *The Turn of the Screw* was banned in Boston. But the *Washington Post* (22 February, 1901, 6) knew and echoed Twain in a laugh at the expense of Boston propriety. Under title "Poor Literary Outlaws," the writer for the *Post* offered sympathy for "the literary waifs excluded from the esteemed Boston Public Library." The writer wants to know the identity of the censors of "the mental food to be absorbed by Boston's cultured readers," and makes the appropriate conjectures as to Boston's collective Mrs. Grundy—"ministers, laymen, jealous authors, university professors, or store clerks?" In any case, the company of the banned is apparently honorable—Capt. Charles King, Mary E. Wilkins, Paul Leiscester Ford, and Gertrude Atherton join James in ignominy: "Gertrude Atherton's 'Senator North' goes to the guillotine with the 'Two Magics' of the irreproachable Henry James." The writer admits that Baltimore once incurred the wrath of New England by castigating E. D. E. N. Southworth, but at a time when she was at the apex of her career and thus invulnerable; whereas Boston has censored the local Molly Elliot Seawell, whose "The Loves of Lady Arabella" the writer now worries will become a victim to other libraries "patterned after Boston's queer institution."[5] At least, then—though the act seems less particularly refined than, for instance, the banning of Joyce's *Ulysses* or the sending up of Lawrence's *Lady Chatterly* on a writ—someone somewhere had the prescience to ban the volume bearing that "lurid, poisonous little tale," as Oscar Wilde called it (Gard 1968, 277), and thus offered us the judgment that the volume in part, if not as a whole, offended the virtues of public taste.

The period from 1898 to 1908 incorporates the reviews of the late novels, sometimes with side reflections on the relation between these works and *The Turn of the Screw*. Reviewers will say a few forgiving things about *The Sacred Fount*—for example, that it is an important study of human nature for those who are interested (Shipman 1901, 148)—but the more characteristic attitude is expressed in H. T. Peck's review as editor of the *Bookman* (1901, 442), in which he complains that the novel is full of supersubtlety about nothing in particular and concludes with his nose in the air: "we cannot quite endure the sort of thing that he is writing nowadays." Even Cornelia Pratt, whose review of James's career in 1899 had been so enthusiastic, is now questioning the value of *The Sacred Fount*: it is wonderful, she suggests, "but is it worthwhile?" (1901, 370).

The reviewer of *The Sacred Fount* for the New York *Tribune* (1901) makes a direct connection between that novel and *The Turn of the Screw*. The unnamed author calls the ghost tale a masterpiece, and finds in it a "train of speculation" that the author indicates a wish to see exploited in more of the novelist's fiction. *The Awkward Age* was a weakening in James's creative process, as was the collection of stories in *The Soft Side*. But *The Sacred Fount* had promise of returning fruitfully to the "spiritual airs of creative imagination." While the new novel borders on the supernatural with its vampire theme, it ends by dealing with an essentially sterile problem. The vampires should thrill us as had the ghosts in *The Turn of the Screw*, but here James "clothes his vampires in evening dress"—"where he might have made them shapes of dread he leaves them figures of fun." While few enough subsequent readers seem to have discovered the fun, the vampire tale has baffled its readers about as persistently as has the ghost tale. The reviewer is content to think that *The Turn of the Screw* is undoubtedly a great book that promises even more power of insight and penetration in James's later work; *The Sacred Fount* is a disappointment that merely "bids us to a Barmecide's feast." The reviewer's principal objection is that James does not explain the nature of the sacred fount—a manner of complaint that anticipates much of the later critical uneasiness over James's problem fiction generally, including *The Turn of the Screw*. James's narrator in the vampire tale is concerned only about trifles, the reviewer protests, and not about the urgent matters of how the transfers of youth and brilliance from donors to recipients are effected. That narrator, the reviewer says, engages in acts of analysis that remind us of the author's own penchant for such activities. But the reviewer makes the same mistake that many critics of the ghost tale make—that of being too sure where to find James himself in the text, sure, then, that James is to be identified with the narrator of the tale.

In this era James will be fair game for those odd vestiges of total-immersion Victorianism that might account for the banning of *The Two Magics* by the Boston Public Library. A writer called Frank Moore Colby coldly recoils from the sophisticated slant of James's work, citing the very indeterminacy that troubles so many of the later readers of *The Turn of the Screw* as James's warrant for sliding by without being locked up for indecent (verbal) exposure: "The man's style was his sufficient fig-leaf, and ... few would see how shocking he really was" (1902a, 396). James hides, Colby says, "behind that verbal hedge of his," and the public simply does not know what he is about. Though his language has grown into "deepening shadows," one has but to follow him into these to discover how many guilty secrets one can find there. The greatest horror for Colby's delicate sensibility is that James counsels women to break the proprieties. His particular quarrel is with James's article on George Sand (*North American Review* 1902) which is "a wicked one indeed." In James's celebration of the coming age of emancipation great new days will dawn: "halcyon days they seem to him, and woman the harbinger of a powerful Babylonish time when the improprieties shall sing together like the morning stars." For his offenses, any other man would be suppressed, Colby says, but James perseveres in his "sheltering vagueness" (1902, 397). "Whatever else may be said of James," Colby continues, "he is no tempter"—precisely because, though the most horrendous immoral and illicit things are depicted, "it is a land where vices have no bodies and the passions no blood, where nobody sins because nobody has anything to sin with." It is safe, Colby says, in an echo of Howells's Grundian dictum, to leave James's books wide open in the nursery: not even the most prurient child could make head or tails out of the mass of verbal hedge. Once James wrote of human things, Colby concludes, but now he has left us only with "the discreditable amours of skeletons" (380). Much of what Colby has to say is reminiscent of the most appalled of the comments on *The Turn of the Screw*. The bafflement is also a cry of frustration over the density and apparent intractability of the texts that these readers face. Colby neatly anticipates Brownell's much more extensive comment on James's work, its late style and the apparent desiccation of the work. He is saying a good deal about the critical uneasiness over James in the period and about the aspect of the ghost tale that most distresses its critics.[6]

This irritation with James resulted in a sort of general journalistic twitch. It was a nuisance in the American or at least the journalistic estimation of his work to decide whether the better conversational strategy were to focus on James's powerful international reputation or on his difficult style or his even more difficult subject matter. The writer for *Outlook* (1904) could thoughtfully decide that James was the "most accomplished American man of letters" of his time; nonetheless, James seemed to this writer to be in need of some of his own advice about an artist's relation to his country, since James in his biography of William Wetmore Story had said that the sculptor's art had suffered from his expatriation. Notwithstanding his absence from the United States, James had seen deeply into his culture and its ails in *The Ambassadors*, his most recent novel, as the writer says. Claude Bragdon in the *Critic* (1904) worked the same sort of hedging comment on James. He produces a lovely sophism in adding his mite to the litany of pricklings over James's return: "Henry James is too great to be ignored; yet he is too ignored to be great." *The Ambassadors,* Bragdon informs us, treats "the amorous predicaments of people belonging to the most idle and depraved society of the land of his adoption." Dwight, providing the antiphony on this litany, says of Bragdon's plum that it is "but the mildest of statements" (1907, 434), and goes on to uncover a good supply of more violent ones. But Bragdon, after he explodes his squib, goes on to show that he really means to praise James and recognizes, even before James makes it a central premise of the prefaces to the New York Edition, that James's critics cannot forgive him "his supreme virtue, that he demands of his readers their full attention and presupposes their intelligence" (1904, 147).

E. R. Hagemann in his treatment (1968) of *Life*'s satirical pursuit of James at the turn of the century speaks of taunts that James did not write English and therefore required translation. Following the publication of James essays in *Harper's* and the *North American Review* (1905) that would ultimately become chapters in *The American Scene*, Charles Battell Loomis (1905) made the case for the foreignness of James's style. He speaks with mock awe of a journalist of his acquaintance who claimed that he could read James in the original and then does a bit of swaggering himself: he, too, could read James in the native idiom. But, says Loomis, if one can understand something, one should be able to explain it, and so he promises a translation into common English of a passage from the impressions of James's travels. Loomis does indeed enjoy himself at James's expense and underlines real difficulties along the way. He quotes a passage from the essay on the middle states, here with a focus on New Jersey, finds the first sentence of the original untranslatable and then does, in a sense, render a version of the subsequent sentences: says James, "I had come forth for a view of such parts of the condition as might peep out at the hour and on the spot, and it was clearly not going to be the restless analyst's own fault if the conditions in general, everywhere, should strike him as almost affectingly at the mercy of observation." Or in Loomis's translation, "I had come forth for copy, and there were the things to observe all ready to hand, if I cared to observe them—which I did care" (465). James pushes nuance in an almost neutral setting to an extreme; Loomis reduces it to a bare bones stripped of any sense of nuance at all. One finds it possible to sympathize with both sides: Loomis has seen the attenuation in James's style; James has continued to struggle for a perfect vocabulary of impression. Nonetheless, the environment in which the ghost tale would be seen in this era and the critical aura surrounding James's late work in general advances a double sense of an important occasion that nonetheless promotes an uneasy milieu. Loomis concludes with a sort of wryness that reflects that double sense: "And I cannot help thinking that however we little insects try to sting James, the truth intrudes every now and then that in spite of his obsession in favour [*sic*] of fogginess of expression, the self-expatriated American who has come back to fall in love with the landscape of his birth and to make fun of the figures in that landscape is a man who by virtue of his best work must ever loom large in English literature" (466).

The same vexation that recurrently surrounds the commentary on the novels sometimes echoes in the critics' reflections on *The Turn of the Screw*. In an unhappy review of *The Wings of the Dove*—because, like too many French novels, it seems to find fault with the English— Harriet Waters Preston (1903) reiterates the less pleased opinions of *The Turn of the Screw*: "but there are certain of Mr. James's later and more elaborate novels of English life, such as *The Awkward Age* and *What Maisie Knew*, that are as full of covert suggestions of the foulness as the worst French novel of the last forty years." Setting this as a context, Preston concludes, "and there is one short story of his, 'The Turn of the Screw', which is a sheer moral horror, like the evil dream of a man under the spell of a deadly drug." For Preston, the tale is apparently as evil as it had been for the writer of *Outlook*, notwithstanding the time of seasoning between first publication and this stage some four years later.

The age produces enthusiastic support for James as well as unease and disparagement. In January 1903, the *Edinburgh Review* published a long article on James's work, laudatory at least in its intention and a presumable compliment to the author by its sheer length (it ran, according to Gard 1968, from 59 to 85). This piece was quickly excerpted in the United States, in *Harper's Weekly* in February 1903, and in *Living Age* in March 1903. The writer celebrates James's long career and in a sense proposes that his work showed great achievement; but the writer also finds shortcomings: though James knows the depths of the human heart, "he has dropped a line but rarely into the deep waters of life [though] his soundings have so added to our knowledge of its shallows that no student of existence can afford to ignore his charts" (*Harper's Weekly*. 1903. 47: 273). This student claims to discuss the entire corpus of James's work (without offering any logic to account for some fairly significant exceptions) and includes a discussion of the supernatural along the way. "In the Cage," the writer tells us, was created for too little purpose, but it reflects James's resolution "to retain his correspondence with life." (*Living Age*. 1903. 236: 579). "How far such resolution has been considered in 'The Turn of the Screw' is a somewhat trenchant question, since the answer must pronounce on Mr. James's attitude to the world of apparition. He has shown from the beginning…a fondness for influences which should be rather defined as superordinary than supernatural." This writer then, pushes the discussion of the ghosts and their status toward a slightly clearer focus than the paradigm of the reviews had reached in speaking of the ghost tale, by posing the question of the distinction between the supernatural and the "superordinary." The writer presumes that the latter is something of a literary device, a quasi-lifelike concept, stretching, perhaps, James's 'resolution' to retain "his correspondence with life at whatever cost of stimulating adventure."

In the ghost tale, however, the "correspondence to life" is perhaps the waif and the "stimulating adventure" the legitimate heir. The writer discusses the treatment of the supernatural in James's work and finds some reasonably satisfactory sorts of apparitions prior to *The Turn of the Screw*—in some of his tales of the superordinary, James crosses a border, in others he merely gives us revenants from the dead, in yet others he gives us figures that might have been generated by "telegraphic suggestion." *The Turn of the Screw* is in a category by itself: "the shades of Peter Quint and Miss Jessel are conclusively screened from such an origin, and their author's serious attitude to his art forbids the suspicion that they are merely elements of make-believe. One seems left with no choice but to take them seriously and to consider them as the author's contribution to a speculation which has imposed its interest upon many writers." Though the writer falls short of commitment to "real" ghosts as against the make-believe of the tale because of James's "serious attitude to his art," the writer sees at least the potential ambiguity of the tale in this rather uneasy sketch of his purpose. This short excursion into the problem of the orientation of the tale's supernatural figures recalls the similarly uneasy review of the work in the *Critic* (1898), in which the reader began by suspecting the sanity of the governess but ended by conceding her logic. The writer for the *Edinburgh Review* joins others in emphasizing the centrality of *The Turn of the Screw* in contemporary discussions of James's supernatural.

Montgomery Schuyler, in a review of *The Better Sort* in the *Lamp* (April 1903), corroborates this view. Schuyler's context is a consideration of *The Sacred Fount* in relation to the newly published tales, the interest of which for him is "the manifestly fantastic thesis that there may be such a thing as a physical vampire which feeds upon and absorbs another's beauty, and such a thing as an intellectual vampire which assimilates another's brains" (p231). But he makes an observation perceptive for the study of the works of James and particularly relevant to James's problem texts: "the world of his psychology, a world of theorems and problems, is as far as may be from the world in which the common novel-reader aspires to lose himself." Just as some of the reviewers had struggled with the problem component in *The Turn of the Screw*, Schuyler identifies in *The Sacred Fount* a feature that suggests something of the schematization of puzzles and puzzle bits, of games and their eccentric laws, to such an extent that James seems to take no care to make his work show how the "real" world functions or how it applies the laws of common properties or probability. He shows his understanding of those properties in James's work even more acutely in quoting Winckelmann to the effect that one mustn't trust artists too far since "they look more to what is difficult than to what is beautiful." (232). It is in this frame that Schuyler finds the ghost tale central: "But is the thesis propounded in 'The Sacred Fount' or in 'The Private Life' any more untenable than that propounded in 'The Turn of the Screw'? And is not this latter success a complete vindication of the author's method, the method of slow and patient accumulation of detail and circumstance to make that credible which, stated baldly and crudely, would be incredible?" (232). For Schuyler the fact of intentional difficulty for the reader in a work is no hindrance to artistic achievement.

Oliver Elton also writes a long and encomiastic overview of James's fiction in the *Edinburgh*'s companion publication the *Quarterly Review* (1903) and is also inclined to give an important place to *The Turn of the Screw*. Elton offers an appreciation of the "gift and scope of pure fantasy in this countryman and student of Hawthorne," declaring that these have "hardly had proper recognition" from the students of his work (365). He supports his appreciation in reassessing "The Private Life" and "Sir Edward Orme." But, says Elton, "Mr. James has put far more force into 'The Turn of the Screw,' one of the hideous stories of our language" (365). Elton echoes the reviewers in speaking of the power of the story to wound the reader's sensibility by displaying the torments of the children in their entanglement with the ghosts. "There might," says Elton "seem something wanton in the ruthless fancy—in the reinvasion of our life by the dead butler Peter Quint and his paramour" (366).[7] In other words, it is not the children alone who suffer the ghosts, but also the reader—and the reader is likewise held in the vise of their evil. Like Schuyler, Elton senses that there is a hanging question about the status of the ghosts, however powerful the reader perceives their corruptive hold over the children; he speaks of the "doubt raised and kept hanging, whether, after all, the two ghosts, who can choose to whom they will appear, are facts or delusions of the young governess who tells the story; and in the final defeat of hope by the boy's death just at the moment he may perhaps be saved."

Elton's joining that select group of early readers of the tale who begin to consider its ambiguity—and its density—emphasizes for us how much earlier than Edna Kenton's 1924 essay this dimension of the tale became a part of its critical grid. But just as the reviewer for the *Critic* and the writer for the *Edinburgh* had noticed this hanging dimension without accepting it as inevitable, Elton refuses to acknowledge the register of his own senses, and he shies away from the logic of the tale's ambiguity in the familiar bromide that James is a child of Puritanism and this ambiguous dimension of the supernatural in the tale is the froth of its residue in him: *The Turn of the Screw* "is the work of a symbolist and a puritan" (366). The ghosts can be rationalized as "the survival of the poison, which, living, they had sown in the breasts of the innocents." (366). Nonetheless, Elton will have it both ways: he will see the ghosts as survivals—a kind of persistent moral memory—and as agents, "at once as symbol and as actual combatant." Elton insists that the veracity of the governess's report comes through James's capacity to speak "in the name of women," a postulate in the larger scope of his essay in which James's insight in fiction is seen as deriving from this very special gift. The governess is not only innocent of the charge of hallucinating the ghosts; she also rises from her torments to a kind of spiritual greatness in which, even though desperate in her attempts to shelter the children, she shows a courage which sets at defiance the "distrust with which others regard her story, and the aversion to her inspired by the ghosts in the children themselves" (366). The greater force that Elton attributes to *The Turn of the Screw* in comparison to other James ghost tales, then, derives in part from James's capacity to suspend the ultimate question of both authority and blame, even though the governess appears to emerge as heroic in Elton's reading. This greater force also derives from James's skill in the "feat of drawing children," the subject to which Elton proceeds after completing his treatment of the supernatural.

The same Claude Bragdon who found James too ignored to be great can nonetheless say of him that he shares with Meredith "the effort to render audible the higher harmonics of the fundamental note of human passion and emotion which their predecessors were content more or less violently to sound" (1904, 147). Like Hardy, James is concerned to express the nature of civilization in his characters: but where Hardy is inclined to do so in the raw, James shows "this same human nature, warped, stunted, distorted, or perchance refined and sublimated by the operation of the laws, forms and observances of civilization,—modified, that is to say, by the conditions incident to the highly organized life of the cities." It is a pestilent, predatory world in James's version of which we see without sufficient awareness a quiet sort of cannibalism, or vampirism (since Bragdon also wishes to refer to the context of *The Sacred Fount*): "the difficulty consists in the fact that most of us are blind to life as it goes on around us until Mr. James assists us with his gift of vision, like some obliging astronomer, with telescope focussed on the moon, who shows us mountains and deep valleys where only a mottled radiance was seen before." Bragdon, too, like Elton, is beginning to sense the terrain of games, of schemes whose execution reveals the darker layers of human motive. This recognition focuses the ghost tale for him. If *The Sacred Fount* shows its power in laying bare the vampirisms that are "going on always, and all about us," there is a special immediate relevance for James's treatment of the supernatural: "in nothing does our author better show his modernity than in his not infrequent excursions into the realm of the supernatural" (149). The implications, as reviewers noted, are that *The Sacred Fount* shares the presence of the supernatural with *The Turn of the Screw*. James includes in his work "nothing that might not be found in the 'Report of the Transactions of the Society for Psychical Research.' Yet by example of his art he is able to produce (in 'The Turn of the Screw,' for example) an effect of poignant horror which makes the essays of Poe and Bulwer in this field seem like the claptrap which they are" (150). The juxtaposition of the ghost tale with the metaphor of the jungle, however tenuously sensed, expands James's own sense, to be expressed in the preface, that the world of the ghost tale "reeks with the air of evil" because it is a just analogue for this world.

Elizabeth Luther Cary also surveys James's novels (1904); in the next year she will turn this essay into a sectodecimo treatise on James's work. Her covering observation is that with few exceptions in her time, fiction "is written for the young and by the young" (394). James is one of the exceptions. Dwight, in considering the critical field, declares that she is one of four commentators known to him in recent times whose treatment of James is entirely favorable (1968, 434–35). For her, against the grain of prevailing opinion, James's view of Americans is both penetrating and generous. She acknowledges how small a part the actual experience of America has played in "creating his environment and forming his associations." But she has some sense of the sort of thing James is talking about in "The Art of Fiction," where he celebrates the capacity of the sensitive artist's mind to grasp its material intuitively in a flight of ecstatic awareness—where he distinguishes Anne Thackeray Ritchie for her ability to grasp the conditions of Huguenot life on the basis of a single glimpse of an abandoned dinner table. "He has written between thirty and forty novels and long stories, and in two-thirds of them, at least, is portrayed the American character with the scrupulous care of a mind ardent in the pursuit of truth" (394). Strether is the perfection of James's grasp of the American: "these [virtues] in Strether combine to form that Americanism for which Mr. James has the tenderest sentiment, the most loyal respect" (398). But this is only to see that James's realism is not a matter of noticing the commonplaces of existence; rather, his realism is "merely the solid and tangible envelope of his inherent mysticism. He is too thoroughly an artist to leave his characters in a disembodied state. It is the business of the artist to give form to his thought, to provide illusions that shall convince; and this to the most extraordinary degree Mr. James accomplishes" (399). In the light of her contention of James's mysticism, she will see a special importance in his use of the supernatural. Visions and dreams mark his work early and late, she says, supposing some relation between them and the ghost tales in his corpus: "occasionally he has written ghost stories of undiluted mystery. 'The Turn of the Screw' is a tale of which the elusive horror cannot be exaggerated." Thus, for her, too, the creation of the tale is an enigma—not as respects the functioning power of the ghosts, but in the majesty of the creative power that can communicate to the story such a force of shuddering accuracy about the nature of ghosts and their evil echoes in human beings.

But that spirit world is large compared to the world of ordinary experience, she suggests, and James benefits from his touch with the mystical: "The domain of terrestrial experience is narrow compared to the wide world of psychological conjecture. From the natural phenomena absorbing the attention of most of us, some of us are continually summoned by a vision of miracle, by a ghostly sense of the supernatural breathing upon our lusty materialism." James is, then, the son of the Swedenborgian father whose mysticism finds a place in the ghost tales. In *The Turn of the Screw* a sense of that vastness penetrates the commonplace, which we encounter "in the choice of the little child as the victim of inexplicable evil, in the veil shrouding in darkness the manifestations of the evil, in the sense of overturning divine innocence of heart, in the downfall of the physical under the fierce assault of the spirit" (399). The combination of the child, the shroud of darkness, the divine innocence, and the collapse of the physical under the pressure of malignity admirably fill out the catalogue of James's own later statement of the dimensions of the tale. In her way, Cary is working with the same aspect of the tale that strikes one in the comments of Elton and Bragdon—the recognition, namely, that James is gathering the reader into the creative framework of the tale.

Cary says that there are other classifications of spirits in James's ghost tales cast in a lighter medium: tales in which the ghosts "enlist the imagination without appalling it" and tales with an "eccentric spirit of whimsy." But the narrative told by James's governess at Bly stands alone. The tale's presentation of phenomena with "equal sensitiveness to the visible and the invisible" is the compositional center of its moral worth. Cary, like a number of the reviewers, discovers that even from such a world the Jamesian figure (and the Jamesian reader) may emerge to find the beauty and dignity of virtue "still preeminent." But she advances on the reviewers by identifying the source of the moral worth in the tale when she sees what James has managed in its construction. Her penetration of James's technique of incorporating the reader into the moral environment of the agon together with her sharp sense of the components of the mystery—the shroud of darkness, the fragility of innocence, the collapse of the spirit under the pressure of ambient malignity—spell out some of the stylistic features that even so sharp a reader as Droch could refer to only as images "carried away on a verbal smoke." Cary expresses some anxiety that James's adoption of current idiom to make himself intelligible to his audience might destroy his intelligibility to later readers; she foresees any decline in James's readership with uneasiness since she sees James as an important expositor of the mysteries of the moral universe.

But if Cary is an exponent of the later work and style of James, despite the risks to intelligibility that James has run, W. C. Brownell, his principal editor at Scribner's, is certainly not. Brownell, without mentioning Colby, emphatically seconds him: for Brownell, too, nobody in James's work seriously sins because, in effect, nobody has anything to sin with. Brownell, in his essay in the *Atlantic* for April 1905, tries, like Elton, to summarize James's career. It is a career, says Brownell, that suggests greatness, but is marked, nonetheless, by a damning tendency for the public to ignore him. James resembles Cuvier in being able to reconstruct the entire (psychological) skeleton from a single (social) bone (Gard 1968, 397); but there is about James's meticulous archaeology only a surface grasp. Though Brownell seems to intend a balanced and objective judgment of James's work, his discussion frequently sounds like an aggrieved personal attack: "Like Lessing, Mr. James has 'bowed humbly to the left hand,' and, saying to the Almighty, 'pure truth is for Thee alone,' has renounced the vision for the pursuit" (399). So far does he carry the pursuit in the direction of exposing those who try to sin with no bodily substance to support their vices, that his work becomes "ardently frigid": "he is not merely detached, the detachment is enthusiastic" (418).

There is, for Brownell, a logical if not particularly happy explanation for this phenomenon in James's work: James suffers from the effects of the "spread of culture" (402). Though science, with its penchant for practical solutions, is often accused of being the enemy of the imagination, it is not the real problem; instead, "the decline of the creative imagination in literature, in poetry, and in fiction, is far more distinctly traceable to the spread of culture, with the consequent

unexampled development of the philosophic and critical spirit and its
inevitable invasion of the field of creative activity, the field, that is to
say, of art." James, he assures us, is an outstanding example of the artist
as critic with the reflex in a critical rather than a creative or imaginative
fiction. Thus the thrust of James's fiction is "theoretic"—that is, James
writes in order to illustrate his theory, the result of which is that "his
critical theorizing about the what and how of fiction is a confusion of
life and art, which are actually as distinct as subject and statement." But
if it is legitimate to show the great flair for technique that might be
expected to arise from James's critical bent, one must object, says
Brownell, to what he calls "virtuosity of vision" (405). By this phrase I
suppose Brownell means James's demon skill in discerning the motives
and the inner natures of his characters, his ability to see into the depths
of being, complicated by his great technical innovation of representing
the characters' impressions of their world—minds in the process of first
registering sensory apprehension. If it is that quality that has endeared
James to his loyal following, one can sympathize with Brownell for the
discomfort that he feels.

Brownell seems here almost to be looking at Max Beerbohm's
cartoon of James scrutinizing the shoes left out in the hotel hall for
polishing, pairings that testify to the naughty liaisons of the night. The
two works that best illustrate virtuosity of vision are *The Sacred Fount*
and *The Turn of the Screw*, which, he says, "are marked instances of it."
These are precisely the late works narrated in first person in which
James applies such great pressure to the reader to distinguish the events
of the world exterior to the narrating consciousness from the events of
consciousness. While James's later critics might insist that he is
showing his readers how difficult the concept of reality is, Brownell
responds by suggesting that James is merely revealing his own literary
shortcomings. These two tales, then, are merely particular instances of
the dominant tendency of James's later work: an "overmastering critical
faculty exercised in philosophizing about, even in the process of
practising, an eminently constructive art" (405). In spite of himself,
however, Brownell, in noticing James's constructive art, cannot avoid
an intimation of the technical deftness in the fiction by which James
constrains the reader to provide the specifications of the human
character in the text; what Brownell dislikes in James's work, James
will, in the prefaces, suggest that all readers, including Brownell, have
put there themselves.[8]

The criticism of *The Turn of the Screw* over these years is incidental
to the larger concerns about James—concerns about the sum of his
career and the nature and justice of his reputation, about his return to

the United States after a long period of expatriation, about the rumors of a definitive edition of his works and the critical material that will supplement it. As the "impressions" of his trip appear in *Harper's* and the *North American*, those concerns also focus on James's critical views of the United States, making *The American Scene* pivotal for the contemporary response to his work. The bearings of that criticism are elusive, as we have seen in the reactions of some of the first commentators on the "impressions." When these are collected into the travel volume, however, at just the moment that the earliest volumes of the New York Edition and its prefaces appear, the view begins to circulate that James is deeply critical of the American spirit. The "American scene" reflects James's recognition of the political choices implicit in the victory for industry that the Civil War achieved, a victory that demonstrated to him that the business of America is Corporations, the amassing of capital for the sake of raw power.[9] This view of America makes a reasonable equivalent for the British "scene"— characterized by *The Turn of the Screw* as forcefully as by *Maisie* or *The Ambassadors* or *The Golden Bowl*. The predominant force in each society is the·exultation of the individual in what appeared to be an unhappy modification of the high values of revolution, in the British scene, by doing—to use Arnold's terms—as one likes; in the American by the confusion of might with right, of God with the dollar. The ghost tale's British uncle in Harley Street who leaves the children in the hands of the governess (both a virtual child herself and the uncle's desperate last choice—because in the pursuit of his own pleasures, he can't be bothered with the children) has for a counterpart in James's corpus the revenant monster with the missing fingers, Brydon's doppelganger, the horror he tracks to his lair in "The Jolly Corner." The American scene, and explicitly *The Turn of the Screw*, is the context for understanding James's late work, in the sense that the flaws in society scrutinized in that work are analogous between the two nations. *The Turn of the Screw*, like *Maisie*, is of 1907. What Howells calls Plutocracy exposes the worst of both James's worlds.

Frederick Taber Cooper treats *The Ambassadors, William Wetmore Story and His Friends*, and *The American Scene* as a "trilogy of expatriation" (1907); but Cooper's exemplary expatriate understands that America is about money rather than about the things celebrated in Whitman's poetry (217). The review of *The American Scene* for *Current Literature* in "Henry James as Literary Sphinx," quotes British sources that understand the book of travel impressions to be a "'profound essay in the psychology of the governing classes in America'" (1907, 635). The reviewer for the *Nation* in "Light on

Darkest Games" cautiously suggests that with James, the style is the man: that however dense we may find *The American Scene*, it is the sort of writing for which James has acquired the respect of the greatest craftsmen of the era (344) and it is to be hoped that James, in the prefaces rumored for the forthcoming edition of his works, will add light to the dark places of his work. This is the mixed context in which the little ghost tale was being received in the time before the first major critical statement on the tale—that of James in the preface—was made.

H. G. Dwight (1907) is the appropriate chorus for the critical environment of James's *The American Scene* and the general awareness among critics that it was time to move toward final critical judgment James's career. He was vexed by the American antagonism toward James and his work; he was inclined to designate the late fiction and the travel impressions as the crown of James's achievement rather than as evidence of an erosion of his powers. He was thus prompted to find Brownell's critical treatment of James unsatisfactory and to scorn those who thought that Brownell had said the definitive word on James's work. Loomis's jeu d'esprit about translating James into English with its closing taunt speculating that James himself was about to translate the early work into the idiom of the later focuses the question of James's style, precisely in the context of the travelogue and coincidentally in that of the earliest appearance of the prefaces to the New York Edition. Conrad had said, in "Henry James: An Appreciation" (1905), that James was "the historian of fine consciences." Dwight joins Bragdon and Cary in observing that a principal complaint among James's readers arose because James "demands ... more attention than many readers think a book deserves" (Gard 1968, 444). But the late style itself, according to Cooper, arises from a change in James's perception, not of the sort that Brownell insists upon—that is, a change from lucidity to intentional obscurity—but rather an abrupt increase of concern for the soul: "indeed this interest has superseded all others in him, making all his later work a series of studies in the dark drama of the inner life." The reviewers of *The Turn of the Screw* had caught glimpses of this deep concern for the soul without being able to flesh it out. What Cooper speaks of here is certainly the center of what Jamesians applaud in their author; and it seems to reach the verge of all those profound insights attributed to James in the years in which his work has been seen as monumental, not only from the perspective of his technical deftness, but also from the perspective of his deep search for the roots of spirit in modern life. Dwight comments that James belongs to the great moderns in taking fiction beyond episode and denouement and concerning himself with "that which lies behind the episode and

[with] a growing sense of the continuity of things—a sense that nothing ever really begins or ends" (Gard 1968, 446). As we become more sophisticated in our capacity to see the profound influence of atmospheres, Dwight says, we will better understand James's problem fictions—*What Maisie Knew, The Sacred Fount,* and *The Golden Bowl.* He might just as well have added *The Turn of the Screw* to this list, a book that has troubled its readers because of its refusal to resolve itself into clear beginnings and ends.

But it is *The American Scene* and its technique of converting fictional impressions into social insights that cap his work, according to Dwight. He sees James exploding the comfortable myths, those, for instance, consequent upon the apocalyptic visions of a Whitman—the new nation in its infancy conquering the problems that have beset the race from its first experience with sin; or contrarily, the inheritor race of all the ages coalescing to forge a new language—and thus a new myth—which in itself will reconcile the antinomies of the past. "We are," he says, "rather, the younger sons of the ages with a tradition and a country that do not match" (448). James's grasp of this truth embraces both the passionate pilgrims and the inheritors of Whitman's dreams of cosmic reconciliation; but he can also identify the excesses. That makes him unassailably useful to Americans despite their antipathy to him, to his return from exile, to his later work, and to his recording of his impressions of the country upon his return. Though *The Turn of the Screw* is by setting and by its particular social problem an "English" fiction, it is no historical error that has made it a particularly urgent American problem in criticism and evaluation.

No inclination to reconsider the reviews of *The Turn of the Screw* surfaces during this succeeding stage of the critical tradition of the tale. Only sporadic interest in any past criticism of James occurs. Dwight (1907) surveys the broader criticism of James's work to ferret out his champions. One or two critics recall Colby's frozen contempt for James (1902), and Brownell is mentioned by both Dwight and Frederick Cooper. But concern for the estate of the criticism of the ghost tale awaited James's own challenge to his readers in the New York preface.

THE PREFACE AND THE PRESS

As the New York Edition began to appear, critical assessments accompanied it continuing some of the caviling about James's late style but beginning to show some of the sensitivity to James's work that we find, for example, in Cary and Dwight. It is James himself who is the principal commentator on *The Turn of the Screw*, but we learn a good deal about the positions of his major critics in this era. Writers like Stuart Pratt Sherman and E. E. Hale, Jr., carve a niche for James convenient to themselves.

Edward Everett Hale, Jr., reviewed the first six volumes of the New York Edition for the *Dial* in March 1908 under the title "The Rejuvenation of Henry James." Hale is aware of the revisions in the New York Edition but objects to the late manner. Hale repeats the fixture about translation—"Mr. James is translating his works into his own dialect" (174)—and he worries that the translation will lose us something of the lovable in the elder works. The conservative Jamesian had read *The Portrait of a Lady* with feverish attention but was forced to strive "unto death with somnolence over 'The Wings of a Dove [*sic*].'" He concedes that the changes were of words and phrases rather than of chapters and larger units and that, therefore, the text is reconcilable. He concedes that the changes are small matters of taste and that the outcries against the late style are undoubtedly overwrought. Hale is cautious, uncertain how properly to handle the challenge of James's careful generation of a canon. He does declare that "James wrote better English thirty years ago than he writes to-day" (175). He offers some examples from *The American* with the idea that the superior state of the prose will be obvious. But he quickly sets aside the comparison, suggesting that the issue should be resolved by "university students of literature as material for doctor's dissertations" (175).

But Hale is, after cautious hedging, enthusiastic about the prefaces, even though he disputes the claim in the prospectus that the prefaces constitute "a unique body of criticism of the art of the novelist" (175). For Hale they will serve cumulatively as a "collection of facts which will help the student as a foundation for a science of fiction." He celebrates James's own recognition of the conceptual sources for three of the first four novels, the "conception of the situation" for *The American*, the figure of the lady for *The Portrait* and the life of London for *The Princess Cassamassima*. He is intrigued by the definition of romanticism in the preface to *The American* "by this accomplished realist." He studies the prefaces to find what they contribute to a communication of "Mr. James's sense of life" (176). That sense of life must be a powerful force in the creation of characters such as the lady or the Princess. Hale agrees with the prospectus that "In the works of no other writer have American types of character and ideas appeared with such high relief and been characterized with such definite reference to nationality" (176). For Hale, too, the Coburn photographs incorporated as impressions of scenes are a very special enhancement to the novels, so much so that the Faubourg Saint Germain in *The American* "almost takes the place of the novel." That is evidence that James had a great sense of place and that the prefaces secured this sense for the novels. He judges that the prefaces clarify the context of the novels and thus expand our understanding of their exacting author.

The reviewer for the *Louisville Courier-Journal* reviews volume 12 of the New York Edition separately (3 October, 1908), exactly ten years from the first book publication of *The Turn of the Screw*, one of the four works collected in it. He glances at other entries in the volume—"The Aspern Papers," "The Liar," "The Two Faces"—but his eye is caught by the part of the preface directed to *The Turn of the Screw*. The reviewer separates himself from those who have found fault with the prefaces—"the retrospective studies of the great novelist"—and proposes to find "the pleasure and profit" with which careful readers have greeted James's volumes and their new prefaces. Nonetheless, the preface to volume 12 is less satisfactory than those which have preceded it, and the reviewer anticipates a long recital of critical grievances against the tale with his cumulative complaints. The reviewer has gone to the new volume seeking answers to the vexed questions of the elusive ghost tale: "Particularly in 'The Turn of the Screw' is more light needed, though of it Mr. James says that it rejoices beyond any rival in a like ground in a conscious provision of prompt retort to the sharpest question that may be addressed to it." The complaint is not simply that the preface fails to shed light, but also that its author seems almost to be toying with the reader. Perhaps on the basis of the comments here, this writer enjoys the distinction of being the first to be caught in the trap—not of the tale—but of the preface.

For the reviewer there is no doubt about the "ghosts of two bad servants" who want to corrupt the children; and there is no doubt about the desire of the governess and the housekeeper to save them; but after that, certainty fades: "the governess ... is trying to save the children from something—what is not clearly stated—but it strikes the reader with an awful dread not only of the dead servants but of the living ones." This reviewer joins the small group of early readers who hesitate at some level to credit the governess. Reading the preface sends the reviewer back to the tale only to be appalled and amazed anew. The governess's courage is heroic, as is her love. The children's beauty makes their criminal corruption artistically powerful. Their helplessness excuses them from complicity in their corruption without saving them from the damnation it requires. But this writer, equally caught in the trap of the tale as well as that of the preface, is, like so many of the first reviewers, unable to find the conventions of narration that make the tale so gripping, and likewise unable to find a place at a safe distance where its terrors cannot shake the reader's emotions.

That fails to stop the reviewer from trying to find such an escape, and in the process of the search this writer adds a previously undiscovered surface to the explored geography of the tale: "the flaw in the story will seem to many to lie in the good governess' love for the negligent uncle, who left these tender waifs with servants because he did not like to be bothered." While this critical motif, which renders the uncle a symbol for the abdication of adult responsibility for the needs of children, will make recurrent appearances in the criticism of the tale, this is the first time it is given such pointed expression, so that, according to the reviewer, the uncle is "the criminal who has shirked and played the coward." Even though the reviewer feels cheated by the preface of desired light on the mystery of ghostly acts of corruption, the achievement of the story is monumental and its brilliant intimation of evil is there to delight. The story is worthy of "any amount of study," the reviewer concludes, in unconscious anticipation of the flood of critical interest to come.

For others the picture and the problems were less troubled. Edward Clark Marsh, for example, in the *Bookman* for October 1909, finds the New York Edition and the prefaces matter only for celebration. Marsh reviews the entire collection of twenty-four volumes[10] and thus speaks from a more complete perspective than Hale's or the *Courier-Journal* reviewer's. Marsh says the prefaces are a major critical venture: "he has done the unexpected, the unique thing. With all his ingratiating air of taking the reader into his confidence, Mr. James is the most objective of authors. ... But if he has thus surprisingly assumed the autobiographical role, he is still true to the artistic practice of a lifetime. There is no vulgar personal revelation; there are records of places and dates, but the man himself, as separate from the artist, is to be discovered only obliquely as in his novels" (139). Marsh, then, avoids Brownell's complication by understanding that the author is elusive from the text. He compares James to Clare Vawdrey of "The Private Life," who had no existence except that of a ventriloquist's dummy apart from his life as an artist. That other private life, Marsh suggests, is as unseen as that of a ghost. Unlike Brownell, he does not expect to find the author's personality through an exploration of the work.

The prefaces are written by "one of the great masters of the game making a complete, thoroughgoing analysis of his own 'play' over a third of a century, with the double advantage of the critic and the secure possession of the facts of the man who has actually done the thing"

(140). Prior to the New York Edition, Marsh suggests, "no one has undertaken to tell from beginning to end the origin and growth of practically all the products of his creative effort." In his success in achieving such a stupendous feat, James "has placed his detractors in the ugly dilemma of having to concede that if he is not a great novelist he is a great critic, while his criticism establishes standards which force the acceptance of his fiction as art of a high order" (141). Marsh is among the first to see that the prefaces have a different function read separately along side of the fictions they introduce and read compositely as a unit of the sort that R. P. Blackmur will create with *The Art of the Novel* in 1934. Read separately, Marsh tells us, the prefaces create a rich context for the tales they introduce: "in recording the first hints of such stories as *The Turn of the Screw* and *What Maisie Knew*, he opens doors long closed, and shows us the creative imagination actually at work. He discloses the secret of the sources of the artist's inspiration."

Nonetheless, the papers collectively "rise constantly to the consideration of more general questions"—the principles of the fictional art. Though James has not given these principles the most rigorous or organized statement, they are particularly valuable; and had he chosen to formulate a philosophically competent statement, "the result would have been the most searching analysis of the novelist's art that has ever been put to paper." Marsh offers three substantial quotations from the prefaces, one each from *The Princess*, *Roderick Hudson*, and *The Portrait of a Lady*. From the first he quotes the passage on the economy of interest; from the second he quotes the passage on the geometry of relations that "really, universally stop nowhere"; and from the third the recollection of Turgenev's practice with the eligibility of characters for roles in fiction. Marsh concludes from the prefaces that their process of reflecting the novelist-artist's compositional practice is "rather that of some higher mathematician, dealing with a complex group of elements susceptible of manipulation only in strict accordance with certain given properties" (142). Veeder and Griffin, in their comments on the reviews of the New York Edition, declare that "most reviewers dealt largely, and often harshly with the revisions" (405). Marsh is a clear exception—both in the sense of approving of the later style and in approving the "translation" of the earlier works into this later manner: "It is not to be forgotten in discussing the famous, the much abused 'later manner' of the novelist that the challenged works have passed the severe scrutiny of one of the most finely disciplined critical minds of the time"—that is, of James himself (142). Marsh admires James for having persevered in face of a criticism that would have extinguished a lesser mind. Depth of vision of the late novels is not the source of the problem; it is the "fulness [*sic*] and richness of his exposition of a whole set of relations commonly ignored by the novelist with his convenient abstractions." Such a practice has risks, Marsh says; he designates the point of highest stylistic risk *The Sacred Fount* and the long story *The Papers*. Marsh assumes that the confirmed Jacobin will have despaired of James's capacity to retain his casual reading audience in such flights. But he counts on the faithful to rescue James's more obscure offerings from neglect.[11]

The critical success of the New York Edition, on which James fixed a good deal of his hope for acceptance and general acknowledgment of his achievement, was at best mixed. And yet there were also recurrently those like Cary, Conrad, Howells, Dwight, and Marsh, and now, among the reviewers of the New York Edition, Percy Lubbock, who understood, who showed that they understood, and who appreciated the work in the refined sense that even so demanding an artist as James could wish. While in no sense is *The Turn of the Screw* the complete bellwether of James's final reputation, the critical success of the work, the mixed and sometimes hostile reception, the restriction to a few particularly congenial minds of an enthusiastic critical pleasure in James's work, the proliferation of journalistic howls about one or another of James's irreparable faults all, it seems to me, condition the context in which *The Turn of the Screw* was scrutinized and appraised following the publication of The New York Edition of his works.

"AN EXCURSION INTO CHAOS"

By the time of the New York Edition little analysis of *The Turn of the Screw* existed; with a few exceptions, the readings of the tale were quite straightforward. In short, there was as yet no single comment on the larger structure of the tale: such commentary as there was expressed the pleasure over the story's thrill. Some attention had been paid to the governess and to the menace to the two exceptionally beautiful children and the hovering evil of the spirits. The comments on the style largely favored it. There was a vague sense of the country house in which the narrative was given its first public exposure. There was a hint of Bly. A cavil arose over the title, but otherwise little emerged about the tale's frame and range of reference. To this point Douglas and the external narrator were still fictive shadows. Beyond a twitch or two about the governess's perfect reliability, the problems of narrative ambiguity or indeterminacy remained unconfronted. There had, in short, been a shudder over the horror; there had arisen a clear sense of the air of evil; but the story had not developed a large literary celebrity.

James's preface constitutes the first major critical statement on the novella. Though James by becoming his own first expositor does not become the dominant influence in the criticism, he does pose an interesting problem in criticism in the preface. The author can have no automatic priority or primacy in the criticism of his own work. Annie Dillard gives us the charming account of two authors who in trying to determine the reception of their own work discovered that they could not even dictate the pronunciation of the names of major characters: Nabokov wished to have his Ada pronounced Ah-da so that the name would be perceived as a kind of Anglicism for "Ardour"; John Barth wished to have the Giles of *Giles Goatboy* pronounced as "Guiles" to indicate the wily character of his hero. Both have been defeated by common practice and have left behind the impression that the author's prerogatives are few indeed (1982, 120). Inevitably, James is a special case, since he often anticipated the critical collective on the first major criticisms of his works—in precisely the prefaces to the New York Edition where he achieves primacy as the critic of *The Turn of the Screw* and of some of his other novels. In the process James himself becomes the critic who shows the important differences in the growth of the criticism between the first public readings and the first exposition.

But what does James contribute to the critical tradition of *The Turn of the Screw* in his critical commentary on the text? Does he answer for us those vexed and, more recently, raging questions about the tale's ambiguity? Does he steer us into some quiet critical haven where we can rest content with the lovely tale and its exotic moral beauties? In fact one of the first things James does is to update Hawthorne's Romantic theory in the preface to *The House of the Seven Gables*: he tells us that the tale operates as a romance that proceeds happily according to laws entirely of its own nature. Of course, over the life of the tradition with its intricately woven tapestries of battles, critics have enlisted James's preface on many sides of the critical quarrels almost indiscriminately. Like a painting with mystic eyes, the preface follows the critic congenially everywhere. But the preface does not settle critical issues. Instead, it despairs over readerly inattentiveness that so fatally misses the method of the tale that the critics accuse James of "monstrous emphasis"—conscious moral manipulation of the reader. On the contrary, says James; in a famous passage he declares "there is not only from beginning to end not an inch of expatiation, but my values are positively all blanks." (Blackmur 1934b). He claims the triumph of having made the reader do a good deal of the creating of the work—of having made the reader produce the "air of evil" with which the tale must "reek" so that James as author can spare himself the enfeebling intensifiers of "weak specification" (176). He claims for his tale the "small strength" of "a perfect homogeneity" so that there is no ambiguity, no shearing off into irrelevant corners. He develops his fiction by means of "good ghosts," by which he means malevolent spirits, not at all in keeping with the emanations approved by the Society for Psychical Research (SPR) and reported in *The Proceedings* (PSPR) (169).

The tale came from a "private source," later revealed in letters, notebooks, and other documents to be from the bare outline of an anecdote told by Edward White Benson, the Archbishop of Canterbury, and later disputed, perhaps a bit gratuitously, by his sons.[12] The production is, James declares, a "fairy-tale pure and simple" (171), "an excursion into chaos while remaining, like Blue-Beard and Cinderella, but an anecdote." It does, he acknowledges, return upon itself. From this reciprocal turn he adduces yet another famous ordinance on *The Turn of the Screw*: it is "a piece of ingenuity pure and simple, of cold artistic calculation, an *amusette* to catch those not easily caught (the 'fun' of the capture of the merely witless being ever but small), the jaded, the disillusioned, the fastidious" (172). The tone is of mystification; the governess's bewilderment is to be "kneaded thick"; yet the expression is to be strained "so clear and fine that beauty would result" (173). This last James recalls with an especial pleasure; he has succeeded not only in representing the governess's mystification as kneaded thick while her expression is strained clear, but he has also begotten a numerous rash of baffled responses from readers who have complained to him of his artistic incompleteness, the very quality for which he had striven in his mousetrap-*amusette*. The objection that he isolates for comment is likely the one from H. G. Wells mentioned in James's letter of 9 December, 1898 (k 110), suggesting that James has not given sufficient character dimensions to the governess and has not allowed her to indulge sufficiently in her own story. For the process of writing the tale had taught James that "one has to choose ever so delicately among one's difficulties, attaching one's self [*sic*] to the greatest, bearing hard on those and intelligently neglecting the others" (Blackmur 1934b, 173). Dealing with those few "casts a blest golden haze" over the retirement of all the rest; and the difficulty that James records having borne down hard upon is that of the "young woman's keeping crystalline her record of so many intense anomalies and obscurities—by which I don't mean her explanation of them, a different matter" (173).

Among other problems in James's exegesis of the tale is the "crystalline" quality of the governess's record of anomalies and obscurities. Surely James's contention of her clarity supplies some of the force behind later critical accusations that the governess is sufficiently mature to be liable for what she says and does and fully aware of the degree of her involvement and responsibilities. James does tell us that there is a disjunction between the governess's *record* of the events and her explanation of them, so that the reader is at liberty to take exception to the explanations she offers. But James does not indicate how the explanation should be regarded except that it diverges from the record, presumably, at least, in the degree of its crystalline nature and possibly in the soundness of its logic. Two things result: the first is the answer that James makes to Wells's objection, the substance of which is that "we surely have as much of her own nature as we can swallow in watching it reflect her anxieties"; on these grounds he cannot probe her own nature. The second is "she has 'authority,' that is a good deal to have given her" (174). In the first instance, James says, in effect, the tale is not about the governess, her struggles for lucidity, her passion; in the second instance, James promotes an ambiguity in respect to the problem of authority which has taxed the interpretative community almost to its extremes. James does not tell us whether she has the constitutional authority of an autocrat at Bly or whether she merely has narrative authority over the sovereign state of her own tale only.

James does perhaps assist us to understand the dimensions of *The Turn of the Screw*, but to the extent of his compositional problems only. He lets us know here that we do not have a record of the governess's awareness of herself and her other relations. Perhaps, though not certainly, there is a hedge here against the assumption that the governess is plying her narrative—potentially thus abusing her autocratic authority at Bly for the sake of attracting the children's uncle to the claims of her charms—for manipulative ends that justify the outcome of events: the maker of the whole is simply excluding personal relations of the governess from the narrative. The enigma is not materially illuminated by James's statement that "it constitutes no little of a character indeed, in such conditions, for a young person, as she says, 'privately bred,' that she is able to make her particular credible statement of such strange matters." Once again, James's reader is likely to find more to increase doubt than to clarify intention in this comment. She has been privately bred, a fact of which she herself makes a good

deal in the tale; and her own awareness of this fact of her biography has
not been lost on her interpreters; the mere existence of the "long
glasses" in which she sees herself at full length for the first time in her
life has been the seedbed of a very searching interpretative inquiry.
"Private breeding" is her own what?—euphemism? convention?
evasion? confession?—for the sense of privation attendant on being at
best "a fluttered, anxious girl out of a Hampshire vicarage" (k 4), one of
the world's true naives. But such character as she is to have must
emerge from this background and will lead her "to make her particular
credible statement of such strange matters." It is a "credible statement,"
as James tells us, but he helps us here no more than he does with the
problem of authority. We do not know whether he means the statement
has the credibility of a narrative unified as to subject and treatment, or
whether he means that the statement which comes of her "crystalline
record" is, despite the difference between the record and the
explanation, credible in its own right—a believable statement of the
events at Bly, or even a believable statement of her own experiences as
recorded in the narrative.

What is clear is that James, for all his trembling over the
inattentiveness of readers, has taken a writer's delight in the grip in
which he has held his reader; he is crowing here because, given the
evidence to the present moment—that is, this preface, ten years after the
first publication of the narrative—his trap has indeed caught those
whom he meant to catch, the "jaded, the disillusioned, the fastidious."
He has succeeded in supplying the tone—of "felt tragedy," surely—but
even more importantly of "exquisite mystification." He ends his
paragraph on the compositional limitations he has placed on the
governess in her recital of events by saying "I couldn't have arrived at
so much had I clumsily tried for more." The limitations on the detail in
which the governess is presented create the charm of an achieved
artifact, a thing of beauty, which in a work of art comprehends "the
close, the curious, the deep." In the preface to *The Ambassadors*, James
says "One's work should have composition, for composition alone is
positive beauty" (Blackmur 1934b, 319). The "close, curious, deep"
suggests another set of terms for "positive beauty." In this light James
wishes to go on to describe the fashion in which he met his gravest
difficulty, the potential current popular prejudice in favor of the
apparitions of SPR. Thus his choice of "good" story rather than
"correct" ghosts. The distinction is that "correct" ghosts are by all
official PSPR reports inert; since the tale is, even "desperately," an
action, it must refuse inert ghosts. James works, then, to produce "my
impression of the dreadful, my designed horror" (Blackmur 1934b,

174–5). Once again, the reader is pressed: how, the question might arise, is *The Turn of the Screw* an action? James is quite insistent that it is precisely the ghosts who make it so: "my hovering prowling blighting presences, my pair of abnormal agents." He goes on, however, with the information that "they would be agents in fact; there would be laid on them the dire duty of causing the situation to reek with the air of evil" (175).

Yet again James gives with one hand and takes away with the other. They are, these ghosts, agents and the narrative is an action; but they are agents in the process of making the atmosphere of the tale; and the action is precisely a crystallization of this pervading atmosphere. In other words, for James to solve the riddle he creates for us in his tale, he would presumably tell us that the tale is an action and the action is that of the ghosts haunting the governess and the two children. More precisely, he is telling us that the ghosts, "incorrect" by certain prevailing cultural standards, haunt not the children, the governess, or the mansion at Bly, but rather the atmosphere in which the events will take place. This attenuation of what one usually means by an action in fiction is James's solution to the gravest compositional problem of his tale. It does not mean that the ghosts do not haunt the children in the execution of an active role in the tale; it merely restricts itself to a positive statement of a compositional value severely short of such haunting. Furthermore, James goes on to give the ghosts status in a curious way, one that locates them in a world more like Hawthorne's than James's; they are "not ghosts at all, as we now know the ghost, but goblins, elves, imps, demons as loosely constructed as those of the old trials for witchcraft; if not, more pleasingly, fairies of the legendary order, wooing their victims forth to see them dance under the light of the moon" (175). While Hawthorne's views on society's treatment of the witches of his natal Salem are well known, we have less clear information on James's response to these issues. To the extent that he is a good Hawthornian, James is likely to think that the trials of which he speaks were abominations performed by a society that had lost its humanity to a species of intellectual superstition; that the "goblins, elves, imps, and demons" were figments of diseased imaginations and not to be taken for reliable survivals of dead human beings. But in the compositional sense, the ghosts of this tale are apparently like the ficelles of other fictions—they assist James "to express my subject all directly and intensely" (175). He remains slippery on their narrative status beyond their assistance to him—"the essence of the matter was the villainy of motive in the evoked predatory creatures." But who has evoked them and by what means the evocation has taken place James leaves undisclosed.

And so a new problem arises without the older one having been solved: "Portentous evil—how was I to save that, as an intention on the part of my demon spirits, from the drop, the comparative vulgarity, inevitably attending, throughout the whole range of possible brief illustration, the offered example, the imputed vice, the cited act, the limited deplorable instance?" The instance is deplorable because it is finite, because it lacks the universal appeal of the reader's own irresistible example. The author avoids particular illustrations precisely to make the reader create the evil for himself. But this in turn becomes the paradigm of *The Turn of the Screw*: the reader must make the fiction for himself; must conspire with the author to create the artifact; must help to make the ghosts sufficiently horrible. For James is saying here that no horror of sufficient merit to stand for an exemplary demonic presence can succeed if it is reduced to concrete example: "There is for such a case no eligible *absolute* of the wrong; it remains relative to fifty other elements, a matter of appreciation, speculation, imagination— these things moreover quite exactly in the light of the spectator's, the critic's, the reader's experience." James's answer is to create the ambience of relativity in the tale, the compositional flexibility of protagonist, children, ghosts promoting the alternative readings that have become the hallmark of the critical response to *The Turn of the Screw*. Once left to supply any of the specifications of the tale, the reader is obliged to supply all of them, or all of them that are of pressing concern. And just as relevant is James's lead on what he had to "give the sense of" in constraining the reader to specify the nature of the evil—the sense of the "haunting pair" "being ... capable of everything—that is of exerting, in respect to the children, the very worst action small victims so conditioned might be conceived as subject to." It is this effect for which James worked hardest; it is this effect that he reaches "with a success apparently beyond my liveliest hope" (176).

Thus he does not emphasize; thus he does not explain; he leaves his values "positively all blanks." The exception for which James allows is the "expertness [which reads] into them more or less fantastic figures." But again he does not really tell us who reads into text or context; and he does not really tell us what is so read. He does imply that he excites horror, pity and expertness precisely to fill his blanks with these "fantastic figures," whatever they are and whatever the context that receives them or into which they are forced. At least we know that these effects are those on which "no writer can ever fail to plume himself" (177). The reactions over which James rejoices in this preface are the "artless, resentful reaction of the entertained person" who has "abounded in the sense of the situation." This entertained person has presumably acquired his pleasure not simply from having been absorbed in the tale, not simply from having created the foul air with which the tale must reek, but, so far as one can follow James's elusive prose, from being induced to call divine wrath on James for the vision of evil that belongs to the reader. In this, James finds "a theme for the moralist"—presumably that the artists must anticipate readers' arraignment of them for stirring up the dark places in the readers' own consciousnesses.[13] One wonders how much play there is in James's use of the word *entertained* in the phrase "the entertained reader." The word, considered in terms of its French roots, allows the reading "held between." It is tempting to see in this phrase James's own clue to the poised split in the tale, the tension between empirical ghosts who stalk the vulnerable children and an emotionally unreliable governess who is often recently seen as the real danger. But there is no authority for that reading in the preface, and the critic promotes that position at the same peril as any other. James tells us that the "entertained person" "abound[s] in the sense of the situation,... visits his abundance, morally, on the artist" (177). In other words, not liking the grim vision that the reader is enticed into dredging up, the critic blames the author for it. James declines the compliment. As for himself, he says, "[the author] has but clung to an ideal of faultlessness" and has created no such monsters. He has supplied the reader an opportunity—blanks that urgently enough require filling—and has, like a watchmaker god, gone off to tend other mechanisms. But the laws in this fictive world as in that cosmic system are immutable, and the smutty face is the face of the reader's imagination, not that of the author's text.

It is surely this triumph—this powerful dramatic manipulation of the reader—that gives him such enormous pleasure in the technical achievement of the tale, his "success apparently beyond my liveliest hope" (176). Inevitably he has further lifted the veil shielding us from the dark inner life that troubles our dreams. He has clung "to an ideal of faultlessness"—that state of innocence, of harmlessness, of perfect detachment in which the writer has his being. We could accuse James of some disingenuous behavior here, that he himself is evading the moral responsibility that he accuses the reader of ducking. But he concludes the *Screw* preface with the same elusiveness that infuses it everywhere: "Such indeed, for this latter, are some of the observations by which the prolonged strain of that clinging may be enlivened!" (177) "I haven't perpetrated an evil," James might be saying, "I have merely shown that there is evil in the world. But your finding the evil in me, when I am trying to expose it, to criticize the hypocrisy by which we let ourselves in for it, is the ultimate guarantee that my trap for the unwary has sprung and has caught its portion of the innocent who are the Devil's own children." The "prolonged strain of that clinging" is "enlivened" indeed! And the susceptibility of numbers of readers of exactly the sort that James wanted to catch is reason enough for him to be delighted with the tale.[14]

The dozen or so textual blanks considered above present James as a resourceful student of reader responses. His compositional blanks cover about as many features of discourse as of story in the tale. His entertained reader is about equally likely to be puzzled and annoyed as delighted. Weaving in and out of the textual blanks is James's study of *impression* on three levels: those of the governess in registering experience and then relating it; those of the author in establishing exigent choice among his difficulties; those of readers whose record shows them squirming under the demands of James's excitements to read into the blanks fantastic figures. Among his many tallies with those who understood the character of darkness—Shakespeare, Sade, and Goethe, for example—emerges the tally here with Baudelaire and the hypocrite reader, who wishes to off-load upon the author the guilt of an imagination of disaster.

But if James is a resourceful student of reader responses, he does not necessarily agree completely with later students of the subject such as Wolfgang Iser. Though they agree on the notion of blanks to be filled, Iser presses the concept of an infinity of possible concretizations of the literary work, while James believes in his capacity as author to constrain the reader to fill in the blanks in fairly specific ways. Iser distinguishes between the artistic pole, which he says is "the author's text and the aesthetic [which is] the realization accomplished by the reader" (1978, 21).[15] The aesthetic text "provokes continually changing views in the reader, and it is through these that the asymmetry begins to give way to the common ground of a situation" (167). Iser's emphasis is upon "the text as a happening, and the experience of the reader that is activated by this happening." "Consequently," Iser says, "the aesthetic nature of meaning constantly threatens to transmute itself into discursive determinacy," but in such a way that it is "at one moment aesthetic and the next discursive" (22). Iser proposes that there are innumerable aspects of the text that prompt the reader's responses. But the realization of the text is individual and cannot be prescribed. James nonetheless plumes himself on his success in making his readers supply the realizations of his blanks. He does not proclaim that the readers emerge with identical images—only that the images that they do provide are wholly generated by their imagination, and that the product thus generated is deeply dark.

IN MEMORIAM

Between the publication of the New York Edition and James's death in 1916, commentary on *The Turn of the Screw* was desultory. In spite of what we might see as James's attempt in the preface to fan the fires of controversy over the tale, interest in it waned except as it became an example of one aspect of James's work, as critics moved toward summary in James's late life. Nonetheless, glimmerings of aggressive critical postures that became entrenched later in the critical development began to show themselves in these days of uncertainty about the ultimate status of James as a writer and of his ultimate contribution to the history and theory of the novel.

A group of university teachers show us the shallowness of the academic interest in the tale in this period. Arthur Hobson Quinn writes "The Supernatural in American Literature" (1910), generously covering Hawthorne and Poe and nodding in the direction of Brockden Brown, Longfellow, and others. With James, however, his whole comment is restricted to an obiter dictum: "certain stories of Henry James in his earliest period, like *A Romance of Certain Old Clothes*, have a flavor of Hawthorne, but his later and most powerful story of the supernatural, *The Turn of the Screw*, is not like Hawthorne's work in the least" (133). Walter B. Pitkin (1912) contrasts O. Henry's *Furnished Room* with James's tale, declaring that the two converge in touching "the old hem of the supernatural" (35). He tells us that James's tale is developed in three phases, but he does not see the three formal phases of the tale's narrative structure. For Pitkin these three phases consist of the governess's loyalty, creating a "character story"; the "mysterious power" of the ghosts over the children; and finally the "awful spectres." Pitkin's interest is in a sort of organic quality of the part "played by the governess" because "the whole tragedy is born of her stubborn will" (36).

John Macy in *The Spirit of American Literature* (1913) takes a pragmatic view of literature that holds that it should usher the reader into a world of perfect illusions. He does not distinguish between author and narrator,[16] and when the Jamesian narrator hedges—"what she was thinking of I am unable to say"—Macy's ideal reader turns on James and says "My dear sir, you made her!" (334). James's technique leads

Macy to conclude that "anything is bad art which makes a reader say: 'This is not so.'" *The Turn of the Screw* is a sufficient example: "he takes the governess's story out of her mouth and retranslates it into an unconvincing idiom, so that what ought to be a great tragic parable, a ghost story even more terribly significant than Ibsen's 'Ghosts,' misses fire" (334).[17] Thus James the critic intrudes on James the novelist and makes unconvincing art. He asks too much of his reader when, to the sin of the governess's artificial speech, he adds the burden of asking this reader to accommodate ghosts.

Henry Seidel Canby (1913) recognizes *Screw* as a "study of intangible, loathly horror whose theme is the corrupting of children's minds" (61). Like Quinn, he proposes a comparison with Hawthorne, with James rather more subtly refined. He tells us that James uses the refined situation "as a kind of frame upon which he stretches the minds he is about to dissect" (62). Canby, like Pitkin, fails to see the framing device of the tale, but he declares that the intrusion of ghosts is such a device; he sees James inviting his reader to "suppose [that] evil influences could be exerted after death by evil advisers ... on the minds of children. There is the frame of *The Turn of the Screw*" (62). Henry A. Beers, in an essay on Hawthorne, also sees the force of James's work. Beers takes Brownell to task for his analysis of Hawthorne as well as of James. But he joins the group of early critics who in speaking of the ghost tale impeach the governess's perfect heroism in her defense of the children. He tells us that modern ghosts are more a suspicion than a presence and goes on to observe "the true interpretation of that story I have sometimes thought to be, that the woman who saw the phantoms was mad" (307). He does allow that this perception results from James's play with ambiguity.

Anna Leach says, in a eulogistic piece at James's death (1916), "What group ever spoke of ghost stories without 'The Turn of the Screw' being given as the supreme example!" (562) Leach gives the novella high status, but she offers little analysis in support of her verdict; she says of the preface that "Mr. James's own story of the 'germ of that supreme horror' was so frank; the workman was entirely detached from the terrible work." She is enthusiastic about the "consummate art" with which he built the tale. And she does see, as others will echo later on, that "it is literally a final turn of the screw on nerves which have been brought to an even higher tension, sending shivering currents of horror through the consciousness." She is, in pressing this metaphor, among those who see the turning screw as an instrument of torture. And though her statements seem to reflect mere surface responses, she reacts in harmony with James's perspective. She speaks of being inspired with the sensation of slime from the pit. And she shudders at "the very names of the two demons, Miss Jessel and Peter Quint." Surely she does James the appropriate homage in recounting the preface with its "haunted children and ... prowling servile spirits" and concludes that he is "one of the immortal race of creative artists" (564).

Helen Thomas Follet and Wilson Follett declare that James's death reconverts him to being an American. For them the kind of neglect and bad manners with which James was treated by his countrymen in the late years of his life was an outrage, "the very perfection of his prose being in fact, to our tortured helplessness, the last 'turn of the screw'" (1916, 802). Even before James's death, Francis Hackett, one of the editors of the very new *New Republic* defends his delight in James's later style against the criticism that it is esoteric for the sake of mystification. But while Hackett defends James, his philistine friends balk at the later style. Hackett reports the characteristic comment that his friends "loved the early James of *The Portrait*" and could "follow James through 'The Turn of the Screw,'" but were lost forever after that. Thus the ghost tale becomes for one pulse taker the line of definition between James's "lucid" and "obscure" works (1915). Stuart Pratt Sherman, in "The Aesthetic Idealism" (1917), earnestly pursues the notion that for James, the aesthete, ugliness is evil: "He is not pitiless except in the exposure of the 'ugly,' which to his sense includes all forms of evil; in that task he is remorseless whether he is exposing the ugliness of American journalism ... or the ugliness of murder." The list of classifications of the ugly includes the fate of the children of James's post-theatrical nineties, extending to cover "the ugliness of corrupted childhood as in 'The Turn of the Screw'" (397). Sherman seems to have blinded his eyes to much that goes on in James's fiction to reduce all questions to aesthetics. As Sherman states the issues, what is immoral for James is so only because it is ugly—only because it fails to please the senses. In this sense, no concern for the morality of a circumstance, in the ordinary sense of the term, could trouble James or make its place in his work. Sherman singles out little Effie of *The Other House*, Maisie, Miles, and Flora: "The deep-going uglinesses in the last three cases are presented with a superlative intenseness of artistic passion. If the effect is not thrilling in the first case and heartrending in the last two, it is because Anglo-Saxons are quite unaccustomed to having their deeps of terror and pity, their moral centres, touched through the aesthetic nerves" (399). Like so many others, then, Sherman sees the artistic passion in James, but refuses to acknowledge the power in his work which is weakened, he says, by the inferior range of James's intellectual powers.

In a eulogy which appeared in the United States in *Living Age* but was reprinted from *Westminster Review*, Walter de la Mare barely mentions *The Turn of the Screw* but speaks of its "enslavement" and links it to a splendid style, rather in the sense of *style parlé*— "the best kind of talk, from which, indeed, 'the best writing has something to learn'" (1916, 124). Theodora Bosanquet, in her own retrospective on having been James's amanuensis, recalls (1917) the marvelous thrill of reading *The Turn of the Screw* for the first time with a recollection of a friend's having lost her "nerve for facing the hours of darkness because her mind was obsessed by the horror of a tale she had lately read called *The Turn of the Screw*, by a writer called Henry James." Her response was like her friend's, complete with horror-stricken nights (348–49). But her sense of the tale was that it constituted the proof that Henry James was among the immortals, and that a chance to work for him as amanuensis was a treasure.

William Lyon Phelps in his evaluation of James's life and work (1916) comes to praise and stays to cavil. James's great decade was the 1870s; his later manner was not an improvement over the earlier, nor was the translation of those works of the 1870s into the later manner a success; these books do not sufficiently repay the labor to reward the effort (788–789). Moreover, Phelps is prepared to account for the "decline" in James: as the novelist became more and more sensitive to the clichés of journalism he became "more afraid of obvious words." Thus *The American* or "Daisy Miller" represent for him the accessible James, who has failed to wallow in his characters like Dickens and Thackeray. He does not care for them and thus leaves them to our tender mercies—which we withhold for cause (793). Nonetheless, the year 1898 was an exception in the downward movement of James's work and reputation, because it witnessed the publication of *The Turn of the Screw*," which I found then and find again to be the most powerful, the most nerve-shattering ghost story I have ever read." Phelps can see some of the technique of the tale, the fashion in which reticence, the withholding of what James calls "specification," intensifies the emotional power of the reading: "The connoting strength of its author's reticence was never displayed to better advantage; had he spoken plainly, the book might have been barred from the mails; yet it is a great work of art, profoundly ethical, and making to all those who are interested in the moral welfare of boys and girls an appeal simply terrific in its intensity" (794). Phelps speaks of having thanked James for the tale and records the author's reply that "he meant to scare the world with that story; and you had precisely the emotion that I hoped to arouse in everybody" (794). Phelps then goes on to retell James's version of the story of the iron Scots stenographer to whom James dictated the novella: "I dictated to him sentences that I thought would make him leap from his chair; he short-handed them as though they had been geometry, and whenever I paused to see him collapse, he would inquire in a dry voice, 'what next?'" (794).

In the year of James's death, or so catalogers are inclined to suspect, Ruth Head published, in the form of a tribute to James, a series of quotations from his work. The passages appear under such rubrics as "London," "Country England," "Interiors," and so forth. The quotations are rather striking in their prescience as to what readers would find to take up in James's work as it became more familiar to the critical eye. For *The Turn of the Screw* she finds only the brief passage on the seasonal change from summer to autumn when the leaves fall at Bly: "all strewn with crumpled playbills." There is a drama, then, in the change of seasons, a picture with enough power to attract the abstracter's eye. But it is of some interest that this very passage from the governess's prose will later be featured in the indictments against the governess's reliability as a narrator: for as some of the critics insist, if the governess has never been to a play, a metaphor for strewn leaves created out of discarded playbills erodes her credibility.

A year or so after James's death, John Freeman published a book called *The Moderns: Essays in Literary Criticism* (1917) with a chapter on Henry James. He discovers that "two of the stories in *The Lesson of the Master* have a singular interest inasmuch as they are sketches in apparent anticipation of *The Turn of the Screw*—false starts in the telling of the grimmest of ghostly stories" (228). One presumes that "The Pupil" is at least one of these anticipatory stories. Freeman proposes that a part of James's practice is developmental, and that *The Turn of the Screw* is a high point of the developmental process. Freeman says that the novella "might be reckoned the most typical of Henry James's stories, since it expresses most completely his isolation from all contemporary writers." Though others tended to see its eccentricity on precisely the grounds of its function as a technical experiment, Freeman finds the story a device that isolates James from contemporary authors. It achieves this phenomenon by being "the 'real right thing'" in contrast to contemporary writing that has struggled too hard for the effects of the weird or the unpleasant. James's novella "is a ghastly story, the relation of the imaginative—which is the moral and spiritual—defilement of two children by apparitional criminals. Nothing more horrible has been conceived" (234). For Freeman, accounting for the governess's success is impossible: "whether the courage of this poor woman outweighs the debasement of the wretched children, a question that has not gone unheeded, is a question which I must leave untouched." He sees that there must ultimately be inquiry into just this point. For the moment he contents himself with the conclusion that the governess is a defender; the children are corrupt, perhaps beyond her power to save.

James's death led to unqualified eulogia for the author and his work. W. B. Cairns says that "James's usual method is to give much the same sort of circumstantial evidence that might be apparent in real life. The reader, unaccustomed to such a treatment in literature, hardly knows how to interpret the vague indications, and is horrified at his own uncertainty" (1916, 314). Cairns appreciates the implications of the preface to *The Turn of the Screw*, the problem of honi soit qui mal y pense: "it is those who in their puzzled innocence have inclined to answer the question in the negative that have most blamed the author for his suggestiveness" (314). By implication, Cairns answers Brownell: "Only the most superficial commentators will accuse him, as Browning was sometimes accused, of puzzling his readers for the mere fun of the thing." E. E. Hale, Jr., speaks of James again at his death (1916), associating James's style with the painting of Monet—the "atmospheric vibration" in the environment. He proposes that James struggles to record the "veriest transcript" of life in his prose and finds James's fiction "the most consummate achievement" (261). Percy Lubbock says that James was a "critic who took up the most haphazard of literary forms and turned it into the most ordered and finished; a statement, moreover, even in an age of ready writers, lavishly detailed and voluminous" (1916. 734).

But even speaking of the dead, memorialists cannot be relied on for perfect sweetness. An unsigned comment in *Literary Digest* (1916) tells us that though the effort is now being made "to say the just thing," James nonetheless continues to be "the baffling thing that he has long proved" (714). The writer cites widespread reviewers' complaints of his "abominable style," regardless of his recent death. One of James's harsher critics in these days was the man who now signed himself Henry S. Canby. In his memorial (1916), Canby questions "whether his novels and short stories gained by this 'heroic highbrowism.'" "To get a million of readers," Canby proceeds, with searing logic, "is no sure sign of greatness; but to find only thousands, as did Henry James, is to be deplored." Canby allows that James was popular in a good way as the author of *Daisy Miller* and *The Bostonians,* "but men read *The Golden Bowl* and *The Wings of the Dove* because they were skilful rather than because they were interesting." Canby echoes Brownell in saying, "Henry James was not a novelist at all, at least in the good old-fashioned sense that we usually give to the word. He was primarily a critic; the greatest American critic since Poe," who must, however, "yield first honors as a novelist" (291). Though Canby cannot settle on James's final place in letters, he concedes that it is secure.

Ford Madox Hueffer (Ford) was ready with an appreciation of James in a little book published by Secker in 1913. It is rather a sprawling and leisurely account of James and of the long literary relationship between James and himself. He offers the curious reflection, more or less in opposition to Sherman, that because James is preeminently a Protestant writer, and that for this community, the concern for ethics extends far beyond the concern for dogma, James "may ... be regarded as a purely religious writer. Indeed, occasionally, in such stories as "The Altar of the Dead," *The Great Good Place*, or *The Turn of the Screw*, he has permitted himself what he calls 'indiscretions'—which implies that he has written stories that propagandise in favour of 'his particular interpretation of the Infinite'" (122). Hueffer is among the early commentators who notices in *The Turn of the Screw* the idea of the wickedness of the uncle who exposes "the English habit of leaving young children to the care of improper maids and salacious ostlers." For Hueffer the novella is "the most eerie and harrowing story that was ever written" (151).

Hueffer also echoes Brownell in declaring that the value of criticism, if indeed there is any, is to unearth the temperament of the author. Hueffer seems to disparage criticism, but very much appreciates James's prefaces, quoting with enthusiasm James's comment from *The Turn of the Screw* preface on making the reader's vision of evil sufficiently intense. He analyzes James's method, stripping the passage "to the barest... of bones, in order to show just exactly what the hard skeleton is. And it will be observed that the whole matter—the whole skeleton or the only bone of it—is the word 'things'" (169). Hueffer sees the sort of dilemma in which the story places the reader: "If you will take *The Turn of the Screw*, with its apparent digressions, its speculations, its turns and twists, you will see that the real interest centres round the proposition: Is the narrator right or wrong in thinking that if the little boy can only disburden himself of a full confession he will be saved for ever from the evil ascendency of Peter Quint. And this last hangs in the balance until the very last sentence settles it"—quoting the governess's final sentence. Hueffer anticipates the crisis of the novella that will engage so many minds later on, the problem of whether the boy can be cured by dispossession (exorcism) or not. The problematizing of the text is near at hand.

Though Ezra Pound tells us frequently that he came to regret it, he superintended a special issue on Henry James for Margaret Anderson's *Little Review* in 1918. At the time, Pound was in England and was an associate editor of the *Egoist* as well. Pound was disinclined to worry about a little foolish consistency, and if there were ultimately "commerce" between Pound and Whitman, there was at least this much of it between Pound and Emerson: so long as he barreled along at full speed and cut a swath of sufficient gaudiness to astonish, he cared little to adjust the contradictions that headlong utterance might produce. His own contributions to the James issue of *Little Review* (5 August, 9–39) found their way into his *Instigations* (1920). He sets off at sufficiently astonishing speed in his essay on James: "I am tired of hearing pettiness talked about Henry James's style. The subject has been discussed enough in all conscience, along with the minor James. Yet I have heard no word of the major James, of the hater of tyranny; book after book against oppression, against all the sordid petty personal crushing oppression, the domination of modern life" (107). Without question, then, in Pound's mind, James is a hero, and of a sort to dwell in Pound's own arcana—that is, a hero of aesthetic discernment. James is a hater of tyranny, which in Pound often comes down to the sort of tyranny associated with cultural conservatism, the academy, the Victorian, or genteel, hegemony: "Kultur is an abomination; philology is an abomination; all repressive uniforming education is an evil" (111).

In this vein, then, James's heroism is to be found in "the outbursts in *The Tragic Muse*, the whole of *The Turn of the Screw*, human liberty, personal liberty, the rights of the individual against all sorts of intangible bondage! The passion of it, the continual passion of it in this man who, fools said, didn't feel." James is a hero and *Muse* and *Screw* are heroic texts, texts poised against philistines. Furthermore, James is heroic because, given his grasp on culture, he is a major translator, a man capable of "making America intelligible, of making it possible for individuals to meet across national borders." Pound goes well beyond most of the academics in these comments. He praises James for two virtues: "First, that there was emotional greatness in [his] hatred of tyranny; secondly, that there was titanic volume, weight, in the masses he sets in opposition within his work" (110). In effect the greatness of his masses comes in the fact that "no other writer had so essayed three great nations or even thought of attempting it" (110). Indeed James set his own finger on the pulse of modernity and its anguish: "no man of our time has so labored to create means of communication as did the late Henry James. The whole of great art is a struggle for communication" (110–11).

But Pound will have it both ways. James may triumph with the later style, "in his last, his most complicated and elaborate, he is capable of great concision; and if, in it, the single sentence is apt to turn and perform evolutions for almost pages at a time, he nevertheless manages to say on one page more than many a more 'direct' author would convey in the course of a chapter." But seeming to forget how he had begun, he now rescinds the accolade for *The Turn of the Screw*. He cites with some pleasure the comment of "R. H. C." in *The New Age* that James will be quite comfortable after death, having spent his whole life with ghosts. In this vein of disparagement he recapitulates the central stages of James's career: "In the interim he had brought out 'In the Cage,' excellent opening sentence, matter too much talked around and around, and 'The Two Magics,' this last a Freudian affair which seems to me to have attracted undue interest, i.e., interest out of proportion to the importance as literature and *as part of* Henry James's own work, because of the subject matter." No longer a heroic tale of resistance to oppression, *Screw* has become a side issue and an unproductive diversion. Further, "the obscenity of 'The Turn of the Screw' has given it undue prominence" (150). The prurient interest in such matters is a distraction from the real concerns, Pound suggests, and "one must keep to the question of literature and not of irrelevancies" (150). Pound objects to Freudian psychology apparently on the grounds that the public has not progressed sufficiently to make it a useful exploration of experience. In any case, for what it is worth, Pound, on two sides of the *Screw* issue, is the first commentator in the history of the criticism of the tale to bracket it with Freud and the Freudian analysis of the unconscious.

His assertion that the tale is a Freudian piece and a distraction for being so is all the more interesting in light of the fact that earlier in the year in the *Egoist*, there is another James retrospective, the one that features Eliot's comment that James "had a mind so fine no idea could violate it" (1918, 2). Eliot, like others, promotes the theme of James's critical acumen: "As a critic, no novelist in our language can approach James; there is not even any large part of the reading public which knows what the word 'critic' means." But Eliot hastens to declare that James was not a good literary critic: "his criticism of books and writers is feeble. In writing of a novelist, he occasionally produces a valuable sentence out of his own experience rather than in judgment of the subject" (1). Instead, according to Eliot, in what might seem a rather left-handed compliment, James "was not a man who preyed upon ideas, but upon living beings." His characters are organic to his books because of this keen critical sense, unlike those of other authors whose characters seem to be merely accidental. "Naturally," Eliot proceeds, "there is something as disconcerting as a quicksand, in this discovery, though it only becomes absolutely dominant in such stories as *The Turn of the Screw*." Eliot understands that James sees with a kind of precision that is disconcerting, the kind that leads, one might speculate, precisely to the recognition that the little ghost tale, with its enticements to participation, does indeed rather uncannily find one out. "It makes," he says, "the reader as well as the personae, uneasily the victim of a merciless clairvoyance." It is this clairvoyance that leads Eliot to conclude that "If they understood James both Americans and Britons would have heaved a sigh of relief at his death that he had stopped exposing the flaws in both countries."

But an even sharper interest here for the study of the ghost tale comes in a piece called "'The Turn of the Screw,'" by Arthur Waley, the first critical piece, perhaps, however brief (it occupies less than two columns on p. 4 of the issue), devoted solely to the tale. Says Waley, quite simply, "the story is not Freudian: it does not deal with the 'involuntarily suppressed' memories of infancy, but with experiences (common in this country, where children are in the charge of domestics) which are deliberately hidden from parents and relatives. The children may appear to be nothing that is not nice *now* as Mrs. Grose 'lugubriously pleaded,' but (such is James's thesis) beneath this mask of 'absolutely unnatural goodness,' of 'more than earthly beauty,' the old contamination lurks. It is this contamination which James materializes in the spooks of Peter Quint and Miss Jessel."

Waley comments on the publication of *The Sense of the Past* and *The Ivory Tower*, both published in London in 1917 by Collins, both incomplete works. These posthumous works had been celebrated by critics as providing a special insight into the character of James's craftsmanship by the very fact of their incompleteness (*Tower* at least having been published with James's scheme for its completion). But Waley informs the reader that the prefaces supply another such insight, and that the interest of the *Screw* preface lay in the force of the servant's "getting hold" of the children—that being, to his mind, James's invention. Waley refuses to believe in the tale as "a fairy tale pure and simple," as James had tried to insist in the preface. "The ghosts," he says, "are a mere literary expedient for portraying in a vivid way the lasting character of the early corruption. They are 'influences' lifted for dramatic purposes to a quasi-material plane." In other words, Waley is not only the first to devote a critical piece solely to *The Turn of the Screw*, but he is the first to suggest that the ghosts are allegorical or quasi-allegorical figures for the sense of corruption in an environment. Says Waley, "this device of substituting the concrete for the abstract is well illustrated by *The Private Life* [his italics], in which the public man literally and not metaphorically 'has no home life.' He simply ceases, in that fantastic tale, to have any existence whatever, unless he is facing an audience."

Nonetheless, Waley refuses to accept James's disclaimer on expatiation: "whether indecently or not, he expatiates," Waley says, giving as examples such informative interventions as the governess's comments on Peter Quint's health, her comments on Flora's corrupt language, her reflection on Miles's having "'said things,'" though in the process he too conflates the narrator and the author. And he spots James's blanks: "Does James pretend ... that [a particular passage] leaves the reader free to fill in the 'blank' as he pleases?" But Waley does not pursue James into the arcane territory in which the blanks are substituted for the specifications of the general air of evil with which the events of the tale must be freighted if it is to carry its reader on its violent currents. Arguing from his contention that James is being disingenuous, for all his denial of expatiation, Waley goes on to accuse James of "palpably lacking in candour" in the preface. But he discounts the notion that James was wilfully deceptive. James simply did not know what he had written. Thus, to the reader "not handicapped by having written the story," it is no ghost story. It deals with the hidden interior life of children. And it shows that the nature of that interior life is the appearance of being occupied, like Flora with her boat, in order to dissemble the prying interest in things that they are not supposed to know. Flora is disguising her involvement with the contamination into which Jessel and Quint have led her. It is an ethical question based on adult willingness to allow children to be initiated into the world's sexual mysteries by servants.

Waley, like Hueffer, anticipates future critical development in the problems embedded in the process of the tale. He is quick in seeing James's technique of giving with one hand and taking away with the other, of seeming to solve the ambiguities of the fiction while actually specifying the nature of its conceptual problems. In their anticipation of later critical concerns, writers like Waley, Pound, and Hueffer establish a legitimate priority on original insights often claimed by later writers. Far too often, solemn assurances of a search of the existing critical record is a signal that the critic has ignored it or taken a small part for the whole. At its most comprehensive, the boast is likely to tell us that the critic has consulted either Gerald Willen's *Casebook on "The Turn of the Screw"* or Robert Kimbrough's Norton Critical Edition.

Soon after the memorializing of James stops, the critical wars over the novella begin: the Charles Demuth paintings appear; Edna Kenton claims that readers have missed James's point. But in the interim, other desultory commentators discuss the tale. Maurice Egan (1920) has his quarrels with James in the sense that James is among those of "the Protestant world" who fail to pay sufficient heed to the Catholic sensibility: he lacks "the inward thrust of spirituality." But Egan can praise some of James's insights, including those in *The Turn of the Screw*: "When Henry James devoted himself both to the telling of a story and the creating of an atmosphere, he was an exquisite artist in letters. There is no better short story in the language than 'The Turn of the Screw' and there are other short stories of his that approach it in merit." Egan says that James surpasses Poe and then says, "When you have finished it, you shudder, and thank God that the story of the 'possessed' children is not true" (294). Since Egan's review covers a volume of James's letters, he has availed himself of James's letter to A. C. Benson about the genesis of the tale in order to give structure to his comment.

In 1921 Virginia Woolf recorded her frisson in "Henry James's Ghost Stories" in the *Times Literary Supplement*. Woolf is unimpressed with tales that had moved others—"Owen Wingrave," "The Great Good Place." Others she liked, but she saved her ultimate delight for *The Turn of the Screw*. Woolf appreciates the music of the tale: "'What does it matter, then, if we do pick up the *Turn of the Screw* an hour or so before bedtime? After an exquisite entertainment we shall, if the other stories are to be trusted, end with this fine music in our ears, and sleep the sounder" (71). The power of art, apparently, offsets the power of the imagination of disaster. But if there is music in the composition of the tale, there is silence at Bly: "Perhaps it is the silence that first impresses us. Everything at Bly is so profoundly quiet. The twitter of birds at dawn, the far-away cries of children, faint footsteps in the distance stir it but leave it unbroken. It accumulates; it weighs us down; it makes us strangely apprehensive of noise." And under the burden of silence, the house and garden of Bly "die out," leaving the aftertone of evil: "We know that the man who stands in the tower staring down at the governess is evil. Some unutterable obscenity has come to the surface" (72). Yet Woolf sees that we can only be certain of the evil, not of the exact circumstances of its enactment. For her the questions proliferate about what has been wrought at Bly. Like Waley, Woolf enters into the spirit of James's preface: "Can it be that we are afraid? But it is not a man with red hair and a white face whom we fear. We are afraid of something, perhaps in ourselves. In short we turn on the light." She understands that we insert our own evil into the tale. Thus, though we can see the entwining of "beauty and obscenity" in the tale, we cannot see into all the things that might account for it, and, finally, "we must admit that Henry James has conquered. That courtly, worldly, sentimental old gentleman can still make us afraid of the dark" (72).

PRELUDE

Thus, we reach the period of James's death and the aftermath with the sense that *The Turn of the Screw* is simply one of many Jamesian texts; the critics will tell us that it has notable features, certainly the vividness to stay in the mind after the reading is done. The critics will show a sharp sensitivity to the problem of the text as against the problem of the preface. As yet no critic proclaims a desire to escape the trap of the preface: to distinguish their acuteness from others' density. As yet no critics will feel it necessary to contradict another of their kind. More than one will see, unlike so many of the early reviewers, that James had a clear point in his favor in showing us that there was no specific evil mentioned in the tale, only the general, pervasive air of evil. Two critics have mentioned the question of literary Freudianism in conjunction with the tale, one to affirm its presence, one to deny it. But even though these two, Waley and Pound, are involved in the same literary publications, they do not bother to quarrel with each other, merely asserting their positions and then going on to other things.

By the time of James's death, the substantial power of *The Turn of the Screw* to move the reader was well established. Its intention of confronting the problem of evil had become a commonplace to its readers. Many saw the adroitness of James's technical exercise in the tale, his manipulation of the reader. Only a few saw that the reader would have to take the responsibility for the vision of evil that ultimately presents itself in the tale. In a good many respects we can foresee the critical battles over the text in precisely these terms: critics will try over and over again in the later critical wars to assign variously either to James or to the governess aspects of the evil that nonetheless, at least according to James, originates within the critic's own psychology. Some later critics will even perceive that this result is the natural outcome of James's technical maneuver without being any more able on that ground to escape his trap.

The outlines on which the critical controversy would be waged have been sketched, but the tale has not become controversial except in the pressure toward controversy that James himself exerts in the preface to the New York Edition. The relation of this stage of the critical tradition to the first readings emerges from James's use of these readings as a backdrop to his own comments.

3

Suppressed Text(s)

This chapter will consider the development of the classic Freudian interpretation of *The Turn of the Screw*. The declaration of a Freudian basis of the tale is, in the first instance, critically opportunistic, deriving from what Roland Barthes would call a translation of the critical response into a current ideological position of the critic. In the early understanding of the Freudian view of human psychology anything that has been suppressed by the unconscious mind is ultimately significant to the suppressor. But the development of this hypothesis in the critical tradition of *The Turn of the Screw* is itself full of murky areas and interesting suppressed texts.[1] The development of the Freudian reading of the tale illustrates abundantly the asymmetry of the critical tradition.

One center of this developing critical premise for James's ghost tale is that while the governess offers a revealed text in which she is a moral heroine in her defense of the children against the ghosts, the true significance of her narrative lies in the suppressed text in which she neurotically hallucinates the ghosts in response to her own suppressed sexuality. The classical Freudian reading of the tale is itself a curious sequence in which both chronology and causality are distorted almost as if in a dream. Edna Kenton (1924) is often given credit for founding the Freudian hypothesis regarding the tale, but she never once mentions Freud or psychoanalysis in "James to the Ruminant Reader." H. C. Goddard claimed apparent primacy in the "pre-Freudian" hallucinatory reading of the tale with an essay speculated to have been written around 1920. But his reading remained unpublished until 1957, after his death. The true inventor of the Freudian reading (if we agree to exclude Ezra Pound) is thus Edmund Wilson, with his "Ambiguity" (1934). But the most enigmatic contribution to the development of this reading anticipates all the writing on it, including Pound's, and is executed not in verbal but rather in plastic form.

In 1917 and 1918 Charles Demuth painted, among a large group of
literary subjects, five panels illustrating aspects of *The Turn of the
Screw* as well as three panels illustrating James's "Beast in the Jungle."[2]
The only figure common to the five paintings for the ghost tale is the
governess, possibly as a concession to the fact that she is the narrator of
the whole (though the first panel, taking Harley Street for its subject,
anticipates the narrative of the events at Bly by falling in the frame
tale).[3] The four of these panels reflecting the governess's narrative were
reproduced in black and white with Edna Kenton's essay, though
without eliciting a single word of comment from Kenton in the process
of the writing. In fact, it was the editor of the *Arts* who decided to
include the paintings with the essay, and therefore, for Kenton's essay,
they were mere peripherals. Kenton's reader might be pardoned for
thinking the paintings had some especial stamp of approval or
authenticity behind them. They were, however, not authorized by the
novelist, and it is both a vexed and insoluble question whether they
were in any sense definitive in illustration of James's meaning or
intention in the tale or whether their purport is really reproducible.[4]

But these paintings make a very attractive case for the concept of
the governess as a frustrated old maid; and it is hard to resist the
conclusion that this view of her has its genesis here in Demuth's
illustrations. Demuth's treatment of May Bartram in the series on "The
Beast in the Jungle" shows his idea of a handsome and elegant woman.
His depiction of the governess from *Screw* makes her a frump, a
goggle-eyed fool, a creature aged far beyond the twenty years she
claims for herself in her narrative with support from Douglas in the
frame. If she is pretty, she is only passably so in the last of the four
Osborn panels, when she is down on her knees in front of Miles, asking
him about the act that led to his dismissal from school. If one sees the
governess as Demuth sees her, it is not surprising that one should treat
her narrative as unbecoming, devious, self-deceiving, and ultimately as
hysterical. Historically, however, the two interpretations—Kenton's and
Demuth's—come into being independently. The coincidence is striking.
For Edna Kenton most certainly sees the governess in terms similar to
those of Charles Demuth, and each treatment of the tale harmoniously
resonates the other. The two interpretations are there powerfully
juxtaposed for Edmund Wilson when he sets out to write his essay on
James's ambiguity. He credits Kenton erroneously with founding the
Freudian reading of the tale; and he mentions, at least in the 1934
version of his essay, the Demuth paintings.[5] Though Wilson himself
continues to mention these paintings in later versions of the essay,

virtually no critic after him in the developing critical tradition of the tale joins him in doing so.

It is impossible to determine the amount of influence the Demuth illustrations had on Edna Kenton's reading of the tale or on her version of the governess, if any; it is even harder to assess their influence on Wilson.[6] But in a bizarre way, they illustrate the penchant for a suppressed text, not only in the governess's narrative but in the criticism of the tale as well: whatever degree of influence the reproduced paintings actually exerted on Kenton's and Wilson's readings has also unavoidably reproduced itself in some form in the writings of all those who have used Kenton and Wilson as authority for viewing the governess as a Jamesian "case" of the frustrated old maid, an assumption nowhere explicitly justified by the text of the tale.

GLAZED EYES

If authoritative inference from a literary text is problematic, notwithstanding the codes, conventions, traditions that the artist might exploit to direct the process of reading, then how shall we ascertain the value of a "literary" painting? Charles Demuth executed nine illustrations of James's stories, five for *The Turn of the Screw*, three for "The Beast in the Jungle," and one, rather fancifully, for "The Real Thing." The three panels for "Beast" depict without much ambiguity the sequence by which the beast of the title prepares to spring—the beast of the unlived life. The sketch entitled "The Real Thing" is more an idea for an illustration than a transformatory act. The sequence for the ghost tale, however, offers nothing easy by way of revealing the artist's intention for the paintings. While the "Beast" sequence constructs a number of compositional devices for promoting unity through the sequence of three panels, the *Screw* sequence has only one: the governess appears in all five panels. But even this unifying figure creates problems insofar as she is not always clearly or verifiably the same figure. Pamela Allara is able to say in the abstract to her dissertation, "The Watercolor Illustrations of Charles Demuth," "the 5 illustrations for 'The Turn of the Screw' reveal that in all probability Demuth was the first to discover the story's deliberate ambiguity" (iv). Perhaps there is support for such a claim in the sequence—but there is at the same time nothing to resist a competing conclusion that Demuth sees the governess as a figure with glazed eyes, a figure of a woman who appears far from the pretty girl of James's story, a figure who seems to be substantially removed from the twenty year old we are invited to visualize.[7] The compositional blank is the locution "pretty girl." Demuth's concretization of this term in plastic form tantalizes the viewer with the sense of a potentially "wrong" reading of the blank.

The risk in collocating the Demuth Illustrations for *The Turn of the Screw* with Wilson's article is that once he mentions them at the start of the essay, he is done with them, at least insofar as conscious employment of them as artifacts in illustration of the tale is concerned. He does tell us that the illustrations "were evidently based on this interpretation," that is, the interpretation that the governess is hallucinating in giving substance to the apparitions in her narrative. The comment squints between designating Kenton's essay the primary interpretive basis of the watercolors or vice versa, leaving open the designation of the founder of the general hallucinated interpretation of the tale.[8] Wilson's ignorance of the conditioning environment for Demuth's watercolors unsettles the questions, and for all that we can learn from the published criticism of the paintings, the Demuth watercolors are the first to invent or create the hallucinationist thesis for the ghost tale—if that is indeed what they depict. As a problem in influence this round robin suggests the need of a Livingston-Lowes at the very least. We can say for sure that Kenton's article in the *Arts*, November 1924, did not influence Demuth, who did the drawings in 1917 and 1918, according to both Gallatin (1927) and Haskell (1987). We can infer if we like from juxtaposition that Demuth's illustrations provided some of the environment for Kenton's ideas about *The Turn of the Screw*. Given the directions that Wilson's essay takes, it is tempting to say that he received a general hint about the governess's psychology from Edna Kenton's prose but a major thrust from Demuth's watercolors.

Temptations aside, if we are to understand the critical tradition of *The Turn of the Screw*, we must restore the context of Wilson's "Ambiguity of Henry James." If there is a fault to find with the way in which the matrix of historical evidence about the criticism of the tale has been established, it arises from the recurrent assumption of later commentators that the criticism of the tale is captured or even incorporated representatively in either Willen's *Casebook* or Kimbrough's Norton Critical Edition. But, though both books recognize the importance of Kenton's article by reprinting or excerpting it, neither book includes Kenton's reproductions of the Demuth illustrations with the reprinting of the essay. Kimbrough, in including salient passages of Kenton's article, signals where the pages of the essay containing the Demuth reproductions occur in the sequence. Willen, in reprinting the Kenton essay nowhere even indicates that the reproductions accompanied the original. When Wilson mentions the illustrations at the opening of his article in Willen's reprint, Willen does give a note declaring that the illustrations appeared among the pages of Kenton's text. Strangely enough, Wilson does not cite the Kenton essay as his source for viewing the Demuth illustrations, either in the original *Hound & Horn* version or in the reprint in *The Triple Thinkers*. Thus, by a sequence of historical accidents, both the juxtaposition of the Demuth illustrations with the Kenton article and their intrinsic alliance with Wilson's interpretation of the tale have been suppressed.

A. E. Gallatin (1927) includes the four Osborn plates, that is, the same ones that are printed with Kenton's article in his book on Demuth, and makes a brief summary comment, not particularly useful in solving the riddle of Demuth's interpretation of the tale, but at least responsive to the process of production of the watercolors. "In executing these illustrations," says Gallatin, "the artist has first made a drawing outlined in pencil, upon which he has imposed washes of colour. His line is extremely sensitive and nervous, and the washes of delicate and alluring colour play an important part in organizing the design. The essence of the scene has in each case been portrayed" (5). The pencil lines are still in evidence in the plates from Kenton's article, almost as if the presented works were no more than preliminary sketches. Perhaps one can agree with Gallatin that the "line is ... sensitive and nervous." But it is worth a question to establish the basis on which Gallatin has concluded that "the essence of the scene has in each case been portrayed." Of course, Demuth's work is "literary" in the sense that the artist has also penciled the story text of the scene which he is illustrating onto the surface of each of the panels. It might be argued that Demuth has captured essences; on the other hand, perhaps as with every other artist who has seen fit to transform *The Turn of the Screw* from prose fiction into an alternate art form, Demuth has been forced to choose exactly how to represent the governess; and that has meant reducing the ambiguity of the text to a chosen unalterable reading. In two of the four panels published with Kenton's essay (hereafter to be referred to by the name of their contemporary owner, Frank Osborn), the governess is anything but pretty, and in two, at least, she is indeed an old maid. In the first Osborn panel (the *Arts* 1924, 247), the one captioned by Demuth as, "I can see the way his hand passed from one crenellation to the next," the eyes are besotted with the vision that they see. But the woman fails to strike us as James's pretty young governess. As a possible conditioner of context, it is worth noting that the Gallatin volume (1927) was issued between the time of publication of Kenton's and Wilson's articles.

Robert Lee Wolff in 1941 is one of a series of critics concerned about the relationship between *The Turn of the Screw* and the plastic arts. His article ultimately declares that Tom Griffiths's illustration in *Black and White* in an issue that also contained the magazine printing of James's "Sir Edmund Orme" was a major influence on the visual sense of *The Turn of the Screw*. But he begins with comments on Kenton, Wilson, and Demuth, thus becoming one of the very few critics who ever consciously makes this important juxtaposition. Wolff begins by quoting Kenton's contention that it is the governess alone who sees the ghosts; declares that "this is the view taken by Charles Demuth" in the illustrations; and proceeds to credit Wilson with a step-by-step analysis to achieve his sense of the governess's passion (apparently sexual) "for the little boy" (k 125–26). Wolff sees this line of development as the key support for Douglas's recoil from the governess's narrative with the judgment that it is beyond anything "'for general ugliness'" (126). While Wolff makes no important attempt to analyze the Demuth paintings, he is the first to insist on the relation between the paintings and the Wilsonian "Freudian" reading, and he seconds Wilson in declaring that the paintings support Kenton's notion of the governess's hallucinating the ghosts and Wilson's notion of the gross sexual hunger that moves her.

Sherman Lee in *Art Quarterly* (1942) comments on the Demuth illustrations, noting their literary qualities and declaring these to project a "sympathetic understanding" with Proust and James (158). Lee clouds the context even further by declaring that there were six illustrations: there are the four known to have been in possession of Frank Osborn; and there is the "sixth" which Lee tells us is "the first in point of time, [but] has hitherto been unpublished: *At a House in Harley Street*, in the Museum of Modern Art." According to Lee, "a fifth illustration, *Boy and Girl* not listed before, is on the New York Art Market." The five works now associated with the text (Haskell 1987, 114–116) are covered by Lee's citation of the Osborn collection in the Philadelphia Museum of Art and the watercolor in the Museum of Modern Art. Barbara Haskell, in preparing the catalogue for the Demuth retrospective run by the Whitney Museum in 1988, makes no mention of a sixth painting. (She speaks definitively of the "five illustrations for 'The Turn of the Screw'" [109]; and on 112 n. 19, she speaks of Lee's hypothesis and the ensuing acceptance of a "watercolor entitled *Boy and Girl* [1912] as Demuth's frontispiece for 'The Turn of the Screw'"; however, she rejects it as a companion piece for the tale).

Lee both promotes Wilson's interpretation and extends the tease of the circumstances by speaking of the "fifth," that is, the non-Kentonian panel, as one in which the text of the tale agrees with the designation *The House in Harley Street*: "a big house filled with the spoils of travel and the trophies of the chase" (167). Furthermore, "the woman can be recognized as the governess, the man as her employer." Lee goes on to tell us that the Harley Street panel represents the earlier style of Demuth illustrations, a style "well suited to the Harley Street atmosphere of the first scene with its air of splendor of setting, and solicitude and interest in the figures. The deliberately fussy line adds to the overstuffed air of the interior. Significant details such as the stuffed birds under glass and the owlish moose heads add to this sensation" (168). The tease lies in the interesting but baffling collaboration of fiction writer, illustrator, and art critic in the production of fiction-painting-interpretation as to where anything like artistic intention occurs. The reader of James's text might well question whether such a heavy atmosphere does indeed overlie the house in Harley Street, either as a matter of fact or as a matter of psychological response on the part of the governess. For in Harley Street, the young girl who will become governess is most surely "seduced"—to use the phrase of the external narrator in the prologue to the tale—though everything suggests that she is not suffocated, as Demuth's illustration insists and as Lee follows Demuth in claiming for him, but is rather carried away on currents as flimsy as clouds.

Nonetheless, Lee continues in the same vein, seeing in Demuth a powerful reflection of the "subtle method in James." For Lee the composition of the painting, with the "two figures in the very close foreground," captures our attention and places the power in the hands of the employer, who stands over the governess to carry out the negotiations, leading us at first to suspend our sense of place and then to turn to it as the very image, as later commentators will say, of the employer as predator. Lee declares that these subtle details will suggest the method as well of Proust, who used it in "his long novels of sensation, response and introspection" (167). But the illustrations become "more and more delicate, fragmentary and reticent." Lee's example of this fragmentation is the panel in which the governess sees Flora pick up the piece of wood. Says Lee, "Much more of the paper is blank and the pencil is not heavily used, but lightly with a lacy effect. Especially well caught, in the spirit of the book, is the willful sullenness of Flora as she ignores the vision which appears to the startled governess. Only the three blurs in the upper right betray the presence of the ghostly figure." What is interesting here is Lee's further involvement in interpretation—in deciding the nature of the tale and the definitive direction of the matters that appear as textual ambiguities. That is, in the first panel in Harley Street, the subtle power is that of the employer over the unsuspecting governess. That power seems to suggest to Demuth the force of the master's sexuality in overwhelming the governess; in turn, it arms the fulcrum-piece in the collection of five panels, the governess gazing with glazed eyes at the figure on the roof at Bly. What Lee says here suggests an interpretation of the tale in which the ghosts are real and the children are depraved, an interpretation categorically opposed to that of Edmund Wilson. For Lee, Flora is sulky, willfully sullen; she ignores the vision. The governess is startled by the apparition; the presence of the apparition is "betrayed" by the blurs in the upper right.

Early in his discussion, Lee admits to having seen only two of the panels (and the context leads one to assume that he means that he has seen the originals of the two; the context also suggests that the two that he has seen are the *House in Harley Street* and *Boy and Girl*, the panel that both Barbara Haskell and Pamela Allara reject as an illustration for *The Turn of the Screw*). His visual source for the four scenes included in Kenton's text appears to be the Gallatin book, which he cites on page 166. The evidence from the interpretation suggests that Lee has seen only the black-and-white reproduction, since he does not see the intensity of the pencil intimation of the ghost of Jessel, stronger in color than in black and white; nor does he see, or at least mention, the compositional ring that surrounds Flora in the watercolor. This ring is to some extent created by figures in the landscape, notably the butterflies above Flora's head, but in the color reproduction, one can see that it is made a compositional unit by being executed in a wash of yellow surrounding Flora and excluding both the governess and the ominous figure in the "upper right." Whatever Demuth intends it to represent, it strongly suggests a halo around youth and innocence. And in fact, though both the governess and the ominous "blur" are excluded from the ring, both seem to breach its perfect uniformity: at least the pattern of yellow wash is least in evidence at the point at which the "torso" of the blur and the hand of the governess intrude on the circle. In any case, the governess here appears with wrinkles on forehead and cheeks; her eyes and mouth are wide open, the stare appearing almost witless and her whole demeanor as though struck dumb. In a very important sense, Demuth's governess here is the very antithesis of the figure who narrates the events at Bly. For James's governess is the epitome of verbal fluency; Demuth's seems in all but the final illustration to be devoid both of wits and of words.

Lee comments on the last two of the Osborn panels. The fourth is the depiction of Flora and Miles together on the grounds, Miles reading to Flora as they cross the lawn together. Lee sees four protagonists "extremely well characterized: the bulky housekeeper, the sensitive governess, and the two children acting out their parts as creatures of sweetness and light." He suggests that the technique here is "crystalline blotting" to produce "a mottled as well as a striated texture." It has a "sudden vista" for which, as far as I know, there is no authority in the text, and it features "rising motifs" to indicate the agitation in the landscape.

In the last scene, of the governess with Miles, the composition is characterized by "a suppressed background of vertical angular motifs." The figures themselves are set out with a delicacy that Lee seems inclined to question; but he sees the "uncertain boy" and the "anguished woman" as the figures calling for our attention. If Lee is unhappy with this last of the illustrations, the less skilled general observer of plastic art might well join him. The governess here is, while still not a pretty girl as James's text seems recurrently to insist, almost unrecognizable as the figure represented to us as the governess in the earlier illustrations. Delicate indeed, she seems to have evolved from the old maid of the earlier panels to the sensitive and matronly figure that we find here embracing Miles. She has none of the glazed sexual hunger of the earlier panels; and she importunes the child here with precisely the anguish that Lee suggests. These are not, he tells us, "ghost-like illustrations. ... They are immensely subtle illustrations in a twisted, tortured manner that parallels the style of the novel. Hints are dropped, nothing is demonstrated" (167–68). Thus, as far as Lee is concerned, what we see in the Demuth illustrations "is not obvious eroticism, but rather a type which becomes so veiled and meaningful in the hands of a James or a Proust" (168). No circumstances present themselves under which Lee could accept Edmund Wilson's interpretation of the tale; correspondingly, the Demuth illustrations, in following the "twisted, tortured manner" of the style of the novel demonstrate, its hints but avoid anything obvious and anything so reeking of repressed sexuality as Wilson's Freudian interpretation. Lee puts us on a kind of holding ground between what Wilson says in his own right and what his treatment implies about Demuth. He presses us to keep looking for some other means of dealing with these illustrations.

That other means might have been provided by John Sweeney's article only a year later. Sweeney proposes to talk about "The Demuth Pictures." Sadly, he restricts his attention to the illustrations for "The Beast in the Jungle" (1943). As he says, the two "notable series of illustrations" were "apparently never intended to be 'served on the same platter' with their inspirations" (523). Sweeney is aware from James's prefaces how averse James was to impeding the verbal imagination by the use of props from the plastic arts. In any case Sweeney says that both series of illustrations are presently recognized as superior "examples of water-color painting." And he tantalizes us by telling us that "both these series are of considerable value for the light they throw on James's literary method by illustrating it through an analogous approach in the materials of another art" (524). He does not offer a detailed compositional study of the panels on *The Turn of the Screw* to support this thesis, but rather limits his attention to the other, later series. He does tell us that "neither series has ever been published with its corresponding text, and their peculiar character makes any future likelihood of their [being so presented] very slight" (524). Sweeney recognizes that the alternative art form also remakes the work of art; and that to present them in juxtaposition is simply to challenge the receiver with competing artifacts, an observation crucial to any sound evaluation of the transformations of *The Turn of the Screw* into paintings, operas, dramas, films, or television plays.[9]

Sweeney's commentary on the illustrations for "The Beast in the Jungle" is brightly perceptive. Like Kenton, he includes black-and-white reproductions of the watercolors in the text of the essay. He comments intelligently on the story first and then shows the compositional elements—structure, color, symbol, and tableau—which reflect those aspects of story that Demuth chose to accentuate in his illustrations. In that sequence of panels, Sweeney finds, Demuth has chosen the salient points of the tale—the announcement of the Impending Doom in the boat ride from Sorrento; the revelation of the Beast for May in her drawing room, where she asks Marcher whether he is still ignorant of the nature of the beast; and the scene of Marcher lying in agony across her grave, the beast having sprung at last for him. Even though Sweeney does not analyze the watercolors for *The Turn of the Screw*, he does reiterate his sense of disjunction between prose and plastic artifact: "Demuth's work is a presentation rather than a representation—a *new* thing in which literal reproduction has been drastically subordinated to a presentation in pictorial terms of the text's supporting structure. The artist has added, on his own initiative, where the addition would fortify his composition and implement the author's intention" (531). All that he says here of the illustrations for the story is true, and in some respects even more intensively true for the novella. That is, Demuth's choice of enhancements for the sequence of panels illustrating the story represents the alteration of relatively small matters from the literal, textual facts of the narrative. In the illustrations for the novella, Demuth has recurrently gone farther afield in his attempts at a unified "presentation" of the issues of the tale. There is little ambiguity in the focus of the story; there is little but ambiguity in the focus of the novella. Perhaps it was on these grounds that Sweeney undertook, so intelligently, to provide a commentary on the Demuth illustrations for "The Beast in the Jungle"—and why he declined to do so for *The Turn of the Screw*. Sweeney recognizes that there was a freight of possible misinterpretation in the illustrations he has analyzed (531). But he concludes by suggesting that James was likely to have celebrated the artistic effort "to do the complicated thing with a strong brevity and lucidity," as he quotes James's preface. Very likely the same problems would have held if he had chosen to treat Demuth's illustrations for *The Turn of the Screw*, possibly more intensively still.

But Sweeney at least puts into perspective the artistic problems surrounding the use of the Demuth illustrations of James as a springboard for the interpretation of the tale. If those illustrations are presentations rather than attempts to render the exact sense of the fiction—what Sweeney seems to mean by "representation"—then they become new artifacts in themselves requiring response in the same sense as would any artifact that exploits an earlier artifact in its process of composition—Joyce's *Ulysses*, for example, or Wolf's *Kassandra*. The sense of competition is not salient here; only the sense of the evolution of an artistic idea. To whatever extent the provocation of an interpretive act might be identified as a goal of these artifacts, such a goal would be distinctly secondary to the artistic concerns of the act of creation. Ultimately, this state of things is true of virtually every transformation of *The Turn of the Screw* with the exception of Mariette Lydis's illustrations for the text of Mark Van Doren's 1949 reissue of the novella—illustrations that would likely have left James speechless with disgust at the sentimentalizing and trivializing of his tale.

Thomas Cranfill and Robert Clark, better known for their excursion into criticism with their *Anatomy of "The Turn of the Screw"* (1965a), give an overview of the "provocative" nature of the tale, which has led to so many re-creations of it in other art forms. As they declare, "At least three other artists, Charles Demuth, Mariette Lydis, and William Archibald, have, in their own way commented on the story by illustrating it. James himself would not have welcomed their efforts. He is quoted on the subject in a note probably by Forbes Watson, the editor of *The Arts*, prefatory to Edna Kenton's well-known article in that journal. ... To the superimposition of another's illustrations on his own 'pictures' James was rigidly opposed: 'Anything that relieves responsible prose of the duty of being, while placed before us, good enough, interesting enough and, if the question be of picture, pictorial enough ... does it the worst of services'" (1970, 96). Cranfill and Clark tell us that Archibald (who did sketches to accompany the play text for his adaptation of the tale *The Innocents*) and Lydis clearly subscribe to the "conventional" reading of the tale with real ghosts. Demuth they find quite different. The editorial that prefaced Kenton's essay declares that the "results of two quite independent excursions into the haunted labyrinths of this famous story by a curiously critical reader and a critically curious painter. In his own medium Mr. Demuth offers, not 'illustrations' for the text, but a criticism and an appreciation of it" (97). Cranfill and Clark go on: "The coincidences of values between Miss Kenton and Mr. Demuth 'make it diverting to set this particular picture and text side by side.'" Their purpose in pursuing the Demuth illustrations is to declare that only Demuth has managed somehow "to translate from the medium of the novelist into the medium of the graphic artist the dreadful impact of the tale." These authors seem to know only the four panels associated with the Kenton text, and they summarize the sequence with the governess as ghost ridden in all four of the panels: "alone, scrutinizing the spectacle of Quint on the tower; knitting on the terrace as an obese and coarse-looking Mrs. Grose stands by in cap and apron and the pathetically frail children walk in the distance; sitting agape as the apparition of Miss Jessel looms across the lake and Flora unconcernedly plays; clasping Miles in the final appalling scene of the novel" (97). But Cranfill and Clark conclude more certainly than do either of the art critics quoted above; and they illustrate the problem of the art criticism of the Demuth watercolors in declaring that these works show "that Demuth shares the view of Miss Kenton, Edmund Wilson and others that the governess is grimly deranged." Only if one starts from the premise that Demuth is portraying madness can one positively conclude that Demuth intends to show a deranged governess. He offers his ambiguous and difficult version of the tale in pictures and without explanation.

Pamela Allara's doctoral thesis is the most ambitious entry in the critical tradition of the Demuth illustrations for *The Turn of the Screw*. She offers some quite striking insights into the technical matters of the paintings—the use of pencil, the manner of Demuth's washes of color, the implications of composition. She tries hard to honor Demuth's own apparent desire to balance his interpretation of the tale between a guilty governess and ghost-corrupted children. She seems to some extent to have been susceptible to fashionable critical persuasions in various of her "literary" interpretations of the texts—both James's and Demuth's.

Allara recounts carefully the aesthetic views of both James and Demuth that inscribe a bridge between them—each artist having considered the other's mode before taking up his own. Allara's inquiry extends to cover the skepticism of the artists about the conversions of each art into the other, James believing that prose must make its own way; Demuth believing that "across [an imposing work of art] is written in larger letters than any printed page will ever dare to hold what its creator had to say about it."[10] She shows in addition, however, James's view that when a work of art prompts another work of art, not as a competitor, but as a separate entity, it can become a "glorious tribute."[11] Allara says, simply, that this parallel work is precisely what Demuth achieves. If most of the transformations or versions of the tale in other art forms have by necessity reduced the tale to singular meanings, it is at least tenable, as Allara says here, to suggest that Demuth alone of those who appropriate the tale has achieved the same kind of ambiguity as the tale. That is, there are suggestions of ghost forms in two of the panels, in the first Osborn panel by the fixation of the governess's eyes, and in the second Osborn panel, where Flora is the focus. In addition, there is a highly suggestive phallic shape in the background behind the governess in the first Osborn panel that we can take for a ghost if we like. But there is no necessity that we should see any of these graphic forms as particular or, more intensely, restricted meaning-forms. In this sense Demuth can, perhaps, have it both (or all) ways, as does James.

Allara is frequently acute on the contributions of the technical execution of the Demuth illustrations to a view of their meaning. Speaking of the first panel, *At a House in Harley Street*, Allara shows the imposing nature of the master who dominates the painting's center as well as the seated, foreshortened applicant who seems almost to kneel before the dominant figure. She suggests to us that the fireplace drawn here recalls the fireplace around which Douglas tells the story in the frame narrative. She shows us that the "trophies of the chase" emphasize the predatory nature of the master and suggests to us that the birdcage is both a symbol of the coming isolation of the governess and a powerful reflex of the "fluttering girl from the Hampshire vicarage"— all matters of the tale's prologue (183–85). She shows us that the landscape behind the governess in panel 2 (*The Governess First Sees the Ghost of Peter Quint*) is both dun and bleak to suggest the winter with which the governess associates the first vision of Quint; and that it seems to fall away beneath the governess to suggest the "succession of flights and drops" that condition the opening of the governess's narrative (188–89). She draws our attention to the framing yellow sky in panel 3 (*Flora and the Governess*), a ring that surrounds Flora but almost completely excludes the governess and the suggested ghost. She shows us that the flowers in the ring locate and symbolize Flora within it. She shows us the composition in panel 4 using the two adult figures in the foreground to frame the children (*The Governess, Mrs. Grose, and the Children*). She points out that the landscape is abstracted and almost suggests the back of the governess's tapestry. She shows us that the circular compositional motifs of panel 5 (*Miles and the Governess*) serve both to move us restlessly through the scene from the governess to the blank window while at the same time suggesting the circle in which the two figures are caught. And she shows us that compositionally this panel completes the series because in the pressure applied to Miles by the governess, the sequence offers us a reprise of the pressure brought to bear on the governess in the first panel by the master of Bly. Allara thus gives a strong argument for the existence of a unified compositional structure for the series that stands as a force behind Demuth's own composition.

Her interpretations seem less compelling than her commentary on technical matters—sometimes, even quite unconvincing. She makes it clear very early that she is aware of both Kenton's and Wilson's treatments of *The Turn of the Screw*. Though she disavows their influence on her readings of James and Demuth, the influence tends to show itself in her interpretations, especially those involving the Osborn panels. The governess, she tells us, speaking of panel 2, is cast by Demuth with a rubbery neck, half-closed eyes, a twisted smile, as though she were drugged. Here she is ugly, masculine, even by parallel with the other Demuth paintings, showing lesbian tendencies (190–91). While nothing in the panel explicitly forbids these observations, nothing supports them either. Unlike the comments on form and design, these prompt us to think of critical impressionism. The interpretive commentary on the third panel suggests much the same thing. While there is no denying that Flora's eyes are downcast in the panel, there is nothing to show us why. She is not in a position to see the suggestive ghost form, but Demuth seems to be allowing the viewer to see in Flora either the shame of the governess's molesting presence, the shame of her consciousness of the ghosts' successful corruption of her mind, or—and there is nothing in the panel to exclude it—mere maidenly modesty. Allara makes this panel fit a scheme of her own making in which Demuth is accommodating the ambiguity of the tale by having alternate panels favor the competing interpretations of the tale: "the two illustrations, when compared, present the two equally convincing interpretations" (193). She acknowledges residual ambiguities in the two panels. With respect to panel 4 Allara tells us, without citing any internal evidence to support her view, that the adults appear 'weightless,' that the governess appears thin and teetering and that Mrs. Grose is recoiling from the back of the governess's tapestry. With respect to the final panel she tells us that the governess is pleading and profoundly concerned; that Miles reacts with disturbance and annoyance. Allara invites us to discern that Demuth is portraying the governess instead of the ghost as Miles's destroyer; the panel shows us that Demuth has made Miles replace the master as the object of the governess's regard. Though Allara covers with an appeal to the panels' general ambiguity, she joins this interpretation with the majority of her other interpretations, which favor the earlier Freudian reading of the paintings and, in turn, of the tale of which they are a version.

Barbara Haskell is, if not the most expert of commentators on Demuth's work, at least the most recent. Haskell's interest in Demuth's illustrations in general seems to rest in her interest in his use of sexual, including homosexual, themes. She tells us that the two stories of James that he illustrated reflect parallels between the lives of the author and the painter—fastidious privacy, passiveness, especially in sexual matters, the sufferers of suffocating childhoods (1987, 108). Haskell believes that the novella evoked a sexual pattern that suited Demuth; and she does not hesitate to solve the novella's traditional ambiguity: the governess's "hysteria in trying to make the boy also see [the ghost] frightens him to death." She allows as how originally the tale was read as a ghost story, but now, she can assure her reader, we know better. She cites Kenton's observation that the governess is the only one to see the ghosts, with the implication that "the source of these apparitions is terror about sexuality"; and that "this sexual subtext is established initially by the governess's infatuation with her employer" (108). She does not go quite so far as Wilson's declaration that the governess is a case of neurotic sex repression, but the final scene of the novel is "charged with sexual energy" (109). Demuth's illustrations capture the sexual currents in James's text, according to Haskell. We see the evidence of the overwhelming impact of the employer in the Harley Street panel; the gazing sequence reflects the governess in her state of quasi-sexual rapture; the gaping governess of the pondside tableau "can be read as a terrorized recoiling from sexual encounter," as we can see in the relation between Flora's piece of wood and the phallus; in the lawn scene with all four principal inhabitants of Bly present, "the housekeeper stands back from the scene with her mouth ajar as if to question the relationship between the governess and her charges"; and in the last of the five scenes, Demuth renders the governess's sexuality by depicting her interrogation of Miles "as seductive."

To the extent that she is trying to cover masses of material in a book given more to reproduction than to analysis, perhaps Haskell can be forgiven the leaps that she takes in her descriptions of the panels. But her demonstration of the purport of the panels is by asseveration only; she does not trouble to explain to her reader just how the illustrations "capture … [the] subtle evocation of sexual currents" (109). It is apparently massiveness in the House in Harley Street that overwhelms the young woman who will become governess at Bly. The junk, the preserved dead animals, and the young man's leaning over her somehow project the current of sexuality in Demuth's watercolor. But Haskell does not show us why the painting does not simply impress us with an impact of suffocation rather than seduction. A case could easily be made that the painting represents the gentleman's predatory habits, with the governess as a mere further exhibit in his triumphs of the chase. One would be less inclined to quarrel with Haskell's discovery of the "quasi-sexual rapture" of "illustration number 2," the governess caught looking at the apparition of Quint for the first time. But her glazed eyes are not the salient effect of the watercolor in this painting: rather her dowdiness, her plainness, her appearance of wasting age is salient. Demuth knows how to convey a pretty woman; the evidence for this skill need be sought at no greater distance than in Demuth's illustrations for "The Beast in the Jungle": May Bartram is both a pretty girl (in the first scene) and a handsome woman (in the second). The reader has not even the faintest hint about how to read the governess's sexual terror from the apparition in the background or from the piece of wood that Flora holds. Similarly, one is at a loss to discover how the bulging and coarse Mrs. Grose achieves the intelligence to judge the proceedings in the fourth panel. Again, Haskell baffles her reader with the charge that Demuth's last scene is seductive. If her pose with Miles shows anything even vaguely suggestive of seduction, this reader at least still awaits a careful demonstration of where the interpreter finds it in the artifact.

While one still recognizes the plastic artifact after looking at the commentary of Lee and Sweeney, Haskell, on the other hand, seems seriously lost in the tentacles of the critical tradition of *The Turn of the Screw* in her attempts to comment on the Demuth illustrations. She does as much as any single commentator in the whole long critical development to show the pitfalls of taking an absolute stand. Moreover, what might be forgivable in 1924, when the whole inquiry was new, seems at best questionable in 1987. Haskell has not even approached Lee and Sweeney for the intelligence that they showed in dealing with the way in which art conveys its ideas;[12] and she has fallen into the griefs of the partisans in the long battle over the meaning of *The Turn of the Screw*. She starts from the premise that Demuth's literary illustrations "revolve almost exclusively around sex and sin, death and salvation" (98). Her list of themes is interesting because it is cast in a form that suggests that these matters are all of a piece or, if not, are so clearly related to each other that there are no clear lines of separation. Indeed, Haskell, in summary, speaks of these four problematic and not necessarily harmonious themes as "this preoccupation." She has done a reasonable job of locating the usual subjects on which the critical battles over James's novella are waged, but she has not seen how widely separated the treatment of sex and sin, for example, might be from the treatment of death and salvation. The criticism of *The Turn of the Screw* contains a fairly significant number of items featuring the problems of sin and redemption and relegating the subject of sex to the subterranean stratum of the novella. For such critics, the force behind the tale is perceived as moral because it is concerned with the purgation of evil and the purification of the soul.

The intentions of Demuth's watercolors of *The Turn of the Screw* seem to me to be as perplexing, though in different ways, as the novella itself. That there are alternative ways of reading these powerful illustrations is evident from the variant views presented here. That they are powerful can be seen from their vivid impact on various interpreters over the years. One can easily agree with Sweeney that these illustrations have no verifiable affinity for the tale itself in illustration of the facts of its plot. But as respects the subsequent critical development of the view that the novella is about the suppressed life of an Anglo-Saxon spinster, it is hard to resist the notion that the reproduction of the Osborn panels with Edna Kenton's article have a significant if shadowy role. The illustrations need to be judged as part of the context of the "Freudian" reading of the tale. Demuth and only Demuth has made the governess into an old maid in the interpretive history of the tale to the moment at which the watercolors are executed. To the extent that Demuth's watercolors depicting the governess as an old maid, whether sexually depraved or not, gave direction to Wilson's vision of the tale, they are fascinatingly submerged in later Freudian readings of the tale. Not one of these later readings ever shows awareness of the watercolors that appear so teasingly to have prompted the earliest notions of the governess's abnormal psychology.

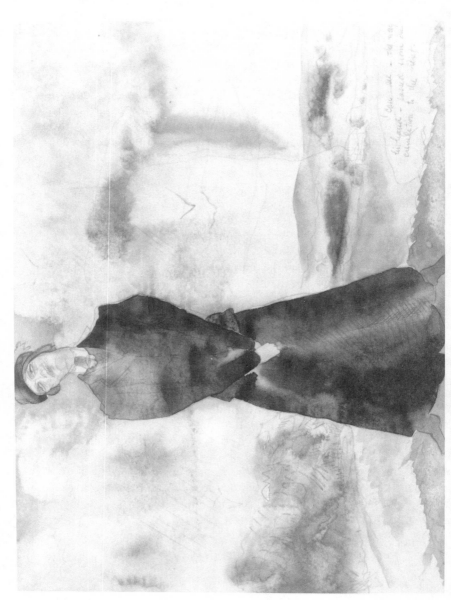

Demuth, Charles. "The Governess First Sees the Ghost of Peter Quint." Philadelphia Museum of Art: gift of Frank and Alice Osborn.

Demuth, Charles. "Flora and The Governess." Philadelphia Museum of Art: gift of Frank and Alice Osborn.

Demuth, Charles. "The Governess, Mrs. Grose and the Children." Philadelphia Museum of Art: gift of Frank and Alice Osborn.

Demuth, Charles. "Miles and the Governess." Philadelphia Museum of Art: gift of Frank and Alice Osborn.

EDNA KENTON AND THE SUPERIOR READER

Kenton is the first critic to declare in print that she reads James's tale with more acuteness than others. Nonetheless, Kenton seems to me an essayist, not a thesis-ridden fury. She sets out to entertain an idea rather than to ravish the world with the splendors of her prose. Furthermore, she has taken some consideration of the earlier critical treatment of the text before offering her view. She searches James's tale; she probes his preface. She offers by way of epigraph what will become the preface's most provocative thrust: that the tale is a trap set by the author. And she looks at some more of James's conditioning prose, the author's use of the reader's natural love of wonder, the author's insistence on the reader's attention and his assumption of it in the creation of the tale. She surveys the critical record for the Effect of the attention that James demanded and finds everywhere in that record clear evidence that "from the 1880's on ... James had to endure from his devotees the poor tribute of mere reverence," settling for the certainty of an "abiding mystery" that lurked behind his art, but bringing likewise "an abiding bewilderment before it" (Willen 1960, 103). Thus, she says, *The Turn of the Screw* "caught every one in its trap." That is, Kenton says, they all knew or believed they knew what he was writing about in the tale but did not read closely enough to see the submerged story.[13]

In the best possible sense of presenting a critical muddle, she introduces what she supposes to be a typical case, that of William Lyon Phelps (cited above, chap. 2, 96–97), whose experience with the tale and whose sensation of evil, whose lovely chill apparently pleased James so thoroughly. She cites the tale of the iron Scots stenographer and declares that he is the only one in James's world who could read the tale without moving a hair. She cites the years of the publication of the New York Edition as "the two marvellous years [1908 and 1909; she doesn't know that the New York Edition began to appear in 1907] in the Jacobites' calendar" that broke the silence on the compositional method and gave us the insight of the prefaces into the unfolding of the Jamesian career. But for Kenton the prefaces have not served their turn historically, and have rather obscured than illumined the Jamesian horizon. In this unfortunate and persistent ignorance of James's meanings, *The Turn of the Screw* "remains today what it has been declared for a quarter of a century to be, 'a relation of the imaginative— which is the moral and spiritual—defiling of two children by apparitional criminals'" (w 1960, 105). And she continues with a list of quotations of the sort that I have cited above from the early critics of the tale. She hoots them to scorn for the very inattentiveness to the tale that

James complained of generally in his readers. She wishes to cite the preface as evidence both for readerly inattentiveness and for her own acuity. "No one," she says, on reading the tale "was baffled by it; it held no secrets. It was simply a gorgeous ghost story, ethical, of course, profoundly moral, involving as it so evidently did, the problem of corrupted childhood" (105). But she declares that James warns his reader in the preface and then proceeds to illustrate how the reader will be trapped. She sees that James's response to Wells on characterization was a clear and unequivocal disclaimer on his way to declaring that the evil is not specified and that there is no expatiation in the tale, that "authority" is a good deal to have given to the governess.

Kenton confesses that on her first reading she had done the conventional things with the tale—had read it in a first edition in a country house at and past the hour of midnight and had shuddered beautifully over the harshly beleaguered children. Her one claim to difference from the readers she quotes, as she recalls, was her "wondering over the portentous Evil that, from the first page to the last, floated through the great room of the story" (106). She says that she saw all the conventional things that the ordinary reader would see, but that she saw as well the problem of the way the evil came into the story. Inevitably, over time, she came to feel that much of what happened in the story came through "the exquisite little governess": "There was the thickly painted picture of horror—but where?—on the pages or in the mind?" (106). Kenton settles quite serenely for locating the horror in the governess's mind. She calls the settled spot of requited wonder "an oasis in the wordy desert of fiction" (107), where she might share with James some of the fun he speaks about in the preface.

But now she ventures into the criticism of the tale up to her own moment and discovers that the professional critic "fell somehow always short of going behind" (107): "Critical appraisement of The Turn of the Screw has never, indeed, pressed beyond the outer circle of the story where the children and ghosts dance together, toward any discerned or discernible inner ring where another figure may be executing some frantic dance of terror, toward any possible story behind the 'story,' toward any character protected by its creator to the very top of his sardonic, ironic bent." Thus does Edna Kenton fire the first salvo in the long and exalted tradition of the criticism of *The Turn of the Screw*, which from this moment onward complains at more or less great length of critical inattention, not to say critical imbecility, on the part of the speaking writer's critical forebears. Though she has eminently more justification for her cavil than do many of her later echoes, she, too, apparently falls into the Jamesian trap. As more than one of the later

critics in review of the criticism will say, she attempts to prove her
point by appropriating the tale to herself. The point that she will press
here is the one she has just made about James's "protecting" his
characters.

Though Kenton does not mention either Frank Moore Colby or W.
C. Brownell (cited above in chap. 1, 68–69), she contradicts them by
what she says about their sort of assessment of James's relationship to
his characters. James loves his characters, she says, and he protects
them because he loves them, especially the wayward and wildly self-
deceived ones. She wants us to recall the paper on Balzac in which
James had declared that Balzac loved his Valérie and in which he had
denounced Thackeray for scorning his own Becky and Blanche. James's
cavil is "a straight little tip that James is never so guileful, so suave and
so honied as when his is busily engaged in protecting'" (w 107). The
reader might recall that Colby had said that James had created a land
"where the vices have no bodies and the passions no blood, where
nobody sins because nobody has anything to sin with" (1902a, 397);
and that Brownell had said, using precisely the image of Balzac's
identification with Valérie Marneffe, that it was unlikely to occur to
anyone "that Mr. James 'loved' any of his characters" (Gard 1968,
417). That is the context in which Brownell found James "ardently
frigid" because of the excessive zeal of his disinterested curiosity.
Kenton, on the other hand, looks at the same matrix and finds quite the
opposite result.

For her, in fact, that "honied" handling of those characters whom
James is inclined to protect is a perfect reflection of his understanding
that they are wayward and wildly self-deceived: "And it is only painting
the gold of the lily to add that if one is making a collection of his agents
of evil, they are not to be found among those endowed with the usual
stripes and markings. He loves them even more than Balzac loved his
Valérie, and protects them with far finer dexterity" (107). For Kenton
the deduction is inevitable: the protection of character reached its
"apotheosis" in *The Turn of the Screw*. She even anticipates another
hotly contested Jamesian battleground—the marvelous battle over the
morality of Maggie in *The Golden Bowl* as a counterpart to the wars
over motive in *The Turn of the Screw*. But she will patiently argue for
her *partie* here, her own "attention of perusal" in the uncovering of the
mystery of the ghost tale. The puffs for the present speaker, at the
expense of the obtuse others, she indulges in to the perfect satisfaction
of the later reader: James would write the tale "primarily for himself
and for the reader for whom he must always write—the reader not
content to have the author do all of the work—but he would make this

particular work a supreme test, of attention and inattention alike" (108). He would do so by baiting traps in successive levels so that even the most alert reader ran risks: "Let some singularly astute reader avoid one and yet another of these—others would lie hidden or beckon invitingly ten steps ahead." According to Kenton, James set the trap for both the wary and for the dull—to see whether the reactions might be identical; she crows to herself in an echo of James's preface that "as a little matter of critical history they were" (108).

Kenton is among the first to notice the prologue to the tale, the frame, which becomes increasingly important as the criticism develops.[14] This prologue she refers to as "the submerged and disregarded forward to the tale," though she continues to leave it submerged and disregarded except as a context for giving a "bright setting" to the tale and for sticking a stray spur into her fellow readers, few of whom "remember this at all." She knows that it is the governess who tells the story and that therefore the narrative responsibility is hers. Thus, says Kenton, "we have got nowhere near the 'story of the story' until, pressing resolutely through her irresistibly credible recounting of the horrors at Bly, we come into closer quarters with the secret causes of her admirable *flair* for the evil she finds there" (109). In recounting the process of the governess's accepting the post at Bly, Kenton cannot help slanting the recital toward her own position: the gentleman in Harley Street is "'such as had never risen, save in a dream or an old novel" and the governess is "'the fluttered anxious girl out of a Hampstead [*sic*, for "Hampshire"] vicarage'"—and Kenton quotes these bits of the prologue; but for her the governess merely "hesitates" over the offer, and Kenton renders the hesitation inconsequential.

Nonetheless, for the strictest accuracy in reporting she might better have given the prologue verbatim: "'The prospect struck her as slightly grim. She was young, untried, nervous: it was a vision of serious duties and little company, of really great loneliness. She hesitated—took a couple of days to consult and consider.'" That amounts to something more substantial than the mere "she hesitated, but she was under a spell" (109)—the words used by Kenton to re-create the context of the prologue. The prologue tells us that even though she is under a spell, she understands with great clarity that what she undertakes is to be arduous and lonely—and very likely thankless: the master has insisted that the prime condition of the job is that she "should never trouble him—but never, never" (k 5). For whatever it is worth, these reflections condition the opening of her narrative with its recollection of a series "of flights and drops." As others have since pointed out, Kenton insists

on calling the narrator "the little governess," the diminutive suggesting
attenuation, perhaps to the point of nonentity.

Kenton can thus see the governess as pleasantly surprised by her
early days at Bly, but undertakes that there is a change "'actually like
the spring of a beast.'" The change comes, as Kenton notes, in the train
of the governess's daydream about the master, and she is prepared to
quote the governess's own rather brave declaration that "I do not in the
least shrink from noting now" that the daydream was about coming face
to face with the master in some sudden rush of re-cognitive love.
Kenton makes most capital of the subject of this daydream whereas
critics who will ultimately exonerate the governess of at least the most
malign of the intentions assigned her by the exponents of Kenton's view
will emphasize the governess's perfect willingness to disclose the
information, making it anything but repressed. Kenton now quotes
several hundred words, the governess's account of the exact
circumstances of the first "visitation of Peter Quint" (111). She quotes
the second visitation as well, the words in which the governess first says
that she has known the specter for years and records his stare into her
eyes. Then she impeaches: "So the little governess says, and upon it she
acts." It is convincing, Kenton says, and the little governess sweeps the
reader along with her into a process of living her nightmare. This is the
standard interpretation of the tale, "the traditional and accepted
interpretation of the story as it has come down to us through a quarter of
a century of readers' reactions resulting from 'a cold artistic
calculation' on the part of its highly entertained author."

But, Kenton says, the authority for this understanding is the
governess's narrative alone; and we must see that only the governess
sees the ghosts (111). Flora does not see the ghost of Miss Jessel; the
ghost is behind her and visible only to the governess. Thus "there are
traps and lures in plenty, but just a little wariness will suffice to
disprove, with a single survey of the ground," that unworthy version. It
is the governess who is haunted by the ghosts, not the children, and the
force of the ghosts is that they will act merely as supports for James's
intention "'to express my subject all directly and intensely'" (112). She
is somehow to blame for the aberrances that she has created: "So she
made the shades of her recurring fevers dummy figures for the delirious
terrifying of others, pathetically trying to harmonize her own
disharmonies by creating discords outside herself" (112). This is so
explicitly James's intention in the tale that Kenton can now declare that
"he is explicit as to just how the screw was tightened, revelatory as to
the calculated cause of his calculated effects" (112). She reverts to the
preface for support for her idea of the sprung trap and avails herself of

James's provision for the process by which the reader must supply the evil in order to relieve the novelist from doing so. This, she says, is an aesthetic moral whose "'sinister agent, be it man or ghost, must be, in the last analysis, capable of *anything*, the very worst conceivable action.'" Thus the governess cannot specify, the "fantastic figures have been read into" the tale, and a generation of readers has unconsciously and ironically supported James in the protection of the governess—ironically, because she has in fact performed the function of promoting the evil that has not been specified.

It has been a war, Kenton will conclude, or at least a game. For there are winners and losers, James being ostentatiously the winner: "James has won, hands down, all round; has won most of all when the reader, persistently baffled, but persistently wondering, comes face to face at last with the little governess, and realizes, with a conscious thrill greater than that of merely automatic nerve shudders before 'horror,' that the guarding ghosts and children—what they are and what they do—are only exquisite dramatizations of her little personal mystery, figures for the ebb and flow of troubled thought within her mind, acting out her story" (113). Although we recognize that for Kenton the ghosts are not real—are some form of projection upon the surface of the governess's surrounding reality—we are not able to see how fully they are removed from reality until the children join them in that isolation from reality as simply another "exquisite dramatization" of the governess's projection. But what James has won, according to Kenton, is the battle to focus the attention of the alert reader and to force this reader to do a substantial part of the work in the creation of the tale. It has "verified James's earliest contention that there was a discoverable way to establish a relation of work shared between the writer and the reader sufficiently curious to follow through" (113–14).

Kenton has the authority of James's preface for the approach she takes to the tale. James has been seen from early in the critical response to his career as demanding a critical eye and an attentive consciousness to his text. Recurrently he also calls for the reader to perform part of the labor of creating the literary artifact. In her essay, she shows how this might be done, how one might refuse to accept a surface line and dig deeper to the level where consciousness itself is in question—not in focus, because it is never in focus—but in prospect where in all its tortuous meanders, it can be seen to be moving. She shows her reader that indeed one can supply an alternative approach to the text under scrutiny, and she can make it attractive to follow her into the fields in which she has been observing the meanders of consciousness. Though she nowhere mentions Freud or the new psychology, one can see where

Edmund Wilson, for example, found in her essay the keys to his own Freudian reading of the tale. He merely extrapolates and extends the logic of Kenton's piece. Surely there is some justification for her in the great pride with which she thrusts forward the achievement of her essay. She has read closely. She has followed buried clues. She has considered the dictates of a reading of the tale variant from the sort of comment that has uniformly characterized responses up to the moment at which she writes; and these, once discovered, certainly seem to establish an authority for her vision, her engagement with the tale. She has reverently acknowledged the reader's own obligation to participate in the creation of the text.

But if Kenton's essay is the first salvo, in what will become the battle for the clear ownership of the tale, with the title in fee simple (Peter G. Beidler's study of the SPR, published in 1989, for example, begins with the claim, not of the decently modest author, but of his prologician that, having written the following exercise, the author has become "the new Master of Bly and its inhabitants"), it is necessarily the first shot fired in a warfare of parallel and often brilliant aberrations. As Shoshana Felman later points out in her own shear of brilliance, the history of the criticism of *The Turn of the Screw* consists by and large of the critics trying desperately to substitute themselves for the central absence of the tale—that of the disappearing master. Here, Kenton sees that James's invitation to the reader is to probe beneath the surface of the tale, while being certain to remain forever watchful, as though against the most direful misstep, which nonetheless awaits at every turn. Dutifully she does so, looking at the text and then continually checking against the preface to see whether her direction is the one in which James intends to take his reader. Kenton believes that she has taken the hint from James in the process of her reduction of the governess to the "little" creature that she becomes in this treatment of her. Once impeach her at all and the process of selected emphases becomes a mere minor adjustment to the initial critical act.

It is not, then, at all out of keeping with her assumption about James's permissions to the critic to downplay the degree of the governess's sense of the ominous in both Douglas's representation of that sense in the prologue and in the governess's own sense of it at the opening of the narrative. To say that Kenton misrepresents the governess by the nature of the choice of critical emphasis, or even that she distorts the context in which she places the governess for us critically, is perhaps less important than to say that Kenton has made a clear critical choice about the tale, has presented it not only as an alternative version to the orthodox standard but as the *right* version and has solved the mystery—at Bly or wherever the locus of the mystery rests (for Kenton it is possible to argue that the mystery is located within the mind of the governess solely)—with no appeal from this present version possible (she visualizes herself as "the reader who has won for himself a blest sense of an extension of experience" at the end of her essay). While it may appear unfriendly to suggest it, Kenton seems indeed to have fallen into the Jamesian trap. That trap might be said to operate on the mere fact of choosing. Thus, Kenton's choice of the solution in which the ghosts become projections of the governess's abnormal psychology is not wrong because it is an aberrant choice of solution—while, for instance, the "traditional" choice that she scouts is the "right" one—but rather because in choosing at all she restricts the tale to a necessary solution. As far as I can see, James's trap is precisely the trap of "rightness," "accuracy," "correctness." The tale seems to yearn for the freedom of the optical illusion, which on given occasions and without any particular reason will now appear to carry the eye one definitive way, now another, never both together. Perhaps the configuration of the story most definitively Jamesian is its stimulus to the critic to search it for the things that are stable in any interpretation. At least those things include human nature and what, under one label or another, we agree to call evil.

WILSON AND THE NEUROTIC CASE

According to this interpretation, the young governess who tells the story is a neurotic case of sex repression, and the ghosts are not real ghosts but merely the governess's hallucinations.

The theory is, then, that the governess who is made to tell the story is a neurotic case of sex repression, and that the ghosts are not real ghosts but hallucinations of the governess.

The two statements above are variants, the first from the original *Hound & Horn* publication of Edmund Wilson's article on James's ambiguity (1934), and the second from *The Triple Thinkers* in its 1948 redaction as reprinted in Gerald Willen's *Casebook on Henry James's "The Turn of the Screw"* (1960). These variants occur among hosts of others in the tortuous process of Wilson's saying what he is going finally to say about *The Turn of the Screw*. In the original, there is no Austrian novelist (Franz Höllering) to sit in judgment on James's

morals; but that happy addition finds its way into the 1948 edition of
The Triple Thinkers, along with an attenuation of the original claims
about the governess's sexually repressed neuroticism. In addition,
Willen includes Wilson's note of 1959 in the *Casebook*, in which
Wilson, basing his judgment on further critical statements, returns to his
original premises. One becomes tempted, on seeing all of Wilson's
revolutions and squirmings on *Screw*, to adapt his own language to
describe his critical practice: A neurotic case of critical compulsion in
which the urgency to seize critical hegemony makes the effort
inevitable, regardless of the difficulties of establishing critical validity
beforehand. Wilson shows some of the weaknesses of the school of
psychoanalytic criticism that wishes to use the literary text as a
substitute for a dream in a proposed analysis of the psyche of the
narrator. But this weakness has not stopped Wilson's "Ambiguity" from
becoming an admired text and the source of a continuing strain of
Screw criticism.

In the above variants we can see the move from "interpretation" to
"theory"; from the "young governess who tells the story" to "the
governess who is made to tell the story"; and "the ghosts ... who are
merely the governess's hallucinations" to "the ghosts [who] are not real
ghosts but hallucinations of the governess." The variants move from the
more casual to the more confirmed, as from "interpretation" to
"theory," from a kind of acknowledging of the governess's
circumstances to a flat statement of the case. In the later version, the
governess is no longer young and she does not tell the story, as the first
statement leaves us to assume, voluntarily, but is now "made to tell the
story" under some form of compulsion that Wilson does not specify and
that we cannot see. In the early version,
the ghosts are "mere hallucinations," as though a whim of the
governess; in the later version, they are nakedly and unmixedly
"hallucinations of the governess"—a kind of neurotic gesture converted
into a fact. In other words, as Wilson moves into the corrections of his
text, he moves toward a harder and more entrenched statement of the
governess's condition.

If Kenton is the first in the line of critics to dispute the generality of
the prior readings of the tale, she does so at least from the perspective
of one who has bothered to read the criticism that she is disentangling
herself from, a feature of the critical practice that becomes increasingly
rare as that criticism proliferates. But Wilson is already inclined to
"know" things without study, by some special magic of intellectual
intuition; and besides, he has Kenton's work on which to draw for his
ideas. Enigmatically he glances at the Demuth illustrations that he

knows in reproduction from Kenton's article for attitudes toward the conditions under which the governess narrates her adventure. He makes himself Kenton's ally with more positive forward reinforcement than she asks for. He makes himself Demuth's ally, if at all, in ways that are more enigmatic still. He gives the reader this information at the head of his essay in his declaration that, though he knows of the theory of a mystery behind the surface mystery of the tale, "I do not know who first propounded the theory" (385). Here, at least, Wilson does not need to know the critical annals of *The Turn of the Screw* to write about it. But though he refers his reader to Edna Kenton (without, in the first edition of "The Ambiguity," citing the source in which the reader can find her statement), he will insist on giving his own version of the "plain sense" of the tale.

His version is similar to Kenton's but with his own set of accents. He too sees Douglas, but like Kenton, does not give him any critical play. Douglas is simply a source of textual information (385), the man who tells us who she is. Wilson quotes the passage about the handsome master and the fluttered anxious girl but goes on in his own prose to tell us that the governess has become "infatuated with her employer" (385–86). His method of procedure (385) is instructive: it shows us that Wilson, in his position as reporter of the facts, selects his accents with care: the employer "lets her have the job" (386), cautioning her against consulting him about the children. Wilson's language implies that the master of Bly is doing the governess a favor—he *lets* her have the job, not, as the only text we have declares, begging her to accept, and holding her hand and "thanking her for the sacrifice" when she does (k 6). If the owner of Bly is doing the governess a favor by letting her have the job, then it is only a small additional burden on her that she is never, never to approach him with problems. But Douglas's recollection of the governess's response to the condition suggests something much more intense in her awareness of the issues: the master "told her frankly all his difficulty—that for several applicants the conditions had been prohibitive. They were somehow simply afraid. It sounded dull—it sounded strange; and all the more so because of his main condition"— which is the nonintervention pact (k 6). The coolness of her going down to Bly is also a selective accent: Wilson, like Kenton, cannot allow the governess to have her "succession of flights and drops," her series of hesitations, if she is to turn into the insane child killer.

If Wilson is unprepared to subject himself to a reading of the prior criticism of the tale in order to fortify his critical position, he is equally unprepared to read the tale itself accurately. We have seen above how selected accents slant his treatment away from inconvenient aspects of the tale. Now, when the governess travels to Bly, the boy has already been sent home and awaits her, as do Flora and Mrs. Grose. Wilson tells us that Miles has been sent home from school; that the governess "colors" this event as "sinister without any apparent justification (386). Of course the governess thinks she has evidence—the headmaster's rather evasive directive that says they cannot have him back. In what follows, we find that the boy admits to having "said things," though it is true that neither the governess, according to her own account, nor we who are dependent on that account for all we are to have of the facts, ever learn what the boy has said or how his utterance has led to his expulsion. But she understands that the child of privilege cannot be expelled from school for no cause at all. Someone later, in defense of Wilson's idea, suggests that the reason for the expulsion might be neutral, might simply be that Miles has been found too young, or as we might say today, emotionally immature. Aside from the lack of any evidence in the text for such a conclusion, we have the evidence of the governess's reports that Miles is, if anything, emotionally and socially precocious, and not the opposite.

Wilson proceeds along the same lines, that is, by way of insinuation, about the other characters that make up the drama of the governess's narrative: she is gratuitously suspicious of her predecessor; she is left alone with the "illiterate housekeeper"; she becomes attached to the charming children. And she wanders about the estate, conjuring up pleasant fantasies of a sudden appearance of the master (386). She doesn't see the master; she sees apparitions. Wilson first summarizes Quint's apparition. Though Wilson suggests that "the valet had been a bad character" whose influence on Miles has not been wholesome, the burden of proof is on the governess to justify his presence: "the governess believes that he has come back to haunt the children" (386). In the same fashion, Miss Jessel's ghost is impugned: "she concludes that it is the former governess." Once again, Wilson acknowledges the text. He accepts Mrs. Grose's hint of the affair between the servants and of Miles's companionship with Quint and then observes, "The governess concludes that the boy must have known about the valet and the woman—the children have been corrupted by them" (387). But we are to observe, says Wilson, that only the governess ever sees the ghosts; that sexual significance lies in the governess's interest in Flora's pieces of wood; and the tower and the lake as the first locations where Quint and Jessel appear are unmistakeably sexual (387). Wilson concludes that there is only one circumstance that opposes the notion that these emanations are the governess's hallucinations: the description of the male apparition by which Mrs. Grose recognizes Quint. This problem he waves aside by suggesting that the governess has inferred Quint from Mrs. Grose's slip in recounting the history of the place about the creature "who liked everyone young and pretty" (388).

In the remainder of his summary, Wilson simply chooses among possible solutions to the problem. He tells us that the governess "continues to see the spirits" and as she does, "the atmosphere becomes more and more hysterical." He chooses, that is, against the governess. The children get up at night; they "give plausible explanations for their behavior." The governess becomes a virtual thumbscrew herself, driving Flora to seek asylum elsewhere, and pressing Miles to an exorcism in which "she has literally frightened him to death" (389). There seems to be no room left for doubt in Wilson's perfect acceptance of "the theory": "When one has once been given this clue to *The Turn of the Screw*, one wonders how one could ever have missed it" (389). But Wilson allows that James, good artist as he is, does not "unequivocally" give the game away: "everything from beginning to end can be taken equally well in either of two senses" (389). At least, in Wilson's reading, the power of the ambiguity is present; that is, after all, the subject of his essay. But Wilson will also cite the preface, those lines about the governess's authority as against her attempts at explanation of her record, citing James's disclaimer about her explanation as the proposition that confirms his own hypothesis out of James's prose.

Wilson sees that the placement of *The Turn of the Screw* is in volume 12 along with *The Aspern Papers* and "The Liar," in both of which fictions there is a narrator who is to be doubted rather than trusted.[15] But he parts company with the preface when it comes to James's declaration that he had not characterized the governess because in the course of her narrative we get about as much of her as we can stand. Wilson now says that James has spent his energies characterizing the governess; that if we disregard the ghost tale convention we can see her in her proper character: a parson's daughter with a Victorian outlook, deeply susceptible to the social disfavor with sexuality and, in the middle class way, attracted to social power (390). *Screw* is not a great ghost story, but a profound psychological sourcebook, which, like *Moby-Dick* and *Alice* "has ... a profound grasp of subconscious processes." In fact it is a characteristic Jamesian tale about "the frustrated Anglo-Saxon spinster" (391). The particular Anglo-Saxon spinster to whom the governess is to be compared is Olive Chancellor. But one can really pick and choose, since they abound in James and include Francie Dosson, Adela Chart, who destroys her father's second marriage, and Milly Theale. In some important respects we might indeed compare the governess with some of these characters. But we would be unlikely to refer to any of them as spinsters, if the definition of the term is a woman unmarried and beyond the usual age for first marriage.

Wilson cannot make up his mind whether *The Sacred Fount* plays a game identical to that of *Screw* or whether the two books merely remind him of one another—whether there is an identity of hallucinations between the two narrators or whether the two narrators are merely alike in being both annoying and persistent in their beliefs in their own fundamental soundness. He goes on at some length about the prospects for conflating the treatment of the two tales, but gives it up and returns to the problem of the ambiguity of *Screw*, raising the question of what James meant us to find in it and going on to discuss James's letters on the subject of the evasions and side glances; he concludes that James might be merely amusing himself at the expense of his readers (396). But Wilson returns to his larger theme, the ambiguity of James's work in general, and suggests that the vagaries of the governess's talks with Mrs. Grose are child's play compared to those of the late novels. In fact Wilson begins to sound like many of the disaffected journalists of the first and second decades of the twentieth century in his air of complaint about the late style—"his long sentences with their circumlocutions" (397). He wants in a desultory way to inquire into this ambiguity that had "come to blur the whole effect of his work." He proposes to pursue this question, but proceeds without clear lines of development to assist him.

He starts with James's work and then moves outward for comparisons, to the obvious sources—Balzac and Flaubert. According to Wilson, James had a quarrel with Flaubert over Emma and more strongly over Frederic, to the effect that these characters were not worthy the attention of the great artist. But Wilson objects that James has himself given us a Frederic in Hyacinth Robinson. He satisfies himself that James's issue with Flaubert is merely that Flaubert got there first—"After all, Frederic and Madame Arnoux are the best people of Albany and Boston" (401). But the style, when the central consciousness "has undergone a strange diminution" (403) becomes "for the first time distinctly gamey." And so we have the telegraphist; Nanda; the governess; and the narrator of *The Sacred Fount*. And all this gaminess comes about through the problems of "their concealed and only guessed-at sexual relations" (403). The nadir appears to be James's unconscious creation of the "disembowelled crew who hover around one another with sordid shadowy designs in *The Awkward Age*" (404). An exception is made for what Matthiessen had not yet called "the major phase." While for the earlier reviewers, that had become the heartland of the stylistic obscurity, Wilson finds in it something of interest. He likes the "phantasmagoria of dream-like metaphors and similes" (404) in the late work.

But Wilson in this first version of the essay can neither solve the problems of ambiguity in *The Turn of the Screw*, nor finally account for the fashion in which James completes his career in the period after the theatrical debacle (1895 and after). Wilson allows that James gets the job done in a shy, cautious, circumlocutory way, but for Wilson the "blur" remains a fixed characteristic of the late work. James was both controlled and forthright as a novelist. Thus the ambiguity in his work suggests unresolved problems and perhaps an underlying malaise (406). But Wilson did not let it go at that. He republished the essay in the first issue of *The Triple Thinkers* (1938) and then again in the second issue (1948) with the addendum to Willen in 1959. I shall not undertake a line-by-line analysis of the differences between the earlier and later forms of the essay, but some points need to be made.

By 1948, when the counterblasts to Wilson's "Freudian Reading" of the tale had begun to appear, Wilson was backing down from the unimpeachable reading of the governess's hallucinatory sexual repression. "The truth is," he tells us, "that Henry James was not clear about the book in his own mind." So intense is the ambiguity that it becomes necessary to believe that James does not want the reader to find the deep meaning (w 125). It does not matter that, only a few pages earlier, he has repeated the conclusion of the *Hound & Horn* version that the reader's discovery of mental disorder in the governess automatically "solves" the mystery (w 120). The section of the essay dealing with James's style is much more thoroughly elaborated in the book version, with a careful study of James's interest in the 1880s with social questions; and Wilson is more careful with the figure of consciousness in this version of the essay. But in 1948, he is compelled to return to *The Turn of the Screw* at the end of the essay—to try to wrestle out the problems that intermediate criticisms have posed.

He begins by saying that in the body of the essay, he has left the treatment of the tale largely as in the original (145). The point of recantation is based upon Wilson's having been forced by Fagin (1941) and Heilman (1947) to reconsider Mrs. Grose's identification of Quint from the governess's description of the apparition. And he allows that the notebook sketch of the origins of the tale supports the notion that James had intended to write a ghost story (145). The notebooks also give Wilson a number of analogies on which to base the notion of what James did in the process of converting an anecdote into a tale. Using a number of stories from the middle to late nineties—notably "The

Friends of the Friends" and "Maud Evelyn"—Wilson deduces that the self-deception of the narrator is a characteristic Jamesian theme in this era. Thus "one is led to conclude that, in *The Turn of the Screw*, not merely the governess is self-deceived, but that James is self-deceived about her" (147). He uses the notebooks to secure the idea that James is not a ruminative author and that what essentially happens in a Jamesian fiction is that the characters act out various portions of James's fantasy life. Thus Wilson's reader follows him into bafflement; and he leaves us in the dark because of what he does not know. It is in this context that Wilson impugns James's morals. He takes Austrian novelist Franz Höllering's view that the author of *The Turn of the Screw* was a child violator and uses it to summarize James's work of the late 1890s as a prototypical assault on childhood (149). Wilson has turned away from a study of the tale to analyze its author.

When Myfanwy Piper created the libretto for Benjamin Britten's opera based on *The Turn of the Screw* (1954), she needed a key line for the sense of ominous event in the ghost mystery. She borrowed from Yeats's "Second Coming" the line "The ceremony of innocence is drowned," a line that repeats in the opera with the recurrent apparition of Peter Quint. There can be no doubt, as Wilson says, that the violation of innocence is the pressing Jamesian theme in the fiction of the era— but it seems that Piper and Britten understand more clearly than Wilson seems to do that for James the destruction of innocence is the outrage of the times. Rose Armiger kills little Effie in the name of love; the succession of parents abandon Maisie for the pleasures of adult sophistication; Nanda is sullied by excessive handling. And yes, for James, "the ceremony of innocence is drowned." But what about the governess? If her creator is a child violator, is she also—is she a participant in the drowning? John Macy had speculated (1913) that James's ruffled reader would always recoil from the narrator's hedging about what he or she knows, and declare loftily, "'My dear sir, you created her'" (332). Wilson might be seconding the motion with the additional accusation that the creation of the governess falls little short of a criminal act. Wilson shows some of the heady thrill, in the 1920s and 1930s, of being there at the head of the class of literary Freudians: he rejoiced in the experience of liberation that the new method brought him. We cannot be surprised then that for Wilson the reader's excitement from James's stories arises from the violation of innocence. Nor can we be surprised that for Wilson, Longdon's interest in Nanda "is given a flavor of unavowed sex" (149). As a corollary "there was always in Henry James an innocent little girl whom he cherished and loved and protected and yet whom he later tried to violate, whom he even tried to kill" (150). But Wilson ignores James's own angry denunciation of the widescale social abandonment of the child when he attributes to James rather than to the society that James criticized the callous disregard for the child.

So Wilson veers between alternatives at the end of his series of ventures on *The Turn of The Screw*. He wishes not to give up his explosive toy, that lovely, shocking Freudian missile under whose aegis the literary world had shuddered at its annunciation; but he cannot have it on the easy terms of fifteen years before. His response is to assault James or to praise him with left-handed compliments. Edna Kenton had written a thoughtful essay that concerned itself with the text of James's story, that looked at the fashion in which James treated the text in his preface, and that, in preparation, had consulted the criticism of the tale to the moment at which she wrote. Wilson, in turn, had looked at none of these things except at Kenton's piece from which, on the evidence of his own text, he benefited little. But the year turns: it is 1959; Gerald Willen is putting out a collection of critical essays on *The Turn of the Screw*, in which Wilson is a featured contributor; essays on the other side of the controversy have surfaced; it is time to rejoin again: "Since writing the above [the surrender of 1948], I have become convinced that James knew exactly what he was doing and that he intended the governess to be suffering from delusions" (153). It is a comfort to the anxious critic to know that when Wilson is in doubt, it is because James is in doubt; but when Wilson recovers his certainty, James does so as well. Part of this comfort comes from finding James at last so flexible, following one like the moon when one is in a moving vehicle. Wilson recovers his certainty through the aid of intervening statements by other critics who have cleared his path. Marius Bewley is one of these: Bewley discovered that the narrator of "The Liar" is the real liar at the center of the title configuration, and that that makes the case for *The Turn of the Screw* as a tale revealing the unreliability of the narrator unanimous, since the narrator of *The Aspern Papers* is already clearly denounced as creating his narrative to serve his ego rather than to recount the truth. The narrators of the two later tales in the New York Edition, volume 12, are "warped." John Silver (1957) assists Wilson to return to his first stance, and once again, when the proof is offered, "one cannot think how one had missed it": "The governess, Mr. Silver suggests, had learned about Quint's appearance from the people in the village with whom we know she had talked and who had presumably also told her of the manner of Quint's death" (153).

Willen's version of Wilson's "Ambiguity" in *The Casebook* runs to approximately twice the length of the original *Hound & Horn* essay.

Included in it are particles of four stages of the genesis of the piece, and, as I have suggested above, some of that process involves revolution in the latitude Wilson allows himself in applying the Freudian model to the tale. Wilson is candid in his 1948 redraft when he concedes that the question of the identification of Quint appears to have defeated him. But the model of himself that emerges from the process of readjustment required by the revision to his hypothesis is distinctly unprepossessing. In the end he very weakly attributes the problem that he cannot solve himself to some compositional flaw in James. As other critics will point out later, both some who dispute the applicability of the hypothesis of psychosis to the governess and some who express disapproval of Wilson because he is not Freudian enough, Wilson is not particularly attentive to the actual text that he is reading. He is himself dazzled by the hypothesis that he imposes on the text to solve its riddles. And those later critics who declare him insufficiently Freudian will also declare that he is insufficiently aware of the implications of Freudian theory to have produced good psychoanalytic criticism. But it remains a curiosity that the Demuth panels form at least some part of Wilson's consciousness of James's tale through their place in Edna Kenton's essay. They are an elusive influence in this context, as elusive as a sled with Rosebud as its trade name.

GODDARD AND TARDY PRIMACY

While Kenton, Wilson, and Demuth belong together for the purposes of the critical tradition of *The Turn of the Screw*, Harold Goddard is another text suppressed or at least displaced by historical accident.[16] Thematically he belongs with the group here who controversialize the tale; but chronologically, his essay does not reach print until long after the immediate furor over Wilson's "Freudian" reading had subsided. According to Goddard himself, he was reading his paper to students around 1920. According to Leon Edel, who introduces the posthumous paper as it was printed for the first time in *Nineteenth Century Fiction* (1957), he was the only reader of the tale until the late 1950s to be intensively concerned with the psychology of the governess in the tale. Edel supports Goddard's case for the governess's deviant psychology on the basis of Goddard's own experience with a governess in his youth.

Goddard's sense was that there was a single reading for the tale, that is—the governess is insane—and he declares that he was astonished when he found that not one of his students read the tale as a record of insanity. Goddard summarizes the events and begins to question the "authority" of the narrator. She is passionately attached to the master of Bly. She is moved to a state just short of ecstasy by the beauty of the children. She develops insomnia and then "more serious symptoms" (w 249). Among these latter is her ominous reading of Miles's dismissal from school, which with the other phenomena she reports sends her off into an "orgy of myth-making" (250). Mrs. Grose slips and lets fly a shady character who might suggest Peter Quint; the governess is swift in pursuit of such a figure for the sake of her orgy: "it supplies the one character missing in the heroic drama that the governess' repressed desire is bent on staging." Thus Quint comes out of the governess's own repressed love for the master of Bly. Goddard requires no other authority than the text itself to justify his reading—no Freud, no Demuth, no Edna Kenton. Since others have argued the question of Goddard's reading pro and con, I will restate that process later. Suffice it to say that for Goddard, the governess is insane (258); the children are victims of her very affections; James is weaving a spell to keep us from seeing that the governess is trapping us into her redefinition of the world. What ultimately stands out about Goddard's interpretation is the satisfaction he expresses in finding that he could, with his persuasive powers, make the "majority of my fellow readers ready to prefer [my reading] to their own" (246). Goddard shows the familiar penchant among critics of the time for capturing the tale, for making it in some inscrutable way his own.

The current theory of aesthetic reception of students like Stanley Fish, Hans Robert Jauß or Karlheinz Stierle might do us a valuable service by showing the mechanism that prompts both critics and general readers of a problem text like *The Turn of the Screw* to wish to possess the artifact, to establish some form of interpretive hegemony over it. This urge is sufficiently strong to make it a fit subject of inquiry for a critical survey of the tale. While we might accept that some of the obvious promptings for such mastery are implicit in the mere aggressive nature of human beings as consumers of the artifact, the idea at least teases us with the sense that there is something more to it. Goddard's terms for his pleasure in his triumph might illustrate at least something of the environment of the phenomenon. He tells his reader or hearer that he saw only a single way of interpreting the tale and then to his surprise, he found his scheme uniformly contradicted, both by his students and by some eminent minds: "my faith in what seemed to me an obvious way of taking the story would have been shaken, had I not, on explaining it, found the majority of my fellow readers ready to prefer it to their own" (246).

We may not wish to take quite literally the notion that the speaker's "faith" is at stake here, or that faith is "shaken" by the prospect of a challenge to an interpretive idea. We can see the writer committing his sensibility to the issue and feeling some achievement at the victory of his idea. But something further still is at stake: the notion that Goddard not only convinces people about the validity of his idea, but causes them to "prefer it to their own" suggests that something more than a mere coup in the critical game has taken place. Perhaps something like "faith" *is* at hazard here, and something like the demonstration of the mysterious unknown has resulted from the process of argumentation that Goddard has mounted. For he claims to have altered the perception of an artifact for a substantial quantity of readers; and even more, he has undertaken to convert large numbers of skeptics and has done so with what he reports as a very substantial success, notwithstanding an occasional unmoved skeptic, or "now and then a strenuous objector" (247). Of course the audience that he describes as being overwhelmed with the logic of his views is a sequence of classes of his own students over a number of years; and, in not publishing his essay in his lifetime, he did not subject it to the risks of academic and critical quarreling that surrounded, for example, Wilson's deliberately provocative essay on some of the same lines. It is worth noting that upon its posthumous publication the essay both enjoyed support from the proponents of the "hallucinationist" theory of the novella and suffered antagonism from its opponents. But for his own satisfaction, and in relation to the audience that he selected for it, Goddard could report the narrative of, as it were, surprising conversions that arose from some aspect of his argument or its presentation. To the extent, then, that converted readers join Goddard on his ground, they certify his proprietorship of the interpretive ground of the tale. He is only the first (as a writer in 1920) in a long line of interpreters who will be moved by the same impulse.

But while the first salients in what will become the continuing battle over *The Turn of the Screw* have been deployed in the period between 1924 and 1934, conventional criticism continues to appear, also a recurrent feature of the critical tradition of the tale. Controversy over the meaning of James's career continues as part of this continued criticism. Dorothy Bethurum, for example (1923), takes issue with Stuart Pratt Sherman's reduction of James's career to a mere aesthetic imperative with no explicit morality and a paring away of "the thick rotundity of life." For Bethurum "the entire body of his work is informed by the very spirit of judgment" (325). The virtue of James's work as she sees it is that it takes the hapless puritan and abrades away some of the harshness of his outlook without costing him "his homely virtue." Isabel is a better woman at the end of the book than at the beginning because "with James as with the Greeks, wisdom and virtue are synonymous" (328). In fact, for her, the moral and aesthetic senses are intrinsic to each other (330).

Grant Knight's *Superlatives* (1925) wanted to interest students "in outstanding characters of fiction" (vi). James's children are among these extraordinary successes, and Miles and Flora are among the most moving of James's children. Kenton's article to the contrary, there is no ambiguity in the tale for Knight: he believes the governess and looks to Miles and Flora for an explanation to the mystery. Their charm, he tells us, lies in "their appalling mixture of normality with a suspected abnormality or supernormality, their terrifying turns from sweetness and light to rebellion and harshness that sear them upon our consciousness" (150–51). These sweet children consort with demons that remind us of Coleridge's Geraldine. They emerge as "the most memorable children in fiction" (152).

Pelham Edgar (1927) is largely unimpressed with James's fictional children, remembering, as he says, a mere four of them: Randolph Miller, Morgan Moreen, and Miles and Flora, "the perverted and haunted children of *The Turn of the Screw*" (125). This tale, he concedes, "will stand in permanence with the malign influence exercised on two exquisite and brilliant children, Miles and Flora, by two dead servants, the valet, Peter Quint, and the governess, Miss Jessel." He sees the governess as narrator and appears to accept her as a reliable reporter of the events. But she operates under "somewhat strange conditions" in agreeing never to communicate with the master of Bly. She stays at her post heroically, for only she can save the children. For Edgar, the children are deep in the toils of evil, Flora beyond the reach of the governess, but Miles still sufficiently uncontaminated to have a chance to survive morally. Edgar gives some amplification to what is being called the conventional reading of *The Turn of the Screw*. He is neither aware of critical controversy nor sensible of ambiguity in the text.

Aside from Wilson's essay in the *Hound & Horn* James issue, treatment of *The Turn of the Screw* is scanty. R. P. Blackmur in his essay on James's prefaces, which became the introduction to *The Art of the Novel* (1934b), declares of those prefaces that they ought, "collected together, . . . to form a sort of comprehensive manual or *vademecum* for aspirants in our arduous profession" (445). Nonetheless, Blackmur recognized acutely something of the problem of criticism raised above in respect to ownership of the ghost tale, for he had James's own word from the prefaces that "'To criticize ... is to appreciate, to appropriate, to take intellectual possession, to establish in fine a relation with the criticized thing and make it one's own'" (1934b, 445–46, from the preface to *Maisie.*). He saw that the evil in *The Turn of the Screw* "had to be represented, like the ghosts who performed it, in the consciousness of normal persons, but it could not be described." Newton Arvin, in the same issue of *Hound & Horn,* tries to assess the nature of the novella in terms of current literary realities and suggests that *The Turn of the Screw* is closer to Faulkner's *Sanctuary* than to Hawthorne's "Rappaccini's Daughter" (1934b, 438). This phenomenon arises, Arvin suggests, out of James's acts in chronicling "a festering society" in his later years. Glenway Wescott, in his "Sentimental Contribution" (1934b, 523–34), comments that James had an "exceptional success or effectiveness, especially on a small scale characteristic of the Suetonian rather than the Plutarchian sense." Wescott also acutely sees into the nature of the problems of form and technique of the novella: "*The Turn of the Screw* provides more explanations than it requires" (530). Like many another of these early and offhanded comments on the tale, it foresees something of the battleground to come without as yet recognizing the potentially controversial nature of what is being said. In essence what Wescott must sense here is that the excess of explanation must be explained either by suggesting that James lost some degree of control of his technique here, or that there was some compositional reason for the excess. He does not enter into an inquiry of the governess's narrative for evidences of its reliability.

By the time a third of a century has elapsed, then, the little ghost story is still achieving some degree of note and comment, and has begun to generate controversy. But while earlier criticism had merely foreseen some of the battle lines on which later critical axes were to be swung, the Kenton thesis had actually begun the process of claiming to have discovered the nature of James's trap for the unwary. Demuth, whether with an ax to grind or merely out of the sort of interest that he seemed to take in literary texts at large, especially when those texts battled social restraints over explicit sexuality, gave us a governess who was neither pretty nor twenty, and without necessarily intending to, submerged that quantity into the context of the criticism. Wilson struck to the core of the matter and declared that James had anticipated Freud in showing us something of the seamy side of suppressed sexuality. Goddard staked out the critical territory of the tale as somehow his own. And in the meantime, general readers went on happily "generally reading" *The Turn of the Screw.* But it was not only the novella that was becoming controversial: James himself—that ambulatory ambivalence for Americans—was likewise becoming controversial. Was his art an aesthetic without a moral fiber? It was possible to claim so in this era of criticism. Van Wyck Brooks was among those who would do so in his *Pilgrimage of Henry James* (1925), making him a traveler who lacked the passion of his puritan forebears, according to Brooks, and whose work by and large lacked the reality of life itself.

4

Freud-counter-Freud:
Screw Criticism, 1934–1959

By the time Gerald Willen's *Casebook on "The Turn of the Screw"* appears in 1960, it is possible for him to assume that the principal concerns in that criticism are in fact incorporated into the quarrel over the center of focus: the abnormal psychology of the governess versus the corruption of the children. The criticism that emerges from the era is characteristic of this heyday of the New Criticism: it produces close readings of the text; it argues toward ineluctable conclusions, as though critical insight were susceptible of perfect logical verification and mathematical proof; it tends toward critical brilliance. The New Criticism having reached its era of hegemony, the *Screw* criticism of the era is typically New Critical. Inevitably, it is also highly imaginative in the New Critical vein and enters into a virtual competition with the original text for imaginative control. The Freudian context of literary study might be seen to belong to a medium of inquiry external to *The Turn of the Screw*; on the other hand, James's ghost tale makes a useful ground for exploring the virtues of the psychoanalytic model in explicating the literary text. In a sense, however, the psychoanalytic model seems merely to substitute for the repudiated Victorian standard of morality: ostensibly Freudian psychoanalysis is a science and offers insight into the workings of the human mind; covertly it creates a framework in which judgment—frequently with very intense moral implications—can operate under the guise of a science.[1] Certainly this strange combination of science and morality colors the method of early literary Freudianism. It runs as a strong undercurrent of the psychoanalytic view of *The Turn of the Screw*.

SKIRMISHES

The first serious attack against Wilson's presentation of the governess as neurotic victimizer of the children comes from the pen of Nathan Bryllion Fagin ([941]; rpt. w 154–59). Fagin, like Kenton, argues from the preface; but he argues to the effect that the trap of the tale has captured the Freudians. Fagin argues historically that since James could not have known Freud, he could not have intended to write a Freudian tale. This denial in 1941 might make Fagin seem rather an innocent in joining these games of conquest: for it was general knowledge that the literary text came first and the Freudian implications afterward—as with Oedipus. Furthermore Fagin does not know that the Freudians will later return on him with a Freudian sorites about the nature of intention, always ending in the conclusion that one never resists against a line of thinking unless one has a guilty secret to hide.

According to Fagin, if Freud is irrelevant to the criticism of a James tale because James could not have known his work, then Hawthorne is obviously relevant because, as Rebecca West and Cornelia Pulsifer Kelley had observed, Hawthorne was the power behind James's persistently puritan view of the nature of life: "in simple terms, *The Turn of the Screw* is an allegory which dramatizes the conflict between good and evil" (w 157). The appurtenances to this allegorical theory are that the governess is merely a point of view, a figure without a name, and that the apparitions are merely personifications of the principle of evil. The children gravitate toward them for the love of evil as the governess declares. Flora is beyond help; Miles is still amenable. When Miles dies, almost cured of the penchant for evil, he dies as does Beatrice Rappaccini, "exhausted by the ordeal" (158). Miles is also like Georgiana in "The Birthmark"; but Fagin does not find Georgiana sympathetic: she is like Beatrice Rappaccini, Fagin's Hawthornian counterpart to Miles. She is "too corrupted to live without evil"; the blemish is in her heart. Since the Hawthornian tales are the "highest point that Hawthorne reached" in the territory of allegory, we are to conclude that *The Turn of the Screw* is James's echo of Hawthorne in the same vein. This, says Fagin, is distinctly different from the Freudian text that we find in Wilson. It may well seem to the reader that this is limited to argument by assumption and by declaration. But Fagin's response already suggests that Wilson has sown the wind, and that the contra-Freudian whirlwind is gathering.

Fagin seems mildly amused at Wilson's position and sees his own as both entirely sane and unassailable. Wilson, after all, according to Fagin, does not pay very much close attention to the text. He makes a to-do about Flora's sticks of wood, but then finds Miss Jessel an inconvenience, Fagin suspects, because Jessel's sexual personality risks displacement of the sexual issue from the governess-narrator to the disgraced predecessor. For this reason, Wilson drops the Jessel-Flora connection and deals exclusively with the Miles-Quint connection. Because Wilson does not pay very careful attention to the structural details of the text, Fagin finds it relatively easy to discover and expose the holes in the logical design of Wilson's argument. Fagin treats the matter lightly and ends by virtually dismissing Wilson and the Freudian argument out of hand. But the heat of battle is nonetheless rising as critics on opposing sides entrench their positions and even stake their reputations in the war that follows.

The reality question surrounding the ghosts and the governess in *The Turn of the Screw* remained unresolved insofar as the Van Doren symposium of 1942 was concerned. Mark Van Doren tended to take the ghosts at face value; Allan Tate tended to see them as having an unincorporated reality; Katherine Anne Porter tended to see them as a projection of the governess's imagination (w 160–61). Porter anticipates during the symposium what will later become the critical commonplace that the principle of causality in the tale, instead of being restricted to either a Wilsonian projection or a Faginian allegory, squints between them: "When I first read this story, I accepted the governess's visions as real, that is, that the ghosts were real in themselves, and not only the governess, perhaps, but others might have seen them; they had a life of their own. But as I went on reading the story and studying it through the years, and I read James's notes on it, I decided that the ghosts were a projection of the governess's imagination and were part of her plot" (160–61). Like Kenton, Porter is flirting with recognition of James's trap. But she goes from one "right" reading of the tale to another, from one absolute truth to an alternative truth that must contradict it. Her comments make it difficult to resist the conclusion that she has in the meantime read Wilson's "Ambiguity."

During the Van Doren symposium the force of Wilson's argument, whether in its own right as an influence or merely as the new form of currency in the critical exchanges on the novella, asserts itself even against the better judgment of Tate and Van Doren. The latter, at one point in some dismay, declares, "We have almost imputed to [the governess] a plot to corrupt the children herself. Now I'm willing to believe that it is she who corrupts the children and brings about the death of the little boy. Nevertheless, this is precisely my way of understanding how potent the evil in this story is" (w 165). Tate responds that in his view the spirits use the governess as a medium; that she performs their will for them, is an unconscious agent of the evil pervading the tale. But both are following Porter, who has declared that "the governess constantly attempts to draw the children into her orbit of evil and force them to share it and prove them guilty." Tate moves to dissipate the Freud-counter-Freud quarrel by saying simply that James knew all that Freud knew before Freud ever wrote (167). But Van Doren advances the thesis that James's governess is a prophet without honor: "Living in our time, which usually does not take stock in either good or evil, [James] was able to construct in the governess a creature almost like Cassandra, through whom evil tears its way without any instigation on her part at all—without, so to speak, her permission" (166). Once or twice again in the long unfolding of the critical tradition of *The Turn of the Screw*, the link between the governess and Cassandra will surface, but perhaps never as strongly as the context seems to demand.[2]

Among those who generate some heat over the Wilson thesis is Robert Liddell, whose *Treatise on the Novel* (1947) offers an appendix refuting the Freudian view. Liddell's challenge reflects his belief that the hallucination theory is a multiple fabrication and that it achieves its force by disregarding the internal evidence of the tale. He is sufficiently incensed to feel that he must deny Wilson categorically, calling him disingenuous, for example, in his explication of the morbidity of the governess over the expulsion of Miles from school (138). He takes Wilson to task over the governess's description of the apparition from which Mrs. Grose easily deduces Quint. He declares that the governess herself anticipates Edna Kenton (and of course, by way of logical extension, Wilson) in considering the "hallucination" theory, but he says that it is the governess herself who first explores and then explodes it: "'She was there, so I was justified,'" he quotes the governess as proclaiming; "'she was there, so I was neither cruel nor mad'" (140). Liddell sees the governess as suspecting herself of the mad projection of the ghosts from her own imagination; he exonerates her from any malignity, using as evidence the confession that she has been troubled about the nature of the apparitions. Liddell makes much of the final colloquy between the governess and Miles. As he suggests, the "natural reading" tells us that he dies worn out "by the struggle between good and evil" (141).

If we reject the "natural reading" in favor of the hallucination theory, says Liddell, we can do so only if we

1. disbelieve Douglas's estimate of the governess's character
2. give a very strained explanation of her description of Quint

3. believe she is deluded about the very sense-data experienced in Miles's room, not only about her interpretation of them

4. believe, on no evidence, that Miles had got into touch with Flora after the scene by the lake (141–42).

But even more profoundly, Liddell suggests, general impression tells us that what the tale is about is the problem of evil and that Wilson's notions are like Verrall's "brilliant perversities about Greek tragedy" (142). He answers Wilson's contention that the preface supports the hallucination theory by arguing that the preface removes from the governess all semblance of personality—except for her soupçon of courage. Wilson claims that the analogies for the governess in James's work are the character from "The Marriages" and Olive Chancellor from *The Bostonians*; Liddell claims that the appropriate analogy is Morgan Moreen or Maisie Farange (143). She is the observer, not the perpetrator.

Liddell makes his own commitments, and he bases them on a careful attention to details of the text. In his own mind what he has said is definitive and determines that there can be no legitimate grounds on which to credit Wilson's reading of the tale. Liddell rather brushes aside Wilson's thesis, declaring that after close examination of the novel, nothing remains of the hallucination theory except the sexual grounds on which the theory is based, an interesting but far from definitive source. In fact Liddell finds the sexual imagery a feature of the surface of the text with the corollary that one should avoid calling the tale "a sexual fantasy," using such imagery as justification (144). His further corollary is that James was unaware of the sexual significance of the tale's imagery. James was taking a very dirty tale and making it into great art, the very art that has drawn, by Liddell's time, such a quantity of appreciative readers. Liddell crows in triumph in an addendum to the second impression of his treatise two years later, asserting that the notebooks (1947; the same date as the first release of Liddell's *Treatise*), with their account of the ghosts as creatures trying to lure the children into the pit and with James's declaration of the governess's role as spectator, observer, simply lay to rest any further claims of Wilson's theory. But Liddell is seldom mentioned in the later comments on *The Turn of the Screw* and thus does not figure very strongly in the critical tradition of the tale.

MORALITY, EDEN, SALVATION

The first salvos in the Freud-counter-Freud feud seem to have been little sputters of musketry, designed to indicate hostility, but too weak and sporadic yet to draw much blood. It is true, as Robert Heilman will point out in his more vigorous attack of 1947—"The Freudian Reading of *The Turn of the Screw*"—something has caused Wilson to begin retracting some of the positiveness of his essay by the time he is writing on horror story anthologies for the *New Yorker* in 1944. The governess is still not defending the children and is still frightening them with projections from her own mind. But Wilson is troubled by "points in the story which are difficult to explain on this theory" (69); the trouble is already with James and not with the interpretative model: "It is probable that James, like Kipling, was unconscious of having raised something more frightening than the ghosts he had contemplated" (69). With Heilman and others, however, the contra-Freudian persuasion will begin to drop some powerful explosives on the contour of the critical tradition of the tale. They will do so with the sort of positiveness that characterizes Kenton and Wilson in their initial assault.

Among these will be A. J. A Waldock with his "Mr. Edmund Wilson and *The Turn of the Screw*" (1947). For Waldock begins with a simple and categorical negation of Wilson's thesis: "no one," he says, "as far as I know, has troubled to point out that the theory is quite untenable, that—apart from general considerations—there are details within the story itself that decisively negative it" (332). The force of his extinguishing detail derives from Mrs. Grose's identification of Quint from the governess's description. For Waldock, the fact that the governess fails to recognize Quint in the first apparition on the tower and yet refrains from reporting the incident stems from her imperfect information and thus her inability to place any of the details in a context appropriate to recounting the incident. But by the same token, the second sighting gives close and detailed information, and furthermore, takes place near the house. Now it becomes urgent for the governess to take responsibility.

She makes her report, and on the basis of the report Mrs. Grose identifies the dead valet. Again no doubts trouble Waldock; he is positive beyond cavil: first, "the identification is absolute"; second, "up to this moment the governess has never heard of Peter Quint" (332). Waldock notes Wilson's admission of the doubleness of the tale—that

almost everything can be read in more than one sense. But Waldock
says that the positive identification of Quint is unambiguous and is
unanswerable in Wilson's terms. He scorns Wilson's attempt to "steer
around" the difficulty by intimating that the governess has seized Quint
from Mrs. Grose's vagrant pronoun—"*he* did like them young and
pretty." Waldock, according to his own record, sticks to the facts: (1)
the apparition wears his master's clothes; (2) the apparition is described
in detail. On the basis of fact, Wilson is preposterous: "Has Mr. Wilson
...ever really tried to make quite clear to himself what he means by that
concluding sentence about the possible likeness between master and
ghost?" (333). He takes Wilson and the reader back through it: "How
did the governess succeed in projecting on vacancy, out of her
subconscious mind, a perfectly precise, point-by-point image of a man,
then dead, whom she had never seen in her life?" (333–34). He rests his
case on its perfect unanswerability. Not all later critics, though, would
agree that Waldock's argument was unanswerable.

The first big gun directed at Wilson was Robert Heilman's
"Freudian Reading of *The Turn of the Screw*" (1947). Heilman will
follow up with an idealized reading of the tale in the much reprinted
"*The Turn of the Screw* as Poem" (1948). Heilman's intention in the
earlier piece was to demolish Wilson's reading on the basis of the
internal logic of the tale. He, too, like Waldock, reads the tale carefully.
His reading, however, demonstrates again how elusive the tale is and
how clever James's trap. Perhaps the imperfections of close reading as
absolute proof are already in evidence when Heilman starts with an
error in attributing the genesis of the Freudian reading to Kenton. His
response to the Kenton-Wilson thesis of the governess's hallucinations—their contention that it is in the submerged hallucinations that we
find James's trap—is to declare that James prides himself on having
secured the willing suspension of disbelief on the part of "the jaded, the
fastidious, the disillusioned" (1947, 433), those who might be expected
to have grown beyond susceptibility to the ghost tale. His first highly
incensed reaction to Wilson occurs in his quarrel over Wilson's
understanding of James's comment in the preface that he has given the
governess "authority." Wilson has taken this to mean that James has
made the governess a tyrant over the children; Heilman takes it that
James is merely giving her *narrative* authority, the gift to be credible in
delivering her narrative. Wilson believes, according to Heilman, that in
distinguishing her record of events from her explanations that "James is
giving it away that the governess has hallucinations" (434-5). But for
Heilman, James is only distinguishing the process of the technique of
the novelist in establishing perspective.

Wilson says that the tale exists to characterize the governess; but Heilman points to the preface and declares that James intends precisely the opposite, that is, the ghosts and the children are the subject of the story and the governess, not always equal to the occasion—but not for that reason any more the subject of the tale—is its vehicle. Heilman approves of Graham Greene's comment (1936, 245) that James believed in the supernatural and was a Manichaean—"saw evil as an equal force with good" and thus denies that there is any sly wink in favor of the rationalists in James's concern for the technical exercise. He attacks Wilson vigorously on Wilson's justification of the emphasis on sexuality in his reading of the tale on the grounds of the "fallacy of insufficient cause" (436). Heilman maintains his stand that James is concerned with technical problems in the preface when he speaks of the governess's yearning for the master of Bly. Her failure to seek help after she sights the apparitions must be accounted for on the assumption that except for her promise not to disturb the uncle, such oversight is unthinkable. Heilman is willing to concede that James imperfectly motivates the governess in this failure, thus perhaps failing to solve the technical question perfectly: "But a technical procedure should not be mistaken for a psychopathological clue" (437). Heilman takes the governess's utterances of self-praise as ironical considering that she formulates her narrative after the events and therefore knows that Miles is dead—has died in her arms—before she begins the narrative of the events that lead to that death.

Heilman reconsiders Waldock's argument that Mrs. Grose's identification of Quint is definitive in obliterating Wilson's argument about the unreliability of the governess's narrative. He is scathing in denouncing Wilson's hypothesis that the governess confuses master and man, she whose narrative shows such a sharp eye for distinctions (437–38). Mrs. Grose is indeed gross, says Heilman, but in the sense of her plainness and dullness of vision and not, as we might say after looking at the Demuth illustrations, in Wilson's sense of the grossly sensual and appetitive. She is a mere foil for the "sensitive, acute governess—Cassandra-like in the insight which outspeeds the perceptions of those about her" (438). But the very grossness of her vision is what secures the credibility of the governess: it is Mrs. Grose who reports and interprets Flora's coarse language when the clash with the governess occurs. Over the letter of dismissal, Mrs. Grose has a knowing recoil about the imperfection of little Miles, and thus reinforces the governess's sense of significance in the occurrence. Heilman goes further and discovers that what is plausible to Wilson—the explanation of the children's behavior in the last phase of the novella—is really an "index to their corruption" (440). These charming little ones cater to the governess while doing, as Heilman says, exactly as they wish (441). In the essence of the tale, the ghosts are symbolic of the evil in the air of James's world.

Heilman returns to Kenton's essay to pick up her very fleeting reference to the "disregarded forward" to the tale.[3] She is referring to the frame tale, and except for a scattering among the early reviews of stylized references to the Christmas practice of telling ghost tales around a fireside, Kenton is the first to make any use of the frame tale at all in the criticism. Even as Heilman was writing it had received little notice by critics. Kenton's citation had assisted her to laugh at her fellow readers' inattention to the tale; Heilman's assists him to laugh at Kenton: "had Miss Kenton herself read the foreword more observantly, she would have found the evidence that makes her interpretation untenable" (442). This untenability arises from the evidence of what the governess has become some ten years later under the eye of an exacting critic: she passes muster as "the most agreeable woman" this observer has ever known in the role of governess. Indeed the evidence shows us that the governess has survived both emotionally and occupationally for the ten years after the incidents at Bly. Heilman takes the testimony of this "graceful middle-aged gentleman" for unadulterated sterling, and further becomes virtually the first critic even to acknowledge the existence of the external narrator of the tale, the figure whom Douglas addresses: "the perceptive first-person narrator" who is "completely *en rapport* with the middle-aged gentleman" (443). Thus is James's picture of the governess incompatible with Wilson's reading, and one conclusion becomes obvious—that at twenty, the governess is "a perfectly normal person" (443). Nonetheless, Heilman asserts that the debate can be defended: because it is important to challenge the doctrinaire and the facile; because the novella is worth saving from the reduction to mere clinical record; and because the tale "'illustrates James's extraordinary command of his own kind of darkness ... the darkness of moral evil,'"[4] Heilman concludes by praising Wilson for the power of his literary insight, but offers a caveat on the critic's prospects when he allows his science to overwhelm his imagination.

Each critic in the war over *The Turn of the Screw* is proposing a solution to the poised mystery of the preface—falling into the trap that James has set for the reader in the tale—and the solutions are based on categorically sound logic and therefore unimpeachable evidence. We can, by following the course of the arguments, decide something about the relative success of the logic or of the argumentative structure in each case. Proof is another matter. Each of these contenders for critical hegemony has added something to our knowledge of the tale by way of observed detail or critical insight. At the same time, each controversion seems definitive, seems momentarily to have made its point unanswerable, regardless of which "side" of the argument it takes. The effect is like the effect of the apparitions on the governess herself, a bewilderment of vision.[5] Much of the critical experience of the tale reflects this bewildering tendency to swing from one position to another in attempting to solve the tale. It is tempting to think that had James been alive to observe these developments, he would have continued to be as delighted by its production of alarms as he had been in the ten years leading up to his writing the preface. Whatever trap he may have designed in the beginning, he seems to have caught readers indiscriminately, regardless of rank. In any case, Heilman, in the secure belief that the trap has not caught him, will pursue the next logical step: having demolished the Freudian reading by a demonstration of its mere untenability, he is prepared to give us the proper definitive reading: "*The Turn of the Screw* as Poem."

In fact, he joins Kenton in an attempt at summary of the critical tradition of the tale. Kenton had indicated an awareness of the critical past, but Heilman will give a theoretical summary—one that in one form or another will echo down the years: "Since the book first appeared, there has been a series of interpretations; as these come forth periodically, and as the alterations in them show the different decades endeavoring to adjust James's materials to new interpretative methods, what is unmistakable is that James has hit upon some fundamental truth of experience that no generation can ignore and that each generation wishes to repeat in its own terms." Critical developments will attempt over time to uncover this "fundamental truth of experience" but without ever achieving critical consensus. Heilman's statement runs parallel with that of Roland Barthes in "What Is Criticism?" already quoted, perhaps with the intention to say that the translations are not restricted to restatements of the same matter in revised terms. Heilman attempts to develop some perspective in dealing with the criticism of *The Turn of the Screw* by raising the question of the extent to which the developing controversy over the tale is simply a matter of conflicting critical vocabularies—the measure of incommensurable things by an instrument which is only apparently uniform. In fact the student of this particular interpretive wrangle eventually wants to know whether the quarrels come down to anything more than the celebrated differences of opinion that are credited with having created horse races and/or semantics.

The terms that Heilman wants to "adjust" for his criticism of the tale embrace the problem of defining evil. Since he has satisfied himself that the Freudian interpretation no longer enjoys wide critical acceptance, he projects that the source of the evil must lie elsewhere than in the psychopathology of the governess's everyday life. Thus the apparitions are real; the governess sees them, and the children know of their existence. The argument takes the form "I am convinced" of these things. As in the article on the Freudian reading, Heilman sees the governess as Cassandra-like, an adept in the intuitive mode. The issue is indefeasibly one of salvation (w 175). Heilman is careful to assume the posture of humility in the form "if this reading...be tenable" (175). The formal statement of this reading involves the "oldest of themes—the struggle of evil to possess the human soul." Heilman does not in the least shirk the Christian implications of this theme. There is a "highly suggestive symbolic language" in the story, a language that constitutes itself intelligible in poetic form (176).

Our focus must be the children. They are preternaturally beautiful, the beauty a type of innocence. James arranges the text so that the force of the shock will intensify through the contrast with the beauty of the children, so that it will occur for us as it does for the governess. But the alert reader has already seen between the lines: the beauty is accompanied with misery; the natural man in Miles will shine through, and the beauty will tarnish. The beauty, we are to see, is real and suggests the allegorical sense of the power to which we might rise: the setting of Bly is idyllic, is a re-creation of Eden itself. But they are Miltonic children, and they carry "the seeds...of their own destruction" (179) within them even as they appear to the governess in angelic radiance. The setting itself reflects the nature of the idyll—the opening scene in the embrace of spring; the closing in the glooms of November, an arc that Heilman sees as describing a renewal of the fall from innocence (179). This process is enhanced figuratively by the appearance of aging in the two children—the blight, the onset of death. Correspondingly, the description of Quint is such that Heilman concludes that these are "the characteristics of a snake" (181). The fixed eyes of Miss Jessel perform a like figural function of haunted remorse. The governess surrenders her teaching responsibility for Miles because she has nothing further to teach him—with the surmise that he has already tasted of the apple.

Heilman issues himself a caution: that one must not press the analogies, so light in the text, too strenuously. The job instead is "to trace all the imaginative emanations that enrich the narrative, the associations and intimations by which it transcends the mere horror story and achieves its own kind of greatness." If by any chance Heilman has been able to avoid the Jamesian trap up to this point, his claim lapses with this statement. His caution is, of course, well taken; his incaution—merely to trace all the emanations—marks the moment of his pitching over the precipice. He does not and cannot exhaust the implications everywhere in the text: he must ultimately become as selective of his evidence as Wilson; he runs the risk of being equally manipulative with it. He concludes from the transcendence of the mere horror story that "by now it must be clear from the antipodal emphases of the story that James has an almost religious sense of the duality of man" (181). The duality is to be derived figurally from the ambiguities of beauty and depravity in the two spirits, but primarily from Miss Jessel, who seems in some way more fully than Quint to have exercised a choice in the evil nature that shows through her, and to have paid for her lapse in an appropriately painful manner. This leaves Miles in a role suggestive of Faust (184).

Thus the recapitulation of the Fall-in-Eden at Bly. The governess, so important to Wilson's psychopathological reading, is central. In her plight, Heilman sees the religious imagery of the tale, imagery of sacrifice or atonement, of suffering, of salvation. She has a "priestly function" (185). In her role as priest, her most sacred obligation is the duty to hear confession. Her acting as confessor of Miles is to be the purgatorial device by which he escapes from the passion at Bly. But the evil is indelible, in the Miltonic sense of original sin, which the governess must accept as a truth of existence. In fact, in Heilman's view, the force of the religious imagery in the tale comes precisely from its quiet assertion rather than from a kind of noisy or garish display. The imagery of passion and fall is dissolved in the text, as Heilman sees it, and impresses us precisely because its force mounts so quietly. Yet the image of the church and of Sunday as the Lord's day begins to assert itself in the later stages of the narrative so that the Christian theme becomes more explicit. Heilman sees that James gives "forty percent" of the action of the tale to the remarkable last three days of Miles's existence, the era of Miles's passion. Again, Heilman questions whether the interpretation will hold up; but the implications, finally, are sure. There may be some danger in declaring Bly a Garden of Eden, but the parallels are more than persuasive. The story is a version of the struggle between good and evil.

The reader may well be moved by the interpretation. The imagery itself is powerful and there is a sufficient quantity of it to support Heilman's reading. It is as though we had another Goddard on our hands with another reading to which its author could not see a legitimate alternative. While we read, we do indeed tend to see Heilman's coverage as exhaustive, and thus to see contending views as mistakes. And yet Heilman ignores large segments of the tale to create the consistency of his evidential grid. Since others have considered this second of the two Heilman essays in detail, it is needless to repeat that work. But one must credit the complaint that Heilman, for all his desire to exhaust the significant imagery of the tale in supporting his argument, ultimately cannot do so, and it is devastatingly clear that the gaps are serious when, for example, he ignores the agonized self-reflection of the governess in her last moment of doubt about the guilt of Miles: "if he *were* innocent, what then on earth was I?" (k 87) Behind that moment of doubt is a massive range of imagery in the governess's own text, ambiguous at best, but full of suggestions of doubt, darkness, unhappy knowledge. It is imagery that is not obliterated by the mere creation of a frame in which the agony of the fall occurs. It extends to include the wavering of the governess's descriptive terms for the children in her care, who do indeed manage to traverse the ground from angels to demons in the governess's imagery.

PITCHED BATTLE

Once we see the contours of the battle over the narrative perspective in *The Turn of the Screw*, we can begin to see where the critical assumption arises that there is only a single dividing line between the contenders. We have already noticed variants in the emphases of the opposing sides, but the problem of the governess's frame of mind is the constant in the division. By the time Robert Heilman has mounted his complex reply to Edmund Wilson, much of the future character of the critical tradition will be set until the first major summarizing occurs in the course of the 1960s with Willen's *Casebook* (1960), Cranfill and Clark's *Anatomy* (1965a), and Kimbrough's Norton Critical Edition (1966). Since much of that commentary comes to little more than a footnote to one side of the controversy or the other, it can, for the most part be summarized.

E. E. Stoll's essay (1948) taking issue with the pursuers of symbolism in Coleridge—especially Kenneth Burke and R. P. Warren[6]—concludes with an excursus into Wilson's "Ambiguity." In fact, he does little that goes beyond Heilman's more painstaking exercise in challenging the "Wilson-Kenton" thesis, but he is also pleasingly incensed, is also inclined to carp at the two principal hallucinationists for inattentive reading—especially of James's preface—and is sharp on the governess's authority: "If all these matters as reported by the governess are to be discounted, discredited, then we have indeed, a story behind the story, but one told us only by Miss Kenton and Mr. Wilson, not by the governess, supposed to be telling it (and what other, really, is there?), nor consequently by James himself" (231). He recognizes Wilson's thrill of discovery by juxtaposition in showing the displacement of the tale in the New York Edition from the ghost stories to the tales of deceit and mendacity in volume 12, a fact that he allows as proof of nothing. He cites the comments of Matthiessen and Murdoch in the preface to the notebooks (1947), in which the notebook entry is seen as definitively certifying the story as a ghost tale. According to his view, the critics have damned the governess. But a note at the end has spotted Desmond MacCarthy, who in turn declares that Robert Liddell has given an "unanswerable refutation" of the Wilson thesis (233). It is noteworthy that Stoll does not mention Waldock or Heilman in his commentary.

Glenn Reed and Oliver Evans are similarly caught out. Issuing in early 1949, both have missed Waldock and the earlier Heilman as well as Stoll's comments in the Coleridge essay and speak as though they are the first contributors to the contra-Freudian argument. Reed (1949) catches his neglect of the prior work while his essay is in publication and offers a propitiatory footnote. Evans (1949) merely sails on in the ignorance that is bliss. Both are strikingly reminiscent of Waldock and Heilman, Reed putting his emphasis on the preexistence of evil in Bly—and therefore impeaching the Kenton-Wilson claim that the governess imports that quantity when she arrives—and Evans pressing the preface as an unambiguous statement of the narrative authority that James gives the governess. Evans declares that ghosts through history have had the privilege to appear to whomsoever they choose, and that their failure to appear to particular observers does not in any sense negate their existence (w 206).

Marius Bewley and F. R. Leavis quarreled over the novella in *Scrutiny* in the early 1950s. Bewley begins, wishing to talk not about James's ambiguity, but about the problem of appearance and reality in James. Bewley is very much at his leisure in the essay and covers the territory that will ultimately make its way into the part of *The Complex Fate* that treats James. He introduces his Platonian theme broadly in Hawthorne, with a number of Jamesian parallels and analogues and eventually comes to the "horrible governess." His mandate for a view of the governess as frigid is Hawthorne's Gervayse Hastings ("The Christmas Banquet"), whose likeness to the governess resides in his

Wakefieldian exile from the feeling center of life, the man of substance who calls himself a shadow (1950b, 113). We are in Hastings's world at Bly, where "nothing is real and we are sure of nothing" (114). In this view, the governess is at fault for the horrors of Bly and the children are exonerated. He pardons Miles on the grounds of Miles's replicating the behavior of Maisie in protecting illicit lovers—that is, in his view, the only notable issue of the corruptions of Bly.[7] Moreover, Quint the man cannot be tarred with the same brush that applies to Quint the ghost, because we lack the evidence necessary to judge. Bewley uses James's "evoked" to suggest that the spirits are projected by someone "living at Bly"—the governess and not the children. For Bewley, the evidence involving the children is identical to the evidence by which we might indict Maisie for corruption: if we let Maisie off the hook, we must do so for Miles and Flora. He can conclude that "the governess is intent on possessing the children in a way which, for both Hawthorne and James represented a violation of human personality" (109). Furthermore, the governess insists that the children shall confess to seeing "her own vision" (111). It is the governess, then, that moves the children into the world of Quint and Jessel. But while Bewley quarrels with the exponents of the paradisal thesis about Bly, he does not accept the Wilsonian reading with its Freudian overlay, and in fact seems closer to the stand of Kenton.

Leavis rejoins with material that reminds us much of Liddell and Heilman. To these, some of which he cites, he adds that the governess cannot be impeached on the ground of her response to the letter of dismissal since the dismissal could not have happened to a boy "belonging to a family of distinguished 'county standing' without being prepared to substantiate against him as grave a charge as the governess divines from the letter" (1950, 118).[8] Leavis defends James's creation of the angelic innocence in the children as a device to accentuate the horror of their corruption. He offers the various ruses of the children to escape from the governess's scrutiny as evidence of such corruption. He is perhaps on less than perfectly solid ground in suggesting that evil had no particular significance for James; and for thinking that James would have been "surprised at the perversity that focuses the evil not in the haunting pair but in the governess" (116), since the problem of evil does indeed haunt James's work, while he seems to have been inoculated against surprise at anything that the readers of *The Turn of the Screw* could conceive of. There is little new in Bewley's further rejoinders.

Charles G. Hoffman (1953; w 212–22) can claim the distinction of being the first to see a link between *Screw* and Conrad, specifically *Heart of Darkness*. Miles's outcry at the end of his agony is to be compared to Kurtz's cry in their parallel wrestle with the dark angel. And yet Hoffman is incompletely schooled—he has read Wilson and Heilman's "Poem" but none of Heilman's "Freudian Reading" or Waldock or Stoll or Leavis and is thus doomed to repeat them. Harry Levin issues a warning in his *Symbolism and Fiction* (1956): "isolating the text in the name of 'close reading,' we can easily be led astray. So sensible a critic as Edmund Wilson has argued that Henry James's 'Turn of the Screw' should be read as a psychological projection of its governess's frustrations" (13). Symbol hunting can indeed be a dangerous game. Earl Roy Miner (1954) opposes the Freudians except to suggest that they show the virtually unsoundable depth of James's ghost tales. Carvel Collins (1955) can claim credit as being the first to suggest that Douglas is Miles grown up, that it is only an illusion that he dies. Oscar Cargill, like Edmund Wilson, offers a dense psychological reading of the tale and then retracts (1956). The tale was one of female hysteria, as Wilson and Kenton had contended; the subject was a veiled recapitulation of the agonizing tale of the clinical hysteria of his sister Alice; the governess is "a demonstrable pathological liar" (w 228). The immediate provenience of the tale is the Freud-Breuer "Case of Miss Lucy R." from *Studien über Hysterie* (1895). The mystifying preface to the tale is conceived as a means of shielding the memory of Alice James.[9] Or in short, not only has the criticism a legitimate Freudian dimension, but it extends to include elements of the bizarre aspects of the author's biography.

John Silver will help the Freudians out in mounting the "insuperable" barrier to the reading of the governess as a case of neurotic sex-repression (1957)—that is, her identification of Quint. He looks at the text, and discovers that the governess is her own voucher for knowing that the apparition was not somebody from the village because she says to Mrs. Grose, "I didn't tell you, but I made sure" (k 22). Silver infers from this that the governess has gone to the village to check and has there discovered the description of Quint that she then foists on Mrs. Grose (w 243). It is on the basis of this note that Wilson spins his final revolution on his essay for its inclusion in Willen's *Casebook*. Peter Coveney, too, wants to come to the aid of the Freudians (1957). The tale reflects James's own delicate and unreliable psychology, and thus the novella is merely a case history of the psychic chaos of Henry James himself. In the same vein, the preface is an index to the sort of unbalanced nature that we ultimately see in the author: "The 'specifications' are—and the equivocation makes them all the more suggestive—sexual depravities, and in particular in the case of Miles, homosexual specifications" (211). The conflict in the tale is thus between the prurient governess, who insists on knowing in graphic detail the things that Miles did to be expelled from school, and, of course, what he did sexually with Quint that preceeded the adventures at school (209–14). Nonetheless, Wilson is specifically wrong—the governess is not a case of repressed sexuality, but of excessive force in the exertion of authority. The novella is a "disorderly fantasy" of the author (214).

John Lydenberg and Joseph Firebaugh, in the same year as Coveney, reflect something of Coveney's views about the nature of innocence in James. However, they stick with the text rather than move the locus of interpretation into James's biography. Each contends, with slight variations in emphasis, that the appropriate reading of the preface is that the governess has been given excessive authority over the children and that she is virtually an allegory of the Victorian abuse of parental power in the treatment of the child. Lydenberg (1957) focuses his complaint on the unexplained aspects of the tale under the analysis of Heilman and the advocates of a Christian conception of the tale. "James's own comments ... make it reasonably clear that he intended neither a psychological study of the governess nor a religious parable," says Lydenberg (w 274). The governess is a "would-be savior" but a false one (276). Her mode of action is to press with increasing force on her inferiors until ultimately they break. The children, mournfully, break also. They do so under the authoritarian rule of the governess who is "hysterical, compulsive, sado-masochistic" (290).

Firebaugh, on the other hand, places his emphasis on the problem of knowledge (1957), the conflict, as it were, between innocence when it means ignorance and whatever we take for the estate of consciousness in the dwellers in paradise. Like Lydenberg, Firebaugh is unimpressed with the Freudian reading of the tale; like Lydenberg, he will not accept Heilman's notion that the tale is James's excursion into the state of idyllic innocence. Moreover, in the cosmos of Firebaugh's *Screw*, the adults are malevolently antipathetic to the children because James wanted to show how the education of the gifted is hampered by those charged with its execution (w 292). Firebaugh suggests that Heilman is correct in his Edenic vision of the children; but Heilman misplaces the emphasis of the tale, which should find its appropriate focus on the bungling governess who carries the ancient consciousness of sin to a fault. Her fault is simply that she sees things in absolutes, the children being, at first, spotlessly innocent; the ghosts and their living counterparts, irretrievably damned. The governess is incompletely schooled, is incompetent in the most basic forms of knowledge. Having nothing to communicate to the children, she resorts to the very sinfulness of knowledge itself. "Flora lapses into hysteria, Miles into death, because their young efforts to know have been forced into the pattern of Original Sin," says Firebaugh. The governess, he concludes, in her fulfilling the contract pressed upon her by the master of Bly, "is the inadequate priestess of an irresponsible deity—the Harley Street uncle" (297), who is inaccessible despite his unfulfilled responsibility for the children. Lack of knowledge is innocence and the governess applies the idea that lack of knowledge is the only salvation in the fallen world (297).[10] According to Firebaugh, she is dangerously wrong in her insistence.

Alexander Jones, turning from the moral issues of the tale and the tactical issues of criticism that seem to cluster around them, wishes to treat technical matters in respect to the tale: the problem of point of view (1959). He knows that a clue to the intentions of James will likely be found in the technique of any fiction, and proposes to clear some of the terms in the equation by a study of technique. In the process, he offers a useful summary of the cleavage points of the criticism to his own moment: aside from acknowledging what Kenton had called the conventional reading of the tale, Jones has descried critical approaches that have called the tale "a sophisticated hoax, an allegory of good and evil in the manner of Hawthorne, a dramatic poem employing Christian symbolism to depict the twofold nature of man ... an attack upon authoritarianism, a rejection of New England Puritanism, an account of hallucination due to terror, a case study of neurosis or even of psychopathology, an exercise in Freudian symbolism—or even as a projection of the doubts and obsessions of James's own 'haunted mind'" (w 298). Jones's summary suggests a good hold of the convergence of critical opinion on the tale by 1959. He does, however, risk the challenge of those other critics who have insisted upon a careful attention to James's technical concerns as the only way to secure one's grasp on the text—for those critics have declared unanimously that James has both announced and achieved the governess's detachment in the tale, while Jones proposes that it is only after one "has analyzed her personality and behavior" that the novella itself becomes intelligible (299). However, for Jones, the establishment of the governess's personality is a labor of the prologue to the tale and the prologue itself is part of its perspective. That is, the prologue exerts a degree of enclosing control over the narrative within it, and therefore conditions critical response.

The personality that survives the prologue is that of the cheerful and brave governess who is perfectly capable of falling in love with her employer, but who represses none of the emotion involved. Jones considers the Freudian approach to the tale and decides to focus his reply on Cargill's interpretation. Jones contends that there is not sufficient evidence to support the conclusion that James's governess experiences the neurosis from which Lucy suffers, the "conversion neurosis" (305). Nonetheless, Jones accepts that the evidence required to exonerate the governess from the charge of malevolence against the children is necessarily evidence that will also uphold the reliability of her narration. Jones impeaches Goddard on the same grounds as extravagant and incautious. He sets aside the Freudian reading of the tale with the remark that it is compelling only so long as the details of the story are read out of context.

Again for Jones, the preface is mischievous in inviting speculation. But Jones has no hesitation in declaring that the force of the preface was singular—to suggest James's desire to draw the rational sophisticate among his readers back into the realm of fancy. Thus the force of the tale is achieved through the "unreliable" perspective of the governess as narrator, who cannot omnisciently know, but who can only "guess and hope and fear" (310). And so Jones takes on Firebaugh and Lydenberg to show that they, too, fall short in the process of dealing with the tale. If the ghosts are real, there can be no impeachment of the governess on statutory grounds. She may be flawed and flaws may lead to mistakes, but if the ghosts are real and she stands up against them, she cannot be declared fundamentally unsound like Lord Jim—for all the similarity of their backgrounds. Jones is quite prepared to cite these flaws, her jumping to conclusions, her construing speculation into fact. But on the whole, Jones finds her reliable within her gifts. He argues a question that will become a recurrent favorite in the 1970s—the question of the absolute nature of first-person narration. He uses what will become for students of narrative from Gerald Prince to Gerard Genette the favorite problem case in first-person narration, Agatha Christie's Dr. Sheppard, narrator and culprit in *The Murder of Roger Ackroyd*.[11] But he will declare that the nature of first-person narration is to communicate a confidence between the narrator and the reader and that even the exceptions tend to honor this rule. Thus, for Jones, the "conventional" reading of the tale is the appropriate one, for the governess does indeed save the children—in the immortal sphere in which the combat is carried out.

RECAPITULATION

While Jones's article was in the press, Willen's *Casebook* was well along in preparation, and the first era of summary of the critical tradition of *The Turn of the Screw* was imminent. Jones, in fact, did some summarizing, listing at least the main antagonists to the "conventional" reading of the tale. His work on summarizing, however, is in no sense systematic, and by and large, he is merely quarreling with those who take a stand different from his. But at the same time, Douglas M. Davis, the first of several graduate students to look skeptically at the criticism of the novella was working in a slightly more systematic vein, inquiring into the very act of criticism, or as he says, citing Stephen Potter, the "explication racket" (1959, 7): "a vast wilderness of interpretations has grown up, each more 'striking' and 'interesting' than the former. They range all the way from Wilson's popular old standby (the governess is a sex-starved neurotic and the ghosts are hallucinations) to Cargill's recent variations of the same (James was writing about his sister Alice in the governess; from anti-Freudians like Robert Heilman (dramatic poem) to Leo Ben Levy (the 'Turn' is James's way of getting revenge on the audience that rejected his plays); from Oliver Evans to Joseph L. Firebaugh" (8). Davis selects for his comments the Freudian reading of the tale, not because he is categorically opposed to the use of Freud in literature, but because the Freudian reading seems to have given rise to excessive critical ingenuity, to a display of cleverness for its own sake in the process of mounting the critical statement (11). Davis's argument is that the force of good criticism must come from the text itself.

That argument will be echoed only a few years later by a voice that has carried more weight than Davis's in the intervening years. In 1972, Roland Barthes will declare criticism only a matter of "validities," not of "truths." Its job is to "elaborate a language whose coherence, logic, in short, whose *systematics can collect or better still can 'integrate'* ... the greatest quantity of [authorial] language, exactly as a logical equation evaluates the validity of reasoning without taking sides as to the 'truth' of the arguments it mobilizes" (258). In summary, "the 'proof' of a criticism is not of an 'alethic' order (it does not proceed from truth), for critical discourse ... is never anything but tautological" (259). Barthes offers, it seems to me, some useful correctives for the critical tradition of *The Turn of the Screw*. Later on these ideas will be

reechoed with growing force. Here, for the moment, the value of what
Barthes says lies in his perception of the pitfall of the explicator—the
penchant for claiming definitive proof, what Barthes calls Truth Value,
for a proposed interpretive idea. A student of the critical record of
James's novella is likely to feel quite strongly that the devices used to
"solve" the novella are by definition inadequate to mathematical
solution. The simplest way of putting the problem is that James's tale is
a captive of its own problematic nature. This is not to say that the
explicative impulse is necessarily pointless. It is only to say that
"proof" and "truth" are not features deducible from arguments from
particular details of the text.[12] While one finds some escape from the
monster of proof in Barthes's repudiation of the alethic intention of the
critical act, one finds, as I have suggested above, some problem with the
historical implications of the reduction of the critical act to the mere
adjustment of shifting critical vocabularies to the logical constraints of
the authorial language of the text. For at least in the critical tradition of
The Turn of the Screw we do indeed witness "discovery" as part of that
process, regardless of how unlikely that achievement may seem. As an
observable fact, the process of discovery of "hidden," "secret," or
"profound" dimensions of the novella will characterize the tradition
from time to time. But the era through which we have just passed
contains the most powerful single example of such discovery. Our
critics may well not have been more "perspicacious" than their
predecessors, as Barthes deprecates, but in this period they do indeed
discover Douglas, the governess's second in the process of transmission
of the narrative, and in the discovering Douglas, they also discover the
frame tale, the prologue to the novella.

While perhaps these discoveries will not seem monumental to the
casual reader of the tale, they are central to any understanding of the
narrative problems of the tale. Before the first substantive mention of
the prologue in Kenton in 1924, a quarter century after the publication
of the tale, the governess and her narrative occupy the entire critical
attention of commentators. The broader questions about whose narrative
we listen to (or read), the circumstances of its delivery, the implications
of this process for the nature of the revelations we recoil from in the
tale, and the larger problems of what the tale is about have remained,
until this exigent concern achieves expression, suspended on an
unreached periphery in the critical appraisal of the tale. Indeed, there is
a dramatic development in the value for the frame tale in the period of
which the reflection is an enhanced critical appreciation of the tale's
depth. Kenton indeed makes the first clear reference to the frame tale.
As others have noted, it is she herself who calls attention to the

disregard with which the prologue has been treated in the prior commentary: "in the submerged and disregarded forward to the tale... lies a little painted portrait of the exquisite young creature who undertook the portentous task at Bly." In my ellipsis lies Kenton's challenge to readers, few of whom, as she says, "remember this at all" (w 108).

Kenton goes on to give a few of the tantalizing details of the "forword" by way of telling us that we are to find the governess "exquisite." It is the "only light we have on her present or her past"; but her own recounting of the events at Bly does not give us the story of the story. The prologue goes on to tell us, Kenton says, that the governess was twenty, a clergyman's daughter, a "fluttered girl out of a Hampstead [*sic*] vicarage." She sees the uncle, the figure of "a dream or an old novel," and all that such a figure must be to appeal to a young girl. She must leave him free to live his life in peace. She hesitates but she succumbs "to ... the beauty of her passion" (109). Kenton gives us little, a mere soupçon of the frame tale, but she has at least introduced it into the context of discussion and it has become an item in the reckoning of the tale. Moreover, Kenton sees at least the salient features of the prologue, the drama of the "seduction" of the governess into her strange role at Bly. And she is aware that at least one interest of the tale is the "story of the story," a notion that she will pursue by investigating the New York preface.

Wilson does not follow Kenton in her interest in the frame tale, so that barring her brief reference in 1924, we wait until the 1940s before the subject surfaces again. Robert Lee Wolff mentions Douglas as "James's fictional narrator, the possessor of the governess's manuscript" and sees that Douglas is made to offer the first statement in criticism of the narrative as its undisputed first reader that "nothing ... that I know... touches it... for general uncanny ugliness and horror and pain" (k 126). But he has nothing to say beyond this about the significance of the prologue. Liddell immediately sees that Douglas assists the governess's credibility by his regard for her: "In the prologue one Douglas introduces the governess's manuscript. He makes it clear that he completely believes in [the governess's] story and regards her as a person of the greatest distinction of mind and character" (138). Since Liddell's concern is to shine light on the darknesses of the Freudian reading of the tale, he treats the frame as a Jamesian device for reinforcing the narrator's "authority." Beyond this, Liddell merely repeats the factual information that one has learned from the prologue and does nothing to improve on Kenton's inferences.

Heilman uses the prologue to buttress his argument that the governess is a credible witness of her own experience. As the prologue "tells us explicitly" (1947, 442) the governess at thirty is still a spinster, still a governess, and thus by Edmund Wilson's standards, still the heiress of all the female psychic ills imaginable. But to Heilman's thinking she must be the very figure that the speaker in the prologue finds her to be: "to challenge this characterization of her [Wilson] would have to challenge the testimony of a poised and graceful middle-aged gentleman; and, in addition to that, the testimony of the perceptive first-person narrator in the prologue, who is completely *en rapport* with the middle-aged gentleman" (443). Heilman thus becomes one of the first to recognize not only the potential role of Douglas as an authenticating voice in the prologue, but also the existence of and possible importance of the external narrator of the tale. Indeed, he is, in his companion essay, the first to declare his awareness that the external narrator supplies the title to the tale as it reaches the reader. He speaks of Mrs. Grose, "whose name, like the narrator's title, has almost allegorical significance" (w 175). E. E. Stoll has spotted Douglas's compliment to the governess—"the most agreeable woman I ever knew in her position"—though he does not go beyond that recognition in his treatment of the tale (1948, 231). Lydenberg, a decade later, still only barely mentions the prologue. He is speaking of the governess as narrator, who as such "is never seen from the outside (except briefly in the prologue)" (w 275). But of course she is seen both more extensively than Lydenberg suggests, and is seen, as Heilman had suggested, by not one but two speakers exterior to her narrative: Douglas in recollection and the external narrator in recollection of Douglas; and in appreciative interpretation of the character Douglas has drawn for his audience.

Reed (1949) and Evans (1949) also comment on the prologue. Reed sees the prologue in the same manner as does Heilman, as one of many hints that we are to credit the governess as narrator. He speaks of Douglas's admission that he "was half in love with her," and proceeds: "Douglas knew her after the events of the story" and attests to her "good breeding with no obvious signs of mental instability" (w 195). He also uses the prologue to support the notion of distance of time and place from the events at Bly with the result that the narrative is not the fiery product of immediate recollection, but rather the seasoned record of events recollected in some tranquillity. For Evans, the New York preface was unambiguous on the purport of the tale, and "the prologue is equally unambiguous" (w 205). He recounts the familiar scene in which Douglas gives his review in advance—the uncannily ugly tale—and goes on to apply James's use of Douglas to the problem of the governess's credibility. On the contrary, says Evans, Douglas is there to supply the governess with a character reference, and after hearing him, we are willing to listen to her with respect (206). Evans inquires, "had James's intention been to characterize her as an irresponsible neurotic, what could have been his motive in having *the only person who knew her*, and was able to vouch for her character, speak in this fashion?" (206) The implied answer is that this challenge cannot be successfully met.

These commentators recognize Douglas, the external narrator, the frames within which the tale is to be contained, the process of establishing distance in time and place, of establishing a witness to the character of the governess, and so forth. But they do not carry the commentary very much beyond the first recognition, beyond the notion that there *is* in the tale a device of creating topographical relief, dimension, distinction. Jones (1959), who has the advantage of their comments, and who is, after all, looking at the techniques of the novel, carries the study of the framing device somewhat further than his fellow commentators. Jones sees from the outset that the tale "does not begin either with the governess herself or with those events which are to be the chief concern of the narrative. Instead, James opens with a sort of prologue in which he introduces the reader to a character, Douglas, who in turn presents the story proper by reading from an old manuscript which the governess has presented to him years before." Jones, then, can claim to have priority in the recognition that one of the potential critical issues of the tale is the progression of its transmission; that, in other words, the prologue not only gives depth to the relief map, but also gives some sense of its spatio-temporal movement. Jones goes on to tell us that the framing device is as old as narrative, but observes that "the device seems particularly useful to writers dealing with the supernatural" (w 299) in its mediation of mood—its seductions to suspension of disbelief. Jones sees that the effects of the fireside scene are cumulative; that what precedes Douglas's tale is prologue; that there is to be a special and notable horror to this tale.

James himself becomes the external narrator, and, in Jones's view, helps himself to establish a verisimilitude by constituting himself a party to the episode of tale telling. He thus escapes being the "omniscient author" (300). There are problems in Jones's equation between James and the external narrator of the tale, but he is acute in his recognition that "no one is left on the 'outside' of the story, and the reader is made to feel that he and James are members of the circle around the fire" (300)—for here is an ultimate and crucial mechanism in the larger concern of the story. Some later critics will contend that the trap of the tale is precisely to constitute the reader a party to the evil contained within it, even to the point of making such reader repeat in *propria persona* the governess's agony in the very process of trying to describe it. One of the grounds for such a contention is the characteristic pose that Jones has discovered here of James's having embraced all parties, including the reader, in the circle around the fire. Jones goes on to declare that James, by promoting himself into that same circle, releases himself from any complicity in the governess's narrative: she has responsibility. Perhaps Douglas does as well, but the external narrator does not. Again, there are possible problems. The narrative is the property of the external narrator to the extent that this ambiguous figure names it—the tale is called *The Turn of the Screw* under the aegis of this same external narrator. For Jones, the narrative, in the form in which Douglas delivers it, first to the audience around the fire and second to the external narrator, becomes a Document, and thus acquires a degree of independent, external, and respectable existence. In the process, the exposition of the principal expositor of the events at Bly can be declared to the reader without fear of accusations that the narrator or her script is a creation out of whole cloth. She is documented down to the inscription of the narrative "in old faded ink, and in a most beautiful hand" (300).

Jones sees the controversy beginning at precisely the point of the prologue at which the question of her nature arises. Douglas has let it be known that she is a "fluttered anxious girl." But as Jones says, "he has gone out of his way to testify in her behalf" (300). His further testimonials ending in the assertion that the governess is worthy of any position whatever becomes itself the dividing line between the readers who accept the testimonial and settle down to a ghost story and those to whom the governess seems "hysterical and even deranged" (300). To such readers, the governess's tale is a long recital of self-deceptions "encompassing the abnormal rather than the supernatural." Toward the end of his essay, Jones looks back to the frame and sees again how substantial a device it is for distancing and authenticating the governess's record of events. He declares that she need not either have written the narrative nor transmitted it to Douglas. But that once having written it, she has done much to display her defects and has little to proffer by way of apologia.

Jones's comments amount to the first concerted attempt to develop the importance of the prologue to the tale. It comes well beyond the half-century mark in the critical tradition of the tale. And instead of exhausting the prologue for its potential contributions to our understanding, Jones has only suggested some prominent points that need further investigation. In other words, whatever Roland Barthes means by his repudiation of discovery as a legitimate aim of criticism, we must see that in the critical tradition of *The Turn of the Screw* the prologue still awaits comprehensive treatment after sixty years of commentary. But if we look to Barthes as a figure who will alter the course of literary studies, and whose comment in 1962 on the problematic nature of truth value will signal at least one direction of change for future theoretical inquiry into the nature of criticism, it is as well to be aware of the publication of a single book of the moment we have reached in which we can root the very axis of change in the treatment of narrative: Wayne Booth's *Rhetoric of Fiction* (1961), a book which also figures intelligibly in the critical record of *The Turn of the Screw*.

Booth wants to write a rhetoric in the most radical sense—he wants to show how the narrative achieves its effects of persuasion in drawing the reader into the experience of the text and he wants to show how it orchestrates the responses that the work is to evoke from its reader. That was no mean undertaking in 1961, and Booth's endorsement of his initial effort by reprinting it almost unchanged (though with an appendix of notes updating his ideas) in a second edition (1983) suggests that he was content with what he had achieved. Nonetheless, apropos of James (and others) in general, and *The Turn of the Screw* in particular, Booth gives way to a kind of exasperation about the critical love of problem texts and the exaltation of interpretive chaos by critical response: "In short, we have looked for so long at foggy landscapes reflected in misty mirrors that we have come to *like* fog. Clarity and simplicity are suspect; irony reigns supreme" (1983, 372). The complications in *Screw* come from a context of composite unreliabilities (339). Booth finds James to fall short of an encompassing theory for his fiction when the narrator is "confused, basically self-deceived, or even wrong-headed or vicious" (340).

Booth, in such a book as the *Rhetoric*, would naturally seek to summarize or to record the summary of the critical tradition of the tale, and he relies on Liddell and Jones to do the summarizing for him (314), with a careful look at Heilman, with whose views of the tale he seems largely to agree. Booth, like others, reviews the exposition given by various parts of the tale on the issues at stake and goes on to acknowledge "that the effects of this story on James's readers have been far from clear" (313). But he "admits" that for him "James's conscious intentions are fully realized: the ghosts are real, the governess sees what she says she sees" (314). Furthermore, "she behaves about as well as we could reasonably expect of ourselves under similarly intolerable circumstances." Booth wishes for a critical practice that shows higher "respect for the standards of proof" (315). *Fiat proba!* But in lieu of proof, Booth recognizes the value of name-calling, and accordingly accuses those who displease him of "galloping Freudianism," only to be met with his opponents' counterthrust of "galloping traditionalism" (315). Unhappily, James's work is highly susceptible to this character of critical wrangling; the effect is that "the critical disagreement revealed by anyone who compares two or three critics on any one [of James's stories] is a scandal" (315). Booth will not be the last to call it so.

The contending views discussed in the prior two chapters tell us something both about readers reading text and about readers reading critics. The same story that had occasioned the pleasures and pains for the first readers confronted the sophisticated critics of the golden age of New Critical analysis. Thus the same compositional blanks remained to be filled. These grouped critics intensely contending with one another wished, as Iser complained, to impose their critical will on all other readers. It is perhaps these readers whom Iser means when he talks of the "traditional form of interpretation, based on the search for a single meaning" (1978, 22). As readers of texts, however, they did not take the same blanks and come up with different readings of them. What they did in fact was to select and emphasize different sets of blanks, arguing that it was the blanks selected that concretized the "pure" reading of the tale. Thus the search for a definitive reading contemplated the notion not so much of compositional blanks, but rather of compositional codes that the members of both parties proposed they could discern either in the text or in the broader scope of the work of the author. These were clashes over how to find the center of the author's thematic directions for the work. The analysts read texts differently and made different assumptions about how to take critical direction from the author. It is clear that a good deal of time would pass before there would be any apparent attempt to mediate between the contending positions and to try to discover the merits of the opposed positions.

In the meantime, the quarreling critics showed us a good deal about the process of (informed) readers reading critics. Because there was such sharp disagreement on how to read and on how to find the appropriate signposts to guide reading, we could say the critics reading critics developed a different sense of compositional blanks from the ones that we discover in fiction or in the literary text. The compositional blanks in the hermeneutic text represented assumptions about the way texts direct readers. Psychoanalysis represented a new analytic science of mind, apparently convertible to the uses of criticism.

The nature of its compositional blanks in the first instance looked a good deal like the cells of dream experience: a highly symbolic language with a delicious substructure of deceit and greedy selfishness. Its practice was suspicion of all motives and of all self-revelations. It made its assumptions about the governess's psychology with ease based on the heightened character of her prose. The Edenists, on the other hand, comprehended the biblical account of the Fall and the permutations of *Paradise Lost*. Their set of compositional blanks would have to contain the yearning for a lost innocence that the suspicious nature of the other party would deny out of hand. The blanks would contain the memory of the idyllic past and the annihilating sense of loss that accompanied the Fall. When the critics read the critics, then, the clash was ideological and the parties were committed to systems that could not be reconciled without a whole new sense of how the text dictates its terms of allegiance.

And yet it is still as though James had anticipated the sectarian quarrels: for though he could not determine the manner in which a particular reader might fill the compositional blanks, he was still catching people in his trap; still making them supply the evil for themselves; still exposing the inevitable reading act of imagining the tale but attributing its horrors to the author. James still understood better than his readers the process by which mere fleeting impressions become the realities on which the human mind operates.

5

Summary and New Beginnings

The movements toward summary of the criticism of *The Turn of the Screw* in the 1960s contain three major texts—book-length treatments of the tale as well as a major revisionary essay—by way of reprint of the tale and critical collection: Gerald Willen 1960; by way of a reconsideration of the basis of the Freudian reading: Mark Spilka 1963; by way of an "anatomy" of the tale itself, with some attention paid to the commentary: Thomas M. Cranfill and Robert L. Clark 1965a; by way of the production of a critical edition with the usual Norton format of text plus backgrounds, sources, and examples of criticism: Robert Kimbrough 1966. That three of the instruments of summary should be book-length treatments suggests that the critical controversy had by this era generated sufficient interest to carry into the major format of critical inquiry, while reflecting at the same time the heady era in which the explosion of knowledge in all fields has led to the need for continual expansions of library plant.

Willen's Casebook, in that vein, for example, not only performed the function of collecting criticism on the tale in a manageable form and, in a sense, engaging in an act of criticism by the mere act of selection of criticism; but also contributed to a growing practice of republishing material in inexpensive reprints in the form of "canned" research instruments as a means of relieving pressure on library resources by young students. Students could engage in the scholarly procedures of dealing with text, background, and criticism without touching the perishable originals. Some evidence of expert knowledge on the part of the compiler would be necessary, but since the purpose was simply to place materials in the students' hands, the need for penetrating and exhaustive scholarship diminished. One saw proliferations of texts entitled *London in Dickens' Day*, *Incident at Harper's Ferry*, *Shakespeare's "Julius Caesar"* and so forth, which would be useful to the undergraduate but which would collect and

178

excerpt materials only within the expertise of the compiler. Undoubtedly, the Norton Critical Editions, which began to appear in the early 1960s with Robert Greenberg's *Gulliver's Travels* (1961), belong historically with this publishing development, though the initial intention seems to have been that the Nortons would produce true critical editions with the estate of the text established by careful scholarship and with backgrounds, sources, and representative critical statements dedicated to the creation of a high standard of critical text.

Of Willen's *Casebook* one can surely say that the author has made both the text and a certain quantity of critical material inexpensively available to the reader. For Willen, the problems of scholarship—problems that made it valid for Norton to issue a rival *Screw* text in its critical edition only six years later, while printings of the *Casebook* were still pouring out—are of little account. He declares that "selecting the critical essays for this book posed the usual problems. Obviously everything written on 'The Turn of the Screw' could not be included" (2). "The usual problems" included the innocent task of making a selection from available materials. "The inclusion of fifteen complete essays" along with the tale and some of James's peripheral remarks "will more than serve to awaken the reader to the possibilities of the subject." There is not even a pretense of scholarship in such comments and the principle of inclusion of the essays seems, from what the introduction says, to have been the weighty consideration of completeness. Instructors are invited to have their students flesh out the essay reading of the *Casebook* with starred books noted in Willen's bibliography to be drawn from their own libraries. Nonetheless, the *Casebook* does make the selected essays available to the reader as they appear here, and whatever scholarly merits the text may lack, it has certainly served many a later critic as though it were the official critical history of the tale. If Willen has oddly chosen to give us Wilson's 1948 reprinting of the original *Hound & Horn* version of "The Ambiguity of Henry James" or if his publishers have decided to save money by excluding Demuth ("The Charles Demuth drawings that accompanied Edna Kenton's article have been omitted" (2)) that is presumably in the interest of making the book available at a reasonable price. And if the criticism of the Willen text is that ultimately it pretends to so little and achieves about as much, one cannot fault it for lacking controversy—for in this the volume abounds, almost as though the hidden principle of construction were to thrust two gamecocks at each other with the idea of creating fruitful outrage. What Willen's *Casebook* seems to propose to its reader is that the criticism of *The Turn of the Screw* is restricted to the Freud-counter-Freud quarrel occasioned by Wilson's "Ambiguity" and to a lesser extent by Kenton's "Ruminant Reader." Willen does not include comments on the novella by writers before Edna Kenton, whose essay of 1924 is the first to appear in the book after the tale itself, and a portion of the preface to volume 12 of the New York Edition. What Kenton calls the "conventional" reading of the tale is left to the essayists themselves to introduce into the text. Thus, while a Waldock or a Heilman, for example, will mention the early reviews and occasionally mention, perhaps, Ford Madox Ford's comments on the tale, Willen's book ignores these sources. And while Wilson himself will mention W. C. Brownell in the earliest version of the essay ("and even years later when Henry James was selecting material for his collected edition, he was forced by the insistence of his publishers—one supposes that W. C. Brownell was responsible—and against his own inclination,[1] to exclude *The Bostonians* from it" [Wilson 1934, 392]; Brownell and all other earlier commentators—even those who might have supported the Wilsonian thesis, which the book seems to favor— are absent from the context. Thus, while one might find fault with its principles of exclusion, the book has been, for better or worse, highly influential in the later critical development of the tale. It has been widely available; has been widely consulted; has been treated as a principal source of information about *The Turn of the Screw*. And within its limits it has done its job. The problem has in fact been the lack of diligence of some later critics: without taking care to inquire into the matter for themselves, later critics have often accepted the *Casebook* as a reprint of representative evidence in the critical tradition of the tale to 1960.

Undoubtedly this acceptance is part of a larger problem about the nature of criticism itself. If we accept the notion of Barthes and others (J. L. Austin is writing *How to Do Things with Words* about this time [1962], and is establishing the foundations on which the speech-act theorists will distinguish between the mere process of describing and the more complex speech-acts of demonstrating and proving) that the critical act is not a process of adducing proof but rather something like an invitation to the reader to entertain a notion of the artifact, there can be nothing wrong in theory with a critic's simply making a further intervention on the text regardless of the extent of the critic's familiarity with the text's critical record—what has been said, what remains to be said, what deserves to be praised, what needs to be contradicted. If we believe, however, that we must also demand coherence in the generation of criticism, some guarantee against mere repetition or attenuation of ideas already on record, then we have a right to expect that the critic survey the criticism before adding to it, a fiction that academics persist in pursuing in the process of sending graduate students off to begin the research for theses. As E. E. Stoll observed, tartly, in his Coleridge essay, "so many who write criticism do not much read it" (1948, 230). His statement has force in the criticism of *The Turn of the Screw*, especially after 1960. One has the sense that fewer and fewer read the tale for themselves, and that the criticism derives more and more from the "canned" context of anthologies.

But Cranfill (and Clark)'s[2] *An Anatomy of "The Turn of the Screw"* (1965) is a different matter. In Christine Brooke-Rose's protest a decade later about the sloppy inattention of too many critics of the tale, she castigated what she called "non-methodology" (1981, 128) a condition in which the critic allows the imagination to supersede the text or encourages critical prepossession to dictate the concept of the tale rather than allowing the tale to dictate the shape of the criticism. The Cranfill (and Clark) *Anatomy* is an exercise in non-methodology. They begin by recapitulation of prior criticism; go on to take a brief look at the preface to volume 12 of the New York Edition; and propose a close reading of the text to discover what James meant by it. They have a look at the various stages of the creation of the text and pronounce the ⋅ revision for the authorized edition to be entirely satisfactory. In fact, without telling us exactly the basis on which they form their judgment, they declare that the changes make the tale more effective (16). If the reader looks and discovers that a large number of these changes were the additions of verbiage in the form of adjectives or adjectival units, such practice is apparently no deterrent to the claim of improvement. They seem to be following Leon Edel, who had suggested that the changes propelled the work from a statement about events at Bly to a statement about the narrator's feelings toward these events. And the novella, which might have had one sort of resonance at the time of its original publication, had a very different one by the time it had completed its revision.[3] It is this difference, according to Cranfill and Clark, that prompts compelling support for the "nonapparitionist" reading of the text. By page 36 of their book the authors have adopted this approach to the tale and will continue from here on to treat it as what Leon Edel calls "a deeply fascinating psychological 'case.'" The governess has not seen ghosts, nor even as Kenton and Wilson have suggested, suffered hallucinations: she has seizures (49), which are the just punishment for her crimes: her "seizures" are "retribution" for unrequited love.[4]

The authors seem to have drawn their conclusions in advance of their argument. They are, after all, the first to offer a critical book entirely devoted to original criticism of *The Turn of the Screw*. They are close readers of the text, and thus one cannot object on the ground of exiguous resources. Moreover, they are arduous in their dedication to their goal. Nonetheless, they run critical risks by falling into a habit of giving credence to everything the narrator says that might allow them to damn her for her crimes against Bly; but to disparage everything she says that might lead the reader to credit her motives. As they proceed they take an angry pleasure in unmasking her with condescending comments like "Poor girl, her nerves and mind *do* treat her to nasty surprises."

Their practice becomes most problematic to the reader when they find it necessary to rewrite the text in order to sustain their perspective. They quote the passage in which the governess indicates that Flora has taken the boat and rowed across the lake on the Bly property. Cranfill and Clark simply declare that the boat is in its usual mooring. The text says, "My companion stared at the vacant mooring-place and then again across the lake. 'Then where is it?'" They walk halfway around the lake and the narrative says "in the course of but few minutes more we reached a point from which we found the boat to be where I had supposed it. It had been intentionally left as much as possible out of sight and was tied to one of the stakes of a fence that came, just there, down to the brink and that had been an assistance to disembarking." (k 68; 69) The *Anatomy* says respecting this passage, "Flora has of course *not* taken the boat." And a bit later on, "Before the very eyes of Mrs. Grose *and* Flora, the governess sees what is *not* there—what she takes to be Miss Jessel's spectre" (63).[5] Though in the text, just after the governess reports the boat to be "where she expected to find it," the searchers do indeed seem to find Flora, and though it is after they find her that the last "seizure" conjuring up Miss Jessel takes place, Cranfill and Clark decline to account for how Flora comes there, a point that would seem to need, if not explanation, then at least explaining away.

The *Anatomy* thus dissolves the text by deciding that it is not stable at all, but rather invites or even demands a sort of voluntary rewriting by the critic, apparently at will. The nonmigratory boat is of a piece with the comment early in the book that considers a gap in the chronology of the events in the prologue: The governess has perhaps spent the intervening years between Bly and the House of Douglas recovering her composure in a nursing home (23). Their nursing home offers a truly miraculous cure, one unknown to Andrew Scull (1981) in *Madhouses, Mad-Doctors and Madmen*. The problem with the sort of argumentation that appears here, argument based on what Brooke-Rose calls extratextual considerations, is that it impugns potentially the entire narrative of the governess, not just the sections that are most fluid or problematic. Once we have accepted the assault on any single part of the narrative, we run the risk that it loses all definitive shape, and random rejection of data becomes the critic's prerogative.

That she has seizures instead of hallucinations or instead of seeing ghosts begs and ignores the question that needs to be entertained. James does not in any sense authorize "seizures" as the appropriate term for what the governess sees; and therefore one expects that the practice of calling her visions "seizures" needs at least to be justified. But in assuming that the story demands to be explained in these psychiatric terms, Cranfill and Clark submerge all of the story's subtleties and ambiguities in a flash of brilliance of the disordered mind so depicted. The announcement that we are to understand the governess's visions in terms of psychic disorder comes on page 49; by page 54 the authors are already concluding that the aftershocks of the "seizures" increase in intensity. Those who dispute the existence of the ghosts, we are told, would like to revise the text to make the governess say, "'Then it was that I was in the grip of further seizures'" (57). It is not enough, apparently, to insist that the governess is already convicted of heinous crimes out of her own mouth: nothing short of the abject language of confession will do. Though these authors are quick to accuse the governess of Inquisitorial behavior, it is difficult to escape the sense that it is the critics themselves who operate the thumbscrew and it is the governess who must be forced to yield by torture. This reasoning allows them to say that "Mark Van Doren is right" and the boy has nothing to confess. They offer no case in support of this conclusion, considering it established, apparently by the mere fact of their assuming it to be so. They do not address the child's reported confession about saying things. Their method might best be summarized in these words: "[they are] seldom inclined to follow even the handful of facts [they are] able to garner to wherever they may logically lead, preferring to sort, rearrange, delete, augment, and otherwise misinterpret them to fit [their] own preconceived theories." These are words (with the change of syntax supplied) that Cranfill and Clark use to describe the intellectual processes of the governess (87).

It is apparent to the authors of the *Anatomy* that the governess, by means of her narrative, is trying to get away with something foul and vile. Thus, the authors tell us of passages "that give her game away" (91) and of phrases that are "a dead giveaway." Not only does she try to fool the reader, but she also characteristically tries to fool herself; and because she is so far gone in psychiatric gore (to borrow a leaf from Edmund Wilson's album), she is undoubtedly successful: "to counter the conscious decision to flee, the governess' subconscious mind conjures up the seizure which makes flight impossible" (93). This adroit gesture comes from the governess's use of "creative logic," as Goddard has called it. "Her heroism challenged, she brings herself round to the same old attitude to which she clings" (93). Part of her fallibility arises from the unrestrained and objectionable obsession for the master; part of it arises from the very center of her own objectionable activity—her strict observance of class distinctions, with which she is also obsessed. Axiomatically she is obsessed with authority; further, an authority of no account in narrative terms, but only in terms of her own assertion of class. The preface, thus, has only a single meaning: that the governess is at Bly to assert the prerogatives of her class, especially as, with respect to the history of British fiction, she can thus answer any Lady Catherines or Blanche Ingrahams, who might venture to sneer at her, that she is a gentleman's daughter, and is a fit match for the master of Bly in spite of the appearances of poverty and unequal rank.

The governess knows her place, but only so that she can remind others of theirs: "Oh the governess is in charge, all right, and moreover exceedingly jealous of her authority" (108). At stake is the genesis of her antipathy to Quint in the first instance and then to Jessel as a companion of Quint. Without ever telling the reader why, the authors of the *Anatomy* have an animus against the governess because of her disgust for Quint. In this matter, they also carry over their animosity to Mrs. Grose as well, though she is otherwise usually enlisted as their ally in their war against the wickedness of the governess: "Why did the arrangement fill Mrs. Grose with loathing and fear? Because Quint was no gentleman and therefore was unqualified to rule the roost? Because Quint was evil in addition to lacking gentility? Because her own station was threatened or rendered equivocal by Quint's presence?" (111).

In answer to these questions the *Anatomy* develops its theory of authority and social order. According to the authors, this question remained unsettled in the narrative: "With Mrs. Grose, Miss Jessel, and Peter Quint—all three of them—on the scene, one begins to suspect that Bly might have been ripe for what labor circles call "jurisdictional disputes" (111). One begins to suspect, however, that the British audience, and at the time the American audience as well, would have understood implicitly that the ranks of the people involved were as fixed as military ranks, with the governess clearly at the top of the hierarchy, the housekeeper next in order and at the head of the corps belowstairs, including the valet and the others in various ranks farther down. If the argument is that the hierarchy is incomplete because there is no adult in full command, it is unlikely that any readers would dispute it. And the relation between the housekeeper and the valet with the master present would be less clearly hierarchical than is suggested above. The critics suggest that they do indeed understand the problem of rank ordering, giving Green's *Loving* and Barrie's *Admirable Crichton* as models. But they seem to have learned little from their models to help them make sense of the politics of Bly.[6]

There is a hint of blame to Mrs. Grose in her refusal to drop the "matter of social propriety in general and Quint's social improprieties in particular" (112). So foolish is Mrs. Grose's objection that the critics hoot at the idea that she should be alarmed at his going about with Miles "quite as if Quint were his tutor—and a very grand one—and Miss Jessel only for the little lady" (112). "So there we have it," Cranfill and Clark rejoin, "Quint did *not* know his place. A gentleman *he*? Never! Yet we find him, not belowstairs with Mrs. Grose, where maybe he belongs, but kiting about like a gentleman-tutor. ... Why, that——that——valet! We can almost see Mrs. Grose bridle and hear her sniff." They record her objection to Miss Jessel about the impropriety and Miss Jessel's snub that she should "mind her business." They record also Mrs. Grose's complaint that Quint had his way with everyone at Bly, but without condemnation of Miss Jessel or of Quint. The only objectionable behavior is that of the governess and of Mrs. Grose that they should object on class grounds to the activities at Bly. About the effects of such behavior on the children they are silent.

This sequence leads to the speculation about the departure of Jessel, about her subsequent death, about the possible sexual relation between Jessel and Quint, and the speculations about a resulting pregnancy. No reader would deny, I think, that these are only speculations on the part of Mrs. Grose and the governess. In addition, the critics seem to be just in feeling that the speculations lack any sort of kindness or concern for the "wronged woman." For their harshness we might condemn the two proper Victorians as uncharitable. But their speculations are at least based on a logical outcome of a man's "doing with [a woman] what he wished"; and the governess is not automatically wrong in saying that these sexual relations were what *she* (Jessel) wished as well (114). But Cranfill and Clark speculate otherwise: "Though the governess declares [Quint] a hound, one wonders whether she does not envisage him rather as another animal, an imperious stallion lording it over *all* the inmates of the stable, including the foals" (114). They refuse to consider the idea that Miss Jessel might have left the post in disgrace, apparently preferring to believe that the pregnancies relevant to the tale are such things as "the pregnant phrase *belowstairs*" (110) and "a pregnant little exchange" between the governess and Mrs. Grose (124). The notion that Quint might have been an unhappy influence on Bly seems to have been ruled out on principle by Cranfill and Clark. The principle seems to be in fact that if the governess thinks something it is by virtue of her hidden agenda at least suspect and at best roundly controverted. Thus if she objects to Quint, they insist on tolerating him even if it seems to their reader rather like hiring a fox to take charge of a henhouse. Only when the narrative adopts their angle of vision is it credible. When the governess raises the matter of Mrs. Grose's illiteracy, for example, the authors say "for once the governess is probably right, as other evidence of Mrs. Grose's illiteracy is plentiful" (118). It is interesting to consider what other evidence beside the governess's narrative they might be drawing on for their canons of reliability in the reports of Bly and even more interesting to be made privy to their principles of distinction between reliable and unreliable reports.

But for Cranfill and Clark witnesses can be conscripted on both sides of an issue. Once they dismiss Quint as a potential danger to Bly, they can engage Mrs. Grose as a witness to the governess's willful wickedness. "Ignorance," we are told, "usually breeds superstition: maybe to begin with she is inclined to believe in ghosts in general, hence in the ghosts at Bly in particular—until the evidence of her own eyes convinces her that there are no such things" (125). It is under such circumstances that we learn about "the governess' sick brain," and her consequent need to be construed as "a patient who needs treating." Mrs. Grose is not only witness to the governess's evil but she is also the nurse to the governess's illness. Inevitably the governess is sufficiently invalided that she is incapable of being a satisfactory teacher, and represents herself as a harassing authority (148). At the end of the tale, the critics tell us that Miles does not steal the governess's letter to the master because the governess takes it herself. Flora not only denies the governess's present accusation but all the other accusations, of which, we are assured—with support from Marius Bewley—there have been many. When Flora speaks horrors—notwithstanding that they are of such a nature that they cancel Mrs. Grose's doubts—these critics assign the horrors to the present governess, not to prior involvement with unsavory company (162). Under the same insight, the governess's final act in the narrative is to frighten Miles to death (168). The conclusion that logically follows for Cranfill and Clark is that "The children suffer prolonged, helpless, lethally dangerous exposure to the mad governess" (169).

Surely the authors of the *Anatomy* can be commended for sticking to their proposed plan. As well they can be commended for looking at a great deal of text in the process of mounting their statement. They are loyal to the conviction that they have embraced as the model on which to understand *The Turn of the Screw*. But for this reader, they have lost track of James's story early in their treatment and have treated themselves to something of an orgy of flagellation of the narrator of the incidents at Bly.[7] One had the notion from various things that Freud says along the way that psychoanalysis was intended to be both a science and a humane inquiry; and that it was to displace the unhappy views of life and of human sexuality preferred by the very reprobatory nineteenth century mind. One had the idea that its purpose was to help find a cure for the ills of the mind troubled by the abrasions of civilization: its stresses, its hidden forces, its insatiable and unfulfillable longings, its terrible experiences of loss. But in the hands of some its literary proponents, critics like Edmund Wilson and Thomas Cranfill, it seems like a new device of torture and torment for the anxious creatures who come under its notice: it seems to put one on the rack in the name of science rather than of religion. It is hard to think of a more punitive use of such a science than that in the *Anatomy*, where first the governess's motives are impugned; then her words are tormented into indictments of her character; then her conduct is judged to be heinous. But again, if one accepts the reading given here, what happens to James's exquisite ghost tale? Under the handling of Cranfill and Clark, it becomes a rather savage and unflattering excursion into the depravity of the character's mind, which makes no allowance for human frailty, self-doubt, or error, and which overwhelms any search for beauty or humanity in its unshakable conviction of human ugliness. It is not at all that Cranfill and Clark invent the governess's faults. She is not without error. But at least this reader emerges from the *Anatomy* with the sense that she is somewhat less appalling in James's hands than the felon that the authors of this critical exercise condemn.

Kimbrough's Critical Edition is the most satisfactory of the books devoted to this stage of summary of *The Turn of the Screw*. In the first place, there is painstaking scholarship here, and nothing is represented that is not also located and documented. The segments of the book are by and large satisfactory, with the scholarly ones having pride of place over the critical ones. Though Kimbrough does not exhaust the early responses, he certainly gives them good representative play. And though he falls short of exhausting, for example, the backgrounds of the tale, again the representative selection is both useful and sufficiently comprehensive. One large area of contribution to further scholarship on the novella is the variorum table as respects the three-to-four stages of the text that passed through James's hands: serial circulation in *Collier's* (January to April 1898); simultaneous publication of *The Two Magics* in England and the United States; the New York Edition. There was a fourth publication while James was alive (1915, Martin Secker), but as Kimbrough reports, Secker was advised to "'conform *literatim* and punctuation to [the New York Edition] text'" (k 89). Kimbrough's own collation shows that that edition did indeed conform literatim to the prior text.

The area in which one might have hoped for something more from the Norton Critical Edition was in its criticism. Kimbrough cannot have been unaware of Willen's *Casebook*, since it was a competing text that had been around for at least five years before the planning of the Norton Critical began. Without question, the Norton Critical would have to take notice of Willen and in a sense decide how to navigate around it. There would be no question about the difference between the two editions, for example, in the area of backgrounds, of textual notes, of sources, of the peripheral letters, and of the Jamesian pronouncements about the tale and about the idea of the ghost story. But the criticism would need perhaps either to subsume Willen—publish all that Willen had done and the more that had been written in the interim—or to publish around Willen, acknowledging by not republishing what Willen had already done. What happened instead was a critical collection that did neither. In the section on major criticism, 1924–57, Kimbrough repeated Goddard entirely; excerpted Kenton and reprinted Heilman's "Poem," thus giving material already available, but ignoring the chance, for example, of increasing the number of available materials by reprinting, say, Heilman's "Freudian Reading of *The Turn of the Screw*," which Willen had decided to exclude. And Kimbrough declines to reprint Wilson's "Ambiguity" either in whole or in part. To this sequence Kimbrough added a new essay by Martina Slaughter (though he does not account for how it was an appropriate conclusion under the rubric of criticism 1924–57); and he adds a sequence out of Edel's *Psychological Novel* (1955), which Willen had also not included in the *Casebook*.

In the material from 1957 to the publication of the Critical Edition, there is no overlap with Willen. Still, given the choices that Kimbrough might have made between his actual inclusions and the ones available to him from the bibliography at the back, it seems to me that he might have preferred, for example, Donald Costello's "Structure of *The Turn of the Screw*" (1960) to Feuerlicht's comparison of *Screw* to Goethe's "Erlkönig." The Costello piece advances the study of the novella, while the Feuerlicht is merely one of a growing number of interesting but merely speculative pieces on it. But perhaps that is a quibble only. If there was one serious omission, it was in my judgment the omission of the Demuth watercolors from the reprinting of the Kenton piece. If Kimbrough's intention was to give a good sense of the history of the criticism of the tale, these watercolors were exigent: if in them the governess that is represented tends to remind me of my grandmother instead of the young and pretty girl that the general information of the text seems to make inevitable, then the paintings are not dispensable to the reading history of the tale.

Nonetheless, by contrast with the other two books, Willen's serenely unpretentious and Cranfill's savagely retributive, Kimbrough's edition is a welcome oasis in what is sometimes the rather arid desert of the novella's criticism by 1966. Perhaps one of its merits is precisely that in its selection of recent criticism are included both the spoof on the detective story aspect of the criticism by Eric Solomon—Sherlock Holmes would have found that Mrs. Grose "did it" (whatever "it" is) because she is the most unlikely character to have done so—and the piece by Mark Spilka calling for a revision of the Freudian reading of the tale.

Spilka's essay is called "Turning the Freudian Screw: How Not to Do It" (1963). He starts off by declaring his astonishment with the "imaginative poverty of much Freudian criticism." He proposes a review of critical essays on *The Turn of the Screw* show a Freudian bias and a revision based upon an improved use of the insights of psychoanalysis. His own review of these essays convinces him that "most of them argue that the governess, in James's tale is neurotic or insane and sees no apparitions: she merely records her own hallucinations and their damaging effect on the two innocent children" (k 245). Spilka applauds Lydenberg's "The Governess Turns the Screws" because Lydenberg carries the commentary out of the range of the narrow conflict between whether the ghosts exist or are a mere projective fantasy of the governess, replacing it with the sense of a generalized evil that is a part of the human composition (245). Spilka is perhaps kind to Lydenberg, applauding his essay for more tolerance of the governess and her plight than Lydenberg allows. Spilka's own revision of the Freudian scheme starts from the premise that the governess has the good of the children at heart precisely in keeping with the Victorian view of human personality. He proposes that the recalcitrancy of that view with respect to human sexuality lies in its promotion of an absolute gulf between the land of the affections and the land of sexuality. According to Spilka, the Victorians were inclined to overheat the affections at the expense of sexual activity, and that the governess's immoderation in her expression of affection for the children is a reflection of the powerful preference of the society in which she lived for behavior of exactly the sort in which she engages. In this sense, says Spilka, the death of Miles may indeed result from the suffocating expressions of the governess, but it is thus the fruit of an unhappy organization of the powers of life in her .

The issue at stake in the ghost tale is thus more complex than the mere requirement for a uniform solution for the ontological quarrel surrounding the ghosts. But Spilka uses the insights of Freudian psychology to pursue his inquiry. The figure on the tower in the governess's vision "supplants another object of romantic fancy" (247). As the governess sees this figure it is the "sex-ghost." "Edmund Wilson," he observes, "argues that she projects her repressed sexual feeling for the master here. Robert Heilman says no: her 'feelings for the master are never repressed: they are wholly in the open and are joyously talked about.' But Wilson is right about repression, if not about projection, and Heilman is culturally off-base" (247). In other words, Spilka might be saying, one senses that while we make gains in the process of the criticism, the gains come in an imperfect progression rather than in the form of an unbroken string of great leaps forward. That is, Spilka's justification for the bald declaration that Heilman is off base culturally is precisely the useful reflection on the disjunction in Victorian society between affections and sexual expression. But he does not otherwise justify his contention. And thus, in spite of his care to avoid the errors of prior Freudians, he does not succeed in extinguishing Heilman's contention denying that the governess represses her attraction to the master. Textually, there is a reasonable case in favor of her forthrightness; and the Freudians—even the more careful ones like Spilka—seem willfully to overlook the governess's sharp criticism of the master in his neglect of the children later in the narrative. Spilka is, on the subject of other Freudians, vigilant in demanding careful use of Freud. He chastises Peter Coveney for his accusation that James exploited prurience in the tale: Spilka contends by contrast that while the tale is about the prurience of some of its characters, it does not itself exploit sensationalism.

Spilka recasts the formulation of the Freudian notions that might be used to illuminate the tale. In speaking of the apparition of the ghosts to the children, he comments on the relation of that phenomenon to infant sexuality and suggests that a legitimate empirical value for the ghosts might derive from their configuration as dream figures: "the spectacle of Freudian critics ignoring or minimizing that principle while conventional critics defend it, is bizarre enough; but then conventional critics ignore it too" (248). Heilman, he tells us, is inexact in his approach to the problems of the text; but then if Heilman is woolly, the Freudians are negligent: "they believe in Original Innocence, in adult harassment of passive or unwilling victims without positive desires.

Hence they minimize or rationalize Miles's dismissal from school, Flora's verbal horrors, and the reports of earlier evils, as childish peccadilloes" (248). They also ignore, he says, all the evidences of the fashion in which the children have indeed expressed their awareness of childhood sexuality. But Spilka's most dramatic revisionary motive is his appreciation of the plight of the governess.

That world of hothouse affections, Spilka says, is a world in which the defenses against sexuality were set up more or less consciously as a defense against the realities of the industrializing world, a world where everything became commodity. The domestic ideal was to provide a sanctuary against this new and disturbing reality. The governess serves the text as a carrier of this dream as she "proceeds to fight the invading evil in the name of hothouse purity and domestic sainthood. That she destroys the children in saving them is understandable: her con-temporaries were doing so all around her and would continue to do so for the next six decades. That James valued her saintliness and recognized the reality of what she fought, yet foresaw her inevitable failure, is a tribute to his artistic grasp of his materials" (252–53). The governess, he says, is much in error in her practice; but her intentions are of the best and are in keeping with the tenets of her society when one considers the nature of the domestic sanctuary. Thus "by turning the opposing screws of sexual horror and idolatrous virtue, [James] has poignantly revealed the moral and psychic cost of hothouse life" (253). The mechanistic process of carving the tale to fit a Freudian bed of Procrustes is the last thing the artifact needs, according to Spilka; but a flexible recognition of the conditions of human life and the dimensions of the artifact might swerve the mechanists, as Spilka is inclined to see them, from both sides of the critical wars, away from the errors of the past. His corrective that the tale's hold over its critics extends to include this sexual element hidden in its recesses suggests a more supple and more illuminating narrative than the one created by the critics who preceded him and who insisted on restricting its prospects either to the entrenched position of the Freudians or to that of the Romancers.[8]

SOME CRITICAL SOPHISTICATIONS, 1960–1970

Mrs. Grose is a villain of the deepest dye, we learn from some of the developing criticism of the tale: is the mother of the children by the master; sets out to drive the governess mad and succeeds. Douglas is Miles now grown up after some mystic survival buried so deeply in the text that we cannot find it with the unaided eye. The governess is fantasizing that she and the uncle are the parents of the two children; she herself, under certain interpretive constraints, is the ghost of Bly; the ghosts she sees are mirror images of herself. Miss Jessel is a mere anticipation of the present governess; she is a displacement of a personality that the governess cannot accept in herself she is part of a paradigm of the whole human consciousness, the female component of which is made up of Jessel-governess-Flora as whore-civilized being-ideal child. The frame tale tells us that little Henry James suffered from primal-scene trauma.[9]

One can say then, that this era in which by chance, perhaps, a number of students of the text began the move toward summary of its criticism and of the results of the criticism in an array of possible meanings, is at the same time characterized by a growing imaginative response, albeit that sometimes this response was more inventive than persuasive. There is, however, an unmistakable sense that this fiction of James, this little potboiler, as he called it himself, held something for the imagination beyond a mere item in an author's work, beyond an addition to the literature of a particular subgenre. From the very beginning it was a generator of grandiloquent emotions as its early readers enjoyed a pleasurable shudder over its horror. But even in the simplicity of first response something seems to have happened to readers that cannot be easily reconstructed from the experience recorded. Reader after reader says something to the effect that the force of the tale is not clear; that the effect of the tale is powerful but fugitive. Perhaps it is this force of what James might call the unspecified that produces the wild imaginative response emergent over the 1960s. But it also begins to lead to more and more inventive responses to the tale's possible significances, as though *The Turn of the Screw* had become a resource text in the very process of generating criticism; as though James had posed the reader a question on a series of levels that would lead to a revaluation of what the literary act contained and what the readerly or critical act might extend to become.[10]

A greater care for the details of the narrative led to an enhanced sense of its suitability for the study of a given artifact as an instrument of understanding. If Mark Spilka was perceptive in cautioning the Freudian critic against mechanizing and simplifying the complexities of psychological causality, he was also seeing in the text the abundance of its modes of presenting the minds that come under narrative notice in it and the corresponding difficulty of reducing the novella to a single "proved" meaning or basis of development. Spilka himself allows for the doubleness, or possible multipleness of the narrative in his essay;

and in fact a number of writers in the 1960s begin to notice that there is evidence not only for a "psychological" reading or an "idealized" reading but rather for two simultaneous readings of the tale, a conclusion that might seem a logical corollary to the controversy that pulls the tale in two opposite directions by opposing "proofs." The idea most frequently offered is that there are two mutually exclusive readings of the tale and these readings are both mandates of the text. Lydenberg, for instance (1957), sees the governess as an evil force not hallucinating the ghosts, but wishing for their appearance because they would justify her, and strangling the children because of her selfish love. He does acknowledge that there are circumstances under which the ghosts might be real, in which case, what she does is necessary even in the light of fatal consequences (w 288).

Lydenberg was the appointed critic when Spilka read his "How Not to Do It" paper to the conference of the Literature and Psychology Association in 1963. He points precisely to Spilka's recognition of the doubleness of the tale: "his is the first reading I recall that gives full recognition to both the sexual and religious overtones of the story" (1964). But Lydenberg particularizes: "Mr. Spilka ... by showing the way in which sexual fears are invested with religious dread in Victorian culture, has demonstrated convincingly how a Victorian governess would, in simple, sober realism, use religious terms to describe her battle against what she felt to be aggressive sexual horrors" (7). While these reflections do not bridge the gap between, say, Heilman and Wilson, they move away from the notion that there is no bridge at all between opposing perceptions of the tale. Thus, the division over the purport of the tale becomes a "false dilemma" and there is no clear evidence that all virtue is on one side of the issue and all vice on the other (7). And yet Lydenberg does not credit Spilka with having solved the tale, adding that "alternative readings we will always have with us" (7). He concludes, "Mr. Spilka has neatly shown us how *not* to turn various critical screws. But for the life of me, I can't see that he has shown us how *to* do it." Lydenberg concludes that James has caught the critics in his trap rather than the ordinary readers. In his reply, Spilka merely raises the questions that a recognition of variables seems to evoke: "How to read [the tale]? As domesticated Gothic, as unresolved dilemma rich with poignant paradox—savior and victims victimized by opposing pulls, savior as forgivably idolatrous" (34). He reaffirms his cautions against both Christian allegory and case study.

Before Lydenberg finishes his commentary on Spilka's paper and the general problems of reading *The Turn of the Screw*, he mentions that Dorothea Krook proposes the same approach to the tale but from the opposite, the religious perspective. In this sense, Krook (1962) is the first critic to pursue the idea that James's novella produces a seamless ambiguity between two absolutely opposed readings. She will propose that the complaints against the governess have at least a degree of validity; but that simultaneously, the evil in the children cannot simply be explained away. Her point is that the problem is ethical and epistemological; because the problem occupies these areas, it is ultimately moral. She attacks Heilman for ignoring the anomalies of the governess's record; she attacks Wilson for his want of restraint. But she sees that Heilman has grasped the sense of the moral problem; that Wilson has done much to discover and accent the anomalies. It is Krook who begins to wrestle with the conceptual problems of the tale, declaring that its perceptual basis is a "metaphysical disaster" (134) because of a distorted posture of reality in it. These moral (logical, ethical) problems come down to some form of "moral infirmity"—the concern that James was rediscovering in his late work (134). In her appendix on Wilson's reading of the tale, however, she categorically denies that the problem has any basis in sexuality, repressed or expressed. The problem here is definitively one of good and evil, as she says, complicated by the "co-existence of good and evil in the human soul" (379). She, too, like Lydenberg, concludes that "what neither Goddard nor Wilson on their side nor Heilman on his appear to recognise is that the text in fact—not possibly or probably but actually—yields two meanings, both equally self-consistent and self-complete" [388]. The term "ambiguous" means exactly this as applied to the tale, as Krook's students Christine Brooke-Rose and Shlomith Rimmon will try to show in a later decade.

But just as Lydenberg had predicted, alternate readings are a fixture of the critical record. A. W. Thomson in a note (1965) on hallucinations starts out by attacking Dorothea Krook. She puts too much reliance on the matters outside the text proper—the notebooks, the letters, the preface, where, since there is "nothing ... which will confirm what James's final intentions were ... Dr. Krook's reliance on them is ill-advised" (28). For Thomson, the Quint problem is paramount and the determination of the tale depends on it: "if Quint is not identified, the theory of hallucination is probably correct and ... if Quint is identified James must still be considered to have given enough evidence on both sides to leave it open" (29). The forms of apparition impress Thomson: Quint appears characteristically fully formed; Jessel is usually conjured up out of clouds. Otherwise, Quint is spontaneous and external; Jessel appears in response to some act of will on the part of the governess.

Thomson is among the earliest critics to say that Quint never appears in full form, but only from the waist up,[11] negating or secreting those parts of himself that represent the male sexuality of which the governess is so powerfully afraid (31). He concludes by declaring that the evidence for the correct reading of the tale is given by Wilson in the original "and none of his critics has really shaken his position" (33). Thomson looks at the prologue to find an equation between Douglas and Miles,[12] and declares that "the parallel is close and I see no reason for supposing that James did not intend it" (34). He finds it "fairly obvious" that the narrator of the prologue is a woman, given the degree of affinity between Douglas and this figure.[13] He sees the sequence of transmission forming an unbroken succession from male to female as from the uncle to the governess, thence to Douglas, thence to this unnamed (female) figure, who conveys it to the reader. Thus only Wilson's reading makes any sense to him. But James is a genius in his managing so that his tale supports such a variety of readings and "gain[s] from every interpretation" (35).

Thomas J. Bontly (1969), on the other hand, wants us to see the disjunct readings as levels of meaning where the governess's record is securely "crystalline," but the philosophical conclusions are much divergent from the record. These conclusions surround the problem of knowledge so that the governess exerts all her efforts to keeping the children from knowing the ghosts, and their evil. She has assumed that her exposure to corruption will make it impossible for the ghosts to corrupt the children—for Bontly, a non sequitur: "the obvious and more logical alternative ... is that the ghosts will corrupt the children *through her*" (725).[14] The governess's flaw is that she imagines depths in the children that are inconsistent with young and inexperienced minds. It is thus the governess who "invests the ghosts with sexual significance" (727). Likewise, for Bontly, it does not stand to reason that the ghosts have a true sexual interest in corrupting the children or preying on the governess on the theory of the grave as "fine and private place" (for ghosts "it is difficult to postulate sexual offences" [727]). The governess's "philosophical reading" moves toward the bifurcation of the sexual and the intellectual; she wishes to keep Miles ignorant of the nature of sex but at the same time to make him her equal in intellectual terms (731). Nonetheless in the late stages of the novella, the relationship between the governess and Miles becomes increasingly sexual in its overtones to the place where the governess translates herself into the sexual horror from which she is trying to protect the children. In this sense, Bontly concludes, through her the ghosts do indeed corrupt the children.[15]

In Bontly's terms "it is this very normality of the governess and the inevitability of her reactions which account for our deep sense of horror and tragedy in the tale. The governess truly loves the children and courageously tries to save them from a real evil, yet because her love is imperfect—because it is haunted by feelings of sexual guilt—it becomes an implement of evil, a destructive force more potent than the ghosts themselves" (733). Bontly sees, then, that the problem of the tale rests not on some terrific abnormal psychology, but on a form of the normal psychology of the narrator focused in terms parallel to Spilka's reflecting the governess's deep commitment to the domestic environment of the affections. Evil results from the human condition and is "limited and temporal" (733). The most unfortunate circumstance at Bly is the absence of masculine authority. Moreover, the children's uncle is irresponsible in his abandonment of the family—rendered his responsibility by circumstances—and the "basic human needs it was formed to serve" (734). Bontly sees in the split structure of the tale the tortured state of the governess's consciousness—and sees it as a reflection of James's own torment that he saw her so completely. But it is this power of insight that "enabled him to draw upon the deep inner anxiety of his readers," the ultimate thrust of the tale. Thus Bontly suggests that the paradigm of the tale is a reflex of its epistemology. James, that is, had no trouble in making the reader supply the dimensions of the evil in the governess's world because of the acute insight with which he penetrated the gray mass of human psychology. The result was that the ghosts in *The Turn of the Screw* remain to haunt us all (735).

Such insights into the effects of the intense enmity of conflicting earlier readings of the tale indicate the sophistication of the newer developments that accompany the deepening critical interest in the tale. Once Heilman has shown how the imagery of the tale can lead to the conclusion that the tale is a poetic flower of the Edenic order; once Alexander Jones has shown us some of the specific features of the point of view in the tale; once Spilka has begun to demand care in the application of models to the interpretation of the tale—the larger problems of technique will begin to receive some careful treatment. Jones himself had introduced us to the interesting problem of what happens to significance when, for instance, we set about impeaching Douglas as interim narrator, or for that matter, when we set about impeaching the external narrator, the one closest to us, the one who claims first person in the prologue and the one who takes credit for having put the story in our hands: "how can we be positive that Douglas is not the liar, forging a manuscript to entertain his little circle of friends; Indeed, what assurance do we have that the 'I' narrator at the beginning of the story is not deceiving the reader by fabricating both the tale of an imaginary governess and also the opening 'frame device,' with its storytellers around a Christmas fire in an old house? Once an erosion of authority begins, who can say where it must stop?" (317) That is, Jones invites us to see that all the questions in dispute seem to surround the reliability of the governess. While Jones's intention here is not to investigate the idea of an unreliable set of intermediary narrators, he at least sees the possibility of such an approach to the tale. And if we take narrative unreliability as a recurrent feature of James's art, it is at least useful to consider whether any narrator in the transmitting chain of the narrative of *The Turn of the Screw* can escape being charged with this fault.

Jones also offers an early insight into the problem of comprehensive inclusion in the tale. He argues that even James himself enters into the narrative when the external narrator employs the "I," with the effect that "No one is left on the 'outside' of the story, and the reader is made to feel that he and James are members of the circle around the fire" (w 300). One might well quarrel with Jones on the equation between the external narrator and James. If there is any merit in Thomson's notion that the external narrator is a woman, and he is by no means the only one to propose such an idea, then it is not James that we find listening so attentively to Douglas in the cozy chill of the fireside. Furthermore, there is no need that "James" be there as character in order that "everybody" be caught within the fiction, since James is even more handily a part of "everybody" than he is the figure of the external narrator intruded into the center of the fiction. Nonetheless, if we are to discover that everybody is within the fiction, we must presume that such comprehensiveness includes the critics and that this interiorization might perhaps contain a clue to the trap that James declares he has laid in writing the tale. If we wish to escape from the implications of the text, we may feel that we can do so by the happy expedient of asserting our distance from it. If it is a text that includes us unawares and unwillingly, then we are doomed to live and relive its passion endlessly as a term uncomprehended in our total gestalt. Nonetheless, we will not forget the Iron Scots Stenographer to whom James dictated the tale and who was as unmoved by it as the chair he sat in while he recorded James's dictation. Not surprisingly, we will find others later on taking up the point of the comprehensive inclusiveness in the tale and finding in it the springs of the trap that James has laid for his reader.

Donald Costello joined Jones in setting out to deal with the technique of the tale in "The Structure of *The Turn of the Screw*"

(1960). He offers a formulation that reaches into the tale and attempts to recover a mode that James used in representing its action. Thus, "scenes in which the governess represents the action usually result in horror; scenes in which the governess interprets the action usually result in mystification." There are thirteen represented scenes: the eight apparitions of the two ghosts plus the letter from the headmaster; Mrs. Grose's revelations of Quint's status and of his intimacy with Miles; Miles's request to return to school; and the final sequence with Miles in which his stealing of the letter is discovered, Miles confesses saying things to others at school, and Miles names both former servants. The purport of such a method is precisely to watch the governess produce the "dear old sacred terror" by struggling to keep "crystalline" her record of the events at Bly (313). The horror is obviously produced by the "very reality of the ghosts." The mystification is produced by a combination of the reader's wonder about the purposes of the ghosts intensified by the reader's uncertainty about the reliability of the governess.

The paradigm of narration then becomes for Costello a three-part sequence fixed in the text: first, a foretelling of the event; second, a recounting of the event; third, an interpretation of the event. Costello sees thirteen events of the novella treated in this fashion; interpretation is always subjective and "challengeable"—to use the term James adopts for the narrators of tales about the supernatural (from the preface to "The Altar of the Dead," Vol. 17, New York Edition, 314). For Costello, then, what happens in the narrative happens unimpeachably; it is the interpretation of what happens that remains in limbo: "Although there is no room to doubt the reality of the *represented* action scenes, the *interpretations* of the governess are open to question throughout. They are presented clearly as the governess' subjective interpretations of what have been given as objective facts. When the governess acts as interpreter rather than reporter the reader is able to challenge her" (321). Costello insists that the Freudians and the Faustians both miss half the tale in refusing to see the mystification that arises from the governess's explanation of events and that leads us to doubt the very facts she is reporting. Like Bontly, Costello is concerned with the tale's success in accommodating the two warring interpretive postures from the earlier critical literature. It is not that Costello finds two mutually exclusive readings of the tale, but rather two phases of narrative presentation at war with one another.

Robert Slabey (1965) comments on the recurrence of ambiguous pronouns in the course of the narrative, especially on the confusions between the use of "he" where the antecedent could be either the master of Bly or Quint. He points to Mrs. Grose's blunder over the "he" who "liked them young and pretty," having clearly in mind the dead Quint because of the past tense, but shifting to the master in the present tense to avoid the appearance of evoking or having to explain the evil presence. James's system, Slabey continues, carries out this confusion of grammatical antecedents in the governess's placing the master in focus in the first apparitional sighting on the battlements of Bly in place of Quint. At the last Slabey sees Miles dealing with difficult pronouns when he goes through the process of identifying Quint at the very end of the tale. What we are to see is that each instant has the force of associating and then dissociating Quint and the master. As Slabey says, "this equivocal association of master and servant is significant because the selfish master's negligence gave the evil Quint an opportunity to corrupt the children. The Harley-Street Uncle is by this device and through other means forcefully implicated in the guilt for the tragedy at Bly" (70). Slabey too, like some of the other critics mentioned above, draws attention to an idea that he declines to explore himself but that will be taken up by later recorders. He suggests that there is some evidence that the governess's narrative is to be taken as a fiction from her (or, we might parenthesize, from somebody's) hand.[16] As a product of such a fiction the ghosts are "true," and as a fiction the tale is "real" (72). This notion that the governess is up to nothing more than creating a playful narrative with a core of imaginative truth will exercise some critical minds in the decades following the 1960s.

John Goode (1966) in "'Character' and Henry James," wants to deal with a broad variety of issues surrounding the notion of literary character, ranging from A. C. Bradley and John Bayley on character in Shakespeare to Leavis's concept of character in the novel in *The Great Tradition* to a (then) new book on character by W. J. Harvey, *Character and the Novel*. The center of his commentary comes in his challenge to Harvey on the subject of characterization in James and especially in late problem fictions—*The Turn of the Screw, The Ambassadors*, and *The Golden Bowl*. Harvey had suggested that character is based upon an impermanent but fairly fixed set of principles; Goode contends that character is unstable in the late work of James and that James succeeds in demonstrating precisely the grounds on which character is essentially unfixable. Strether, he says, risks the loss of character in the process of the search for knowledge—the search for knowledge being the search for the self. But the process is one of immersion in which character as entity is very nearly drowned. In *The Golden Bowl*, Maggie is not heroic in her sense of love, as Bayley claims, but intent on first destroying Charlotte's personhood and then pictorializing her despair—

re-creating her as a "character" in whom Maggie finds no just claim for sympathy or guilt.

Goode thus offers an alternative approach to the governess on technical grounds—she, too, is creating personality in a clash with a reality uncomfortable to her: "The governess creates a fictional world in a highly stylised mode in order to create for herself an identity separate from the identity given her by her social role. She achieves this through a kind of knowledge that is unable to change her and thus threaten her own separateness" (73). As others have also suggested, Goode finds the governess a "do-it-yourself" novelist, but for him she is novelist in order to create a reality consistent with her own egotistical needs rather than for the sake of an illuminating art. Thus, she must "combat knowledge not with love but with symbolism," and in so doing, she becomes the "Absolute in her own creation, dispossessing Miles and Flora of any relationship which is not to her. The *object* of social knowledge attains *subjectivity* through art: this is her social revenge" (70). It is not character, in other words, that survives the creative act, but rather some form of reified symbolism in which the children become adjuncts of the governess's hunger for status and identity. Her preexisting identity is supplied only through her employment and this employment is both impersonal and depersonalizing (68).[17] Goode supposes that the governess produces the ghosts as part of her fiction and that she succeeds in triumphing over the past and spatializing it in the present. And though in such a fashion James tends to sacrifice character to symmetry, according to Goode, he does perform the function of demonstrating some of the qualities of personality (56–57), however discontinuous and disintegrative that factor might seem.

Three commentators in very close succession treat the subject of psychologically reflexive mirrors in *The Turn of the Screw*.[18] Though there is some divergence in their views, the focus on the technique of the mirror image in the tale is central to their studies. Paul Siegel (1968) tells us that James uses mirrors in the tale to reinforce the idea that Miss Jessel is merely a reflection of the governess's psychology. He sees a perfect ambivalence in the governess: she is attracted to Miss Jessel for her sexual knowledge, but is repelled by the social implications of that knowledge. Siegel exposes something that earlier critics had failed to notice: "a fact of utmost importance has been missed, the fact that in each of the four appearances of the apparitional Miss Jessel, she faithfully and unfailingly mirrors the actions of the governess herself, a shadowy portion of her personality which she does not wish to recognize" (30). Siegel is among those who claim to have secured critical rights of possession over the tale by unlocking its ultimate secrets: "That Miss Jessel acts as a shadow of the governess on each occasion in which she appears is, I submit, irrefutable proof that the hallucinationist reading of *The Turn of the Screw* is no critical aberration or irresponsible fancy, no hallucination of the critics themselves. It is a reading which the text is contrived to suggest" (30). However, Siegel reflects the growing knowledge that a collective reading of the tale is evolving in which it is less and less comfortable to claim a perfect hegemony for one or the other side of the classic discord over the tale's meaning: the force of many voices preferring a meaning opposed to the one offered here has now so efficiently penetrated the critical context that claims for the outright triumph of a particular reading have commonly given place to claims for the legitimacy of simultaneous opposed readings.

Siegel proceeds: "It is not, however, I should hasten to say, the *only* reading which it is contrived to suggest: the apparitionist reading is as valid as the hallucinationist reading" (30). He does not seek to show the reader the source of this validity, but he does propose, as others have been doing, that the tale is intentionally ambiguous. He draws attention to windows behind which are horrors, with the implication that the windows are mirrors. If the governess tells us that Miss Jessel fixes eyes upon Flora with "a fury of intention," the reader can be sure that the governess has also done so and is about to do so with more furious intention still (31). The parallel extends to the "young and pretty" attribute of both governesses, both of whom achieve a moment's interest from the master, but only one, Jessel, having the fortune to fulfill her sexual longings with Quint. Jessel is thus a mirror image because she is an object of envy; the Quint apparition appears as a projection of the governess's own yearning. She knows of Jessel's yearnings by way of her own, according to Siegel, because she is quite ready to accuse Jessel of wanting what Quint has wanted (33). Though perhaps the conclusion seems supplied rather than achieved at several points, Siegel contrives to alert the reader to the mirror image in the text and to the textual problem of recurrence—which works in mirror images and in a good many other respects.

Duncan Aswell (1968) tells his reader that the governess is herself the haunting demon at Bly, and that she will perform this role by "carrying out the functions and duties she ascribes to her supposed enemies" (49). Like Siegel, he sets out to claim critical primacy for his discovery: "No other analysis, however, has pointed out that the governess's behavior mirrors that of the ghosts, that the language she uses to describe their activity accurately fits her own gestures and intentions with respect to the children" (49). She is condemned to act out both the parts of the demonic ghosts and of the salvific angel, yielding the "irony" that she "succeeds in the first half of her evangelical errand—she leads the children to an awareness and acknowledgement of evil—but she fails in the second, the salvation of their souls" (49–50). Aswell's focus rests on the replication of the action of Quint in the governess's going out after the second sighting and taking his place, so that Mrs. Grose sees the governess in the identical position, giving the precise mirror image that Aswell wishes to talk about. Following this reflexive scene, the next several, with Miss Jessel especially, are mere confirmations that this pattern of representation by recurrence is James's method in the novella. Aswell echoes Goode in saying that the governess's purpose is to dissociate the children from any history or past not connected with herself. Like Siegel, Aswell sees in the fury of Miss Jessel's intention the fury of the governess's own. The visitations of the ghosts on the staircase and in the schoolroom "impress upon her consciousness the ghosts' relation to herself" (55), with the effect that ghosts and governess are interchangeable, mutually reflexive beings. The tale is thus an agon in which the governess struggles as she must, but coarsens along the way, leaving a "fine intellect destroyed by pride" (62). She is ultimately crippled by her "incapacity to distinguish growth from corruption"; she becomes the agent of the evil she is trying to combat (63). Aswell sees the mirror reflex as essentially an unresolved social and psychological term in the governess's portfolio that prompts her to preserve her world untouched, but that denies the very process of maturing that she herself must have gone through in order to have achieved her perceptions.

Juliet McMaster (1969) sees in a sense the same pattern of recurrence suggested by Siegel and Aswell, that is, the governess's replication of Quint's apparition outside the dining room window for the benefit, as it turns out, of Mrs. Grose. McMaster, indeed, draws her title from the governess's responsive awareness of this recurrence; once Mrs. Grose appears on the inside at the point from which the governess has just seen Quint, the latter can say: "I had the full image of a repetition of what had occurred" (k 21). Much of what she says repeats Siegel and Aswell—the governess continues to do herself what she has ascribed to the ghosts. The crucial recurrence for McMaster is the one in which Flora sees the governess as the governess has seen Miss Jessel, standing on the shore of the lake. McMaster perceives that the governess's experience is one in which she discovers in herself the mirror image of the ghosts. Like both Siegel and Aswell before her, McMaster presses the problem of windows as possible mirrors at dusk casting back at her a reflection of herself (379). But McMaster enlists

Douglas and the frame narrative as support for her discovery in the sense that he has not recorded her narrative, but rather has taken it to heart (380). And this mirror image as textual image presents the reader with a choice—either to take the governess as valid and see the ghosts through the windows with her, or to take her as obsessed and to see the ghosts as creatures merely reflected back at her through the mirror of her estranged optics. Thus there is no right way to read the tale, and we may either enjoy our shudder or recoil from obsessed psychology— decide for ourselves "what to take for substance and what for shadow" (382). McMaster notices the "long glasses"—the full-length mirrors of Bly, in which the governess sees her own full image for the first time in her life. Few others had taken note of the actual mirrors at Bly, but their reflecting agency is to become an enhanced value in the criticism of the next decade.

Roger Ramsay (1971) begins to work toward a summary of some the innovations that we see in *Screw* criticism over the course of the 1960s. The governess shares with Marlow of *Heart of Darkness* the problem of how to deal with truth in the shadowy world of psychological causality. But what interests Ramsay about the two fictions is the even more shadowy external narrators of both fictions, the ones who accept the responsibility for delivering the fiction/narration to the reader. McMaster has solved the problem of this external narrator by calling "him" "James" (381). And we have seen that others have begun to offer quite various identities for this shadow figure. Ramsay sees that this identification is going to be a fixture of future criticism and shows that he knows at least enough of the critical record of the tale to be able to report that "Even Wayne C. Booth, who takes *The Turn of the Screw* as a pivotal example, notorious by now, does not contend with the 'I'" (139). The significance of the external narrator, Ramsay tells us, lies in the degree of removal from the events at Bly that this figure creates for the reader. There are at least four such removes, he suggests, including the 'I,' Douglas, the governess as narrator to Douglas independently of the written narrative, and the governess as the writer of the narrative which is the parent of the document that comes into our hands. Ramsay also adds that Mrs. Grose is a narrator of the tale since it is from her only that we (and the governess) learn the details of Quint and Miss Jessel. But the novella is characterized by an "unavailable narrator," one who disappears from the text and is thus "unavailable" for narrative recapitulation at the end of the tale.

Ramsay's reading discounts Douglas as narrator. He draws attention, however, to the problems of the status of the external narrator in the tale and to the possibilities that it is this figure around whom the uncertainties of the tale swirl: "In disappearing, this 'I' is, I think, tricking the reader into an obscurity which seventy-five years of critical haggling has not cleared up; yet something may be clearer, and that is James's 'sinister' intent." Ramsay satisfies himself that there is no similarity to James in this external narrator. Nonetheless, the condition of indeterminacy of which Wayne Booth complains arises from the disappearance of the narrator of *The Turn of the Screw*, creating "the condition of infinite perspective. He is unavailable, and though the reader may wonder about the validity of what he says there is no way to find out, ever. The secrets of the governess and the 'I' are infinitely beyond reach; this is superbly bodied forth in the format" (142). Ramsay is quite alone among commentators to the end of the 1960s in seeing the problems of the novel from the perspective of its multiple narrators, in seeing that the indeterminacy, which is so problematic to its critics, lies in part in the complication of perspectives, each of which creates a further distance from the events, each of which, in setting out to clarify, potentially obscures. Ramsay argues that this narrator only increases the obscurity of the tale's environment. But the external narrator does indeed set out to clarify: it is this figure who proposes the title of the tale, which in turn comes from two of its internal frames, the prologue, where the appearance of a ghost to a child is represented as a turn of the screw; and in the tale itself, where the governess calls upon herself for a mere further "turn of the screw of ordinary human virtue" (k 80) as the source of courage necessary for ghost fighting.

In the next decade (1974) Bernadine Brown will take Siegel and Aswell to task for not carrying the mirror image far enough. Her contribution to the study will be to suggest that the larger impulse of the mirror image is contained in a sequence of couples developed in the tale. The governess herself is the repressed fantasy beloved of the master of Bly. She projects herself outward into the images of Miles and Flora, who as ideal innocents are all that she wishes for herself and the master; and to Quint and Jessel, who are a kind of reality principle of all that she wishes to avoid. In other words, the fantasy occupies three rungs: the governess and the master are the romantic rung; Quint and Jessel are the sexual rung; Miles and Flora are the idealized innocent rung. She veers away from the notion of Miles being the living original of Douglas, but importantly offers the hypothesis that he is the figure into whom the governess displaces the master. She will use the shared sartorial distinction of the two figures as her key to this identification between them. Thus, if Miles betrays his identity through the clothes of his uncle's tailor as well as through a likely physical resemblance, it is the clothes, once again, that create the symbolic tie to Quint, who does not wear his own clothes, and who is suspected of making off with the master's vests.

Brown also makes capital out of the governess's admission of being carried away in Harley Street, an experience that she expects to repeat in being introduced to Miles (80). Some of these ideas are ingenious and assist in the quest for light on the novella. Brown considers her case as proved, however, and goes on to the less profitable speculation that Miles thus becomes an "uncle-substitute" and that the bridegroom reference late in the tale evokes the "other uncle-substitute," Quint, the "guilty spectre of sexuality" (80). Like others both before and after her, Brown will take authority for this idea from James's use of the word *intercourse* as a sexual term in spite of the anachronism of the assumption.[19] She concludes that the governess destroys the uncle's mirror image, Miles, because he, along with Flora, stands in the way of her realization of the romantic dream of the uncle. At the same time she destroys Quint because she cannot face her sexuality, a part of her that he forces her to notice. Nonetheless, Brown also sees that the uncle is reprehensible for his abandonment of the establishment at Bly both before the administration of the current governess and during this time. His degree of responsibility for the events at Bly is not altogether neglected in the criticism, as I will show later in one of the longer and more fully sustained streams of critical development in the tale.

SUMMARY

Over the course of the 1960s, criticism of James's novella substantially advanced in its sophistication. In the area of narrative complexity alone the decade witnesses the movement from an understanding of the role of Douglas as a mere character reference for the governess to the point where he is implicated in the tale—as a surviving Miles; as the lover of the governess, who thus grows in our admiration; as an offset against the figure in Harley Street, who then sinks in our estimation for his failure to recognize the governess's substantial charms; as himself a transmitter of the narrative; as the playmate in one form or another of the external narrator. The decade also witnessed interest in this external narrator, who in important ways is also seen as implicated in the tale—as a sympathetic female voice in the prologue; as a foil to Douglas in his admiration for the governess; as one of the figures in the chain of transmission of the narrative; as the inventor of the tale; as the author of the title, if not of the entire tale. The increase in critical sophistication in this decade of summary and invention has fostered critical awareness of several dynamic areas of the prologue.

The major sophistication, the subject of the first section of this chapter, is the critical confrontation with the idea that there are two mandated mutually exclusive readings embedded in the tale and that the necessity for recognizing their symbiosis reflects the need to move away from the dogmatisms of the earlier critical quarrels over the novella, its author's intentions, its explicit delimited meaning. The proponents of this revisionary view seem to fall into the practice of replicating the distinguished discord over the tale, only now softening the opposition to urging a preference for one side or the other without insisting on its perfect dominance—the same distinguished discord rather muted in the brass section. It is as though this tolerance of difference of opinion will lead to a truce in the critical hostilities, a movement from heat to light with the corollary that the riddle of the tale will be solved. But into such pacific purlieus strides John Lydenberg to tell us that we will always have variant readings with us. Over the course of this decade the concession to the tale's doubleness in the criticism never gives place to a reconciliation of the oppositions of criticism. Dorothea Krook insists on the urgent split reference of the tale without for a moment surrendering the moral and ethical implications as the central ones in the tale; Mark Spilka insists on the split reference with the conviction that the sexuality of the governess's consciousness is the unpulverized concrete of its foundation.

The same basic critical approaches have taken a more sophisticated look at the governess herself, although the tendency either to blame her for the agonies of the children or to exonerate her for her heroism still survives. Charles T. Samuels (1968), for example, finds a strong analogy between the governess and Hawthorne's Giovanni of "Rappaccini's Daughter," in the sense that each figure sins against the natural order by wishing to make another human being perfect. Giovanni, in Hawthorne's terms, is incapable of love and can demand only things that stroke his ego. Similarly, to support her own ego the governess decides to make Miles and Flora into a unity of goodness instead of allowing them the human ambiguity comprised in the mixture of good and evil that is the human condition (664). For Samuels, in both tales "ordinary human virtue is insufficient and its relentless pursuit is, ironically, a vice" (666). Because in this reading the governess is radically flawed, we can use her flaw to escape the controversy over the tale without having to judge the governess. Muriel Shine, on the other hand, is among the first of the critics who can find some excuse for the governess's behavior in the fact that she is herself "a notable, if heightened, portrait of an adolescent" (1968–69, 132). We need, she suggests, to remove the governess from the realms of major metaphysical inquiries and to take into account her "adolescent characteristics." Thus Shine sees in the governess the evidence that "emotion has engulfed cognition" (134), and she is an unreliable guide for the children in her care. Shine would agree fundamentally with Spilka that the governess has been warped by her society and that the tale is at least in part a statement of the inseparability of good and evil in the human constitution (135).

There are those as well that will begin to look carefully at the tale in generic terms as a representation of the gothic in James's work and as a ghost story pure and simple. C. B. Ives (1963) proposes that the preface raises the problem of the status of the ghosts: whereas James says there that he wants good, evil, active ghosts to raise the good old sacred terror, what he gives us instead are virtually inactive ghosts with Jessel characteristically motionless and Quint only very marginally active (186–87). George Knox (1963) declares that we need to recall the medieval concept of the incubi and succubi in regarding Quint and Jessel. His notion is that the battles in the tale surround the struggle for possession of the children, suggesting an almost supernatural role for the governess. Knox believes that James avails himself of this lore in order to include the sexual components of the struggle without having to do more than suggest sexual acts (122). Margaret Lane tells us that progress has deprived us of our capacity for awe: we can no longer respond to ghost stories because the electric light has obliterated the shadows in which ghosts have their genesis (1967, 137). Raymond Thorberg says that "great ghost stories surround the isolation of obsession" (1967, 186). The force of *The Turn of the Screw* is its use of terror breaking through our defenses "to give insight into our nakedest selves" (196). Everett Zimmerman (1970) suggests that the tale changes literary modes from the Quixotic at the opening to the Gothic in its later stages—from the comic to the fantastic. Zimmerman sees the tale moving towards a reification of the Gothic, a rendering of the problematic in art itself. Rictor Norton goes into detail in the process of declaring that the governess is a form of inquisitor who believes literally in the concept of exorcism (1971). The sophistications are both real and broad ranging.

These critical sophistications of the 1960s will be superseded in the next decade, but only because they have existed in the first place as the basis on which to build. In the years 1976–77 alone, four major contributions on the notion of the tale as an insoluble ambiguity will propel the critical context into dimensions as yet impossible to it in the 1960s. The development of the criticism, thus, will travel some distance farther in the geography of the tale and will enhance the understanding of the geography as it is discovered.

6

Main Currents in Recent *Screw* Criticism

Paul Armstrong (1988) argues for an inevitable connection between history and epistemology in the generation of interpretations of literary works; he goes on to contend for epistemological roots to the choices that we all make when we set out to interpret; and he argues against any ultimate consensus on the hermeneutic act. His text is the critical tradition of *The Turn of the Screw*. In a world where we are bound by choices and where the choices are founded on partiality of perception, we cannot demand absolutes: "In a multiple world of conflicting practices of thinking and speaking, it makes no sense to try to promulgate laws for how the mind should work, because to do so would only be to propose another manner of interpreting and talking about the world, not the way to end all ways" (695). Inevitably we are condemned to an eternal round of critical ventures, none of them definitive.[1] In its recent as well as in its past critical tradition, James's tale has been solved recurrently. That the solutions often contradict each other is incidental: incontrovertible proof is the watchword. Richard Hocks and Paul Taylor, in their review of James studies for 1982 (1984, 182), sigh over so much certainty: "I suppose we had better get used to it. The chance to offer the 'definitive reading' of *The Turn of the Screw* is too attractive." Peter Beidler in his recent study (1989) of the tale in relation to psychic research contemporary with the story's publication begins with a summary of miraculous contradictory solutions for the tale's famous enigmas and concludes that "armed with certain assumptions, [the critics] can prove almost anything by a close reading of the text" (12). The path of the recent criticism is thus strewn with a sequence of proofs interspersed with a sequence of warnings in a ratio, I should think, of about ten (proofs) to one (warning). Dieter Freundlieb uses the "scandal" of the critical controversy over *The Turn of the Screw* as an occasion to decry the luxurious decadence of interpretation itself (1984). John Carlos Rowe warns against the "abuse of uncertainty" in the excessive critical reverence for James's ambiguity (1984). Students of the tale's critical tradition can hardly be unaware of the controversies surrounding it by the time of the first movement toward critical summary in the 1960s with Gerald Willen's *Casebook* (1960), Cranfill and Clark's *Anatomy* (1965), and Robert Kimbrough's Norton Critical Edition (1966), a summary that exposed what Oliver Evans (1949) had nominated "so much distinguished discord." If the record prior to the publication of the Norton Critical Edition is thus fouled in controversy and the more recent path is strewn with warnings about critical excesses, it is pertinent to ask the question whether, in spite of the warnings and the continuing contradictions, the more recent interventions have promoted progress in the interpretation of *The Turn of the Screw* or whether they have only further muddied the already murky waters. This chapter will attempt to answer that question.

Furthermore, the last twenty years have seen the development of several intensive schools of literary theory, leaning toward the human sciences. These schools are often seen operating in modes suggesting that literary matters can be solved in empirical terms—that literature can be made to surrender its secrets as Cosmos had been made to do in the great age of science. Edward Said hints at the underlying attitudes of these schools when, in a celebration of the advances to human knowledge made by the structuralists, he scorns the "appreciation that used to pass itself off as scholarship" (1972). Structuralism, Russian formalism, *Rezeptionsästhetik*, narratology, Lacanian psychoanalysis, semiology, feminist theory, Derridean philology, Marxist aesthetics—all these and more have promoted new systems for assessing language, for parsing the narrative act, for comprehending the workings of the mind, for describing culture. These new schools of theory, then, fortify the question whether recent study has been able to reduce the number of uncertainties surrounding the interpretation of James's tale. The claims to science in their various methods seem to promise a reliable system for dealing with such matters as textual ambiguity. But while there have been some sure gains, the vexed questions of the interpretation of the novella seem to persist as well.

(NOT QUITE) SEAMLESS DOUBLENESS

At roughly the midway point between Kimbrough's Norton Critical Edition of *The Turn of the Screw* and the present, a series of critical-theoretical developments suggest the powers of the new theories. Three works of virtually monographic scale appear in 1976 and 1977. Christine Brook-Rose published a series of essays in *Poetics and the Theory of Literature* (since succeeded by *Poetics Today*) under the covering title "The Squirm of the True" (1976–77), later reprinted in altered form in *The Rhetoric of the Unreal* (1981); Shlomith Rimmon published her study of ambiguity in James, including a long chapter on *The Turn of the Screw* (1977); and Shoshana Felman published her dazzling "Turning the Screw of Interpretation" in *Yale French Studies* (1977). Brook-Rose and Rimmon draw heavily on the developments from Russian formalism, citing Tvetan Todorov's *The Fantastic* (1973); Felman acknowledges Jacques Lacan. All three studies take careful note of prior commentary on the novella and work to correct error and to clarify some of the issues that had previously troubled its critics. All three writers, apparently in complete isolation from one another, reach the conclusion that *The Turn of the Screw* is irresolubly ambiguous, caught between two irreducible readings: the ghosts are real and have returned from the dead to haunt and corrupt the children; the ghosts are figments of the governess's repressed libido and represent her unassuaged sexual urgency. All three writers see the critical discord as, to some extent, repeating the process of the tale itself.

I have called Shoshana Felman's study dazzling. Insightful and provocative from start to finish, it probes the tale, the contexts of criticism generated by it, the nature of the writing act, and the theories of literature on which interpretation rests, with a focus on the perspectives of literature and the goals of psychoanalysis. But it is with respect to her treatment of the tale itself that its students owe her the greatest debt. For instance, in the extended critical development of *The Turn of the Screw* it is the prologue—the tale's frame—that waits longest for acute critical attention. Nowhere in that critical literature is the prologue so carefully and intensively treated as in Felman's "Turning the Screw." Her analysis is in fact her answer to the question implicit in the discord over the tale for the last fifty years, an answer to Mark Spilka's counterturn on the psychoanalytic interpretation (1963), in which he lashes the "Freudian" critics for being insufficiently Freudian. Felman uses the prologue as a springboard to show what a "Freudian reading" of text might be.

In Felman's reading, the imagery of the prologue amounts to a labyrinthine series of passages, chainlike in the sense of linkage, but tending toward an obscurity for all its emphasis on light. Thus the company is gathered around a fire, the seasonal setting is Christmas, celebrating birth, and the festival is only a thin disguise over the ancient ceremony invoking the return of light at the winter solstice.

Nonetheless, the theme of the prologue is death and revenance—ghostly investment. Felman focuses on the prologue's process of loss—of origins, narrators, distinctions, authorities—leading her to conclude that it repeats "the very story of psychoanalysis" (122). "The story therefore," she says, "seems to frame itself into losing not only its origin but its very title" (127). That is, the story, in requiring a prologue from Douglas to make it intelligible, loses its origin both by Douglas's account of things prior to its opening chronology, and by Douglas's projecting the story forward to the time of the setting of his reading at the fireside. It loses its title in Douglas's plea that he hasn't one.

These losses, Felman continues, result in a loss of authority to the point that the tale has "no right to *name itself*" (127).[2] The story is thus again like the narrative of the unconscious, a sequence of unknowing in a context of rising anxiety. Even more acutely, Felman suggests that the major loss disclosed by the prologue is that of the master of Bly, so that the motifs of ship, helm, helmskeeper, and the common lot of those aboard—which recur in the governess's narrative—restate the image of the labyrinth without clue:[3] "Just as the frame's content, the governess's narrative tells of the *loss of the proprietor* of the house, of the 'Master' (by virtue of which loss, the house becomes *haunted*, haunted by the usurping ghosts of its *subordinates*), so does the framing prologue convey, through the reader's (vocal) rendering of an authorship to which he has no title, the *loss of the proprietor of the narrative*" (127). Rudderless ship, haunted house, clueless labyrinth—all these are metaphors for the psyche's journey in and into the unknown. Indeed, to the voyager, the journey itself is unknown.

Reciprocally, the prologue and the narrative reflect the same states of knowing ignorance: the absent master of Bly in both the frame and in the tale evokes the absent master of the unconscious, which is "precisely authorless and ownerless" (127–28). Such reciprocation between frame and tale carries to the central subject of the whole fiction, which Felman has already shown to be the haunting, in the absence of the master, of the narrative's field of vision. As she does recurrently so well, Felman brings this paradox full circle within the frame and within the framed narrative. All depends on a sequence of letters, whose messages are essentially undisclosed.[4] The process, Felman sees as "transferral," once more linked to psychoanalytical method: the governess dies and transfers the narrative to Douglas; Douglas dies and transfers the narrative to the external narrator. Death becomes the agent of narrative transmission, she tells us (128). If the movement of the prologue, then, is from death to life—"the survival of the giver's language and the giver's own survival *in* his language"—the prologue reflects the text of the narrative in a parallel movement: the insistence on the return of the dead as motive force for the narrative (128). Her reference is of course to the ghosts of the servants who confront the governess with her own tormented voyage.

Felman's argument is far too complex to recapitulate here. The core of it, her own first cathexis, perhaps, is represented in this statement of the prologue's reflection of the narrative text. The obscurity of the prologue is reiterated in the "indecipherable letters" of the narrative (141). The ghosts fill out as negations the empty content of the letters of the text and Felman makes another substantial contribution to our understanding of the tale in her focus on the governess's first sighting of Quint: "So I saw him as I see the letters I form on this page" (k chapter 3). "*To see ghosts = to see letters*" she concludes: "But what is 'seeing letters,' if not, precisely *reading?*" The governess is reading her own story and writing a letter to Douglas. In the process she is incorporating the ghosts both as part of the letter to Douglas and as the undisclosed sum of the missing contents of the letters of her narrative (150–51). Moreover, the governess is bent on using letters to reduce her experience to "but one meaning," the meaning essential to her own canons of coherence. Felman uses this important yardstick to measure the critical tradition of the tale: "the governess's method of reading her own adventure is thus not substantially different from that of James's readers, the critics" (154–55). Her own application of the governess's reading process reflects the governess's confrontation with the unconscious, Lacan's phallic signifier, which after all stands for "the incessant sliding of signification" (172). The ambiguity of the text is thus the mirror of the unfixed nature of signification, and the critics— for instance, Edmund Wilson, who, as Felman says, forces the text to surrender its secret—stand in relation to it as the governess stands in relation to little Miles in forcing him to surrender the name of his corrupter (192).

If the text is irresolubly ambiguous because it is a text about the unconscious, the reader is trapped, in the language of James's preface, because the reader is implicated in the text and cannot situate consciousness outside it. The reader "sits at the fire with the company" and hears the tale with a thrill of recognition. The desire to master the text, in the form of a solving criticism, amounts to the desire to take the place of the absent master within it. That, says Felman, is James's trap: "It is with 'supreme authority' indeed that James, in deconstructing his own mastery, vests his reader. But isn't this gift of supreme authority bestowed upon the reader as upon the governess the very thing that will precisely drive them mad?" (206). Thus neatly does Felman summarize the distinguished discord over *The Turn of the Screw*; thus nimbly does she evoke the whole problem of interpretation in literature; thus ably does she caution both theorists of literature and practitioners of psychoanalysis. She has approached the unknowable text with admirable caution to preserve her own record against either "wild psychoanalysis" or "the madness of criticism." She has assuredly focused the important questions about the estate of criticism of the tale in the wake of the first summarizing of the 1960s. But has she herself managed to escape the trap of certainty for which she has castigated Edmund Wilson?

The other two major monographs in this vein shed some light. In dealing with the story's outcome, both Brooke-Rose and Rimmon accept Todorov's summary judgment that the story belongs to the new subgenre "the Pure Fantastic," whose morphology requires that the reader is held in perfect suspension between two opposing and mutually exclusive hypotheses to its conclusion. Rimmon says simply, "*The Turn of the Screw* is written in the pure fantastic' mode, maintaining the ambiguity to the very end" (119). Brooke-Rose says, "The hesitation of the reader... is encoded in the ambiguity of the text, and so efficiently that it has continued for three-quarters of a century, building itself up into a literary 'case'" (128–29). In a note for *The Rhetoric of the Unreal*, Brooke-Rose speaks of Felman's *"Turning the Screw of Interpretation"* as "an excellent essay," "with which I wholly concur" (1981, 319 n. 1). Nonetheless, the ultimate textual ambiguity over which the reader must hesitate between natural and supernatural causes—in Todorov and again in Rimmon and Brooke-Rose—is the death of little Miles. But if the two students of the Fantastic must suspend the cause of little Miles's death, for Felman there is no ambiguity about the event: the governess kills him. Her section on the subject is entitled "A Child Is Killed." While Felman offers some degree of hesitation over the process of Miles's dying, as "it is the governess's very 'science' that seems to kill the child" (163), and indeed, allows that the death might be accidental—"the final paragraph suggests that he is accidentally suffocated by the governess in the strength of her passionate embrace" (162)—her recurrent terms for the status of the death later in the section are "murder" and "crime."

She is still hesitating when she says (175) that James's ghost tale might be read as a detective story. She reaches a stroke of impressive critical ingenuity in her observation that "ironically enough ... not knowing what the crime really consists of, the governess-detective finally ends up *committing it herself*" (175). For this stroke enables her to align the sequences of James's tale with the dramatic issues of

Oedipus Rex, the most central literary text in the exemplary
psychoanalytic lexicon: "In James's text as well as in Sophocles's, the
self-proclaimed detective ends up discovering that he himself is the
author of the crime he is investigating: that the crime is his, that he is,
himself, the criminal he seeks" (175). It seems to me that Felman has
done as much here to "master" the text as Wilson had done before her
and that here if nowhere else in her essay, the text has been trained to
surrender exactly the right secret to exalt the ingenuity of the critic. The
respect for the possibility of error that had lent so much persuasiveness
to the exordium of her essay seems at best in abeyance when Felman
equates the governess to Oedipus. In any case all pretense to hesitation
over the outcome of the tale has vanished by the time Felman declares
that "It is not insignificant for the text's subtle entrapment of its
psychoanalytical interpretation that the governess ends up killing the
child" (193).[5]

I do not question whether the implications of Felman's homicidal
reading of the tale are present. Recurrent treatments in the critical
tradition have taken such a line. What troubles me is that in the very
process of demonstrating the inadequacies of Edmund Wilson's
Freudianism she seems to imitate what she herself calls his worst flaws.
Of Wilson she concludes, "it is precisely by proclaiming that the
governess is mad that Wilson inadvertently *imitates* the very madness
he denounces, unwittingly *participates in it*" (196). Her argument, with
respect to Wilson's failings, comes down to the conviction that while
there are textual implications that would support the diagnosis of the
governess's madness, there is no text that makes it a mandate. But her
own treatment of Miles's death shares something with Wilson: while
there are textual implications to support the governess's agency in the
death of Miles, there is, once again, no textual mandate. However self-
serving we might find the governess's final statement to be—"his little
heart, dispossessed, had stopped"—it accounts for Miles's death in
terms of the exorcism for which the governess has been working from
the moment of her conviction that it was her duty to protect the children
from the corrupting powers of the ghosts. While we may not wish to
credit the governess with the sort of powers of diagnosis that she claims
for herself, the maximum force we can bring to bear toward an
impeachment of her claim is speculative, not textual. There is no more
textual authority for the assumption that the governess has killed the
child than there is for the speculation (made by Cranfill and Clark in
The Anatomy) that she has spent the ten years between her adventure at
Bly and her becoming governess to Douglas's sister in a madhouse.
Felman's ignoring of the motif of exorcism leads me, I'm afraid, to

another cavil with her splendid essay. Two-thirds of the way through her essay, Felman returns to the prologue in an extended footnote of nearly seven hundred words. Though for all its length this footnote still seems obscure rather than lucid, one thing at least is clear: in this note Felman is chastising the text. She has been looking into the title of the tale and its two recurrences in the text, one in the prologue and one in the governess's final resolution to carry out her mission, which will require "only another turn of the screw of ordinary human virtue" (k 80; Felman 1977, 182–83). The footnote focuses the phrase's use in the prologue and concludes that "the expression 'to give a turn of the screw' is not mathematizable." One of the unnamed hearers of the prologue has answered Douglas's question "'If the child *gives the effect of another turn of the screw*, what do you say to *two* children'" (k 1; Felman 1977, 182) by declaring that "'they give *two turns*.'" Now she declares (n. 183), "The listener's interpretation (2 children = 2 turns) is thus a reading-mistake, an error of interpretation. The error lies in taking rhetoric as such (the rhetorical question as well as the rhetorical outbidding) *literally*." Though Felman concedes that the two turns "curiously" reflect the text, she insists that Douglas's listener has made a "reading-mistake." I'm not certain what Felman's quarrel with the rhetoric amounts to. But it seems likely that the hearer has first answered in the vein that Douglas's question evokes, and second in terms that suggest that he or she unhesitatingly takes the screw referred to as the thumbscrew, the Inquisitorial mechanism of exorcistic torture. Whether such an assumption on the part of the hearer conflicts with the rhetoric of Douglas's question or not, I leave to Felman's enigmatic footnote to decide. But surely to the sufferer under the operation of the thumbscrew, its turns are mathematizable: the more turns, the more exquisite the torture, and the more likely the result in a confession that would be taken by the Inquisitor for exorcism of the possessing demon.

It is a curiosity of the criticism of *The Turn of the Screw* that little notice has been taken of the title's meaning or significance. We seem to have assumed that we all understand the title and that it requires no explication. Felman, on evidence such as Flora's applying a stick to a board as a mast for a boat, seems to be assuming that the title refers to a wood screw. So far as I can make out from her note, it is on this basis that she argues that "to give a turn of the screw is not mathematizable," though in my own days of playing with wood and wood screws, I would have felt baffled if somebody had told me that I could not count the number of turns it took to set a screw. While again there is explicit evidence to support this value for the title, there is also compelling evidence at least to support if not mandate the alternative reading of the turned screw as the engine of torture. Leon Edel, in the fourth volume of his biography of James, makes this assumption without qualification (1969. 207). Of course if one is to respect the Todorov thesis of perfect ambiguity, one must credit the images of the wood screw; nonetheless, the unfolding of both the tale and the prologue gives force to the Inquisitorial reading. But Edel is not alone in regarding the title as a reference to medieval torture.

In Rictor Norton's article (1971) treating the unity of opposites in the tale, the title occurs not only as a reference to torture, but as a detailed reference to the very exacting mathematics of medieval torture for the sake of dispossessing demons. The article was published in *American Imago*, the American journal for psychoanalytical research. Norton sees the torture mechanism as associated with the word *revolution* which occurs in chapter 4 and again in chapter 13. He sees the Inquiry into the case of Miles and Flora as taking place in three stages after the fashion of the Inquisition: display of the torture instruments to the prospective penitents (to chap. 4); the *Question Definitif*, in which the governess applies the lighter and less devastating of the machines (to chap. 13); and the *Question Extraordinaire*, in which she applies the most profound of the devices of torture (to the end of the narrative). The *Question Definitif*, according to Norton, is for whom did Quint come? The *Question Extraordinaire* is how much does Miles know? Norton sees Miles as surrendering the answers under the pressures applied: Quint has come for Miles; Miles knows everything.

The question here is not whether Rictor Norton has offered the definitive explication of the title, but whether his contribution to our knowledge of *The Turn of the Screw* should form a legitimate part of the critical record of the tale. Given the disposition of critics to quarrel over the text, to appropriate it to specific uses, I suspect that there are those who would be prepared to dispute his conclusions. But he has based his study on the text, showing images of light pressure to chapter 4, of acute pressure to chapter 13, and of splitting and rending to the end of the tale as linguistic support for the employment of devices of torture implicit in the title and in the governess's agon. He has made a powerful case for regarding the title in quantitative terms or, alternately, for supporting the hearer's answer to Douglas that two children give two turns to the screw. It appears to me, quite simply, that Felman has erred in attacking the text when it reports an answer to a question that seems both to fit the question asked and to fit the implications of the title of the tale.[6]

"Turning the Screw of Interpretation" is only one of hundreds of texts in criticism of James's novella since the era of summary in the

1960s.[7] If I have spent so much time on it, I have done so because it seems so happily to locate and focus the issues of the criticism that have arisen since Kimbrough's edition. Rimmon and Brooke-Rose deserve some comment, since they, too, have made substantial contributions to our evolving understanding of the tale. In one sense the two studies are quite different, Rimmon wishing to anatomize the subject of ambiguity with James's work as an example; Brooke-Rose wishing to explicate the act of reading based on several theoretical concepts, including that of the encoded reader in contrast with the careless critic. In another sense, the two studies converge on their use of Todorov's recognition of the subgenre of the "pure fantastic." Rimmon through her entire essay attempts to disclose the nature of ambiguity in text, using formalist techniques and an essentially descriptive method. Brooke-Rose begins with "an essay in non-methodology," attacking critics for inattention and for imposing meanings for which textual support is lacking.

With respect to her section on *The Turn of the Screw*, Rimmon reads meticulously. She uses the logician's distinction between the *aut* and the *vel* for the strong and weak oppositions between one idea and another, and she looks with care at the text to uncover the ambiguities reposing in two types of clues: first, the singly directed, which support one or the other of the opposed readings of the tale between which the reader is constrained to hesitate; and second, the doubly directed, which perform the trompe l'oeil in which ambiguity rests. The reading process, under her description, becomes a process of veering back and forth between an unqualified support for the governess's own evaluation of her experience and an ineluctable support for the position that the governess is mad. Thus, "*The Turn of the Screw* [shows ... a central permanent gap and ... mutually exclusive systems of clues designed to fill it in" (126). She concludes both that "the last scenes with Flora and Miles are ambiguous, ... and that the gap remains open" (127–28); indeed, "with *The Turn of the Screw* there is a marked increase in the complexity of the system of clues used to create and maintain the ambiguity" (166) over earlier works like "The Lesson of the Master" and "The Figure in the Carpet." She has succeeded in showing that the system of ambiguous clues in the tale is both highly sophisticated and highly ingenious. Like Felman, she hews to the text and reads both it and the prior critics salient to her study with exemplary care.

Brooke-Rose, on the other hand, is both blunt and cutting. The "non-methodology" of which she speaks is nothing short of perfect critical carelessness. Her exploration of critical inattention to detail makes yet another substantial contribution to our understanding of

James's text and its critical environment. In speaking of the "encoded reader" (1981, chap. 5), she declares, in both an extension of the reader-response theories of Iser and Jauß and an expression of doubt about their utility for criticism (chap. 2, 34–35), that certain more or less universal codes condition the reader's responses to the text of a literary work. In approaching the errant critics, she distinguishes between the encoded reader and the mistaken critic: "A preliminary distinction must be rigorously made between the reader encoded in the text ... and the specific individual reader—or more easily available—the specific readings that have been made of a text" (129). She offers lists of areas in which she has observed faulty readings of the text: a faulty sense of textual intentions, a penchant for psychoanalysis of the author, a manipulation of characters and events, and a distortion of textual significance. She gives an abundance of reading errors by way of example.

In a subsection under characters and events she speaks of "rehandling the signifier" (a translation of a term from Lacan), using as one of many examples Oliver Evans's reflections on Miles as the ideal child: "'And *somehow* "the rose flush of his innocence" is never so intense as when he is engaged in *positive evil*'" (Evans. 1949; In w [1970], 211; Brooke-Rose 1981, 134). Her complaint is that prior critics constantly reflect the governess's own movement from doubt to absolute certainty (Brooke-Rose 1981, 132) with "shifters" like *somehow* in circumstances where, according to her, "precision is required" and where the chosen shifter is offered in place of precise thought and expression (132). In addition, the critical penchant leans toward noisy certainty about matters that the text leaves unclear (133). She calls this inclination "a specific version of our general propensity to use the meaning-making machine of language to alter one meaning with a new meaning" (133). Brooke-Rose accounts in this fashion both for the controversy over *The Turn of the Screw* and for the positiveness with which mutually exclusive arguments are asserted. In the example of the brief Evans statement, Brooke-Rose is saying that his *somehow* substitutes for a careful analysis of the text that discloses the paradox of Miles's innocence and the air of evil that surrounds him; and that there is insufficient textual support for the conclusion in such emphatic form for Miles's engaging in *positive evil*. The other two essays (1981, chap. 7 and 8) on the novella, "Mirror-Structures" and "Surface Structures," represent Brooke-Rose's own alternate analysis of the text, showing in careful detail the manner in which the text is fully and seamlessly ambiguous. In the "Mirror-Structures" treatment she, like Felman, focuses on the work of Jacques Lacan, using the governess's rapture over the "long glasses," the full-length mirrors of Bly (with an appropriate bow to Juliet McMaster), in which she sees her own complete image for the first time in her life (160). It is Lacan's concept of le stade du miroir in the psychic growth of the child that Brooke-Rose applies here, emphasizing the mirror stage as the moment at which the child first confronts *le corps morcelé*—"an awareness only of separate parts of the body and never of its totality" (161).

Having declared that "the onus of proof is on the natural explanation [the neurotic hallucinatory view of the governess], for the supernatural cannot be proved" (158), Brooke-Rose now goes on to declare that "the governess's narrative is neurotic in both hypotheses" (156). In the final chapter on surface structures, she returns to the Russian formalist hypotheses associated with Vladimir Propp and Mikhail Bakhtin and incorporated into Todorov's *The Fantastic* (sjuzet as surface structure and fabula as basic structure) to indicate the formal ways in which the two opposing views of the tale function simultaneously. Here, with a care equal to that of Rimmon, she demonstrates point for point how the governess's neurosis intensifies in each reading of the tale, with a certain special emphasis on the governess's own intense movement from supposition, inference, mere vague speculation to an absolute and unchallengeable certainty of the form "'I know! I know! I know!'" (210–13). In her theoretical summary at the end of the last essay, Brooke-Rose uses the device of framing, both in the Gricean sense and in reference to the tale's prologue to suggest the devices of enclosure within which the governess's adventure is itself entrapped (224–25).[8] She confirms Rimmon's conviction of the gap that remains open (227–28).

Brooke-Rose's treatment of the tale, like those of Felman and Rimmon, is a careful and considered statement, of value both in the development of our knowledge of the tale and in the great care she takes to render theoretical concepts available to the student of textual theory. Once again, we may ask whether she escapes the traps into which she has shown others to have fallen. In a sequence on page 138, in which Brooke-Rose has been declaring that the governess does not "repress" her feeling for the absent master of Bly, "nor … does she elaborate it in terms of hopelessness or social impossibility" (138), she says: "In this connection it is interesting to note that James carefully places his narrative (written in 1897) fifty years back, 1847 being the date of *Jane Eyre*, in which a governess does marry her employer." Does James thus carefully date the governess's narrative to that explicit year?[9] Many of the writers on *The Turn of the Screw* have joined Brooke-Rose in saying so, both those who wish to validate the *Jane Eyre* reference and those who wish to see this "psychoanalytic narrative" taking place around the time of James's own childhood. Certainly 1847 is a possible and even an attractive dating for the action of the governess's narrative. Nonetheless, James does *not* positively place it there. He gives time spans separating the events at Bly from the first meeting between the governess and Douglas; separating this meeting from the governess's forwarding the manuscript to Douglas at her death; separating Douglas's receipt of the manuscript from Douglas's reading in the old country house at Christmas. The sum of that time lapse does indeed seem to amount to fifty years (Bly + 10 = Douglas in his garden; Douglas + 20 = the governess forwarding the manuscript; forwarding + 20 = the reading). But the frame gives no time lapse between Douglas's reading and his forwarding the manuscript to the external narrator, and between that narrator's receipt of the manuscript and the transcribing of the manuscript for publication, events that are said to have happened, but which are not restricted to any precise timing. Though we might well declare that fifty years elapses between the events at Bly and the reading by Douglas, we are not given text to restrict the total elapse of time. We are thus as easily authorized to date the setting of the Bly adventure in 1816, coeval with the publication of Mary Shelley's *Frankenstein* (of which it enunciates at least a few echoes), as we are to set it in 1847. Brooke-Rose has been as inattentive to the given text in this instance as she has shown prior critics to be in many others.[10]

Yet again, in her long and careful sequence on the effect of the images of mirrors and framing, Brooke-Rose declares: "For Mrs. Grose is not merely the commonsense foil to the governess that she is always presented as, she is also the governess's mirror, her transfer even, in the psychoanalytical sense that every event is elaborated with her, and that the governess absolutely needs to convince her" (169). Perhaps there is mere carelessness here, because Brooke-Rose has already shown an exception to her general rule disallowing any validity to extratextual reading in her displeasure with C. Knight Aldrich's presentation of Mrs. Grose as the villain of the piece. She had easily at her command the splendid spoof on *Turn of the Screw* criticism in Eric Solomon's essay (included in Kimbrough, which she uses for textual reference), where Sherlock Holmes is put to work to solve the "mystery" at Bly and Conan Doyle's detective comes up with Mrs. Grose as the "villain" because she is the least likely character to have done "it." Mrs. Grose is, indeed, quite variously treated in the criticism, from those who like Demuth treat her as coarse, gross—even grotesque—and Heilman (1949), who sees her as phonically represented—dull witted and conventional—to those who see her sympathetically as the figure that

Brooke-Rose presents here. Nonetheless, in 1974, Arthur Boardman published a reasoned argument that Mrs. Grose "reads" *The Turn of the Screw*, that is, though she has no letters, she has an authoritative and compassionate view of the matters at Bly. Citing Booth ([1961], 1983) and Vaid (1964), Boardman suggests that Mrs. Grose is a "disguised" narrator of the tale. She is a primary "narrator" in this sense, since long before the writing of the narrative, the governess tries all her experiences out on Mrs. Grose: "Thus she is 'first' in that the governess constantly confides in her, and she is a 'reader' in that like us she knows—i.e., we are to imagine her as knowing—only what the governess tells her about what the governess experiences. Further, she is an informed 'reader,' for she knows the characters in the governess's narrative first-hand, both the quick and the dead. And she is a critical 'reader,' for she continually tests the governess's story. As a first 'reader,' she indicates how we, James's audience, must take the governess's tale, and her final judgment of it, coming just before her removal, shows that the story must be taken as true and the governess as seeing apparitions" (621). Boardman concludes by declaring that Mrs. Grose is also a judicious reader, since she constantly refers to the evidence of her own experiences for confirmation of her "reading," rejecting the governess's claim of the presence of Miss Jessel's ghost in the fourth Jessel apparition and accepting the corruption of Flora when she hears the horrors emanating from the child after the fourth Jessel apparition, and declares her "'I believe'" to the governess (k 78; Boardman. 1974, 632–33). While Boardman may say exceptionable things in his analysis of Mrs. Grose, he has treated her character in a manner far different from Heilman's dull-witted commoner and as an intelligence far outreaching Brooke-Rose's commonplace foil. In short, he has anticipated Brooke-Rose in declaring Mrs. Grose to be the sounding board for the governess's own "reading" of her experience.

My inquiry here is not as to whether Brooke-Rose has been attentive to the text, but whether she has been attentive to the criticism in her statement about how Mrs. Grose is "always" presented. It is important to observe that Boardman's essay appeared in 1974 and that Brooke-Rose's essay on the long glasses appeared in 1977; that all scholars are susceptible to missing crucial observations on their subject close to the time of publication of their essays. But *The Rhetoric of the Unreal*, from which I have quoted the comment on Mrs. Grose, appears in 1981, seven years after Boardman's article, and the excuse of proximity to publication falls away for her book. In one sense, this *always* may seem a small point to belabor at such length. In another sense, it is the symptom of a perplexity about the criticism of *The Turn of the Screw.* For Brooke-Rose herself, like so many of the students of the tale, speaks confidently of "consulting the criticism." Much too frequently, this all-enfolding blanket covers only the criticism reprinted in Willen and Kimbrough. For better or worse, these two volumes fail to incorporate the critical tradition of the tale. The three writers are brilliant; they are not conclusively error free.

SOCIAL CONSCIOUSNESS

Brooke-Rose begins her study with a prudential obiter dictum: "And of course, the current interpretation of absolute ambiguity, which I accept, may one day turn out to be itself aberrant, though naturally I hope to show this is unlikely" (128). Well, but what is *The Turn of the Screw* about? For Brooke-Rose's natural hope to be redeemed, it must apparently be about a governess who, neurotic in any case, sees ghosts in one incontrovertible reading of the story and sees hallucinations in another equally incontrovertible. That is the purport of Brooke-Rose's and Rimmon's treatment of the ambiguous text, and, in a slightly variant version, of Felman's Lacanian reading. When John Carlos Rowe warns us (1984) about our tendency to abuse the concept of uncertainty, he warns us at the same time about reducing James's exquisite tale to a mere accommodation of the accumulated psychological arguments about it: "both the narrative structure and diverse critical views of this work seem to concentrate on the psychology of the Governess to the significant exclusion of the work's wider social implications" (123). In other words, he asks, as well, what the tale is about. The "wider social implications" of the tale have not been completely ignored in the criticism.

"Apparitionists" like Heilman (1947, 1948) and Dorothea Krook (1962) tried to show that the governess's narrative and its surrounding apparatus evoked the general problem of evil in the world that James records. Because they selected their evidence as "proof" of such a contention with such partial eyes, they were easy conquests for later commentators, especially the three sharp-eyed critics featured here; and in failing of absolute proof, they seem to have lost the power to enforce on their readers the conviction of a general evil in the tale. But the failure of execution does not necessarily destroy the validity of the premise that the tale is about evil. Nor does the carefully documented ambiguity of the narrative preclude meanings or significances quite at variance with the issue of the governess's neuroticism. The tale, for instance, has been read as a commentary on the issue of class distinctions in the society of its setting; and it has been recurrently read as an imaginative record of the work, contemporary with its publication, of the Society for Psychic Research.

Mark Spilka praises John Lydenberg for being "the only critic, Freudian or otherwise, to discuss the story's cultural implications" (k 249). Perhaps he could be pardoned for not knowing of others, but as I have shown above (chap. 5), Joseph Firebaugh joined Lydenberg in a very similar comment on the governess as a figure of authority. But Lydenberg was not the only important earlier critic of the cultural aspects of the tale. A number of readers from Hueffer onward had censured the master of Bly for his dereliction of duty. Leslie Fiedler wrote in the late 1950s about the importance of the child and of the abuse of the child in literature, including a discussion of Miles and Flora in the process; Albert Stone's "Henry James and the Child: *The Turn of the Screw*" (1961) has been largely and quite unjustly ignored in later criticism of the tale. Perhaps the lack of regard for this essay arises from its being anything but a close reading of the tale: it proposes, instead, to treat the tale as social history, and it focuses on the theme of the child in American literary history. Taking a hint from Leslie Fiedler's essays on the child in literature and especially from his fifth essay in the series "The Profanation of the Child" (1958) (or from *No! In Thunder* [1960], where the essays are reprinted), Stone views the theme as beginning with Hawthorne's early story "The Gentle Boy" (1832) and developing to one important climax in James's tale at the end of the century. According to Fiedler, James's tale permitted later writers to deal with the theme of the child possessed: "Ever since Henry James's *Turn of the Screw* writers have presented as objects of horror children possessed, children through whom the satanic attempts to enter the adult world. After all, 'satanic' is merely another word for the impulsive, unconscious life otherwise called innocent" (28). Fiedler says that the literary progeny of the two haunted children in the tale are legion.

Stone concludes that James is writing about dangerous innocence shared by the governess and Miles and derived from the governess's singular black-and-white version of morality as the express form of that dangerous innocence. That is, he sees the governess as shielding Miles from any knowledge of the adult sexual world, and refusing him the right to the mixed nature which is about all that human maturity can manage. Thus the story discloses not two but rather several children: "For if Miles and Flora personify childish beauty and defenselessness, the young governess is innocence itself, and even Mrs. Grose ... is essentially a childlike figure" (1–2). Notwithstanding its British setting,

Stone claims the tale for American literature and places it in a tradition shared by "three recognizable juvenile roles: the precocious infant (Hawthorne's Pearl or Holmes's Elsie), the bad boy (Aldrich's Tom Bailey, Tom Sawyer) and the virginal maiden (Phoebe Pyncheon or Crane's Maggie)" (2).

To Stone the story is at the very least about the evil that seems to pervade James's world in the late fiction. He does not exclude the concerns of those who argue the psychology of the adults in the tale, but he focuses on the problem of innocence and evil. We must, he tells us, accept the governess's word, but we must not allow ourselves to be restricted to her field of vision, for we find "the sense of evil pervading everything. Corruption is clearly in the ghosts and may have infected Flora and Miles, but there are other and more subtle forms of iniquity abroad. Evil has tainted the thoughts and actions of the children's companion and even the good housekeeper. It also exists in the world beyond Bly. The master in Harley Street bears a share of the general evil which the young lady finds in the ghosts" (5). Indeed, the master, according to Stone, stands for society at large as James tended to see it in the 1890s; he stands for a general defection from responsibility and a willful abandonment of the young: "The result is a wholesale arraignment. James's rich, self-indulgent parents, too preoccupied with pleasure, social status, money or sexual intrigue to bother with their offspring, stand condemned for their abuse of innocence" (6).

The governess unquestionably has a good deal to answer for at the tale's end, according to Stone. But he sees a larger religious question in the abandonment of children: "Something is wrong with a social order ... that allows and encourages the betrayal of innocence deemed sacrosanct by its own religion" (9). If the master is the symbol for society, Bly is the symbol for social order, and "the drifting ship metaphor...reinforces the notion of the house as microcosm of a society lacking proper control and moral responsibility" (10). Thus the house itself contains a hierarchy, a significance that is too often overlooked in the treatments of the tale. For at the head of the hierarchy stand the two children, Miles and Flora—not the governess—with a clear anomaly of distorted social order implicit from the outset of the tale. Only after Miles and Flora in the hierarchy comes the gentlewoman, the governess; then a servant of status, Mrs. Grose; then the house servants; then the outdoor servants. In this hierarchical scheme, Quint manipulates the class situation "to his own licentious ends" (10). The governess properly sees Quint as the essence of social disorder; but it is a corruption that she is ill equipped to deal with: "On each count the weakness of her mere unaided innocence is implied. ... I see the governess...as a child bravely but mistakenly grappling with a problem she does not comprehend" (14). Stone anticipates Felman in seeing the parallels between the governess and Oedipus—"she is like Oedipus who will uncover every secret" (15)—but he applies the parallel suggestively rather than definitively. The governess, thus, can "perhaps unravel the Sphinx's riddle of original sin but she never arrives at Colonus" (15). The child's world—of the governess as well as of Miles and Flora—is morally unequal to the problem of confronting the requirements of the world of adult experience, as Stone suggests; but "*The Turn of the Screw*, for all its ambiguity, pays childhood the ultimate tribute of taking it with utter seriousness" (18).

Is Stone's subject—the disorder of society and the abandonment of moral responsibility—what James's tale is about? There are others besides Stone who have thought so. Within a few years of the publication of the Norton Critical Edition, Claude Tournadre was writing on the social structure of the house at Bly (1969). He objects early to the Freudian controversy over the tale because neither version takes into account the social structure of its world, "une structure sociale fortement hierarchisée" (an intensely stratified social organization) (259). As to the ghosts, he declares "La question n'est pas alors si elles existent vraiment mais quelle valeur elles ont" (The question is not so much whether they really exist but rather what value to assign them) (260). The ghosts operate within the children regardless of their existential status—that is, the original sin that the ghosts signal by their reduction to an idea. But they signal class structure as well, Miss Jessel being a lady while Quint is no gentleman. The governess and Mrs. Grose condemn her because she falls—not so much sexually as socially. The uncle, on the other hand, is the ideal aristocrat, the figure of a dream. But he has the habit of appropriating the liberty of his inferiors, paying for it only with his charm (260). Miles, then, who is dressed by his uncle's tailor, is his uncle's heir: the little gentleman who condescends to women, the little charmer. Crucially, the governess's consciousness extends the palm of royalty to Miles. Thus, like Stone, Tournadre sees Bly as a microcosm of the aristocratic world, a world that must be controlled by masters and sustained by servants. The real danger to Bly comes not from Quint, but from Miss Jessel: "Celle-ci se trouve dans la situation qu'occupe la gouvernante dans le récit et toutes deux sont liées par leur position sociale, leur beauté, leur âge et leur éducation" (We find her in the same position that the governess holds during her narrative and the two young women are linked by their social status, their beauty, their age and their breeding) (262). The governess is the only figure at Bly who can comprehend Miss Jessel, and her recoil against Jessel is like Spencer Brydon's recoil against the ghost of the figure that he might have become had he stayed at home to pursue the dollar. Miss Jessel is the "double noir" (malign alter ego) (263) of the governess, representing the challenge to join the Quint-Jessel revolution or to resist by protecting the existing hierarchy. Tournadre declares that she is already of the master's party: "elle deviendra la protectrice et la sauvegarde d'un ordre sociale dont elle est la première victime" (she will become the protector and the safeguard of a social order of which she is the foremost victim) (266). But the heroism of this role already justifies her in her own mind, and the children are to be saved socially as well as religiously. That the failure to uphold her trust will result in the collapse of the social order is attested in the laideur (ugliness) of Flora when she turns on the governess—an ugliness of language as well as of countenance that transforms the aristocrat into a girl of the streets (268). But if Flora is lost, Miles is saved, at least from the Quint revolution, though at the cost of his life. Douglas's portrait of the governess, Tournadre claims, shows that the governess does not rise socially: but neither does she fall into the leveling movement of Quint. This social question, then, occurs at the point of convergence of the two more familiar contending positions with respect to the tale.

Elliot Schrero, whose work on James is characteristically painstaking and thoroughly researched also looks at the social setting of the tale (1981). He takes a careful and not simplistic look at the critical record of the tale; and he also offers a careful passage through the social history of the governess. His notion is that "specific cultural allegiances controlled the play of textual meaning" in the composition of the tale (261). His essay recovers the literature of servants and corruption in nineteenth-century England (with strong reflections of the same conditions in the United States). After a survey of earlier views, including those of Maria Edgeworth and Anne Brontë, Schrero remarks that "distrust of servants rose sharply in the late 1880s and 1890s—so much, in fact, as to become a notorious topic for the reviews read in cultivated households. The author of one uncomplimentary notice, 'himself a butler' concluded that 'servants' reputation for meanness and general depravity is abundantly supported.'" The problem developed from the passion for social engagements, the butler concluded (265). Schrero finds that it was the governess who was expected to offset the unsavory influence. While there is evidence that governesses in the real world might become sour or captious because of the pressures placed on them to uphold the Victorian ideals of behavior, Schrero finds little evidence that governesses were driven mad by their activities. And even if the pressures were appalling, the governess at Bly is not, in Schrero's view, "especially a candidate for madness." Her position is one of great power, she is not slighted by those who experience her power and "she enjoys the deference of all at Bly" (267). But the key question is exactly how much the governess is under the sway of the master in the unfolding of her record of the events at Bly.

Schrero finds the governess delivering her judgment of the master at four points in the story, with the effect that "with increasing emphasis, she condemns him" (269). First he sees the governess squaring her opinion that the master could not be "a trouble-loving gentleman" (chap. 6); next that "his indifference [to the conditions at Bly with Quint in charge] must have been awful" (chap. 12); next that "we were all, at Bly, sufficiently sacrificed" to the master's own desire for personal pleasure, which allows her to say, "I don't think your uncle much cares" (chap. 14); next that Miles cannot have been entirely at fault in the behavior that led to his dismissal since "'it's their uncle's fault. If he left here such people–!'" (chap. 16). Schrero argues that though we do not have vocal intonations from the governess by which to judge her, we do have "her prose style, her choices of detail, her turns of thought, and her moral judgments." Then, finally, "her handwriting implies what her vocal tone would have been; her tone implies her cultivation and her clarity and 'authority,' as James called it in his preface" (269).[11] For Schrero, too, the issue surrounding the governess is that she has been conscripted for the sole authority: "she is compelled to act as the sole representative of parental authority. If she feels that rescuing the children is her lone battle, she is only recognizing a responsibility defined by Victorian culture and thrust on her by the moral abdication of her employer" (270). As to the character of life at the beastly school, Schrero uses the example of Thackeray's experience at his boarding school: "one of the first orders he received was 'Come & frig me.'"[12] Thus Schrero concludes that the two children have been exposed to the virus of precocious sexual knowledge; and that the governess is exposed to the effects of sexual knowledge in the young. But her exposure is fatal, says Schrero, because "she underestimates the effect of the evil on herself. Her zeal and her youthful vanity, and at length her desire for vindication, carry her too far, first with Flora and then, disastrously with Miles" (274). He says that she represents civilization and that there is a frightening lesson in her failure for that reason. Though he sees her largely as a victim, he cannot finally excuse her from guilt for the unhappy conclusion.

Heath Moon (1982) echoes both Tournadre and Schrero in asserting that the tale is about the governess's holding the line against leveling. He pairs the governess with the telegraphist of "In the Cage" and with

Mrs. Gracedew of *Covering End*. All three Moon sees as saviors of class status and distinctions, a subject he declares has been neglected as uncongenial to American critics. The tale is thus about the effects of allowing social responsibility to slide; it embraces "what happens in a unique world where the moral consequences of an absent master are pushed to metaphysical extremes. The master has abandoned his property, abdicated his responsibility over the most precious but inconvenient embodiment of his inheritances, the burdensome guardianship over his niece and nephew" (22). Moon sees Quint as Fagan, "another demonic character who tries to get 'hold of' another finely tuned, precocious boy fallen into his clutches from a superior rank" (25). But Quint goes beyond Fagan since the tale's "thematic logic" offers Quint as the "anti-master: first valet; then in charge at Bly; wearing his gentleman's waistcoats; then with his consort, fallen 'respectability,' getting hold of the children; finally unassailable, even seen, as a haunting ghost, insurrection achieves exponentially higher power in the supernatural" (25).

The morass at the heart of the tale is the "mutual reinforcing of social subversion and sexual corruption" (26). Moon scowls at the want of sympathy for the governess in her plight as one who sacrifices herself not to a vague religious notion but to a very intense idea of social order. Thus, according to Moon, the tale plays out "on a metaphysical stage James's anxieties over the loss of vitality and social hegemony of the English upper classes" (27). The governess is a gentlewoman, the telegraphist is a Cockney, and Mrs. Gracedew is an American. They are all, in defense of order, more highly devoted to the urgencies of the prevailing structure than the aristocrats they are protecting. Moon concludes that the middle class does not absorb a useless upper class and assume its burdens. In James's vision, as Moon sees it, when the obligations of the upper class dissolve in the general indifference to responsibility, the whole structure collapses, as does the structure of the house at Bly. *Covering End* and "In the Cage" are both comic versions of *The Turn of the Screw*. But the sense of anxiety over the loss of order prevails in all three texts.[13]

PSYCHIC RESEARCH

Is *The Turn of the Screw* an imaginative re-creation of the work of the Society for Psychic Research (SPR). Several students of the text over a long period of time have claimed so. As long ago as 1949,

Francis X. Roellinger gave the SPR reading of the tale an academic imprimatur; Roellinger in turn cited Dorothy Scarborough's *Supernatural Element in Modern English Fiction* (1917) as an original suggestion for the influence of the SPR on *The Turn of the Screw*. Roellinger contends, after looking at the preface to the New York Edition, that James eschews the incredible ghosts of sensational fiction for the more plausible and so-called "veridical apparitions of the reports" of the SPR (k 132–42). Roellinger shows a number of coincidences scattered over the cases reported by the SPR but concludes that there is no proof that James was indebted to these reports for the material of his tale.

Ernest Tuveson (1972) takes a more strongly worded position in favor of the influence of the society. The governess, he claims, is a sensitive, a medium through which the ghosts make known their revenance (794–95).[14] Through the governess the ghosts reach the children. Tuveson suggests that the corruption of the children has already progressed somewhat before the deaths of Quint and Miss Jessel. He takes Miles's dismissal from school seriously, in contrast to the nonapparitionists, and declares that, given the social conditions of the time, the dismissal must have taken place on moral grounds. Similarly, he declares that Flora's "horrors" are the direct result of the servants' corrupting presence. Miles, in his hints at blackmail—his threats to write his uncle to describe the events at Bly to the disadvantage of the governess (790–91)—suggests further evidence of the corrupting power. In the process James uses, according to Tuveson, "just the kind of verification the SPR would require" (792) for justifying the presence and efficacy of the ghosts.

The tale, as his title indicates, is a palimpsest of James's own consciousness, whose upper layer is the work of the SPR, whose next layer is his father's "ideas," and whose deepest layer is the cornerstone of those parental ideas rooted in Swedenborg. This deepest layer is the pivot of *The Turn of the Screw*, for Swedenborg had refused the contention of the angelic in human beings. Thus when the governess sees evidence of the angelic in Miles and Flora, she is already deluded about human nature and the human proneness to evil (Tuveson quotes the elder Henry James to this effect from *The Nature of Evil*). Indeed, according to Tuveson, the governess's recognition of the "little natural man" in Miles for his lying and impudence (k 57) is strong evidence of James's awareness of his father's ideas and Swedenborg's revelation of innate depravity (798). Swedenborg's conviction that the spirits of the dead possess the living when "that person is receptive to their influence" makes an important item in the case for *The Turn of the*

Screw as a phenomenon of James's deep memory (799). These Swedenborgian observations, when engrafted to F. W. H. Myers's belief in the "possession" or "invasion" theory of the revenant spirits (795–96), make the case for the "reality" of the ghosts compelling for Tuveson. He concludes that the complex, deep-seated ideas through which James created the tale find an equivalent in all of us that "responds to the representation of such beliefs" (800).

Martha Banta's *Henry James and the Occult* (1972) takes the position that James used the work of the SPR as a tendency, as a means of exploiting current enthusiasms and thought processes, but only as a casual student of the science of extraordinary mental states. For Banta neither the underlayer of his father's ideas nor the parallel development of his brother William's ravished Henry's mind: "art gave James what he needed, and because his father's systems and the SPR's cases lacked the drama and style of art, their methods were renounced. ... James did not, however, renounce the material explored by both the systems and the cases" (46). Again, "wherever he finds amusement and interest, he makes metaphoric alliances with charlatan mediums or probing SPR men. Whenever they are merely dull, stupid, and uncomprehending of the larger realities of life, he denounces them both" (50). In other words, James is no systematic researcher in the realms of the occult; but he draws on the fund of material that the occult provides to enliven the drama of consciousness. He shows clear awareness of contemporary thought in his own ghostly tales.

In her treatment of *The Turn of the Screw*, however, Banta is perfectly certain that it is the negation of the SPR and its passive ghosts that James is pressing, for he "did not care for what the Society for Psychic Research had done to the novel and the romance" (42). For Banta, James's desideratum in the tale was that "his apparitions make good art, not the kind of authenticity the SPR formulated in its records." She relies on the prefaces for her supposition (a practice that Brooke-Rose would scowl at as extratextual). But Banta, like others before her, believes that the governess internalizes the ghosts so that the Master-Miles-Quint collective phenomenon is the ambiguous object of her desires and the Jessel-(traduced)-Flora phenomenon is the inescapable flaw in herself (122–24). The drama lies thus not in a quandary about whether the ghosts are "real" or "authentic" but in the evocation or reification of the ghosts by the governess herself: "Until she came to Bly the dead seemed not to have appeared" (126). Miles's death is the direct result of the suffocating embrace of the governess. She declares that if the artist succeeds in overcoming "'our grudge against the attempted deceit' [her reference is to Freud's *The Uncanny*], we learn,

to our terror and our delight, that we have been made children again"
(128). But what we witness in *The Turn of the Screw* as newly remade
children is our own "coming-to-awareness" reenacted, but this time as a
failure of love: "The governess ... and the ghosts at Bly work out a
pattern of sin, punishment, and self-hatred that tends to efface whatever
knowledge of self true loving might offer" (131–32). Thus, the cases
and theories of the SPR are for James only a play text, a quarry for
ideas about the idiosyncracies of personality.

    E. A. Sheppard delivered a lecture series in Auckland, New Zealand
in 1970–71 and then turned the material into a book called *Henry James
and "The Turn of the Screw"* in 1974. One rather laments Brooke-
Rose's neglect of this book in her commentary on the wide latitudes
that critics allow themselves, for Sheppard's book is a treasure house of
the extratextual and the speculative. Sheppard finds living originals at
will for the characters and place names of James's tale. Availing herself
of extravagant liberty, she makes Griffin, the teller of the ghost tale that
spurs Douglas to read the governess's narrative, into Owain ab
Gruffydd Glyn Dwr (Glendower, who "can call spirits from the vasty
deep," [31]); Bly is Blythe (29) because it becomes ironic through the
notion that Blythe implies pleasure in locus; and Ballechin (where there
was an SPR cause celèbre, and because Ballechin in Gaelic means what
Blythe does in English; 205); Douglas is not, however, as somebody has
suggested, the Scot of *Henry IV*, but is Edward White Benson, the
Archbishop of Canterbury who gave James the germ for *The Turn of the
Screw* in the first instance. She devotes a chapter to showing that the
"Real Peter Quint" is George Bernard Shaw (61); and another to
showing that the "real governess" might in spite of her clear
indebtedness to *Jane Eyre* have been Henriette Deluzy, governess-
paramour who was the incendiary in the murder of his duchess by the
Duke de Praslin, an exotic flavor further spiced by the fact that Deluzy
became Mrs. Henry Field, socialite, in the United States (104). By the
same process, Sheppard discovers that the proceedings of the SPR and
Phantasms of the Living by F. W. H. Myers and others become
definitive and unimpeachable sources for the events of *The Turn of the
Screw*.

    Sheppard's book is a leisurely and sprawling account of what
interests the author; there is a good deal of learning in it and many of
the connections that she makes are attractive speculations. But she
treats herself to extraordinary latitudes in amassing her evidence for the
importance of SPR in Henry James's creation of his ghostly tales:
"*Publications of the Society for Psychic Research* (PSPR) volume VI
had supplied a good many touches in James's fiction of 1891 and 1892"

(183); "At all events, by September of 1897, the Ballechin episode had effectively coloured James's conception of his donnée for *The Turn of the Screw*" (205); and "we have not independent links in an evidential chain, but independently corroborative sticks of evidence which massed together are unbreakable" in support of James's having read intensively volume 6 of PSPR (276). But no evidence to support any of these claims can be found in the record of James's writing. Not only does Sheppard allow herself the liberty of taking unproven assumptions as facts, but she does so in a context in which she condemns others (Cranfill and Clark, Edel, and Kimbrough) for falling into a progressive "chain of error" in *their* logic (252–53).

Nonetheless, Sheppard gives the most comprehensive survey to her own date of those cases in PSPR that might have made an impression on James during the formulation of the events of his tale and that are, in any case, the most striking as parallels for the events of the tale. Drawing liberally from volumes 3 to 10 of PSPR (for the years 1885–94) and from *Phantasms of the Living*, Sheppard documents the various cases most suggestive of James's tale, conveniently summarized in her notes (241–43). She records "impressions of luminosity," "impressions of sudden chill," the "Phantasm looking in at a closed window," the percipient (i.e., the person who perceives the ghost) at the head of a staircase "sees the phantasm on an upper landing, descending, on a lower floor"; "sees the phantasm … from the waist up"; sees that the "Phantasm of a woman is dressed in black" and sees that a "Phantasm is bareheaded." Like others in the 1970s Sheppard treats the readings of the tale as divided between two possibilities; but unlike Brooke-Rose and Rimmon, she sees the split as between F. W. H. Myers, who came later in his studies to believe that the spirits manifested themselves as emanations of the dead, and Frank Podmore, who in *Apparitions and Thought Transference* (1894) contended that all phantasms arose from living minds projecting thoughts of others, dead or alive (168, 208). She prefers Podmore's explanation of phantasms as accounting for the governess's evocations of the ghosts of Quint and Miss Jessel. She cites the governess's "unconscious clairvoyant faculty," which "shapes these impressions (whatever illicit satisfactions Quint and Miss Jessel have taught [Miles and Flora] to need) into visual images before her conscious mind has begun to take account of them" (209). It is to be inferred, then, that James had also read and digested Podmore's book as well as the thick volumes of PSPR, Myers's and the others' *Phantasms*, his brother William's outpourings on psychological subjects, and heaven knows how many other arcane works during one of the busiest times of his life, devoted not to the pursuit of deep psychological subjects, but rather to his attempts to write for the stage. Nonetheless, Sheppard's useful summary has been at least of some importance to other students of William James and the SPR in relation to Henry James's work.

After Sheppard's book interest in the relationship between the SPR and *The Turn of the Screw* declines until recently. Two studies round out the list, Karen Halttunen's "'Through the Cracked and Fragmented Self': William James and *The Turn of the Screw*" (1988) and Peter Beidler's *Ghosts, Demons and Henry James*: "*The Turn of the Screw*" *at the Turn of the Century* (1989). Halttunen is interested in looking at the relationship of William James's thought to the novella, especially at his series of lectures, *Exceptional Mental States* (1894), reconstructed from the lecture notes as a book by Eugene Taylor in 1984. The governess suffers hallucinations, Halttunen suggests, that reflect what William James called in his lectures hypnagogia, a sort of self-hypnosis coming between sleep and waking moments (474). Characteristic of such a state is, according to William James, a mind seeming to embrace "'a confederation of psychic entities,'" a dissociation from the reality configurations of waking consciousness (w. James [1894] 1984, 35; Halttunen 1989, 476). Halttunen asks whether the governess is "in possession of a 'normal' mind" (though she does not trouble to tell her reader her definition of normality); cites the governess's own confession that she is a "fluttered, anxious girl"; and rejects the notion that she is a hysteric by the terms of Freud and Breuer's *Studies on Hysteria* (1895), though acknowledging the parallels between the governess and the case of Miss Lucy R., an old bromide of the Freudian critics of the tale. One point the lectures rendered acutely was the assertion that "consciousness splits, and two halves share the field" (w. James [1894] 1984, 62; Halttunen 1989, 479). But the burden of the parallels between the governess and the material described in the lectures is contained in the fourth lecture on multiple personalities, with cases cited. It is this state that Halttunen sees in the governess, who in the final scene experiences a division of consciousness between Miles and the apparition of Quint, a division "which would have conveyed clinical meaning" to William James (480). Yet again, she is a medium and can re-create the past existence of others who occupied Bly before her through "supernormal powers of cognition" (481). But Halttunen concludes that William James's lectures do not solve simply the question of how we are to take the governess (483).

Nonetheless, Halttunen suggests, on two territories of psychic states, the brothers are likely to have shared information—on their sister Alice's hysterical lapses and on the findings of the SPR. Myers' comments on "the subliminal self," which he calls a "treasure house" from which we arise enabled to perform "supernormal feats of cognition" (484), lead to his own belief in the survival of personality after death (486). Alice James's illness presses William James to account for hysteria in "infernality," darkly suggestive of demonic possession. But Henry James, in spite of his very real concern for his sister's suffering, treats such ambiguities and implausibilities with "ironic playfulness": "the artist brother took delight ... in two perfectly acceptable and mutually exclusive readings of the same story" (487). Halttunen sees that Henry James had captured by his insoluble tale exactly the ambiguity that the "scientist despaired of explaining" (487).

If we see that so much richness of parallel development between the findings of the SPR and *The Turn of the Screw* has already been developed by Sheppard's book, why, we might ask, do we need Beidler's *Ghosts, Demons and Henry James*? Beidler's own answer comes in the form of a criticism of Sheppard's work: that it verges on the quixotic in its speculation as to sources and connections. Not only is Sheppard's evidence questionable, but her parallels are too narrowly drawn and pay too little attention to the broader range of materials that reflects the status of inquiry into percipience and psychic phenomena in James's time. Beidler does, however, accept Sheppard's evidence for the links between PSPR and *The Turn of the Screw*: "she established beyond any reasonable doubt Henry James's reliance upon the work of the men and women associated with that organization" (1989, 42). Unwilling to let the matter rest with Sheppard's book, Beidler goes about setting the record straight with a much more meticulous account of the state of ghostly narratives and a broader and more neatly docketed study of the parallels between the writers on the subject of apparitions and James's fiction. His intention is to try to re-create the cast of mind of the late nineteenth century and its knowledge of and receptivity to the phenomena of the spirit world.

After a summary of the rise of spiritualism and the founding of the SPR in chapter 1, Beidler goes on to specific cases of ghost narratives in chapter 2, pausing to summarize prior research and then proceeding with the narratives he has considered. Some of these bear marked resemblance to James's tale, notably "Miss B. and the Lady in the Tower" and "Miss Morris and the Lady in Black." But he does no better than Sheppard in proving them contributions to James's tale. His best gesture in favor of their utility to James is to urge the reader to consider them as part of a tradition on which James might have drawn (75). His third chapter draws parallels between reports of ghost sightings and James's tale. The importance of these sightings lies in the apparitions having returned from the dead, since, for Beidler's account, the crux lies in exonerating the governess from the charge of hysteria by showing her reaction to the apparitions as grounded in valid reports of the return of the dead. Cases in abundance he gives us, on every conceivable aspect of the relations between the apparitions of various psychic researchers and James's Quint and Jessel. And if he fails to prove the importance of any particular existing ghost narrative to the genesis of James's tale, he certainly establishes the context for the sightings of ghosts with enough authority to make it a commonplace of late-nineteenth-century experience. But Beidler himself cautions against taking James's ghosts as reliable re-creations of ghost narratives, for these apparitions conform to no set of prescriptions for legitimate ghosts, but rather reflect James's own artistic demands (112).

For his achievement thus far, however, the student of the tale's critical tradition is inclined to repeat Horatio's protest on hearing from Hamlet that villains are arrant knaves, for Tuveson and Sheppard between them have covered nearly as much territory and have come to similar conclusions. But in the remainder of the book, Beidler goes well beyond prior studies—to the point where he exonerates the governess not merely from the charge of hysteria but from all blame in the death of Miles, from all possible opprobrium in her attempts to exorcise from the children the ghosts of Quint and Jessel. Using the less "scientific" publications of psychic researchers, especially those of W. T. Stead, Beidler first shows the passivity of the spirit sightings of the PSPR— ghosts who only make appearances, but never do anything more than appear. But in the findings of the less skeptical researchers spirits frequently show purpose, intervening in the lives of the percipients and on occasion possessing them demonically (chaps. 4 and 5). Beidler gives us William James's account of Mrs. Leonore Piper (150–59), the medium who was host to a spirit called "Phinuit," who under the most scrupulous of tests was almost infallible in his knowledge of the details of the lives of William James's own family—knowledge of both the living and the dead. William James wrote a letter for the British SPR describing his experiments with Mrs. Piper's mediumship and declaring his entire faith in her authenticity; it was this paper that Henry James read to a gathering of SPR members in London in October of 1890. In addition Beidler gives us the case of Lurancy Vennum, a midwestern girl who was reported to have been invaded by the spirit of Mary Roff, a girl of her own community who had died some years before. William James cited this case as an attested incident of demon possession in his *Principles of Psychology* (1890). Beidler, in his application of this material to the great ghost tale, declares that the demonic behavior of both Miles and Flora is consistent with the terms of demon possession treated by William James; and that the governess's attempt to exorcise these demons is not only a tolerable response to the circumstances, but a courageous and necessary one (chap. 6).

Nonetheless, Beidler does see a flaw in the governess's approach to the exorcism: "Because she can see [the ghosts] she thinks that the only danger they present to the children is the possibility of the children's also seeing them" (216). The children's failing to see the ghosts is consistent with the findings of the researchers, since percipients like Lurancy Vennum are reported not to have seen the spirits that possessed them. Beidler suggests that the real danger to the children is demon possession, and that the governess should be addressing her attention to shielding them from this danger. Thus, far from "saving" Flora by allowing her to leave Bly with Mrs. Grose, the governess is very likely condemning her to the "object loss" of her own self-control (195). Beidler shows that Miles does not die suddenly, but rather goes through a series of stages in which the Inquisition of the governess promotes the exorcism of the possessing Quint, on whose expulsion Miles responds with a convulsion that leads to death (202–06).[15] On the subject of whether Miles is saved, Beidler is coy, suggesting that on some notions of salvation, he might well be considered as saved (206–21). He refuses to "join the chorus" of those who blame the governess for the evil happenings at Bly (217).

Beidler rereads James's peripheral comments on *The Turn of the Screw* in the light of his findings and discovers a high degree of consonance between the material he has adduced as evidence of the contemporaneity of the spirit lore and the comments that abound in notebooks, letters, and the preface to the New York edition. The tensions that prior critics have generally discovered between the comments and the tale relax in the light of Beidler's grid of information about the state of spirit manifestation; and specifically in terms of James's eschewing the passive ghosts of the SPR (k, preface, 121; Beidler 1989, 227). He makes a good case for the presence in *The Turn of the Screw* of the active and possessing spirits of the traditional ghost tale, with an especial sense of their embodiment of evil.

Beidler and those who have preceded him in the study of historical psychic research have given us a chance to construe *The Turn of the Screw* in terms other than those imposed by the followers of Todorov in the conviction of perfectly balanced insolubility between the apparitionist and nonapparitionist readings of the tale, or if one likes, to defeat Brooke-Rose's "natural hope" that her solution of the tale will never be overturned. Beidler himself is sufficiently cautious to allow the reader to see that he has not proved that Henry James read a single one of the texts adduced to support the tendency of his understanding of the tale (239). The author of his book's foreword is less so: "Beidler has settled the issue conclusively; he is the new master of Bly and its occupants" (ix). Beidler sees that the dispute will continue; and so it will. The battle to possess the tale carries far too many potential perquisites to be ended in any peaceful fashion.

READERS READING CRITICS

Much of the discussion above surrounds direct criticism of text. Even when the apparent subject is critics rather than text, the intention is to identify problems with reading the text. By the 1980s, however, interest in reading problems replaces at least some of the grappling for critical hegemony. Critics and theorists ponder the critical act and offer some alternatives to the illusion of hegemonic exegesis. James, punctually prior in all aspects of the criticism of his tale, anticipates the critics reading the critics. The psychological warfare over the tale undergoes some important adjustment with the combination of narratological and neo-Freudian revisions in the 1970s; and in turn provides the groundwork for careful reassessments of the 1980s. The movement, starting with James's own reflections on the tale, is toward a recognition of the likely critical confusion between poetic closure and critical closure, the former being a topos of the literary act, the latter being a compulsion of the reader performing critical labors. James taunts the reader of this preface with the close connection of the readerly and the critical postures.

More simply, James taunts the reader of the prefaces with all the problems of being a reader. The problems of deciphering the ghost story reflect the datum that "the critical challenge ... may take a hundred forms" (Blackmur 1934b, 257). Indeed, if one looks to James for a clue as to which of the hundred forms might best solve *The Turn of the Screw*, James is only too helpful. At one point or another he refers to the tale as "a sinister romance ... a simple tale ... an affair of terror ... a pot-boiler ... a shameless pot-boiler ... an excursion into chaos ... a bogey tale ... an inferior, a merely pictorial subject ... a cold artistic calculation ... *an amusette* ... a wanton little tale ... a fantastic fiction ... a *jeu d'esprit* ... a trap ... a very mechanical matter." He also suggests that it might be a tale depicting the tragedy of abandoning children and, by analogy to *Maisie*, a tale suggesting the close connection of bliss and bale. There is more here than the reflection that to James the tale was many things. And as critics from Edna Kenton onward have noted, one of the central of the hundred possible critical forms was the tale as a trap. An Arnoldian, James told the reader of his preface that in the world where ignorant armies clash by night and where the brave new idea is powerless to be born, those critics who, like the journalist-narrator of "The Figure in the Carpet," insisted on knowing things definitively were destined for some disappointments. James as a reader of critics knew how to signify what was beyond knowing.

After a long era of criticism in which the writers declared that they knew how to read both text and critics—with a corpse-strewn critical landscape left behind to prove it—came that window on Todorov's Fantastic with its vista of a naturalizing of opposing perspectives. Felman, Brooke-Rose, Rimmon, taking the cue from Todorov, discovered the reader's hesitation between two possible readings of the tale, incorporating the perspectives on both sides of the governess's responsibility for what happens at Bly. Freud supplies the sense of the disordered or neurotic mind; Lacan supplies the notion of the fragmented personality with its especial rooting in the *stade du miroir*—the governess before the "long glasses" of Bly; Todorov supplied the notion of an indissoluble ambiguity in the literary representation. Brooke-Rose, as we have seen, wished to believe that this incorporative view both solved the question of the ambiguity of the tale and put the controversy to rest. But once Edna Kenton recognized the centrality of the trap in the tale, the critical game amounted to avoiding the trap oneself and assuring one's readers that the opponent had fallen into it. James himself seems always to stand somewhere in the brilliant mastery that Felman accords him and to judge the results of these evasions and seductions. James might well have hugged himself like a character in a Brueghel cartoon at discovering this new trio of solution-bearers sliding after their predecessors into the trap. So in any case alleged the students of narrative in the 1980s.

Millicent Bell (1982) suggests that the attempt to wrestle with the reality of the ghosts is misplaced: that it is the governess, who is besotted by contending absolutes and their interchangeability, whose job it is to determine their reality. Our job is to see that "their irreality functions mythically, to create a profound perception about the structures of human experience" (35). The governess is driven into her own mind and into her own world, where we cannot follow her; what we can do is to appreciate the extent to which she is wrestling with the phenomena of a corrupt world where one can only make choices among evils and hope such choices are the least destructive. Bell sees the focus of that existential agony emerging in the governess's sudden moment of self-consciousness toward the end of her narrative, where she says "'for if [Miles] were innocent what then on earth was I?'" (48), so that "it is *her* innocence, finally, that may be its opposite, that is, damnation." Bruce Kawin (1982) echoes Bell's point here: "not to explain away the mystery but to share the governess' uncertainty as well as her clarity" (183).

Darrell Mansell (1985) rejects the notion that we should apply truth-value to declarations within a work of fiction; instead, matters literary may have interior extension or standing within the world of the fiction, but even this is not necessarily so. As an analogy for the ghosts he cites the figures putatively appearing on Keats's Grecian urn. Keats says that the viewer sees a sacrificial procession moving through the landscape in the third tableau of the urn, an example of interior extension. But then the poet raises the problem of the status of the putative altar to which the procession may be assumed to be moving and of the putative town from which the folk must be assumed to have departed. These last, figures postulated not to be depicted on the urn, are examples of detail that do not enjoy even inner extension on the urn, though they are given inner extension in the poem. In his reading of the critics, Mansell has seen improvement in critical comprehension over time as "extension has been taken away from more and more of the detail" (52).

Mansell concedes that the earliest readings of *The Turn of the Screw* gave the ghosts inner extension, or specification within the tale's reality, and that the ensuing reading based on Kenton's recognition of the trap had permitted inner extension but only by a character "extended in the story's inner world." He insists, however, that the remaining critical need is for "a further stage in which some of the details turn out not to have any inner extension at all but to be merely scared up into being by language defectively going about its job of meaning"—the ghosts in *The Turn of the Screw* and the town posited to be forever abandoned "on" Keats's urn (52–53). It is language that conjures up the ghosts, and when the language that does so is subtracted from the fiction, only the text is left (55). The actual subtraction leaves the qualities of flatness that suggests a two-dimensional world of the governess's imagining. Mansell accepts Felman's pronouncement that the internal landscape of the tale becomes the product of the equation between Flora's row of "*O*'s and the 'nothing' that Miles finds in the governess's unposted letter" (63). It is this movement toward unextended flatness, toward two dimensions, toward a world of ghost words creating ghost texts that characterizes the movement from the prologue to the tale and into the critical enigma that survives the reduction. Those who declare what the characters other than the governess perceive and what thus occurs in the incidental bearing of the tale are caught without possibility of escape in James's trap; those who understand that the world of her reckoning is a word world will understand that the possibility of escape from the trap proceeds solely from the comprehension of the governess's imprisonment in text.

Susan Wells (1985) finds the same sort of reduction occurring in the tale, but focuses, however, on the absent (and pervasive) master of Bly as the vitiating figure in the text, for "he is everywhere present but nowhere visible," she says, "like Flaubert's novelist as god" (82). The uncle or master in Harley Street carries the arch-theme of possession in the tale, but like the narrative itself in Mansell's analysis, this motif of possession pares the novel to a condition resembling the invisibility of the ghosts. The story is so poised on its indeterminate edges that possession is always elusive, whether we regard the children, the figures given us in the prologue, the physical presence of Bly, or the many possible configurations of the ghosts: "To consider the ghosts is to write an inventory of all the forms of possession in the story" (93). And her commentary on the process of the criticism is instructive: "So forcible is James's temptation to the interpreter tha[t] even a reader convinced of the multivalence of the story is likely to follow some association, suggestion, or echo, misled by the story's suggestion of its own awful coherence. Readers of *The Turn of the Screw* not only scare themselves; they also deceive themselves" (93). The critics deceive themselves, she suggests, because they cannot establish sufficient grasp of the whole of the story simultaneously. In other words, they set out to *possess* the story, but in failing to hold it all, they lose the compass points on its reading map. Like Mansell, Wells sees the story fulfilling itself beyond the text of its own words: "The 'tale that won't tell'—[that is, the governess's unbidden tale]—is in fact told" (94). There is no parity in the governess's world, and her tragedy is "too long a labor at making sense of senseless social arrangements" (98).

Tobin Siebers (1983, 1984) also roots his coverage in the trio of exponents of Todorov's Fantastic. Siebers, in both versions of the piece on hesitation in the tale, proclaims that the criticism of the horror tale "has itself grown to horrifying dimensions" (1983, 560; 1984, 50). He discounts Todorov's real contribution to the structuralist study of texts and proposes to use Lévi-Strauss's contrast between myth and superstition to indicate the fashion in which one can escape the Jamesian trap. The trap, he says, in a survey of prior criticism "leads the reader into false choices and the accusatory logic of superstition," the sinkhole of the critics who have pressed the criticism to its horrifying dimensions (1984, 51). Siebers warns that false choices force the reader to find evil either in the children or in the governess. Always, Siebers suggests, the choice between the two elect figures—the governess and, in essence, Miles—accepts the notion that the evil has a pertinent locus. This will to crystallize the evil results in hesitation between the children and the governess as the locus of the evil; invariably this false choice leads to the entrapment of which James warned. Refusing the logic of exclusion, refusing to hesitate over the vulnerables of the tale—or to "hesitate over hesitation," as Siebers puts it—is "to recognize the occurrence of a radical discontinuity" between the perfect logic of a rational world and the perverse logic of a merely human world and thus to allow "literature to teach...what literature is" (1983, 572).

Hetty Clews (1985) rehearses the early controversy over *Screw* from Kenton to Heilman. She disparages the wild readings of critics like Clair (1965), C. Knight Aldrich (1967), and Sheppard (1974) for their obsessive desire to solve the tale and to explain away the difficulties. Like Siebers, she is inclined to attribute the controversy over the tale to the critics' inclination to shift focus from problems of good and evil to problematic psychology (157). Like Kawin (1982) she sees the focus of the trapping gesture in the frame, remarkable for three features: (1) Douglas's claim to sole prior admission into the details of the governess's narrative; (2) "the tonal emphasis on 'seeing'"; (3) Douglas's "attestation to the authority of the governess" (158–59). The governess sees and does not invent the ghosts, Clews says, and then she mirrors them, acting "in ways calculated to inspire terror"; the evil threatening the children operates through her (162–63). Clews seems to adopt the position of some of the speakers in the 1942 radio colloquium, especially Allen Tate, in saying that the governess "has passed through a fire and emerged like Cassandra. Evil has used her, and departed from her because she was an instrument and not an agent" (165). In the process the governess exerts an extraordinary emphasis on the unstable and the unseen, "disturbing...because it involves [readers] in a struggle against rather than with the narrator; their acceptance of the narrator's authority can be accomplished only at the cost of abdicating their own responsibility as careful readers" (166). We escape the trap, she suggests, only if we are able to suspend final judgment and bring continually renewed insight to the reading of the experience that the governess describes.

Paul Armstrong (1988), as noted at the head of this chapter, saw the differences among interpreters of *The Turn of the Screw* as arising from perceptions whose epistemological assumptions operated without being disclosed. Thus he shows that the neat critical closure of an enclosed or totalizing interpretation "depends on the prior projection of a pattern which helps to generate the consistency which justifies it" (700). He uses William James's definition of "truth" as "'what it is better for us to believe,' rather than as 'the accurate representation of reality'" (700; quoted from Rorty 1979, 10). Armstrong pits Wilson against Waldock and Heilman. He rediscovers the ransoming of Wilson's theory of the governess's neurosis by John Silver, who exposed the place in the text where the governess "made sure" by some sort of excursion that Quint did not belong to the village. These conflicts exhibit the toils of undisclosed assumption, essentially here about the nature of the world, Waldock and Heilman emphasizing good and evil, Wilson and Silver abnormal psychology. Armstrong also looks at the dispute of John Carlos Rowe with Shoshana Felman: "where Felman finds in the text an absence of meaning which encourages play and resists mastery, John Carlos Rowe argues that the novella masters the reader for its own ends by playing the game of absent authority" (705). For Felman, thus, the power of the fiction is to encourage the free play of speculation about the meaning of words—those of the text as well as those of the surrounding world—while for Rowe the narrative seeks to establish control over the reader by inserting the reader into the vacuum of authority. Armstrong concludes that if we study the history of reception of the tale, we can choose more consciously the epistemological pattern that forms our hermeneutic choice in quest of what it is best to believe.

Gila Ramras-Rauch (1982) studies a number of protagonists in the novel in transition, suggesting that in the passage between modernist and postmodernist work a separate view must be established—for James's governess, for Conrad's Marlow, for Kafka's Joseph K, for Musil's man without characteristics. For such figures, she says "it is the fabula that is negligible," so that reading errors are likely to arise from attempts to make linear sense out of the story (14). In this interim fictional world the process involves a breakdown of what Ramras-Rauch calls the traditional covenant among author, protagonist, and reader, where the author assigns function, the protagonist acts out the function role, and the reader performs the hermeneutic directed by this role. In the transitional protagonist, the hermeneutic role falls to the protagonist, and the world seen is equally part of the phenomenal world and part of the interior landscape of the protagonist (15–16). For Ramras-Rauch as for Mansell, truth-value in the governess's account of her experience is irrelevant and the question of the status of the ghosts is merely strategic.

Ramras-Rauch makes a careful excursion through the critical quarrels in the tradition of *The Turn of the Screw* toward an appraisal of what the reader's remaining function is after the hermeneutic function has descended to the protagonist. She demonstrates the reading problems that arise from an insistence on reading the transitional protagonist in the same way as one had read the traditional one. Like Brooke-Rose, she resists the extratextual interpretation of the sort that Wilson had offered in the 1930s but sees that the replacement tends to be the "structural approach" of the 1960s and 1970s (93). Reality comes to be seen as more nearly elective than verifiable, and thus James's text becomes an object through which James asks questions of the reader that cannot be answered. In this wise, the tale becomes a "metaphor... for the problem of interpretation" (95). The tale establishes a sequence of watchers from exterior to interior, some of which can be probated, but some of which defy verification. Thus, the reader watches the whole, but perforce starts with the external narrator of the frame (and of the tale), who watches Douglas; Douglas watches the people around the fireplace; they watch the governess; she watches Miles; Miles may or may not watch Quint. When our gaze shifts to Miles, we see his death as "an enigma, like our own inevitable death" (95). James confronts us fictionally with the mysteries of existence.

The structuralist theorists do not solve the tale any more than do the extratextualists; but the structuralists point to some satisfactory openings, says Ramras-Rauch. As with the traditional novel, this one is a mirror, but with a difference: "We now see the parties—the protagonist/narrator and the commentator/reader—standing on opposite sides of the mirror. Whether the mirror reflects back at us or allows a degree of through-vision is left open" (105). And if the governess' own emphasis is on seeing, the ultimate concern of the fiction is hearing. Language fails. Empty dialogue is replicated in the governess's interpretations of her impressions. Her rush into speech has the effect of "concealing the silences which surround the dialogue" (107). Language fails because of the limitations in the world not in the text; "in the midst of innocence, childhood and beauty there is evil and death" (108–9). Readers want assurance, clarity, authority, above all, critical closure; but, says Ramras-Rauch, "against adult interpretation (and interference), the children are representatives of silence" (109). The way to escape the trap, then, is to see the fashion in which the narrative of this narrator-in-transition reflects the problems of seeing, hearing, and understanding the turbulent world it reflects. To escape the trap is to be in sufficient doubt, even distress, and still to maintain the capacity to avoid any irritable reaching after fact or reason.

Hans Robert Jauß had said that literary history "scarcely scratches out a living for itself in the intellectual life of our time." Histories of literature, he suggests, grace the shelves of "the educated bourgeoisie," who use them "to answer literary quiz questions" (1982b, 3). He disparages literary history on the theory that the new views of reading make most hermeneutic gestures obsolete. Wolfgang Iser, Jauß's colleague, attacks the interpretive process because it seeks to totalize and to reach exclusive, definitive conclusions, where he finds instead that the blanks in the text, subject to certain acts of coding by the author, are susceptible of being cleared by an infinite number of possible reading acts, no one preferable to another. Iser resists the notion of a "real" reader, a creature who "is evoked mainly in studies of responses, i.e., when attention is focused on the way in which a literary work has been received by a specific reading public" (1978, 28). Iser's goal seems to be to reduce all readers to a single helpless level suspended by the merciless irreducibility of the textual blank. The experienced reader of literature "remains nothing more than a cultured reader" (28) with no legitimate claims to superior knowledge, no especial skills, no communicable means to make the literary text intelligible. The world would then seem to divide into *readers* held in suspension by the monolithic impermeability of text and *reception theorists* assuring them they can know nothing of the text with certainty.

Gila Ramras-Rauch quotes Iser (1971) with apparent sanction, recapitulating his observations on indeterminacy (1982, 77) and concluding "thus, every one-sided 'interpretation' of *The Turn* will commit a species of the reductive fallacy, unjustifiably dissolving its intrinsic complexity" (78). However, she makes the important proviso that literature is undergoing "an increasing indeterminacy," proposing that there are important distinctions between degrees of indeterminacy and countering Iser's generalization that *all* texts are inherently resistant to uniform interpretation. For Ramras-Rauch, *The Turn of the Screw* holds special status among the texts in transition between modern and postmodern texts employing first-person narrators. She concludes that the governess's function is to apply pressure to the very act of interpretation. Thus though she concedes Iser the reductive fallacy, she contends against its universal application.

Darrell Mansell yields to Iser that "there is no concrete object corresponding to [the ghosts] in the real world" (Iser 1971, 7; Mansell 1985, 51). But he does not capitulate outright: "Nevertheless, even literary texts must say either that the types or objects referred to by the words exist in the extensionless, imagined inner 'world' of the text itself, or that the types do *not* exist there" (51). Mansell is bent on limiting the indeterminacy of referents because the character of the degrees of extension is more important than the broader fact of the textual blank. His demonstration uses the governess's urgent appeal— "'He [Quint's ghost] did stand there'" and says that this posits him as standing there even if the *there* has no extension in the real world, "but only in the inner extension (as it were) in the imaginary world created in the text" (51). Mansell, in support of "deficient" language that creates ex nihilo—or rather out of mere words—works to reduce the mere indeterminacy of texts by showing that determination in fiction occurs by the imaginative use of language, a process that the reader *can* follow.

Paul Armstrong cites Jauß to illustrate the importance of historical perspectives in exposing the shifting emphases on meaning: "understanding brings about a meeting of horizons of past and present in which the meanings of the past will vary according to the different presuppositions and interests which define the standpoint of the present" (1988, 694). He nods in the direction of Iser when he says "the history of *The Turn of the Screw* provides classic evidence of why the goal of achieving a single right reading is elusive and misconceived" (694). But Armstrong refuses to accept the notion that because a text is variably seen from reader to reader and from time to time, it is therefore hopelessly indeterminate and indecipherable. He also cites Dieter Freundlieb's angry rejection of criticism's claim to legitimacy based on the "scandal" of *Screw* criticism (1984, 79; Armstrong 1988, 696). Armstrong acknowledges the problems in the criticism and uses them to propose that "accurate representation is a less useful model for describing understanding than variable conversations concerned with shifting, often incommensurable problems" (696). But he goes on to say "that it also demonstrates that there are fundamental epistemological reasons for these developments and discontinuities which we cannot understand if we stop asking theoretical questions about knowledge" (696). Armstrong's conclusion that literary history properly discloses the alternatives from which readers can choose "what it is best to believe" challenges Jauß's claim that literary history is both obsolete and inutile. His support for multiple readings challenges Iser's notion that reading is at best a solipsistic exercise with slender prospects of producing illuminating interpretations.

These students of narrative/readers of critics then support the notion of the usefulness of interpretation. But for *The Turn of the Screw*, at least, they seem to have reduced the geography of possible explorations and perhaps to have taken away some of the pleasures of the hermeneutic quest. They suggest that critical closure in the sense of total solution of the problems of the literary work is beyond the scope of the hermeneutic process. We might question whether their reduction of scope leaves anything to build on. But perhaps the most we should ever have expected from hermeneutics is good pointing.

GOOD POINTING

We recall John Carlos Rowe's rather enigmatic comment on "the book's wider social implications," enigmatic because Rowe does not indicate or enumerate what these wider social implications might comprise. But it is well worth noting that some aspects of the tale still await careful consideration. What are the implications, for example, if we read the narrative not only as coeval with but also as echoing Shelley's *Frankenstein* with its modern Prometheus and its ancient and honorable tradition of creating monsters?—for there are monsters in *The Turn of the Screw* somewhere, and somebody is responsible for creating them. What are the implications of the tale if we construe it as a fiction wholly of Douglas's creation, remembering the long and hoary tradition of the "manuscript (or book) of which I hold the only extant copy" (as in Sterne's *Tristram* with his Slawkenbergius; Melville on Euroclydon in *Moby-Dick*; Hawthorne clutching Mr. Surveyor Pue's yellow parchment; not to mention the endless repetition of the motif in the Gothic tales)? What are the implications of the tale if the script is wholly the work of the external narrator, who writes *The Turn of the Screw* at least as far as the title is concerned? And what are the implications of the tale if we see the governess not as the bogey of James's bogey tale but as the victim of her society; not as the murderer of Miles but as James's Starbuck, who has to face a terrifying world with even less conviction of faith than Starbuck but with her "mere unaided virtue" equally vulnerable; not as the wholly responsible adult, but as the female child of a society that spurns the female in any executive role—the unamused queen to the contrary notwithstanding— refuses to educate her except in needlework, trains her for nothing except household management under the thumb of the paterfamilias, sits in judgment on her morals and behavior from birth—and then thrusts her into a position of total authority with no provision for support in her difficulties? There are few enough who will champion the governess on the raw ground of her courage in the face of monumental catastrophe and with no systems of support, however the story is read.

But it seems to me that in the mania to solve the text and in the restless desire to make the study of literature a science, we have risked forgetting what reading is all about. A few voices, especially from among aesthetic commentators looking at speech-act theory, have tried to recall us to our purpose in criticism. In 1977, Robert J. Matthews makes a stab at giving us such a reminder. Focusing on Mark Van Doren's 1942 radio forum on *The Turn of the Screw,* Matthews declares that there is a disparity between "describing and interpreting a work of art," a difference that is "epistemic in nature": "in order to be able to interpret an object (event) the interpreter must be in a weaker epistemic position vis à vis the interpreted object (event) that [*sic*] is required if he is able to describe the same object"; "interpretations ... are as a general rule epistemically weak ... because they are radically underdetermined by the interpreted work" (5). What Matthews was trying to do was to show that the process of interpretation demanded that the interpreted item have the fullness and completeness of an object or event in nature, something that a work of art with its selective process cannot. In this context, Matthews says, Van Doren's panelists disagreed with one member's commentary because it was an interpretation that paraded as a description. Though Matthews makes a good attempt to show the shortcomings of interpretation, he lacks some of the terms he needs to make his idea clear, and he becomes an easy target for Michael Hancher (1978) in a subsequent rejoinder, who merely declares that the "claim that 'interpretative statements in art criticism are as a general rule underdetermined and hence neither true nor false' is itself false" (485). The problem is that too many of the sorts of statements that might be made as matters of taste or preference cannot be efficiently excluded by Matthews's formula.

Marcia Eaton (1983) does it better. There has been a great deal of ancestor worship in the recent years of intense critical theory. The semiologists have revived Pierce and de Saussure; the Lacanians have offered reverence for Freud; the formalists have made their bows to Bakhtin and Propp; the reception-aestheticians have celebrated Ingarden—and so forth. But only Marcia Eaton, to my knowledge, has recalled Arnold Isenberg, who in "Critical Communication" (1949) holds the view that criticism does not argue from premises to firm conclusions, but rather "points to features of works of art" (343). Critics bedevil themselves, she declares, when they promote their observations under the cloak of logically derived conclusions, for the work of art, as Matthews tried to say, does not contain the coherence of a fully articulated world of experience. Eaton applies to the problem the language of speech-act theory: critics, in attempting to argue logically, are attempting to convert *perlocutions* (effects on an audience of various speech-acts rather than of the acts themselves) into *illocutions* (the acts of assertion, command, or interrogation on the part of a speaker) (343–44). Thus, she suggests, "the argument form ... which deals with passages in *The Turn of the Screw* can be construed as a compound illocution which has the form of an argument but the perlocutionary effect of pointing to... specific words in *The Turn of the Screw*" (344). In other words, argument form to the contrary, the true critical act is an attempt simply to interest the reader in an approach to a work of art, not to prove an hypothesis beyond a doubt or to solve the text in some definitive way. Hence Eaton's corollary: "If criticism is primarily a matter of pointing, then good criticism is good pointing" (344).

One analogy between *The Turn of the Screw* and *Jane Eyre is* seductive; we have, in the process of generating the criticism of the text, converted the slender volume into a *Bewick's British Birds,* which we can fling at one another's heads to draw blood. Perhaps it is time that we began again to regard criticism as the attempt to render light instead of an occasion for generating heat. Along the way in Brooke-Rose's preamble to her assault on the critics of James's tale, where she expresses her "natural hope" not to be superseded in her mode of interpretation of the tale, she offers an obiter dictum: "I have also to say that 'aberrant' readings are necessary, are part of this life, and that it is also thanks to them that the text lives and gives rise to greater understanding: Bacon is necessary to Shakespeare" (128). If her natural hope not to be superseded extends to this forgiving gesture, it seems that she runs little risk here, at least among the fair-minded, of disappointment.

Coda

However much I might prefer to write a conclusion to my study, I must settle for a mere tailing off: the labor that it treats is still incomplete. To this point, however, a number of things can be summed up about the critical tradition of *The Turn of the Screw*. The first readings make an important though discontinuous contribution to the understanding of the tale. James as first interpreter established the course for the problematic character of the critical tradition. The blanks of which he speaks in his preface do indeed justify the contentions of response theorists that fictive text contains indeterminate elements. The study shows some points of sharp critical concentration as a recurrent feature of the critical tradition. These critical concentrations in turn suggest some orderly progression in the genesis of the critical understanding. Competing lines of development uncover the asymmetry of the critical tradition. And a succession of bizarre occurrences renders the asymmetry of this tradition its salient feature. The whole of the critical tradition to date, however asymmetrical its development, shows a clear progressive gain in understanding, which amounts to a good deal more than mere casual adjustments of critical vocabularies and theoretical styles.

The first readings have their highest degree of focus in the fleeting but useful summary responses to them in James's preface. These become the form in which the first readings are best known to later readers and critics. Perhaps even authorial intention is involved, since it is still possible to argue that James's conception of the tale as a trap is generated in the preface for the first time, and was not in his mind in the writing of the tale—for his earliest responses to his correspondents suggest that he had no subtle motives at all in writing the tale. While he was coy on his intentions in the aftermath of publication, it is certain that he exulted in his triumph over his readers in the preface. Though James is not necessarily reliable—that is, wholly candid and wholly without irony—in writing this or any of his other prefaces, he leaves the impression that the readers' enigmas were the effects for which he had

striven in the writing, that all of it was "déjà très-joli"—well in hand—
as James himself delighted to say. In any case, it was out of the first
readings (without our knowing how many of the reviews if any he is
likely to have read)[1] that James inferred that he had set a trap in the tale
willy-nilly in which he had caught clever readers. Their baffled prayers
to him to help them to escape from it fell on deaf ears. Whatever he
may have intended, his preface has tormented the critical tradition from
then on. Other critics paid attention to first readings as well as to
James's use of them in the preface—Edna Kenton (1924), Cranfill and
Clark in the *Anatomy* (1965), Robert Kimbrough in the Norton Critical
(1966), Shoshana Felman in Turning the Screw of Interpretation (1977),
Susan Wells (1985), Allan Lloyd Smith (1993)—but James remains the
major conduit of them in the critical tradition of the tale.

Just as important as the marshaling of the first readings of the tale
in James's preface is his ambiguous declaration of the value of his
compositional blanks. This present study of the critical tradition
acknowledges its debt to the poststructuralists for their illumination of
the problems of authority of text, critical hegemony, absolute meaning.
Variant readings of a text, they show us, come from conflicting
assumptions about the appropriate ways of reading the compositional
blanks, of responding to the encoding of the text. Just as one eyesight
does not countervail another, one reading does not extinguish another.
Nonetheless, as John Carlos Rowe pointed out, there are limits to
indeterminacy. Contending readings can also be accounted for by
recognizing the different systematic assumptions from which they arise:
assumptions about the nature of art, about the nature of evidence, about
the mindset of characters within a fiction, about the logical constraints
of the world depicted. We come to understand that we can learn from
contending readings even though they contradict each other. Thus one
disputes the apparent corollary of the poststructuralists that every
reading is equally valid and is true only for the "reader" at liberty to
give perfect free rein to the dictates of the imagination. For critics there
are limits—even rules. Nothing stops a "reader" from envisioning the
faithless who desert Goldsmith's doomed village by rushing off on
trains. But the "critic" must respect time, place, and the logical
constraints of the world created within the fiction.

Moreover, the critical tradition evolves and augments from earlier
to later readings: we do learn from each other, however unwillingly.
The tradition of *The Turn of the Screw*, though discontinuous,
asymmetrical, and contentious, is exemplary in its progressive
development. Starting from the origin in the reviews, the criticism
shows the tale's evocative power, its might in making the reader feel

the evil and shudder under the horror and cower in the face of the governess's great test. These readers wanted more—and less: more of the governess, more exact specification of the evil, more of the life that followed the catastrophe at Bly; but less of the unmitigated horror, less of the discomfort of an evil that James forces the readers to supply themselves, less of the sense of manipulation at the hands of the author. One reviewer, we recall, uttered a plea for the prevention of cruelty to fictional as well as empirical children. That evocative power, and not the critical enigmas, accounts for the persistence of readerly interest in the tale and the pursuing critical interest, which is at least in part a response to the prodigious power of the tale over readers.

James, in his preface, delighted at the bewilderment of first readers, offered the most potent critique of the reading act: when the reader is forced to scare up into being the causative constraints of the created world, the author can claim clean hands, sublime innocence of what is thus created. The reader with an innocent mind, we might infer, will see nothing irremediably evil in the tale. One can posit authorial intention in the forcing of the reader's response; one can see the awful subliminal awareness of the gestation of evil in the reader's mind. Wherever else the ghosts may exist, wherever else they may achieve extension, they exist because they are created in the reader's mind. It is this that Ramras-Rauch is insisting upon when she gives the governess as a protagonist-in-transition the textual function of applying pressure to the very notion of the hermeneutic act. The reader wants the act of interpretion to create a sanctuary where consciousness can shelter from the harsh facts of an external reality. James's demand that the reader confect the specifications of the evil places the responsibility for the ghosts squarely on the reader's shoulders. Quite simply, all critics are readers first: some accept the responsibility for what they join with the author to create and speak sadly of the evil rampant in the world; others deny the responsibility and speak angrily of the evil outside themselves. Out of these opposed postures of response a critical tradition marked with contention and animus is born.

The oppositions in this critical tradition descend with modification, separately and in a fairly orderly fashion. Kenton and Wilson picked up adherents for the side that favors the tale as an excitement of abnormal psychology. At first that progression attracts exponents like John Silver (1957), who helped Wilson to restore his faith in the governess's neurotic character by reporting her assay into the village; and by Oscar Cargill (1956, 1963), who finds Freud and family at the root of James's creation of her. Mark Spilka's correction of the Freudian approach appeared in 1963. Cranfill and Clark (1965) adjoined to the chorus of detractors their demonstration of the governess's irredeemable delusion. With the emergence of critical interest in the psychoanalytic theories of Jacques Lacan came the sequence of studies of the tale from the perspective of "the French Freud." Shoshana Felman's elaboration (1977) of Spilka's critique of "wild psychoanalytic" reading of the tale, and her own ingenious reading, especially of the frame tale and of the psychology of the reading act, constitute a profound explication of the nature of the trap in which James caught his clever readers. Both Brooke-Rose (1976–77; 1981) and Rimmon (1977) join Felman in finding the governess neurotic no matter how the story is read. The neurotic reading finds a later champion in Paula Marantz Cohen (1986), who returns to Freud, this time to the analytic tale of Dora, for corroboration of the theory. The progression of the neurotic reading is orderly, though it cannot avoid contradiction within its development.

Sophistications in the comprehension occur with the profound advance in the reading of the frame tale by Felman and to some extent by Brooke-Rose and Rimmon. In turn, their reading is enhanced by their reconsideration of Juliet McMaster's study of the mirror motif in her "Full Image of a Repetition" (1969). McMaster exposes the force of the mirror image first as an effect of the tale, showing its internal reflective value, and second, as an example of reading effect. The mirror springs James's trap; it prompts readers to look for the figures of the tale that might be reflected there. Since the tradition tells us that the mirror will not reflect the image of a ghost, the readers' attempts to avoid finding their own image there amount to making themselves textual ghosts, deeply implicated in the malign ambience of the hallways at Bly. All three of Felman, Brooke-Rose. and Rimmon make use of McMaster's conclusions as tools to expose the governess's neurosis. Thus one can see not only a progression in the development of a general critical premise about *The Turn of the Screw*, but also how the idea becomes enriched by ramification through related ideas. If we add further branches, like, say, the artistic treatment of the Demuth illustrations by Pamela Allara and Barbara Haskell, both of whom accept Wilson's view of the neurotic governess, we can see that the branches continually enhance the lines of the tree. That sort of movement is characteristic of the critical tradition of *The Turn of the Screw*.

In the trial of her virtue as against her malignity, the jury of reviewers and other first readers returned a verdict for the governess. Relatively little of the mythic sense of the earthly Paradise emerges from the reviewers' presentation of the experience at Bly; the closest approach to it comes from those who see the children as sublimely beautiful and the demons as indelibly monstrous. But myth criticism had reached a high point by the late 1940s, and when Robert Heilman first attacked Wilson's representation of the governess's neurotic character (1947), it was essentially in the mythic terms of the earthly Paradise that he did so. Wilson, he suggested, failed to appreciate the ineluctable contest between good and evil in the world, especially in James's puritan version of it, and therefore Wilson wished to move the locus of the contest from the world to the particular person, from the traditional stage of the conflict between good and evil to the perverse or perverted psychology of that particular person. Heilman had been anticipated by Fagin (1941) and Waldock (1947) in quarreling with Wilson; and refocused his argument in "*The Turn of the Screw* as Poem" (1948), turning away from the attack on Wilson and deliberately emphasizing the diction in the tale that confirms the battle in Paradise. Robert Liddell joined in the attack on Wilson (1947), and a group of others joined over the course of the 1950s, concluding with the gravely illuminating article of Alexander Jones (1959) and only slightly later with James Gargano's article in 1961.

From that point on, the battle tended to rage back and forth with a growing number of opponents on both sides of the question. The first movement toward summary of the critical tradition of the tale in the 1960s showed how frayed the lines of development had become and how intensely the contentious developments illustrated the asymmetry of the tradition. The reviewers had promoted James's puritan background as a conditioning force in the story. The mythic view of the tale, using the idyllic character of Bly as its equation for Paradise and the ghosts as its equation for the serpent, proposed that James's subject was the fall from innocence with an intense accent on the abandonment of beauty in the quest for knowledge. But it was just as much James's reputed puritan background which gave aid and comfort to the adherents of the party of madness and hysteria: the puritanical was precisely the impulse that fueled the theory of neurotic sexual repression. Leslie Fiedler's "Profanation of the Child" (1989), with its applause for James's inquiry into psychology in the tale, suggests that James's great contribution to the development of ideas in fiction was his forthright representation of the "natural man" in the child Miles: what was called satanic under the puritan aegis was simply the urgent adolescent need for growth out of the nullity of nonknowledge. Dorothea Krook gave the governess a Faustian cast in 1962. And so, like the chain of studies supporting the neurotic view of the governess, the mythic also branched out and surrendered some of its purity to further insights. The interesting structuralist premise of the 1970s that the reader must hesitate between the two readings—hallucinant and revenant, both equally embedded and encoded in the text—concluded with the extension that the governess is not the saint of salvation, as she had been to Heilman and the other mythic critics, but that her narrative is "neurotic in both hypotheses" (Brooke-Rose 1981, 156).

Certain anachronisms, developmental anomalies, interesting extratextualisms enforce the asymmetry of the tale's critical tradition and crystallize the sense of the bizarre with which James invested the tale in writing it and which he reinvigorated with his preface. The anachronisms surround matters like the putative primacy of Goddard's "pre-Freudian" hallucinant reading of the tale dated around 1920 and the emergence and subsequent submergence of the Demuth paintings in the critical tradition. But there are other quite wonderful anachronisms in the tradition. In 1988, when Paul Armstrong was wrestling with the battle between an outmoded literary history and a suspect epistemology as a kind of summary of the contentious hermeneutic issues of dealing with the tale, two essays appeared, both solemnly declaring that the studies arose out of a careful consultation of the existing criticism, and both sublimely unaware of the intricate developments of the accumulating tradition—of the summaries of Willen, Cranfill and Clark, Kimbrough; of the invention of "the Fantastic" and its train of corollary readings in Brooke-Rose, Felman, and Rimmon; of the application of Lacan to the issues; of the advances of narrative theory and the treatments of the tale under the notion of the governess's unreachable character. The two essays could, with a few modifications, have been issued as reprints respectively of Wilson's argument in 1934 and of Heilman's in 1948. They represented very exactly what has annoyed readers like Susan Sonntag, Wolfgang Iser, Roland Barthes, and Dieter Freundlieb about the very claims of interpretation to add anything of use to our collective knowledge.

As Shoshana Felman suggests, readers who merely attempt to resolve the tale automatically join those around the fireplace who listen to Douglas's combination of seduction and complicity in the events at Bly. More than one critic understands that the tale was created to titillate the reader with those worst things that could be conceived of to happen to the children at Bly (Preface. k 122).[2] One important developmental anomaly in the critical history is the fading away of the mythic or Edenic reading of the character represented in Heilman's essays (1947, 1948). It survives the 1960s to some extent in recurrent studies of the beautiful garden at Bly—in Eric Vogelin's return to his mythic interpretation of the 1940s (1971),[3] in the putative suspended reading of the adherents of the genre of the Fantastic, and in an occasional essay reasonably innocent of the developing critical tradition. Yet another developmental anomaly is the surprising fact of the relative lack of rejoinder in the criticism. Vogelin returns to his former statement to revise substantially; Wilson, of course, returned again and again; there was the sharp exchange between Marius Bewley and F. R. Leavis in *Scrutiny* in the 1950s; and Millicent Bell gave her paper in 1982 and returned to rejoin in her book 1991; and a few others used essays as part of books later without much change. But for the overwhelming majority of the commentators, once was enough, and clarification or rebuttal or response to new approaches seems to have enticed very few into subsequent comments.

The reading aberrations in the extratextual sense are the most fascinating area in the asymmetry of the development of *The Turn of the Screw*. In one sense, all readings are aberrant because none can ever become the perfect reflex of the tale itself. But once the notion occurs that there is a controversial reading, the idea of controversy for its own sake begins to become a part of the critical tradition. A sequence of critics, for example, decided to award pride of place in the tale to Mrs. Grose, so that she became the focus of the tale instead of the uncle, Quint and Jessel, or Miles and Flora. Eric Solomon (1964) laughs at the controversy by making Mrs. Grose the natural villain of the tale because she is the least likely candidate for the honor. John Clair (1965) makes Mrs. Grose the deceiver who keeps from the governess that the master is the father of the children, Jessel is their insane mother, and Quint her keeper. C. Knight Aldrich (1967) declares that Mrs. Grose drives the paranoid governess mad in the process of protecting the status quo at Bly. Arthur Boardman (1974) finds Mrs. Grose a "reader" despite her illiteracy—a first reader of the experience at Bly and an accurate reporter of it, a source of succor for the embattled governess. Where Mrs. Grose is seen as the evil presence in the tale, the subtext is all villainously sexual and in some fashion points back to Kenton's and Wilson's early suggestion of the governess's hallucinations deriving from some sexual disorder. Perhaps this is the area of the most intense extratextual readings in the tradition.

The broad Freudian reading of *The Turn of the Screw* moves ever more surely toward a narrower application. Wilson was content with the general application of the theory: the governess was neurotic and repressed and much of her behavior derived from this sad disorder. As we have seen, Mark Spilka (1963) wanted the students of Freud to exert themselves more fully and to account for behavior in a more rigorous fashion than had Wilson. He wanted these critics to respect the conventions of language and behavior in the time of the action of the governess's narrative and to acknowledge the tendency of the Victorians to engage in overheated affections as a displacement for the sexual. But no matter who the critic, as long as the governess could be designated only neurotic, she was likewise merely misguided—with whatever results. Once this vision of troubled consciousness is carried to the next level—so that she becomes psychotic—the extratextual readings seem at last to reach the goal toward which they have been striving. Two strands represent the coalition: in one, psychotic, the governess is a sphinx, confronting the children with her own sexual fantasies, her own distortions of reality, her own fanatical notion of the cure for what she devises as their disease. In the enactment of her fantasy, she squeezes the life out of Miles. The sexual component of this strain of critical insight is unmistakeable.

Muriel West (1964a) is an early contributor to this hypothesis. The governess is carried away and finally handles Miles with too great force. Cranfill and Clark (1965) agree that the governess is unbalanced and that her condition contributes to Miles's death. Rictor Norton shows the governess to preside over the child's death, but as an exorcist. Byers (1971) sees the governess as an agent of the Devil, destroying the children and deceiving readers. A. E. Dyson (1972) sees the governess driven by the madness of puritanical zeal and by equally mad notions of sin and redemption in ecstasies of murderous innocence. Felman (1977), as we saw, spoke of the killing of a child. Peter Dyson, in the *Explicator* (1978), declares that she becomes the beast she has denounced, that she is "the white face of damnation" in the final scene. Clark (1978) says simply, "Then the governess squeezes him to death." Matheson (1982) agrees. Stanley Renner (1988) sees the malignity of a despicable hostility to sex and sexual maturity as the progenitors of murder in the governess. In all of these the governess is a malign force with more or less sexual thrust to her behavior. But there is a finer dimension to this motif in which the governess lusts for the child Miles, sometimes in lieu of the vanished master, sometimes for his own sake.

In one sense, the list of examples of those who favor the governess's sexual penchant for Miles is as long as those who share in the commerce of the governess's abnormal psychology. A few writers make the sexual penchant explicit. John Clair (1965) suggests that when the ghost of Quint reappears at the window in the final scene of the tale, his purpose is to observe "what must have appeared to be a twenty-year-old governess attempting to seduce a boy half her age" and suggests that the figure who appears to the governess is more likely to be Luke or the bailiff (56). Bernadine Brown (1974) is a bit more coy, suggesting only that "this innocent child, an uncle substitute, is the bridegroom that she desires," and that this function in Miles evokes the other uncle substitute, Quint (81). M. Karen Crowe (1982) makes her application a bit more oblique: "To love him as a surrogate son, a student, a child is not only understandable but is sanctioned by society. But to love him as a newly-wed husband, a surrogate lover, an adult is the romanticized fantasy of an inexperienced, sheltered, blushing, potentially dangerous individual" (45). Stanley Renner (1988), too, displaces the sexual into the psychosexual when he concludes "but the male child, trapped in the psychosexual undertow of the mother-son relationship, is destroyed" (194). But surely this aspect of the tradition has been yearning in a very specific direction ever since Wilson gave the psychology of the tale its sexual component: in the direction of a sexual consummation between the governess and Miles. Happily, this dimension is now supplied. In a recent article (1994) Sämi Ludwig has offered the thesis that "the conclusion of *The Turn of the Screw* enacts a scene of culturally enforced sexual initiation, and such a 'dreadful' reading of the 'climax' of the narrative is forecasted and called for by James's diction" (36).

* * *

Shoshana Felman is undoubtedly right when she tells us that a mere reading of *The Turn of the Screw* places us with Douglas's listeners at the fireside with the difference that it is likely to depend with most readers whether theirs is a first or subsequent reading. Placement at the fireside is exactly the condition of first readers. We see with the governess, beautifully unfolded by the fictive covering of Douglas's smitten praise: the country seat holds ghosts and beautiful children, villainy of motive, sympathy with the children, and horror of their false friends. If we don't know by our first reading, surely we do by the subsequent ones that we have watched things with the titillation that more than one student of the tale has mentioned. Ramras-Rauch suggests that our presence contributes to the children's uncertainty. She concludes that our reading the manuscript and arguing about it not only places us at Douglas's recital, but also at Bly with the ghosts and the living, all of whom have something at stake in musing the children's lives. Wells mentions that the "audience seeks to be horrified," that it enjoys "recreational horror" (1985, 88). If the audience is attracted by what it also deplores, then its responses will fall into either of the two main reading categories that the critical tradition has developed: either a recognition of complicity in the evil by identification in the events, with a correlative need to expiate; or a recognition of evil by reflexive guilt with a correlative need to accuse the governess of vile deeds in order to distance itself from her failings. If any part of the audience finds the governess haunted by the eternal ones of the dream—neurotic, that is, no matter how the tale is interpreted—the desiderative posture is to find her categorically different from itself, and therefore obnoxious, as the nineteenth century liked to say, to its censure.

The poisonous little tale is full of horrors that spread out and infect the landscape. For the governess, there is the horror of apparition; for Mrs. Grose and through her for the governess, there is the horror of corruption; for the children, there is the horror of the presence of evil; for Bly, there is the horror of the ghosts as presences; for the reader, there is the horror of the world from which they came. Are they real? Somewhere and at some level of the tale they are real. Do we know why they have come? Surely in whatever form they appear they have come because of unresolved torments, revenants from some imagination full of disquiet. Felman says that to see letters (on the page; through the post) is to see ghosts; merely to read is to see ghosts. Mansell says that language creates ghosts, that the defects of language rest in its capacity to make unicorns that will not go away; he sees the governess in her narrative disestablishing the vanishing point and reducing the narrative to two dimensions, the mere mirror with only an illusion of depth. Clews says that the governess "sees [the ghosts], and whatever has conjured them forth, they are real to her. They do not appear solely at her instigation, nor always in places where she expects them" (1985, 162). She sees the governess overturning Whitman's premise that one eyesight does not countervail another by believing that if she performs the act of seeing the ghosts, her performance will somehow exempt the children from seeing them. Wells says that the ghosts are the (negative) clearing terms in a series of equations involving substitutions. The tale does give us ghosts, and they have status, even if that status is a negative that cannot be expunged once it makes its appearance. But she sees into the paradox of the governess's power in the tale—"the tension between her apparent power and her real helplessness" (1985, 84).

Felman says that the narrative is transmitted by means of death: Miles dies and becomes the occasion of the narrative; the governess dies and transmits the narrative to Douglas; Douglas dies and transmits the narrative to the external narrator. Lurking in this combination of deaths and ghosts is an unexpressed theory of revenance; it seems, however, to evoke the laws by which King Hamlet roams, an unquiet grave, an unshriven death, an undisclosed murder. The governess dies; she stands accused of murder at the critical bar: yet she seems to rest in peace. Douglas dies; he has broadcast the governess's secret for no better purpose than to earn himself the prize for storytelling—yet he seems at peace. Quint and Jessel die; they are doomed to walk restlessly, to return to Bly, to haunt the house, to haunt, perhaps, the children, to haunt the governess. We know two characters who die and seem to be at peace; we know two characters who die and seem to be doomed to an anguished return. But another character dies—Miles. The governess says that she has exorcised his demon; many critics say that she has murdered him. But what we need to know at last is whether the story says that he sleeps quietly or whether he, too, like the ghosts at Bly, will be forced to roam for a season. But if he is condemned to this more horrid hent, he does not, in the lovely enigmatic movement of the tale, haunt the governess's beautiful script.

Notes

Introduction

1. This protest has generated some vocal censure. Douglas M. Davis, in *Graduate Student of English* (1959), condemns what he calls "the explication racket" and implies that the whole history of explication of *The Turn of the Screw* exists for the purpose of thrusting academic names into print. Dieter Freundlieb (1984) calls the *Screw* critical tradition a scandal and uses it as a reason to condemn the whole practice of textual explication.

2. This is the inescapable inference from his comment in "What Is Criticism?" (1972a) when he denies the power of later critics to advance our knowledge of text based on what earlier critics have said. This is a favorite postulate of recent critical theory. What Barthes says and what he does, however, do not necessarily coincide. In *S/Z*, the gnostic text of deconstruction, Barthes proposes to "cover the text with its own meaning." His application of a broad range of codes to the "lexias" of the text proposes to open out the text endlessly—to allow for an infinite number of virtually unrestricted impressions of the text, none definitive. Those who have applauded Deconstruction have done so precisely for the effect of its liberating force. Richard Howard, who introduces the Hill and Wang translation by Richard Miller, boldly proclaims that the sins of the academy will finally be brought to retribution by this escape from the sort of definitive claims of those who have wrestled with problem works such as *The Turn of the Screw*. However, Eve Tavor Bannet, another student of *S/Z* is quite prepared to challenge the claims of liberation: "In *S/Z* Barthes inverts a well-known nursery story, The Emperor's New Clothes. In the nursery story, everyone was told that the Emperor was wearing new clothes when he was in fact naked. In *S/Z*, Barthes does the opposite. He tells everyone that the Emperor is naked: instead of clothing Balzac's short story *Sarrasine* in a single totalising meta-meaning, as criticism of all kinds is wont to do, Barthes is going to open the text to multiple possibilities of meaning. ... Despite all these pluralising and liberating gestures, however, 200 pages of lexes shows [*sic*] not only that Barthes's text has been clothed in a single totalising meta-meaning from Barthes' first commentary but also that what Barthes has been doing is weaving a cast-iron dress for it" (Bannet 1989, 58–59). The meta-meaning is in his "rather enigmatic title. ... Z is the 'initial of castration.' According to the rules of French philology, SarraSine should be pronounced SarraZine; but this Z is transposed from Sarrasine's name to that of Zambinella, the eunuch with whom Sarrasine falls in love, mistaking him for a woman. ... Sarrasine contemplates in Zambinella his own castration" (59). "The discrepancy between what we are told the lexes and codes are going to do (open the text, constitute a plural) and what they in fact do (close the text, lock it into an

inescapable singular) is an anamorphic reflection of the structuration of the Balzacian text. The classical text is a 'game with two partners: the decoy and the truth' and so is Barthes' text" (60). While Barthes has indeed accounted for everything in the text in his reading, he has wound up according to Bannet, in a place very suspiciously like that of the New Critics; and indeed, very much like that of the appropriators of the text of *The Turn of the Screw*. What Bannet says does not revoke the power of Barthes' insights into literature, or, indeed, into this text; it merely raises the question that must be raised about the advance of the Deconstructive system as represented here over what Barthes and Richard Howard proclaim the work is superseding. The New Critics, too, believed in close reading; and swore that a valid reading must not ignore any salient points in the systems of the artifact. As the new theorists were swift to assert, close reading could not guarantee against critical error. But neither does Deconstruction solve all the problems of the reading act—or correct all the sins of the academy.

3. "Literary History as a Challenge to Literary Theory" appeared in *New Literary History* 2:1, in January 1970 as a translation of chapters 5–12 of the book *Literaturgeschichte als Provokation der Literaturwissenschaft* of 1967; it appeared later in translation in an altered form in Jauß's *Toward an Aesthetic of Reception*, 1982. Both texts have been consulted for this discussion.

4. Reviewing as a subset of the more general practice of criticism needs more attention than it has received from theorists of all stripes. In the fall of 1992 appeared a newly published version of a work in existence for almost forty years, Jack Green's *Fire the Bastards!*—a fair portion of the reviewers of William Gaddis's *The Recognitions* (1957). It was originally published in Green's *newspaper*, an underground sheet from Greenwich Village in the 1950s. Part of the interest arises from the fact that the staff of the Dalkey Archive published the book without the author's permission: the material was never placed under copyright (confirmed in conversation with representatives at the Modern Language Association meeting in New York in 1992). Green makes an idiosyncratic excursion into the dimensions of reviewing, accenting at least one strain of the indignant response the practice has bred since its earliest days—that of harsh and uninformed reply. Green had thought Gaddis's book a work of great character and achievement, and found that the overwhelming majority of the initial reviewers had misread and had executed their responsibilities to author and public negligently; some thirty-three of the fifty-five he had come to notice having done so poorly that they deserved to be fired. Here, in its own particular way, is both a critical history and a history of "naive public reading." It provides some good material for a test of the values of historical criticism. The implications of Green's readings and denunciations are far-reaching but are too complicated to assess fully here. He implies a high standard of reviewing that offers infinite respect for and care of literary effort. He intimates a ready, automatic identification of creative merit, which, however, he cannot make absolute. He finds Gaddis's novel filled with the sorts of things one should hope for in a novel—an epoch maker like *Ulysses*, with which both he and the reviewers are disposed to compare it—but he renders this judgment problematic when he says at the end of the third (and last) paper in the book: "the *ny times* failed to get with it, just had a para quoting hicks 1955 con*" and in a note "*they were busy preparing the book coup of the year in may the *times* was actually able to locate a novelist whod write a favorable review of herman wouk's *youngblood hawke* (commercial antisexual filth!) to go with the 2p ad in the same issue (im proud to say i instantly reading wouks 1st novel *aurora dawn* spotted him as the worst writer in the world)[.]" For Green there are good books and bad books; this condition of being is a matter of fact; there is no appeal from such final judgments. Green does not tell his reader how he has established his infallibility.

Thus, from his own perspective, Green proposes that reviewing should be conscientious and that reviewers should have the competence to distinguish between great books and the ordinary run; and that they should always know the difference between competent literary work and trash. Green is unsystematic and is unconcerned about the implications of his demands if they were really carried out fully. He is, in fact, very much concerned to make as broad a wash of color as he can in the process of writing his exposé. He suggests, quite contrary to the fact, that reviewing is an occupation and that reviewers' incompetence should be rewarded with occupational decapitation. With few exceptions, reviewing is an amateur act with all the problems attached to it that Green shows in his scorn for Wouk. But his study of the competence and conscience of the reviewers of Gaddis's work is a careful, painstaking collation and is exemplary for the sort of discussion that theories of reviewing require.

5. Walter Graham ([1930]; 1966) dates the first such journalism from about the year 1666, reaching its first moment of consummation with the success of the *Edinburgh Review* in the first decade of the nineteenth century. The sense that emerges from Graham's treatment is that virtually from the beginning, the questions about the limits of responsibility were mingled with the injured laments of those who came under reviewerly notice. Each generation of reviewers emerged with solemn answers to the questions about limits; and each generation discovered its own set of wretched victims.

6. Graham quotes the "Introductory Address" of the *London Review* (1809): "'The Man, who in the genuine spirit of criticism impartially distributes praise or blame to the work he reviews, has no more need to hide his name than the tradesman has, who records himself over his shop door....Everyone must confess, that there is a dangerous temptation, an unmanly security, an unfair advantage in concealment" (240). Nonetheless, Graham reports, the public was not ready for identified reviewers and the *London Review* failed within a few years.

All but eight of the twenty-eight reviews of *Screw* considered here were anonymously published. This phenomenon gives a sort of promotion to the idea of a composite first reading of the tale. On the other hand, the whole question of anonymity is a long-standing and difficult one as Graham's commentary on the *London Review* suggests. The practice of anonymous reviewing undoubtedly harkens back to the early days of the *Edinburgh* and the *Quarterly* when it was argued that there was a single standard either observed or implied in the critical operations of these two formidable journals and that mere descent into names would reduce the majesty of the standard to particularity and accident. It has been argued that the anonymity of the reviewers served handsomely as a cloak for reviewerly excesses as well as personal attacks masquerading as the stern imposition of the house style. Tennyson's cowering under the lash of "Christopher North" (Professor John Wilson of the University of Edinburgh) is almost as famous as Keats's injury at the hands of Croker. Jennings (1882, 83) quotes Tennyson's bitter reply in which the poet forgives the blame but cannot forgive the praise. Jennings also reprints an anonymous slash at anonymous reviewing:

> How much an editor would lose, if he,
> Abandoning mysterious incogs,
> Wrote little 'I' instead of mighty 'We!'
> For when a man the public memory jog
> In a critique severe, or slashing article.
> To stamp upon the thunderbolt 'Tim Scroggs'
> Would spoil its efficacy no small particle!
> There is much wisdom in that same plurality
> It neutralises personal rascality,

And shrouds from scorn his individuality! (153)

7. Only a few years after the publication of the ghost tale, Theodora Bosanquet became James's stenographer and typist. Her own remarks on reading seem to represent the casualness of the early first readers' responses. She records her own special shudder at the encounter with the ghosts, but does not enter into any detailed response or reason for her reaction. Her own critical emphasis falls upon the reading error of the friend who first drew her attention to the book: her friend had termed Quint a butler rather than a valet, and Bosanquet had decided that the tale could not be a menace since butlers in literature were comic figures. In reading for herself, she discovered that Quint is a valet, and her friend, she said, "was delighted to learn that my nights were as horror-stricken as her own had been." She comments on the heroine of *Covering End* and her charm for Bosanquet together with the comment that James confided in her that the heroine, Mrs. Gracedew, had been based on Ellen Terry. ("Henry James" 1917, 347). James received a number of letters from first readers on the tale. One must infer their content from James's replies and from James's summary riposte in the preface. Dr. Louis Waldstein had apparently found some significance for the nature of the subconscious self in the volume; H. G. Wells had apparently objected that he did not find enough about the "subjective complications" of the governess; F. W. H. Myers had apparently put "a principal question" to James about his intentions for the tale, one that James ducks in reply in favor of declaring his intention to "give the impression of the communication to the children of the most infernal imaginable evil and danger," matters of sufficient weight to constitute an answer to the chief of the Society for Psychic Research. Oscar Wilde captioned *The Turn of the Screw* "a poisonous little tale." James, in the preface, seemed to refer to these letter writers as those who were not usually easily caught in literary traps—but seemed to have been caught in the toils of his ghost tale.

8. But Rachel Salmon was already quarreling with Brooke-Rose about the validity of divided reading before Brooke-Rose's articles had reached book form in *The Rhetoric of the Unreal*. Salmon's argument is too complex even to summarize here, but she does observe that the division is defensible in the diachronic sense but that her unaccepted marriage of opposites takes place in the synthetic sense of the synchronic. Arguing about "The Figure in the Carpet," Salmon observes: "The apparent ambiguity of 'Figure'—that the figure both does and does not exist—can produce, eventually, a simultaneous perception: the figure exists for those capable of seeing it, but not for those incapable. It can never be extracted from the carpet of text or life; it can never be told as abstraction"; and again, the figure is an experience "rather than a paraphrasable hypothesis" (1980, 801). She criticizes Brooke-Rose for failing to tell why the ambiguity in *The Turn of the Screw* exists rather than simply showing how it got there (789). Salmon's interest in part is to show something about the nature of the reading experience, the sense of a criticism that develops exactly the hidden matter that Brooke-Rose and even Rimmon (1977) give too little consideration. Vereker, the novelist who claims to have included the Figure in the pattern of his fiction, does not, after all, make a major howl about the general failure to read him fully; he merely sorrows for the chasm between intention and reception.

Chapter 1. Naive Public Reading

1. So displeased was James about the state of American criticism that he could single out a particular critic as a virtual sole exception to the rule of flawed practice. In an

"American Letter" for *Literature* in 1898, James praised Norman Hapgood as an exception worth noticing: essay to the work of Henry James. Moreover, Hapgood came closer "I can speak but for myself, but nothing, in the United States, appeals so to the attention at any moment as the symptom in any quarter of the world of letters, of the possible growth of a real influence in criticism. That alertness causes me to lay a prompt hand upon the *Literary Statesmen and Others* of Mr. Norman Hapgood, and to feel toward him...a conscious warming of the heart" (Edel 1956, 227). Hapgood was among the early critics to devote a long to understanding James's style and his achievements than did many of his contemporaries. Hapgood can write good, tangled, Jamesian sentences himself: "To explain what is meant by saying that, while everything is expression, everything is also form to Mr. James, may, after one has denied him any remarkable eye for line and color, be rather difficult" (201). However, this observation comes en route to the perception that James himself felt that "the most definite thing about an emotion is its surface," going on to show that a particular emotion showed its surface in behaviors that did not need to be named but could simply be recorded. Hapgood saw that James stood "alike in the world of art and the world of sympathy, [and that] he has been the interpreter of each to the other" (207). Hapgood went on to a distinguished literary, editorial, and politically active career. He edited *Colliers* from 1902 to 1910.

2. By the time of the major phase, the disaffection with James's style and the perception of the seamy side of life that he insisted on dealing with turned away many Americans who had been faithful readers up to the time of *The Turn of the Screw*. But the American reviewers of, say, *The Ambassadors* or *The Golden Bowl* recognized that British reviewers were still treating James as though he were both making sense and extending his literary reputation. It was not uncommon to hear American reviewers say that the British pretended to like James, but as for themselves, they did not believe it.

3. H. G. Dwight, only a few years later (1907), in an impassioned defense of James from critical disparagement over style and in defense of James from the accusation of anti-Americanism, declared that James was deeply aware of the anomaly of American cultural experience, returning to James's comments on Hawthorne's imperfect cultural soil in the biography. Dwight proposed that "no other country could have produced him" on his way to saying that it was a precious illusion among Americans to think of themselves either as a "legendary race in its infancy face to face with the primal problems...[or] a historical race rich with the accumulations of ages." Instead, Dwight says, "we are...the younger sons of the ages, with a tradition and a country that do not match." (Dwight, 1907; Gard 1968, 448) James, he says, faced this cultural anomaly without blinking. Santayana said it as well: "we are a young country with an old mentality" (*The Genteel Tradition* quoted in O'Connor 1952, 32). Oscar Wilde said simply, "the oldest tradition in America is its youthfulness; it's been going on for three hundred years" (*A Woman of No Importance*).

4. I am indebted to Linda J. Taylor's bibliography of writings about James for the bits from the *Portland Morning Oregonian* and *Dixie*.

5. This is the Society for the Prevention of Cruelty to Children, founded in New York in 1874.

6. On this point Leslie Fiedler (1958) has made some useful comments, suggesting that *The Turn of the Screw* is itself a cultural turning point that heralds the loosening of the stranglehold on the subjects that literature can embrace. Fiedler points out Hawthorne's representation of child nature in "The Gentle Boy," where the Quaker child, Ilbrahim, is shunned by the community at large for his parents' unwanted views, at least until he comes to the notice of the Puritan children, who savage him in a fashion quite in keeping with the best traditions of the scapegoat. Fiedler sees the Ilbrahim

pattern recurring through American literary history until the time of James, when he believes it comes into the mainstream as a recognized if regrettable configuration of the human personality. To some extent, Fiedler palliates the depraved sense by suggesting the presence of Satan in the young, as in all human beings, is merely another word for the presence of nature—as the governess finds in Miles when she calls him the "little natural man."

7. Reviewing in general was not necessarily a kindly activity at the time, so that there is a genuine quality of shocked response to James's work very different from the response to the standard sentimental romance of the moment. James the writer first came to public attention not as an author of fiction, but as an author of reviews. The majority of his early reviews have been collected in *Notes and Reviews*, ed. Pierre de Chaignon La Rose. In a review of Harriet Prescott's *Azerian*, January 1865, James said, among other charges, "from beginning to end it is a succession of forced assaults upon the impregnable stronghold of painting; a wearisome series of word-pictures linked by a slight thread of narrative, strung together, to use one of Miss Prescott's own expressions, like 'beads on a leash.'" Or, a bit later, "her paragraphs read as if in composition she completely ignored the expedient of the eraser." James suffered his own version of harsh reviewing of his late style by being accused of some of the faults that he had brashly accused others of perpetrating in the swashbuckling days of his early twenties. His reviews were, of course, anonymous.

8. Her figure is in fact a Chinese architect: "In his 'Artist's Letters from Japan,' Mr. La Farge tells of a famous Chinese architect who lived more than two thousand years ago. When asked how he conceived his marvellous works, he replied that it was very simple; he put out of his mind everything but the thing he wished to do and his sense of relation to the divine mind. At the end of the first day he had forgotten the money he was to receive for the work; at the end of the second, he no longer remembered the applause which would be given him, and very soon nothing was present to his consciousness save the Thing Itself which he desired to create. Then he was ready to go out into the forest and choose the timber of which his building should be wrought. Now and again, in art and in literature we come upon works of such extraordinary vividness, so completely seen, so detached and independent, that we know instinctively they have been shaped with the aid of this eternal formula" (341). She is speaking of John La Farge, who did the decorative art work for the *Collier's* serial publication of *The Turn of the Screw* in January of 1898.

9. Katharine Lee Bates, by this time president of Wellesley College, is a critical voice coeval with the publication of *The Turn of The Screw*. She states, in *American Literature* (1898), perhaps as well as any critic of the time the prevailing notion of James's work most in harmony with that of the reviewers. "The interest of James's books mainly lies, however, in the microscopic observation of men and manners, in the labyrinthine discussion of men and manners, approached from the side of taste rather than of conscience, and in the beauty of detail, the elegance and accuracy of the workmanship." Thus in a work on American Literature, written, one notes, while James was still alive, James deserves two pages, mostly for the purpose of declaring his excessive emphasis on technique. "For plain people," Bates continues, "James's style is overwrought; there is too much sauce for the pudding; but those upon whom its fine fascinations has once fixed, think better of themselves ever after. The author is, as he says of one of his own heroes, 'much addicted to conversing with his own wit'" (322–23). There is more, but this is the substance. James is refined to the point of desiccation and therefore fails to perform the function of writing democratically for the mass audience. Of course Bates offers the legitimate notion that the criticism of an author should await the successful survival of the test of time. And Bates gives only a sketch of

appraisal here, quite content to leave the enduring judgment to posterity. But she says, finely, that even when James "achieves the ethereal and passionate" he is still "cold, watchful, analytic" (323). That is a perfect restatement of the summary judgments of James's reviewers at the turn of the century.

10. "Droch" is the pseudonym of Robert Bridges, a fixture of the literary columns in *Life* in the 1890s. Patricia Marks, in "*Life*," included in Chielens 1986, 213–17, speaks of *Life*'s running argument with Victorian usage, lashing out at the stylistic character of Thackeray and Trollope and denouncing James and Howells for their imitations. But of Droch she says, "Amid the proliferation of satirical columns, parodies and quips, the reviewer Robert Bridges alone quietly assessed James's importance in the development of narrative point of view" (215). E. R. Hagemann (1968, 207–25), also places Bridges among those who understood the later James and offered some consolation for the continual lampoons of the variety represented in the mock announcement that "Messrs. Bigtype and Sharper" will publish some things to solace the "long-suffering public": "*A Plain Tale.* By Henry James. Written in real English. No sentence over eight words long. Every sentence begins with a noun and has a traceable verb and guaranteed object. Would make a good primer. Easily understood plot." (*Life* 1901, 38:415).

11. Of which more anon. But for instance, William James was much interested in psychic phenomena and included study of these phenomena in *Principles of Psychology* (1891) and elsewhere, and was a founding member of the American branch of SPR. See Beidler 1989 and Halttunen 1989.

12. The problem of authority—either the integrity of the author or the authenticity of the text—is not solved by merely answering no to the question "is there a text in this classroom?" with the implication that we might as well take all texts—narratives—as anonymously generated. The concept of authentic text is easily challengeable—and nowhere more so than in the work of Henry James, who revised his fiction for the New York Edition. Tzvetan Todorov illustrates the problem as it is often perceived by modern theory. In the preface to the English translation of *Introduction to Poetics* he accounts for his unwillingness to rewrite the text or to register his current views, much altered from the original. He speaks in terms of estrangement from the text that bear directly on the point of authority: "Obliged to reread my text, I experienced it as somehow external to me, as if someone else had written it" (Preface. xxi). Edward Said distributes Todorov's principle: "Thus in the written statement, beginning or inauguration, augmentation by extension, possession and continuity stand for the word *authority*." But *authority* is "bothered by *molestation*": "By that I mean that no novelist has ever been unaware that his authority, regardless of how complete, or the authority of a narrator, is a sham" (1985, 83-84). Said uses James's own treatment of Isabel Archer in *The Portrait of a Lady* as an example of writing himself out of the text by giving Isabel narrative authority over the world she creates alternatively for herself. The extreme form of challenge to narrative-authorial primacy is stated in reader-response theory where the "reader" not the author makes the work: there are as many texts under a particular title as there are "readers" to create them; none of them has authority or primacy and there is no definitive text or interpretation. Karl-Heinz Stierle says it as well as any: "Since different readings do not necessarily follow the same thematic scheme, it seems difficult to derive from the history of readings the meaning of a specific work (in Suleiman 1980, 88).

But if Todorov cannot decide on an authentic version of his poetics—he visualizes any possible revision not as creating authoritative text but only as an act "to erase [the] signs of time"—he does authorize a work called *Introduction to Poetics* to appear in English. I do not expect anybody to challenge the contention that I have consulted this work as the product of this writer and in this translation no matter how variant from any of its prior states this text may appear to be—even if it should be argued that the original were wholly absent from what I have read. There is some residual text, however imperfect, challengeable, variant, corrupt. Merely declaring the text's virtual anonymity does not address any of the significant questions about the nature of text. Variant text, corrupt text, translation, emended manuscript—however problematic, some state of the text is available to teachers, to their students, to colleagues to discuss. Leon Edel speaks of the changes in James's *The Portrait of a Lady* between the original Harpers' edition and the revision for the New York Edition, stating his preference for the original book-form of the novel (Edel, Intro. 1977. Henry James. Portrait of a Lady. Boston: Houghton-Mifflin). Edel, a good and an influential reader of James, cannot, however, make his mere preference for the original definitive. On the other hand, the differences between the two versions do not keep exponents of either from saying that they have read the book or from understanding the salient features of it.

13. See Levy 1955, 286–88. Where Levy suggests that James's bitterness at the failure of his work erupted in this intractable novella, "he had now retrieved the full power of his narrative skills and offered an ambiguity-ridden novella in order to baffle his readers in turn" (286). Levy suggests that there are a sufficient number of theatrical bits in the tale to support the idea that theater is on his mind in the execution of the tale.

14. The *New Orleans Daily Picayune* also offers a moment on the novella, but Jack Green would surely say that this reviewer must be fired. It was not necessary for the reviewer to have read the novella to mount the collection of generalities that occurs in the hundred words. James's ghost story is "a fascinating tale of mystery" and Mr. James adds "all the delights of his style." It is his best since "The Bostonians," "instinct with his peculiar charm."

15. Shoshana Felman is a minor exception in that she mentions a few of the reviews, using Kimbrough's brief references as her source. Needless to say, she shows no sense of the reading issues for the reviews as a collective first reading of the tale or of the breadth of the recognitions that the reviewers comprehended in the reviews.

16. Jack Green 1992, Green lists his grievances against the reviewers of William Gaddis's *The Recognitions*. One of the reviewers, Edward Wagenknecht of the *Chicago Tribune*, who despaired of making sense of Gaddis's *The Recognitions* (1955), justified a sketchy review by saying "I'm like the Vermont farmer listening to the New Deal spellbinder. 'What's he talking about?' his neighbor queried. ... And quite without perturbation, he replied 'He don't say.' Gaddis don't say neither" (Green 5, 1992). There is a striking similarity between the reviews of James's late fiction and the reviews of Gaddis's first novel. The similarity illustrates intensely the problem of reviewing taken as a responsibility divided between respect for the work and a judicious reading of it. It is ironic that Green says that the reviewers can't take the time to review Gaddis because they are too busy measuring Henry James's fingernails. The reviewers' carelessness with James's late fiction was of a piece with the reviewers' treatment of Gaddis's first.

17. Croker had confessed that he had not read past the first of the four parts of the cycle and that the poet was careless with the application of his rhymes to his sense, presumably with Pope's injunction about the relation between sound and sense in his ear and not Wordsworth's liberties with blank verse. The era in which James was also roughly handled by the critics was not unaware of the Keats-Croker collision. It came up in Jennings's gossipy *Curiosities of Criticism* (1882); and it surfaced again in the *New York Times Saturday Review of Books* in the high season of critical antagonism against James in an essay entitled "Poets and Critics," 7 February 1903, 88. The anonymous author begins by saying that we all now agree that the poetry of Keats is immortal; and that for all the hyperbole of the age, nobody still believes the myth that

Keats died of Croker's review: "'men have died from time to time and worms have eaten them,' but not for harsh criticism." The subject has arisen, however, because the writer has just learned that at a recent sale, Keats's autograph sold for $187.50 while "a well-informed and chipper writer in The Literary Collector [stated that]... an autograph of John Wilson Croker... 'would be dear at $3.00.'" Croker was "a very decent fellow in his time. He was a man of splendid attainments and his services to literature were considerable." But, says the writer, he was the victim of harsher criticism than any he delivered, suffering at the hands of Macaulay, who was his political as well as his literary enemy. The writer concludes by saying that the longevity of the Croker cause célèbre is indebted to its use as "a preliminary to the puffing up of very small literary fry." Along the way, the writer says that some of the reluctance of critics to discover greatness in every new claimant "is rather a good than a bad trait in any critic." Thus, it is indeed a safer course to condemn than to praise.

Chapter 2. The Genesis of a Critique

1. A mere casual notice in Advance (weekly, the journal addressing the concerns of Congregationalism out of Chicago) for 26 May 1904 (47:673) under the rubric "Literary Small Talk" informed its readers that "Henry James, after many years' absence from America[,] has been induced by an American publisher to revisit his native country in order to study the new social conditions which have arisen during his prolonged stay in England. Mr. James expects to make his visit in the coming autumn, and will plan to remain here a year, traveling about. The result of his observation will probably be embodied in fiction." This last prediction was accurate to the degree that the late stories, "The Jolly Corner," "Julia Bride," and "Crapy Cornelia" might have arisen from his observations. Edel says that the arrangement for the return was made with Harpers (1985, 590), though the "Impressions" came out in the North American Review; however, the finished book, The American Scene came out under the label of the Scribner's, James's publisher for the majority of his late work, including the New York Edition. Advance does not say where its information comes from. But Edel in the same context reports James chiding Grace Norton for broadcasting the idea that he was antagonistic toward the United States (589), and apparently returns with every intention of renewing fond remembrance. The reviewery response to The American Scene tells later readers once again how much that work broke new ground in applying the techniques of painting to the observations of travel; how James could see passionately through the painter's eye when the painter was, for example, Monet; and how skilled he had become in the recording of impressions through his late novels.

As a matter of interest, James's return did not escape conversion into fiction. No less a figure than Edna Kenton, who in 1924 released the squib that set off the *Screw* wars in her "Ruminant Reader," wrote a story in 1906 called "Love Laughs at Lions," in which her heroine wishes to publish art novels but finds herself married to one of the 'damned mob of scribbling men,' a husband, a lawyer, who secretly publishes bestsellers. Ellen's alliance with Howells and James is unmistakeable: "The Dean of American Realism had openly praised her two novels and several of her shorter stories, and the Master of Subtleties, who refused to dwell in unillusioned and disillusioning America, had written her direct about her second book, and she had walked on air for days therefore" (1906, 334). Then the Master returns to the United States—"The Master of Subtleties had come, like a homing bird, at last unto his own people, for a lecturing tour and an impressionistic view"—and gives a lecture after which she is invited into the august presence. This is to have been the high point of her existence. But the master denounces two popular writers in the millings of the crowd after the address, one of them being her husband, and loyally Ellen prefers her husband, snubbing the Master (442–43). Along the way Kenton's protagonist praises The Master for the sorts of achievements that had annoyed Brownell: "He deals altogether in situations...psychological difficulties in people and between people. More and more I feel that plot, in the old definition is n't [sic] the vital thing" (341). Kenton's interest in James, therefore, long antedates the pivotal piece on *The Turn of the Screw*. She poses some interesting challenges to the reviewers of James during this time of assessment.

2. Gertrude Hall Brownell recalls that Brownell believed he had paid James a "significant tribute" in making James one of his *American Prose Masters*. Brownell had reported that after an extended and cordial talk about literary matters, James had "at leave-taking wound up with a smile, 'Don't despair of me. I may do something yet.'" Mrs. Brownell assumes that this colloquy took place after the publication of Brownell's *American Prose Masters* (1909), whereas it took place during James's stay in New York in 1904–5 to take his impressions and to make arrangements for the New York Edition of his work, and certainly not in 1910, after the prose masters volume appeared—when James was so gloomy about his health and when he was despondent over the death of his brother. Gertrude Brownell's comments appear in "Impressions of the Later Years," 1928, 366.

3. For an account of the complex presence of Matthew Arnold in the strained relations between Brownell and James, see Raleigh 1957. Raleigh recognizes three major Arnoldians around the turn of the century: James, Brownell, and Stuart Pratt Sherman. James's debt is constant and acknowledged; Brownell attempted to build Arnold's ideas of the best that has been thought and said into all of his own critical work, especially into his *Victorian Prose Masters* and its companion volume, *American Prose Masters*, where the prevailing idea was always the majesty of style and its relation to cultivated graces. Sherman carried the Arnoldian premise to a sort of logical conclusion in his treatment of James's own concern as "Aesthetic Idealism," in a well known essay published soon after James's death, which declared that James cared nothing about morality, but only about aesthetic perfection, so that the great artistic achievement was its own vindication and nothing merely conventionally moral need ever trouble the horizon of the idealist. It is strange in the long retrospect how variant this judgment seems as respects James and how closely it fits Oscar Wilde, at least in the latter's defense of literary exemption from ordinary morality.

4. One notes that it is in the interim between 1900 and 1905 that James writes his most comprehensive denunciation of newspaper journalism in the long story "The Papers." Added to such prior outbursts of displeasure at the excesses and heartless invasions of journalism as his treatment of Matthias Pardon in *The Bostonians*, of Flack of *The Reverberator*, of the aggressive young lady in "Flickerbridge," and of Chad in *The Ambassadors*—who is, after all, to become a creator of advertising copy—this description of a pair of young Cockney idealists who execute their own defrocking after the disillusionment of a long and increasingly pointless "novitiate" crowns James's rough handling of the press. Howard Bight summarizes the unhappy position of the press as fourth estate when he observes to Maud Blandy that "the press is the watchdog of civilization, and the watchdog happens to be—it can't be helped—in a perpetual state of rabies." Nothing could say more profoundly for James how Siamese-twinned he found the values of necessary surveillance of public activity and the arrogation of privacy by the ravening of journalistic publicity. James's difficulties with reviewing are inextricably linked with his general views of the press as a mixed blessing of a free society.

5. The writer needn't have worried: Molly Elliott Seawell shows up recurrently on the best-seller lists of the day from this time forward, is well and enthusiastically reviewed, is prolific. Others also noted Boston's excursion into literary rituals of purification. At about the same time as did the *Washington Post*, the *Atlanta Constitution* also noted the event. "The Lounger," Joseph B. Gilder, an editor of the *Critic*, received a circular from C. M. Clark Publishing Company celebrating that their publication, *Quincy Adams Sawyer*, by Charles Felton Pidgin (1901), had just been accepted by the Boston Public Library, a mark of its distinction as well as of its moral purity. The Lounger wondered "just how much of a compliment has been paid to this 'famously popular novel of New England Life' when I read among the novels rejected are Mrs. Humphrey Ward's 'Eleanor,' Mr. James's 'Two Magics,' Mrs. Wharton's 'Touchstone,' Miss Wilkins's 'People of Our Neighborhood,' and Sir Walter Besant's 'Changeling.' It is after all a matter of taste, but I think that in the circumstances if I were the author of a novel I should feel it much more of a compliment to have my book rejected than accepted by the Boston Public Library. In the former case I should at least be in good company" (1901, 403).

6. Colby supplies a perfect analogy for the critics' displeasure with James's late style by conflating him with Marlow of Conrad's *Heart of Darkness* or perhaps Sir Henry M. Stanley when he entitles his review of *The Wings of the Dove* "In Darkest James." Colby thought enough of these two reviews to include them in *Imaginary Obligations* (1904). His bludgeoned sensibility does not allow him to see the differences between *The Sacred Fount* and *The Wings of the Dove*. He is very much inclined to attribute the faults of the characters to the author—again, the best single indicator that a particular work has broken new ground technically and has confronted readers with a new calculus.

7. Elton is a careful and intent reader of James; he is here calling for readerly attention of the sort that James later conditions for in the prefaces to the New York Edition. But Elton falls into a significant error here in designating Quint a butler. When Theodora Bosanquet, James's secretary and amanuensis for all of the late work after 1900, first heard of *The Turn of the Screw*, she heard that the ghost was that of a butler and declared that the tale could not thus be frightening—because butlers were uniformly comic characters. But when she understood that the ghost was that of a valet, she could easily accept the menace. She reports that she read the tale the first time after midnight and that her hair stood on end from start to finish. It is all the more surprising that Elton misses the status of Peter Quint because his perspective is English. But this matter of textual mistakes plagues the critical tradition to the extent that later students wag angry fingers at inattentive critics.

8. The relationship between Brownell and James is too complex to go into fully here. In an article on Brownell in 1982, René Wellek says that he seems today "not only neglected but forgotten," listing a number of discussions of critical development that might well have noticed Brownell's contributions to the development of critical judgment and standards in the early years of this century. He is the man of whom Edith Wharton said, "we have lost our greatest critic" at his death (Bell 1966). Wellek's complaint goes too far—there was a good deal of discussion of Brownell's critical place in the strong revival of interest in the history of American criticism in the 1950's. Raleigh gives him respectful and extended treatment in *Matthew Arnold and American Culture*, and, for example, O'Connor does so as well in *An Age of Criticism*: "Among the best of these critics was W. C. Brownell, who apparently wanted to be an American Matthew Arnold" (13). In *The Development of American Criticism*, Stovall and the authors of the sections around 1900 know clearly of Brownell's importance. He was branded as a blue-law Victorian by Mencken; but that only means that he was important

enough to brand. His biographer in *DAB* says that he remained puzzled by and never came to terms with James either in their long official connection or in the sequence of critical books that Brownell wrote from 1909 until his death. The issue of the author's personality in the artifact, so central to Brownell's literary theory, had some substance at the time; and has arisen since his death on some notable occasions. James gave an oblique answer to the quest for personality in his 1907 essay *"The Tempest"* where he says of Shakespeare "The man himself, in the Plays, we directly touch, to my consciousness, positively nowhere: we are dealing too perpetually with the artist, the monster and magician of a thousand masks, not one of which we feel him drop long enough to gratify with the breath of the interval that strained attention in us which would be yet, so quickened, ready to become deeper still" (Shapira 1965, 300). One can't miss, here, the implication that the *artist* is not to be found in the work—or not corporeally so; and that James numbers himself among those who challenge the absolute authority of author or narrator in text. The sense is perhaps that the artist is dissolved in the text, but cannot be reconstructed from it. For an extended discussion of the problem see C. S. Lewis and E. M. W. Tillyard *The Personal Heresy* (London 1939). However tenuous the assertion that the artist's personality is recoverable from the artifact, Brownell held to the idea persistently. Brownell needs further study and reconsideration and the complex relationship between him and James needs more careful exploration and elaboration.

9. It is true that James needed to return to the United States to gather the full force of this revolution; it is likewise true that he reflected his sense of it in the late stories collected in *The Finer Grain* (1910). But before his return he was already troubled by the implications of unbridled power, gathered, presumably, from many sources—not the least, the depiction of it in Howells's socially conscious novels of the 1890s. He made plain his sense of the specific ills of American society in, for example, his "American Letter" of 25 June 1898, principally devoted to comments on E. L. Godkin's *Unforeseen Tendencies of Democracy*, in which the editor spoke at length of the anomalies of power accumulation unforeseen by the founding fathers. Of these, the Boss System, with its corruption of the procedure of nominating candidates for public office in the United States and the general decline of interest in public service against the larger attraction of reaping wealth on the open markets, came in for some scrutiny. In the process of the essay, James comes up with his own version of Arnold's Mary Wragg: the pictures of "stupid" faces of "groups of congregations of athletes and games players" peering out of newspapers and store windows as the underlying inheritors of the actual as against the theoretical democracy (Edel 1956, 250, 241–50).

Arnold bursts out, in "The Function of Criticism at the Present Time," against the complacence of "Roebuck and Adderley," two shallow optimists and uncritical boosters of the greatness of British life. His fury falls on the piece in the local paper that reports *"'Wragg is in custody.'"* In a paper given in New York (1992), Terence Hawkes explained. Arnold was "erupting," and the nature of his eruption was precisely over the failures of criticism at the present time. The paper was entitled "I Should Never Have Done It If I Had Had a Home for Him"—Mary Wragg's words in defense of the murder of her child. Hawkes went on to show Eliot bursting out in a similar disgust for an overrated civilization in his collision with some footballers returning on a train. The grounds on which Americans sometimes found James elitist are represented in observations such as these. They nonetheless ally him with Arnold in the general views of the anarchy of modern life. All three would have had something to shout at in the recent political cartoon that showed a long procession of people leaving the White House carrying what looked like diplomas with the caption, "The Law and Order Administration Leaves the White House Clutching Its Pardons."

10. In spite of the limitation to twenty-four volumes and in spite of James's desire to include *The Bostonians* in a projected revision, the set is completed only with the posthumous addition of two later volumes by agreement with James's first literary executor, his sister-in-law, Alice. Volume 25 was the unfinished *The Sense of the Past*; volume 26 was the also unfinished *Ivory Tower*. I have not seen these Scribner volumes in many places (most libraries have the Collins versions, published in London in 1917), but the Firestone Library at Princeton, where the Scribner Archives are housed, has these volumes.

11. In fact the expected sales of the New York Edition, especially in the United Kingdom, were disappointing both to James and to his publisher. The projected second edition that would have included *The Bostonians* and possibly several other works excluded from the first edition was abandoned early in the Scribner's planning; and James's hope that the New York Edition would sustain him financially through his declining years was simply another disappointment for him at the end of the first decade of this century. See Edel 1985, 663.

12. Their denial was based on the rather circular assumption that if there had been such a tale, their father would have told them. Since he had not, there could be no such tale. See Benson, 1930. James's description of its unformed structure and highly fragmental nature suggests the plausible hypothesis that the subject of the occult had come up some way in conversation and that the archbishop had used it by way of illustration of a point. Since James was much engaged in excursions into the occult in the early 1890s, it is not at all unlikely that such an event might occur. At the same time, if the Benson sons are correct, it would go to show only that for a master like James, the genesis of a tale out of a suppositions document would not exceed possibility. He did after all write a biography of Hawthorne in which he focused careful attention on *The Scarlet Letter*, a tale whose authenticating document belongs to the upper story of the fiction rather than to the museum of fact.

13. Many years ago, Lorna Berman (1968), speaking of Sade and the ambiguity of his influence on the development of Western thought, remarked on his having lifted the veil from the dark consciousness of humanity after the happy flirtation with the ultima ratio regum of the eighteenth century. We have been living with the creatures who were in hiding behind the veil ever since Sade undertook to strip away their covering. Freud knew this and explored the creatures for the extent of a career. So did James. It is not pleasant to find that there is evil in creation, not in some remote hell of the imagination, but in the hell of consciousness. But as Sade knew, it would not hide; it would not remain imprisoned behind some bleached curtain of righteousness. The Victorian division of women into angels and whores was one such curtain. And the creation of what Mark Spilka called the hothouse of family affections (k 251) was its reflex: "On the one hand, domestic affections were cooked up to a high pitch; on the other, sexual feeling was severely repressed and talk about sex forbidden. ... In the meantime prostitution flourished in the cities and, in covert and open ways, prurience seems to have flourished in the home." Spilka proposes that the problem in *Screw* is overheated affections. James, more covertly, merely ratifies the Sadean dictum: The evil lies in the human mind. It is undoubtedly a subterranean sense of *this* horror that so agitated James's readers. Some application of it operates in the development of the tale's critical history.

14. Perhaps the most acute of the interpreters of the tale, besides the author himself, to this point was his doctor, Sir James Mackenzie. Edel, in *The Treacherous Years* (1969) speaks of James's visit to Sir James at a time when he was much troubled with angina pectoris. However, Edel quotes the part of "Case #97" from Mackenzie's *Angina Pectoris*, in which the emphasis is on Mackenzie's complaint that James failed to

particularize the ghosts with some of James's explanation of his technique. R. McNair Wilson, in his recounting of the same incident (1926, 49), stresses Mackenzie's own explicatory use of the tale. Wilson has been discussing the problems of the diagnostician versus the patient, Mackenzie having been scrupulous not to issue a diagnosis where there was doubt. He proceeds,

> A friend of the late Henry James, the novelist, told me a story of Mackenzie, which shows how keenly he was alive to this consideration. Henry James suffered from a pain, and desired to consult Mackenzie about it. When he entered the doctor's room in Harley Street, he was met with a question:
> "What is it really that the children saw outside the window which so greatly terrified them?"
> The reference was, of course, to a story by James himself. James raised his hands, and in that voice of his which, had it not been sincere, must have been incredibly pompous, replied:
> "My dear Sir James, do you not know that the whole basis of terror is mystery? The children were afraid, because they did not know what they were looking at. Why, then, should I tell the reader what they were looking at?"
> Mackenzie nodded and proceeded to examine his patient. Then he asked:
> "Of what are you afraid?"
> "I don't know…"
> "Like the children in the story."
> James saw the point, and went away comforted.

15. Iser creates some problems with this distinction between the "artistic" and the "aesthetic" that he does not solve in this book. If the "aesthetic" text constitutes the "concretization" of the "reader, then the result is that the word aesthetic has been exhausted in the mere activity of any form of reading. Nothing in that case is left over for what are normally thought of as aesthetic values—our ideas of beauty and virtue. In speaking to his hypothesis, Iser uses the example of the contention between C. S. Lewis and F. R. Leavis over their opposing aesthetic responses to *Paradise Lost*. Iser quotes the sequence in Lewis's preface to Milton's epic where Lewis says, "It is not that he and I see different things when we look at *Paradise Lost*. He sees and hates the very same that I see and love." (Iser 1978, 25). Iser concludes: "It is evident that they have identical criteria, but draw totally different conclusions from them." But surely love and hate are not conclusions drawn from evidence; surely these are aesthetic reactions dictated by the emotions. The larger context of Lewis's discussion illustrates the problem that Iser has created for himself. Preceding the passage that Iser quotes, Lewis has said "Dr. Leavis does not differ from me about the properties of Milton's epic verse. He describes them very accurately—and understands them better, in my opinion, than Mr. Pearsall Smith." In the strictly formal sense of the text, in other words, the two students reflect at least some homogenity of values for the text; and it is in the sense of its beauty that they part company. Lewis says, following Iser's quoted passage, "Hence the disagreement between us *tends to escape the realm of literary criticism*. We differ not about the nature of Milton's poetry, but about the nature of man, or even the nature of joy itself" (emphasis supplied). Lewis's discrimination belongs to the sorts of distinction that must be made in the evaluation of literature. Its submergence in the general act of reading in Iser's "aesthetic text" might support his contention about the difficulties of definition of the literary text, but at the expense of those areas of evaluation that can indeed be used to distinguish between achievement and banality.

James's pleasure in the aesthetic of "the good old sacred thrill" derives from his assertion of power over the reader but always with the sense that the careful reader may learn from aesthetic responses, may learn to distinguish between the evil that is out there in the world and the evil that resides in the reader's own consciousness.

16. Recurrently through this recapitulation of responses to the narrative structure of *The Turn of the Screw* we have seen the critics conflating the narrator with the author and the character with the narrator. Though it seems manifestly absurd to do so with the governess, that conflation nonetheless recurs broadly in the criticism. It is simply a commonplace of the criticism of the time to ignore the possible stances of the narrator. Bragdon, for example, in the part of his review that refers to *The Ambassadors*, says that James makes his hero say: "there was something in the great world covertly tigerish, which came to him across the lawn in the charming air as a waft from the jungle." Though this remark is clearly the narrator's and may easily represent the narrator's and not Strether's choice of words, Bragdon is complacent in attributing it to the character. The problem of narrative attribution is acutely discussed by Janet Holmgren McKay (1982) where she wrestles with both the attribution of narrative deixis and with the locus of narrative sympathy in *The Bostonians*. McKay refers back to Dorrit Cohn and ultimately to Lubomir Dolezel (1977). See McKay 1982, esp. 40–41, 86. In a note to her article "Formal Coherence of Represented Speech and Thought" (1978), Ann Banfield reports that "the term *narrator* entered the critical vocabulary as a legacy of the New Criticism and of Russian Formalism as the first person who recounts the story, a persona quite distinct from the author. The distinction was once necessary because Romantically inspired literary criticism often assumed that any first-person in the text represented the author." But the need for the distinction between author and observer internal to the narrative becomes increasingly necessary as one sees more subtlety in the organization of point of view. In his authorial probe of the psychology of impression—virtually the grasping of light as form—James places his narrator like Pope's Ariel where this narrator can see a character's ideas arise from the initial processing of the sense-data of impressions. The significance of the author existing at a distance from the third-person narrator becomes more intense as one sees the limitations under which the narrator or internal observer and reporter operates. The puzzlement of the narrator of *The Golden Bowl*, for example, who cannot decide on a conclusive focus for narrative sympathy or character morality and remains divided between competing applicants for that sympathy at the end of the narrative, is inconsistent with a masterly and artistically secure Henry James as author. See Austin-Smith 1992.

17. This is a fairly frequent complaint over the development of the critical tradition. But does James take the story out of the governess's mouth? Edwin Fussell argues many years later that James has given the governess a novel "to be proud of" (1980, 122). He goes on to say that within the limits of stylistic matters, "James wanted to discriminate novelistic styles. There are similitudes which James did little or nothing to obviate. There are also differences. Both writers are given to the long sentence, but hers are far less frequent, less convoluted, perhaps less periodic. Her mode of perceiving and expressing tends to brevity; incident, conversation, reflection are cut short by the energy of her narration. This mannerism of hers, this telling of past events as if they were just about to happen is another reason why *The Turn of the Screw* sometimes seems as if it were delivered to the front door in present tense." He goes on to tell us that James's governess gives us a masterpiece, "but is not literary" (123); and that her narrative contains very clear examples of breathless naïveté.

Chapter 3. Suppressed Text(s)

1. Later students of the text, with a psychoanalytic bias, will declare that the process of suppression is the powerful underlying force of the novella. Thus, for instance, Shoshana Felman (1977) proposes that the governess keeps the whole of her sexuality poised in the interstice between a kind of protracted infant erotic personality sustained by her sense of herself in her first view of herself at full length in the "long glasses" (full-length mirrors) of Bly (what she refers to as the Lacanian *stade du miroir*) and the sort of fantasy life that is available to a "fluttered girl from Hampshire" from reading the local papers and from reading the romances that are permitted such children of the local clergy. Those who approve of the changes in psychology represented in Lacan's redefinition of signifiers tend to look back with skepticism to the easy conclusions of the first literary Freudians, and Edmund Wilson becomes an easy target for demonstrations of an improved understanding. A further step back will suggest, however, that the murky areas of the mind are not subject to simplification, and however pleasingly complex Lacan's diagram of the phallic signifier—or indeed of Jacques Derrida's representation of consciousness as mere tracings—the unsolved questions of human psychology still remain to plague us. Felman's analysis is more painstaking than Edmund Wilson's and is, in my judgment, more penetrating. It is not, however, flawless. See her 1977 work and various other discussions of a poetics for the relation between psychology and literature; for example, the one under the direction of Mieke Bal in 1984 in *Style* 18.

A delicious sectarian exchange arose over Virginia Woolf, psychobiography, psychobiology, and psychopoetics in the October 1988 Forum of *PMLA*. It takes one happily back to the sectarian arguments of a century ago about the right nature of God and sect—back to Isaac Bickersteth and *The Rock of Ages*. Thomas C. Caramagno had, in "Manic-Depressive Psychosis and Critical Approaches to Virginia Woolf's Life and Work," swung wild, denouncing the psychopoetics of both analysis of authors and analysis of texts. Three replies and a rejoinder appear. James Glogowski charges that "quoting any particular biobehaviorist does not provide enough support. It is uncomfortably like a clerical appeal to ecclesiastic authority, not unlike the tactic of analytic critics who invoke the authority of Freud" (808). Glogowski would like to see a brave new future in which the psychiatrists and psychoanalysts would come to literary scholars "to learn something of the context within which to assess the significance of their findings." Shirley Panken defends her book point by point against Caramagno's criticisms. Point by point Caramagno is wrong, or has altered context. "Caramagno," she says "alludes to 'Panken layering one neurosis over another' (Caramagno 10). More accurately, I say Woolf evidenced character traits of a 'mixed' variety, 'depressive, obsessive, masochistic, psychosomatic'" (809). She attacks his findings in saying that "early studies pointing to high or low levels of neurotransmitter at critical synapses have not been validated" (810). Robert Seaman calls Caramagno's study "misguided," singling out especially Caramagno's apparent disdain for "the Freudian method of the 'talking cure' in the struggle to alleviate even somatic-induced symptoms" (810). But the ultimate issue is hermeneutic: "Caramagno finds reductionism and simplification in what Freudian critics do to a text, the bringing to consciousness of unconscious content," with an excursus on the nature of the fictive reality of reality. But the anguish of the antagonists is poised on Caramagno's contention that psychoanalysis operates on a practice of blaming the afflicted for their disordered states. The counterargument is that there is warmth and human concern in psychoanalysis, but only cold science in psychobiology. Caramagno gets the last word and so has the tactical advantage. He tries to sort it out in a series of responses—that Freud had it wrong when he applied diagnoses of sexual and familial guilt to Dostoyevsky's epilepsy; that the cold science is a hedge against psychoanalytic "overreading" (811). He admits that there is "no unified theory for mentality, either biological or psychological" (811) and concludes that there is some merger necessary between the two modes of analysis in the future. But cold or not, the "new discoveries about neurological mechanisms in the hippocampus and limbic systems suggest that dreams are not distorted by an unconscious censor but expressive of a kind of adaptive thinking"; that "split-brain studies are even now challenging our notion of unconscious life and the structure of the self, denying introspection its customary epistemological privileges ... and that the dominant hemisphere, a specialist in linguistic signifiers, is debarred from direct knowledge of the nondominant hemisphere, the signified, where a separate structure processes many important perceptions and feelings. Perhaps, then, the 'Other' that we most struggle to know is not the unconscious part of one self but another conscious self, coexisting in our shared body, mute and unavailable to language, yet responsible for processing the visual cues that the dominant hemisphere may misunderstand because mistranslations are inevitable between two minds that do not speak the same language" (811). The question is not whether Caramagno uses his tactical position to defeat his adversaries; rather the question is about the nature of the truths that the various branches of analysis of minds have been assuming. One wonders about the nature of the Other under this new set of hypotheses; and over the shape of the barred signifier. Caramagno quotes a clinician, a biologist and two philosophers in his construction here.

2. Panel 1, in the collection of the Museum of Modern Art, the gift of Abbey Aldrich Rockefeller, is called *In a House in Harley Street*, and depicts the master of Bly thanking the governess for accepting the post; panels 2–5 are in the collection of the Philadelphia Museum of Art, the bequest of Frank and Alice Osborn (as are the Demuth panels for *The Beast in the Jungle*), and comprise 2, *The Governess First Sees the Ghost of Peter Quint*; 3, *Flora and the Governess*; 4, *The Governess, Mrs. Grose and the Children*; and 5, *Miles and the Governess*. The three panels for *The Beast in the Jungle* are 1 *The Boat Ride from Sorrento*; 2, *The Revelation Comes to May Bartram in Her Drawing Room*; and 3, *Marcher Receives His Revelation at May Bartram's Tomb*.

3. Barbara Haskell (1987) tells us that Demuth himself remembered only four panels, those in the Osborn collection, and suggests that the attachment of the Harley Street painting awaited recognition at a later time; the subjects of the panel make it certainly one of the sequence executed to illustrate *The Turn of the Screw*.

4. The whole question of illustration of James's work is vexed. In the preface to *The Golden Bowl* James allowed that he was prepared to accept illustration of his stories— but only if it left them untouched. In fact he proposed that illustration would be acceptable to him if it were executed separately from a work and not included with it in publication, precisely as Demuth had done. James worried that if the fiction was illustrated with the publication, the fiction runs "the risk of finding itself elbowed, on that ground, by another and a competitive process" (AN 331). But in this preface he was talking about the Alvin Langdon Coburn photographs that accompanied the New York Edition and about accepting them in part because they did not represent the painter's art and in part because they signaled rather than represent the texts and were thus not competitive. The relevance for *The Turn of the Screw* is that in the serial publication in *Collier's* the story was indeed illustrated, and by two artists: John La Farge, James's friend and sometime mentor, and Eric Pape. The La Farge illustration was included with eleven of the twelve installments of the tale; Pape did indeed set out to engage in solid specifications in competition with the prose of the tale. For a lucid and admirable account of the issues, see the note by S. P. Rosenbaum in k 254–59. The question of the Demuth illustrations is a good deal more complex. On the one hand, these illustrations

do not compete with James's work; rather they respond to it and necessarily, and in two important respects, interpret it. That is, James offered certain impressions of the characters, impressions that seem to be ratified by the characters within the tale. An example is the governess's own view of her "slighted charms" added to Mrs. Grose's supporting text that "he [antecedent ambiguous] liked them young and pretty," a compliment that embraces the governess, added to Douglas's supporting text that the governess was to be seen in a variety of ways as pretty, distinguished, extraordinary. But James enters into no more weak specifications of the governess's beauty than he does of the nature of evil environing the ghosts. James sets Demuth free to find his own specifications, and these emerge from his illustrations. He seems to make some far-reaching assumptions about the physical appearance of the governess, assumptions that support something other than conventional ideas of female prettiness of the era. If we are speaking of illustration, we could say that convention rises to the concept of Charles Dana Gibson, or perhaps updates to the image of art nouveau, as, say, in the illustrations of Lily Bart by A. B. Wenzell in Wharton's *House of Mirth* (1905). Demuth's governess does not strike us as a figure that Mrs. Grose would risk characterizing as pretty.

Adeline Tintner (1979) has an important note on La Farge's illustrations accompanying the *Collier's* serial publication of *Screw* in which she analyzes the friezelike illustration. She says that the central figure of the governess and Miles shows the governess with two right hands on Miles, one, a white one, on his shoulder, suggesting the comforting and shielding mother figure she projects for herself and one, a black one, around his head imprisoning him. The other forms of the frieze triptych suggest animals, beasts of the springing variety. The whole leads Tintner to suggest that La Farge anticipated the duality of the governess before the book publication even occurred.

The question of illustration of story reflects upon the question of reader response. James sees the illustration as a direct attempt to re-create the verbal description in the story: and he sees it as a competing artifact. In one sense he supports Iser because he seems to feel that illustration reduces the figure to singularity rather than leaving it an open-ended figure for the reader to create—exactly his notion of the reader's part in the creative process. In another sense he resists Iser's notion of multiplicity of possible gap fillings because the important feature of blank filling is precisely the reader's commitment to the creative or conceptualizing process as James's own aesthetic pole, leaving the reader at liberty to discover that the process of acquisition of data is by way of impression, and to know is to understand what impression has shown about the world—about form and light.

5. Wilson delivers the essay many times: first in *Hound & Horn* in 1934; then as a chapter on James in *The Triple Thinkers* (1938); then in something of a repudiation in the *New Yorker* (1944); then again in a second edition of *The Triple Thinkers* (1948); and finally as an item in Gerald Willen's *Casebook on Henry James's "The Turn of the Screw"* (1960).

6. Allara says tantalizingly that in the Bohemian teens of the current century Demuth took rooms in Washington Square in New York and that he frequented the various notorious watering holes of the artist group. She speaks in particular of Christine Ell's restaurant: "Among the people who frequented the Brévoort, The Hell-hole and Christine's were Eugene O'Neill, George Cram Cook, Edna Kenton, Edna St. Vincent and Norma Millay, Polly and Louis Holliday, and Terry Carlin" (1970, 40). It is not possible from this to tell whether Kenton and Demuth ever met, or if so, whether Kenton had ever seen the *Screw* illustrations before they appeared with her article in 1924. A good deal depends both on whether she did see the paintings, whether she ever discussed them with Demuth, whether she acknowledged any influence on her own

thinking from early views of them. Hutchins Hapgood, the brother of Norman Hapgood, of whose critical work James had approved in the 1890s, mentions Wilson and some of the places and people of this era, but fails to mention Kenton. Robert Crunden, in *The American Salon* (1993), mentions both Wilson and Kenton but not in juxtaposition.

7. Again, it is a matter of some difficulty to decide how one finds value in plastic arts. Is Demuth's governess pretty? In our own time, aesthetic values or perhaps aesthetic norms are very much conditioned by forces that package "beauty"—the fashion industry, the advertising industry, the world of cosmetics, all of that world that benefits if we allow ourselves to be made discontent with our current lot so that we will provide ourselves with one form or another of happiness by taking direction from the creators of these desirable things. If we look from our current norms to those of the Renaissance painters, we can see substantial areas of variation without being able to say that either ours or theirs are absolute, that either ours or theirs waver from some identifiable standard. If we listen to Barbara Herrnstein Smith (1988), we will hear her tell us that all aesthetic values—indeed, all values of any kind—are economic values first: that we reverence the surviving classical artists or the heroes of the Arnoldian dictum about the best that has been thought and said (and depicted?) because they promote our economic interests. If we listen to Marcia Eaton (1989), on the other hand, we will find that however difficult aesthetic values may be to render absolute, they are nonetheless intrinsic to aesthetic objects and are valuable directly, that is, aside from economic implications in the first instance. Smith's views are the center of her own thesis; Eaton's are the result of her study, but can be inferred from her chapter "Applied Aesthetics" (chap. 4), where she probes the reasons for an engineering firm's inability to recommend on the aesthetics of damming the upper Susitna Valley. It is reasonable to say that both of these commentators use *aesthetic* variantly from Iser's use of the term.

8. We have no way of knowing how much Edmund Wilson may have known of the Demuth illustrations independent of Kenton's article. He moved in circles that included some of the people mentioned as associated with the New York Bohemia of the 1920s and 1930s and may have acquired knowledge of Demuth and his illustrations before seeing them with Kenton's work. The discussion of the paintings in the *Hound & Horn* version of "The Ambiguity of Henry James" suggests strongly that Wilson did not know the painter. On the other hand, his acquaintance with Edna Kenton occurred some time before they both appeared in the *Hound & Horn* issue on Henry James. In a letter of 1925, he addresses her on the subject of her review of Brooks's *Pilgrimage of Henry James* (1925) conceding her superior knowledge of James's texts and wishing to meet her to discuss James because he had "contemplated writing something about him myself" (1977, 236). Likewise there is a letter of 1925 expressing his admiration for her "Ruminant Reader," in which he says "I believe you are right—though I don't think, as you seem to do, that both the ghosts and the children are imaginary. I think we must accept the children as real. The point then would be that though they have actually been exposed to rather bad influences in the groom and the former governess, whom, I take it, we must accept as having existed, too, it is the new governess who makes the real trouble. She has been fluttered by the uncle; but isn't it the boy that she really falls in love with?" (236). In a letter to James Thurber of 1959 Wilson makes his only reference to Demuth and the paintings outside the article on James's ambiguity (239).

9. Cranfill and Clark (1970) provide a selected list of transformations of the tale into other art forms. It is indeed characteristic of these transformations that they determine one aspect of the multiple possible readings of the tale and reduce the tale to that reading. Benjamin Britten, for example, in his opera of *The Turn of the Screw*, must decide how the ghosts will be represented in the music-drama form. He decides to corporealize them at least to the extent that he gives Quint both singing and verse lines.

One could decide that this is symbolic in the same fashion as a number of the *Screw* critics have done, but Britten goes even further (or his librettist, Myfanwy Piper, does) and gives highly conscious lines representing awareness of guilt to Miles. This is not to say that the opera lacks either dramatic effect or some of James's intentions for the original. It merely dispenses with the seamless multiplicity of the text. For a more recent "artsography" consult Anthony Mazzella 1981.

   10. Allara's note: Charles Demuth, "Across a Greco Is Written ... ," *Creative Art* 5:634. The complex relationship between allied arts, which has a history going back at least to Gotthold Ephraim Lessing's *Laokoön*, figures strongly for Demuth, who had wanted for some time at the beginning of his artistic life to be a writer and who did indeed publish a bit of imaginative writing early in his life. But when he moves to painting, he also moves the idea of the concept of proselike statements in his painting, supporting his idea with, among other things, this comment about the nature of and inscribed meaning in a Greco or a Velázquez or a Cézanne. Allara says that Demuth found a powerful sympathy with Walter Pater, agreeing strongly with the views attributed to the writer by Eugene J. Brzenk in his introduction to *The Imaginary Portraits of Walter Pater* (New York, 1964): "Pater attempted ' ... to demonstrate that each art strives to overcome its own limitations and to pass over into the realm of other arts. It is this *anderstreben* which he hoped to achieve in his Portraits,'" quoted in Allara 1970, 123 n. 18. By the time of the article on Greco and other painters, Demuth had lost faith in words, as Barbara Haskell, (1987, 195): "Words ... 'explain too much and say too little.' From the beginning of his career, Demuth had asserted that painting was as capable as literature of communicating ideas. Color and line 'said' something; they were not simply elements of a formal composition. 'Across the final surface—the touchable bloom, if it were a peach—of any fine painting is written for those who dare to read that which the painter knew, that which he hoped to find out, that which he—whatever. Pictures, he believed, were 'painted sentences.'" What Demuth says more than a decade after the literary paintings is that the subjects provided him with occasions to engage in the private language that was inscribed for the daring to read. The sense of private messages is certainly at least part of the implication of the illustrations for *The Turn of the Screw*.

   11. Allara's note: "Henry James, preface to *The Golden Bowl* in [Blackmur AN] p. 332–33."

   12. Interpreters like Erwin Panofsky in his *Meaning in the Fine Arts* show us that there was once a shorthand lexicon to meaning of plastic forms in the works of Alciati or Ripa; and that when these lexicographers were working at the end of the sixteenth century, the language of forms and colors was so well known that, for example, Ripa's *Iconolgia* (1595) could be published without illustrations and be perfectly intelligible to his audience—a very circumscribed one, certainly. Already by the last quarter of the eighteenth century that broad knowledge no longer pervaded, and when Johann Hertel decided to reissue the *Iconologia* in Augsburg in the 1760s, it was already necessary to assist his audience with illustrations, which for his edition were supplied by Hans Eichler, an engraver of that city (see Ripa 1971). But at least there survived a common language for interpreting works of art at that time. As surely as all classical languages have fallen into disuse, so has that language, and we are currently either at liberty to or reduced to matters of form as our index to meaning—or to ad hoc treatments that do not necessarily depend on consensus of the community of interpretation.

   13. Kenton's first novel, *What Manner of Man*, was being reviewed at the same time as James's *Ambassadors* in 1903. When her second novel, *Clem*, was published in 1907 a writer for the *Bookman*, in a brief note entitled "Edna Kenton," observed dryly, "Edna Kenton, whose novel *Clem* is being published by the Century Company, was a Chicago

newspaper woman before she began writing fiction. Her first two or three years as a freelance were exceedingly lean years, her total earnings amounting only to a few hundred dollars. The turning of the tide came with the appearance, about four years ago, of *What Manner of Man*, her first novel" (3). So apparently the novel was a financial success. But the critics were not particularly kind to her. There was, for instance, an accusation that she had stolen her plot from a current best-seller, *A Princess of Thule*, by William Black. J. B. Kerfoot, *Life*'s veteran reviewer after the departure of Robert Bridges, observes "A book by Edna Kenton... shows what a poor thing William Black might have made of *A Princess of Thule*. ... The truth is that plagiarism by a genius is a compliment; by a bungler it is a joke; it is only a crime when perpetrated by an equal" (Kerfoot 1903, 344). It is clear that for Kerfoot Kenton is a bungler. Others were not so unkind about her achievement. Eleanor Hoyt in *The Lamp* (26: 161–62) says that the story "is distinctly unpleasant" but goes on to say that "It is also distinctly powerful. Both characteristics will win readers for it." Even though she seems to make a success at writing fiction, she goes back to journalism, writing on a variety of subjects. She comes out with a very strong feminist position in the mid-teens with an essay on all the blessings that woman's liberation will bring (*Delta* 85: 1914) and also with a book on Feminist issues. It is in this role, undoubtedly, that she shows up among the denizens of the Village in the teens. Her memorable intervention in the history of *Screw* criticism seems to emerge from this long involvement with journalism. The essay is mature and certain, and her mind is sharply trained for the venture she undertakes in it. She participates along with Edmund Wilson in the *Hound & Horn* James issue in 1934.

14. This constitutes preliminary evidence that, at least for James's novella, there is a demonstrable area in which the criticism of the tale is progressive over a period of time, that is, literally undertakes matters that were previously unobserved, untreated, and unincorporated into the body of the criticism. Kenton here at least exposes the fact that public readers had ignored the prologue in prior criticism, and suggests that the prologue is important to the execution of the tale. She does relatively little with it herself, but she does credit Douglas with deepening the context of the governess's account of herself. Wilson, ten years later, also sees some distance into the prologue without realizing any important gains on Kenton. If I suggest that the coverage of the tale's geography—its mere factual materials—emerges only slowly in the course of the tale's critical history, then this is a profoundly important area upon which to base a judgment of the progressive development of the critical process in this tale. I suggest that this area of the tale's geography reaches cartographical accuracy only in the account of it given in Shoshana Felman (1977), fifty-three years after Kenton hooted at her predecessors for not paying sufficient attention to the preface. I suggest as well that there are areas of the prologue that still await full critical treatment, but that these are matters of topography—of the depth or vertical corpus of the prologue instead of its surface or horizontal geography.

15. The whole subject of what Edward Stone (1975) calls "Edition Architecture" needs to be reconsidered in the light of the correspondence in the Scribner Archive at Princeton University over the publication of the New York Edition. The burden of the correspondence suggested that the leading idea was chronology—that where no conditions prevented, order of publication was to dictate order of inclusion. But there were important further considerations: James, as Edel says (1985, 625), wanted to produce the edition in twenty-three volumes as a gesture of solidarity with Balzac, whose collected edition of the *Comédie Humaine* ran to that number of volumes. Already the process of production had necessitated a twenty-fourth volume to accommodate the length of the stories. But in addition, as the correspondence in the archives shows, there was the awkwardness of the length of *The Ambassadors* in its

running to a rather slender two volumes; and thus, though chronology was broken to a fairly substantial degree with volume 12 of the edition, constraints of space rather than elaborate thematic placing was a ruling consideration. Henry James/W. C. Brownell correspondence, 1901–ca. 1909, the Archives of Charles Scribner's Sons, box 81, subfolder 3, passim, Manuscripts Division, Department of Rare Books and Special Collections, Princeton University Libraries.

16. It is fascinating in this succession of subterranean replications of the textual movements of *The Turn of the Screw* that it should be Edmund Wilson who forwards the Goddard piece to Leon Edel for publication and inclusion in the critical history. In a letter to Edel of 21 November 1956 Wilson writes "You seem to know everything, so I suppose you have seen Oscar Cargill's paper on *The Turn of the Screw* in the summer *Chicago Review*. But do you know about a man named Harold C. Goddard of Swarthmore—now dead—who before Edna Kenton had published her note, assumed on first reading the story was about a disturbed governess and was surprised to find that other people took it as a conventional ghost story? His daughter has sent me his essay on the subject by him. I think it ought to be printed. ... You and Cargill and he all, I think, have quite distinct ideas about how the governess was able to give, or appear to give, an accurate description of Quint. Cargill's seems to me the most plausible. She had found out from the little girl." Only ten days later Wilson is writing to Edel, "Here is the Goddard paper. If it is published, it ought to be explained that it was a pioneering work—written before Edna Kenton" (1977, 538–39). Thus for each surface move in the succession of developments there is a corresponding depth move, once again like the story of psychoanalysis (and like narrative and Chomskyan grammar).

Chapter 4. Freud-Counter-Freud

1. In a Rousseauesque gesture of the 1860's James C. Jackson, an American physician, declared, in effect, that humanity was born healthy but was everywhere diseased: "That human beings are sick,—much more frequently so, than in good health,—is a fact known, or if not known, easy to be known, by all who can lay the least claim to the quality of common observation; for in truth, sickness has come to be the ruling condition of our people, while health is their exceptional condition. For this, in the nature of things, there is no sound basis. The laws of life, as exhibited in the human organism and made manifest through its economy, are just what they profess to be: their influence, their tendency, their effects, their operations, are to *preserve* life" (1862, 5–6). His challenge to Victorian America was a call to break the chains of illness and rise to robust health. Jackson virtually accused his countrymen of choosing disease over health. He argued that this was a poor choice that distorted normality.

Sherry Turkle, reviewing the first two volumes of Lacan's *Seminar* (1989, 3–4), suggested that Lacan answered Jackson by tendency in the first year of his seminars in 1953: "But Lacan argues that the ego cannot hold the solution [to the problem of will], because it is the problem: 'the ego is structured exactly like a symptom. At the heart of the subject, it is only a privileged symptom, the human symptom *par excellence*, the mental illness of man' I, 16." In other words, Jackson is wrong in his opening assumption about choice or the exertion of will in the control of the conditions of life. Humankind is not born healthy; it is born diseased. The normal state of humanity is abnormal. It is interesting that Jackson's views should so anticipate the study of psychosomatic medicine, since what Lacan suggests to us contemplates an ineluctable psychologically generated pandemic illness. It is hard to escape the impression of doublespeak in the paradox that Lacan produces. But the underlying accusation of moral unsoundness—of the ego as evil—pervades the discourse: "Lacan made it clear that the ego was the carrier of the neurosis, and that allying with the ego is like consorting with the enemy." The ego is, in short, Satan's own slave; and the distinction between what Lacan says here and what appears in books of Jackson's time declaiming against the dangers of self-pollution is virtually only one of vocabulary. Not only is the ego a conscript of the psychoanalytic Satan but it is likewise a recruit of Chaos: "The ego is built out of misidentifications, confusions and alienations of a pre-symbolic, pre-Oedipal stage of development. It can do no better. The only psychoanalytic approach to the ego is with daggers drawn." But it is precisely this heavy moralistic subtext that pervades the language of psychoanalysis in the Freudian and Lacanian branches. The psychoanalytic estrangement of the ego from the psyche in the rite of possession of the Other is inescapably reminiscent of the Christian estrangement of the soul from its God in the rite of possession of the Antichrist. Brooke-Rose, indeed, says, in a footnote, "I use 'illness' rather than evil to obviate the curious puritanism of some Anglo-American critics, for whom 'hysteria' and other psychoanalytic terms seem merely to have replaced 'sin.' I can only insist that Freud only spoke of an original lack" (1981, 397 n. 2).

It is only fair to say that Dr. Jackson also had a single-minded approach to the problem. For him the whole problem arose out of self-pollution, that demon of nineteenth-century medical hypothesis, along with its involuntary companion, "nocturnal emission," or, as it was dignified, "spermatorrhoeia." Imperfect control of sexual fluids led to the legendary nineteenth century abysses of madness or death. Cure this expense of spirit in a waste of shame and the cure for the endemic illness is at hand. The text is the same regardless of the faith: there is a state of perfection; that state of perfection belongs to a lost golden age; an appropriate gesture will bring us back toward the lost paradise.

2. It depends on one's textual source representing Cassandra how her role is perceived. She has variant functions in, say, Homer, Aeschylus, and Euripides, Homer's perspective favoring Achilles, Aeschylus' favoring Agamemnon, Euripides' favoring Helen. But uniformly Cassandra is marginalized in the classical versions of the myth. In an obscure though significant fashion, she has outraged the subcode of the immortals; to some extent she is perceived as justly excluded from acceptance by the other Trojan women; and to some extent, her execution at the hands of Clytemnestra is a logical equivalent to her spurning of or her resistance to Apollo. It is not hard to see why she should become a symptom figure to modern feminists, who see in her plight all those who are abused for imperfect subjugation to male force. It is exactly this effect in Cassandra's experience that Christa Wolf uses in her redevelopment of the legend (1984). Thus the parallel between James's governess and Cassandra is complex and is slightly differently viewed by the various critics who propose it. For some, Cassandra is a vehicle of the imperfect apprehension of disaster; for others, she is the stained prophet without honor where she lives. Clews (1985) says that "theories of hallucination attendant upon Freudian repression do not seem to capture the actuality of evil that the tale bodies forth. The apparitions have too much power to be invented, and it is they, working through the possessed governess, that do indeed accomplish the impairment of Flora and the death of Miles. If the governess herself is unimpaired—indeed rather strengthened, as Douglas's account of her suggests—it is because, having unwittingly housed the conjunction of evil forces, she has passed through a fire and emerged like Cassandra. Evil has used her, and departed from her because she was an instrument and not an agent" (165).

But to the extent that the governess is a vehicle for James's themes of the moral movement of society, she is a prophet without effectuality in proclaiming the abandonment of the child and the evil that crawls into the vacuum of such abandonment. If Hardy in *Jude*, two years before *Screw*, could give us a vision, in Little Father Time, of the "coming universal wish among the young not to live," James's governess seems to go a good way toward providing a motive for that horror—that the child is of no use in the modern world. Henry Adams, a mere decade after Hardy, watches the collapse of marriage among the laboring classes because of the economic burden of the young. Swift, of course, had seen it all ages before; but his proposal was addressed to a subject nation, not to the two nations acclaimed as the most powerful since the beginning of time, both feeding on ideologies of progress.

3. The importance of the prologue to the tale and to its critical history is the subject of the last section of the present chapter. However, it is worth taking note of the number of procedures the criticism performs in the process of appreciating the prologue. If this procession is steady, it is certainly slow as well. But the importance for criticism is that over a period of time it is progressive, even if not in an unbroken line. It becomes clear that as critics take the story more seriously and understand more fully the problematic nature of the composition and of the represented psychology, the need emerges to search the text more fully and to avoid polemic unless some newly discovered aspect of the tale's geography becomes apparent. The study of Douglas particularly and then of the prologue as a device more generally indicates to us the single most important feature of the progressive property of the criticism.

4. Heilman's note for this quotation cites Matthiessen 1944, 94. It is the Matthiessen of *The American Renaissance* who is speaking here, and for him, significantly, the tale fits the context of New England, the athletic morality, the Hawthornian darkness of the quality of evil, the figure of Ethan Brand looking into the lime pit or of the minister behind his black veil. For Matthiessen in *The Major Phase* James joins the New England fraternity of dark visions. Though Matthiessen is reported as uneasy with James in such a context, at least he joins the group of reviewers who see James as more a conscript of Hawthorne than of Emerson—or indeed of his own father—in the view of human nature developed by the fiction.

5. Shoshana Felman says (1977) that the effect of the tale upon the reader—the reading effect, or inevitable response to its agonizing absence—is to force the reader to become a figure within the tale, precisely at the stage of the gathering about the fire when the tale is given its first public exposure through Douglas's reading it. That is, for Felman, at least, the need to acquire the tale, to become its possessor or, more darkly, the possessor of its meaning, is James's appeal to the depths of human psychology. The absence is the void, or as Felman would show Lacan saying, the place of the Other, the figure who dominates consciousness, who accounts for the diseased ego. James has done nothing short of re-creating the primal sense of the alienation of the self. Hence bewilderment of vision—on both the governess's and the reader's part. By extension, under these terms, the creation of the critical model becomes a lever by whose use one can pry the tale loose from other claimants and secure it for the questing and incurable self.

6. Both, of course, eminent statesmen of letters in the late-twentieth century. The attack of Stoll on these two writers—especially on Warren, who was at that time his colleague at the University of Minnesota, underscores that aspect of the criticism that Barthes does indeed uncover in his skepticism over criticism as a progressive undertaking. The passing of generations occasions powerful antipathies, the new characteristically seeming to the old to have developed a diseased sense of language and critical vocabulary, and to want things very much their own way, a way startlingly

unlike the old. It is that in part that fuels the exchange between Douglas Bush and Stanley Fish in the 1970s and any number of the battles over critical terminology, theoretical orthodoxy, and Truth. The fact that the old order changes—that there are petulant quarrels over critical vocabulary and the appropriateness of alternate methods—does not in itself mean that there can be no progress in the development of the criticism of a particular artifact over a period of time.

7. The parallels between Maisie and the Bly children go back, of course, to the reviews. They do indeed share in the functions of illustrating James's exposure of social corruption represented in the abandonment of the child, and they are strongly parallel in their being exploited by adults whose sexual impulses are stronger than their sense of responsibility to the children who rely on them. But there are important differences. We learn from the governess's account that Mrs. Grose believes that Quint was far too free with Miles, a view that leads the governess to conclude that Quint has contributed to Miles's corruption. While the extent of Miles's depravity may be open to interpretive emphasis, the governess gives us at least a tangible clue to it in his confession that he was rusticated from school because he "said things" to people he liked (we recall that the index of Flora's possible corruption is verbal as well: that Mrs. Grose has heard language from her that she cannot ally with innocence; and her conversion to the governess's party is based upon this experience). Since the text gives us no more, we must be satisfied with this inconclusive admission. It permits the conclusion that his dismissal arose from his corruption, without either mandating it or giving the substance of it. It seems on the other hand that Maisie does indeed escape corruption, though the people among whom she moves are at least as contagious as those associated with Miles and Flora. In fact, in the matter of Maisie's knowledge, it seems convincing that she does indeed know corruption without being stained by it. Thus, when she engages in "protecting illicit lovers," as Bewley suggests, she adopts the vocabulary supplied her by Miss Overmore/Mrs. Beale—the vocabulary of salvation. If the irony comes from our understanding Mrs. Beale to mean "saving appearances" while Maisie understands spiritual salvation, that does not weaken Maisie's own claim to be honorably and disinterestedly engaged on behalf of others. And to the extent that Maisie is concerned about the salvation of the endangered, she would seem to belong to the governess's party rather than to Miles's, if indeed one must choose.

8. Leavis's observation here is one of the recurrent features of the critical tradition: the significant difference between British and American response to the tale. The one issue on which so much of the controversy turns is precisely that of the dismissal from school. For the American reader, any number of reasons might be proposed to explain the dismissal innocently. It is well worth while to keep in mind the American tradition of the bad boy—Peck's, Aldrich's, Twain's, Tarkington's, and so forth into legion. The bad-innocent equation is at least as deep an American tradition as its youth. On the other hand, if we look at, say, Dickens, who must give us the most reliable view of youth from a British perspective, we find it difficult to see a replication of the bad-innocent equation. Pip, David Copperfield, Oliver all seem to have the innocence but not the mischief. Steerforth has the mischief but not the innocence. Tiny Tim is simply ideally vulnerable. Little Nell has the innocence, but it is perishable. Perhaps Joe, in *Bleak House*, carries the symbol of Dickensian youth for us: innocent though he may be, he carries the smallpox that Esther Sommerson contracts and is disfigured by. In any case, the recurrent British view, carried by critics as diverse as Hueffer, Waley, and Leavis, is that the habit of leaving children with servants is a detestable British habit; and that however pestilential the child, he could not be sent down from school without a salient reason. The American indifference to this state of affairs represents an important divergence of cultural views. Since James's setting is British, however important the tale

for American literary history, the conventions of the cultural context must make at least part of the critical assumption about its purport.

In its first form Cargill's piece on *The Turn of the Screw* appeared as "Henry James as Freudian Pioneer," (1956) *Chicago Review* 10:13–29. Cargill gave Gerald Willen reluctant permission to reprint the essay in *The Casebook* [w 223–38]. Cargill then rewrote the article and published the revision in *PMLA* (1963) 78:238–49 as "*The Turn of the Screw* and Alice James." In turn this revision was reprinted in Robert Kimbrough's Norton Critical Edition (1966) 145–165. Cargill expresses his reservations about the earlier version in a headnote to this revision: "when Gerald Willen asked my permission to reprint this sketch in his [Casebook] I wished greatly to revise. ... I had previously recognized that I must repudiate the sketch (which I do now) and provide a more adequate statement" (k 145).

9. Alice James died in 1892 amid all the agonies that the recent revival of her biography has made plain. There can be no doubt that her death had a profound effect on both of her illustrious brothers, and subsequently on their writings. It is interesting, for instance, that the figure memorialized by Milly Theale in *The Wings of the Dove* is always and only conceived critically to be Minny Temple. The case for Minny is of course accentuated by the identity of initials. But the notion that there must be a restriction to a singular source in the genesis of a character is, it seems to me, misleading. Alice died in England with Henry James present at her death. He was powerfully moved by it and was reverential in his report to William. If we are looking for parallels between characters based on accidentals, then it was Alice James, not Minny Temple, who left a cash legacy to the novelist—not the millions of Milly Theale, but a substantial amount notwithstanding. That Alice might have been in James's mind in creating the governess is not beyond possibility, but the martyrdom of the Dantean epitaph chosen by the brothers for her Italian marble tombstone seems a more likely subject for his consciousness of her than the desire to convert her hysteria into fiction. What seems interesting about Cargill's speculation is that the governess of Douglas's creation (or re-creation) is as far as possible from a clinically hysterical invalid when Douglas knows her. See Edel, 1985, 393–94.

10. These comments by Coveney, Lydenberg, and Firebaugh on the plight of the child in the novella evoke some powerful images to a later reader of the criticism without seeming to address the larger problems of the text or of the cultural context. The possibility of attributing a psychopathology to James, or of using James's tale as a means of impeaching improper authority, skirting the edge of an unhappy world that James seemed to dwell in, strikes the reader as the sort of issue that inevitably arises in James's environs. The Max Beerbohm cartoon of James scrutinizing the telltale shoes or the report of Thomas Beer (1925) that James appeared white-faced at a friend's apartment because he had just burst in on de Maupassant naked in bed with a woman reflect the sort of thinking that James was unbalanced on the subject of sex. Edel's biographies tend to foster this idea, and the new biography by Fred Kaplan "unbuttons" James, confronts the sexual issues in James's life, as the *New York Times Book Review* suggests. The nagging problem of knowledge in James's fiction of the 1890s, especially sexual knowledge in the child, focuses the social function of James's work of the 1890s, implicit in *Screw* and scattered broadly in his work. Critics like Leslie Fiedler and A. E. Stone dealt with these social issues in the late 1950s, but the study of their work is more fruitfully left to development in the era following the summary of the first stages of the critical history of *Screw* in the 1960s.

11. Hercule Poirot must break through the narrative line and lay a hand on Dr. Sheppard's shoulder in the process of the tale. Thus he seizes the narrative line from its possessor as a final gesture of the tale, as the figure of narrative closure. As such he is

inevitably also the figure of the Nemesis, the carrier of the sense of poetic justice, yet another rhetorical gesture announcing closure. When Poirot breaks Sheppard's narrative line, Sheppard dies, or at least begins the spiral downward to darkness. He completes the cycle that Scheherazade, according to Tzvetan Todorov (1977), evades because, though as for Scheherazade, narrative is life for him, he loses the right to the narrative in failing to keep a sufficient watch over narrative control. If the governess is guilty of using her narrative to protect murder, then she belongs with Sheppard rather than with Scheherazade among narrators and the symbols of closure. Once again, one must go to the frame tale in all three fictions to decide the fate of the narrators. Scheherazade survives and restores the potential for fidelity to the Sultan; Sheppard dies in the frame for deviating from the character of his fictive substitute in the main narrative. The governess survives in sunny innocence in the frame. In some sense one must judge closure from this circumstance. If one argues that the frame is incomplete, is a broken cadre allowing for seepage or imperfect closure, then one has discovered the problem of solving the tale: if one had a place to stand, one could move the world.

12. I can remember in my own early days coming across a piece in the *Explicator* on Joyce's *Ulysses* in which Charles C. Walcutt (1956) was setting out to read a very minute passage of prose that cropped up in the text of the tale and seemed inexplicable on any ordinary grounds, namely, Stephen's repetition of the table of vowels: "AEIOU." The explicator searched the biography intensely for some sense of what the repeated unit might mean beyond the vague indication of the vocables by which words might be sounded, perhaps as a valid vehicle of significance for the writer who meant for his own words to be sounded, but lame as an explication of the unit. In the biography at around the time of the *Ulysses* idea, the commentator discovered that Joyce was using George William Russell's ideas in *The Candle of Vision*, and in addition that Joyce owed Russell a small sum of money. He surmised that Joyce wished to acknowledge his reliance on and more properly his debt to Russell. Recollecting that Russell was characteristically known by his pseudonym, A. E., the explicator put the values together: "A.E.I.O.U." meant simply "A. E. [Russell], I owe you," the common form of a promissory note. The point is that this particular explication seemed to me automatically and immediately convincing, seemed to lack nothing of perfect proof and therefore of unarguable truth. It was a deep, hidden value in the text and in the biography of the author which could be unearthed only through the painstaking process of explication and the practices of literary inference.

Chapter 5. Summary and New Beginnings

1. As we have seen, the exclusion of *The Bostonians* was not, in the first instance, against Henry James's inclinations. The desideratum to keep the collected edition to the number of volumes in Balzac's *Comédie Humaine* (twenty-three) had already been abated by the time of the completion of the first (and only) edition. Wilson's perception of a disaffinity between James and Brownell is both perceptive and historically justified. His notion that Brownell went so far as the appearance of spite in his editorial involvement with the New York Edition is unfounded. For details on the shaping of the New York Edition, see Edel 1985, 624–29.

2. Clark is written out of the preface, which is narrated in first person and signed only by Cranfill.

3. This again is one of the areas of criticism that raises the question about the validity of the interpreter's process and the proof-value if not the truth-value of a developed line.

The paradigm here is that Leon Edel, one of the elders of James criticism and scholarship, made an observation about the nature of the changes from one edition to another. The observation appeared to be authoritative to the authors of the *Anatomy*, and they adopted it. But proof is harder than assertion.

4. Thus Cranfill and Clark join the literary Freudians who take a punitive view of psychological disorders. The governess suffers "retribution" for having loved baselessly and excessively. In this sense, we can say that they also reflect Roland Barthes's proposition that criticism undertakes to translate the critical aperçu into a currently fashionable language. The punitive view does, however, seem to move from the territory of literary criticism and into the realm of moral judgment. In 1976 David Timms gave a vigorous refutation of Edel, Cranfill and Clark, and Kimbrough on the subject of James's revisions. He counts carefully, indicating that many fewer examples of revision to "verbs of feeling" from "verbs of perception" take place than Edel suggests (198). He looks carefully at James's actual usage in the tale and asserts that "a false antithesis is being made in both terms" (200), since James is concerned with cognition equally with the use of each. And he refers to the especial use of "felt" in the late style, citing the preface to *The Portrait of a Lady*, where "he does not mean 'felt' as opposed to directly perceived and physically observed', or 'provable'. A novel demonstrates 'felt life', James says, in so far as it is 'valid ... genuine ... sincere, the result of some direct impression or perception of life'" (201). Timms does not "prove" his case either—but he does argue it. Clews (1985) citing Edel in a generally perceptive and valuable section of her book on *Screw*, ignores Timms and repeats Edel's notion: "James seems to have taken pains to emphasize the strength of his narrator's feelings by expunging such terms as 'perceived,' 'I understood,' 'I observed,' and replacing them with 'I felt' and 'I fancied'"(161). She does not do her own counting.

5. And here we are in the perplexity of the higher criticism. If there is none—in literature as in theology—we are reduced to fundamentalism and all the embarrassments of orthodoxy. But once we encourage it, because our sense is that the critic engages in an imaginative act that helps to give a satisfactory account of the artifact, we also risk disputes over matters of right and wrong, over legitimacy and illegitimacy, over, in short, the critical history of all problem texts. As Maisie discovers, there's something behind everything as there is color behind the undiffracted light of Wordsworth's rainbow. The pleasure of discovery must have place in this process. Thurber twits the searchers after elusive literary truths with his good lady who wishes to detect the culprit in *Macbeth*. We are stuck with the irreducible ambiguity of *Rashoman*, no matter how partisan we are in the preference of one or another perspective.

6. Placing emphasis on the question of the social hierarchy at Bly, the *Anatomy* ignores the implication in the preface that James might well have been talking about narrative authority in his preface when he says "she has authority and that is a great deal to have given her." The point at issue is exactly that Firebaugh and Lydenberg had also wrestled with the problem of the interpretation of the tale as an issue of social authority; that the *Anatomy* cites the two critics, but does not sufficiently work out the problem of the relation between the governess and Bly as against her relationship with her own record of events. James had said about that, at least, that it was "crystalline," with, indeed, the possibility of irony in this designation. But if the critic wishes to impeach, one at least expects the impeachment to take the form of a structured argument, not simply an assumption. The authors themselves are deeply aware that they have plunged themselves into the middle of a controversy. Merely to set it aside and to declare their values weakens their critique as illustration. Juliet McMaster (1969) challenges this in a note (378 n. 4)—"[Cranfill and Clark] in *An Anatomy of "The Turn of the Screw"* (Austin, 1965), suggest that Flora's abduction of the boat is another of the governess's

delusions; however, there is no doubt about the location of the confrontation: at the far side of the lake, where the governess had first seen Miss Jessel."

7. Moreover, in the sense that the governess is a character, or as I am inclined to suggest, a character-metaphor, she is unavailable for appraisal as an empirical body. Käte Hamburger speaks of the "intransgressible boundary which separates fiction from reality" (1979, 151). This boundary separates the truth-value that inheres in an organic unit from the systematically imperfect *ens* comprehended in a literary character. The boundary that Hamburger speaks of is "established solely in that a given material becomes 'fictionalized': the persons in action are portrayed as being so 'here' and 'now,' and therefore necessarily experiencing 'here' and 'now,' concomitant to which is the experience of fiction, of non-reality." The narrative yields its values, but its values are restricted to the represented and cannot be projected beyond the confines of narrative. It is amusing to engage in literary detection—to carry out the implications of character activities to a conclusion logical to organic life. And this amusing activity can be useful in the matter of supplying the narrative blanks that perforce the narrative leaves. It is easy, in fact, to confuse the filling in of the blanks with the act of literary interpretation, where, pace Hamburger, the boundary line is not so easy to draw. The effect of Cranfill and Clark's projections for the governess amount to reification, to an assumption of perfect systematic wholeness for the character. The nature of their evidence against her is precisely the evidence that one would bring to bear in a "case"—either legal or pathological. The difficulty comes when we object that all we can have of the character is what is in the text—in a first-person narrative from the narrator. The reification of the governess in the *Anatomy* extends the character beyond any textual evidence to subject the character to the rigors of psychological analysis: large sectors of her psyche are supplied by the interpreters as though it were indeed organically whole. But James suggests that her very want of wholeness is what assists him to enmesh us in her life, or restated, in his art. As later commentators have suggested, we cannot escape the impulse to complete the organic unity of the governess by supplying her with our own psyches. In this lies James's genius. Our only escape is to follow the Iron Scots Stenographer into perfect immunity to the governess's textual appeal. Otherwise we follow Douglas and the external narrator into her net.

8. If the governess is really certifiably insane in a Victorian "real-world," as, for example, Cranfill and Clark speculate, there is little hope for a cure and little skill with which to produce it. Mary Daly (1978), in *Gyn/Ecology* describes the characteristic cure—a surgical procedure in the form of female castration, or clitoridectomy. The madhouse understanding of female psychic disorders was indeed inclined toward a sexual explanation. Literarily, of course, the most famous case is that of Bertha Mason: and after we have climbed down from the excursus into the condition of the madwoman in the attic, we might well raise the question of Charlotte Brontë's intention in creating Bertha, or, if one prefers, of exactly how to determine the inclination of narrative regard (sympathy or aversion) for this character. The essays in Andrew Scull's book on madness indicate generally the sense of desperation associated with madness (1981). Brooke-Rose, with characteristic good sense, says in a note (1981, 396 n. 8) "Even on the level of psychoanalysing a non-existent fictional character this is confusing: hysteria is the only neurosis that can become a psychosis, and hallucinations can occur in both conversion hysteria and psychosis, but if the governess were psychotic she would be wholly unable to work, or relate to reality in any way, and would certainly not have found a job later, or told Douglas so calmly and charmingly about her experience. Psychosis was, and maybe still is, incurable." The problem of the governess's ten intervening years—or indeed her own narrative regard for the events at Bly in these ten years—is unrecoverable because it makes no part of her narrative, which ends with her

report of dispossession. But the speculation of "real-life" incarceration for mental illness seems not to fit any of the narrative facts that the tale does disclose.

9. Grose is the villain—C. K. Aldrich (1967–68); is the mother—Clair (1965); is driving the governess mad—Aldrich, Solomon (1964), Clair; Douglas is Miles—Collins (1955), Rubin (1963), Trachtenberg (1965); the governess fantasizes the mother role—Katan (1962); is the ghost—Aswell (1968); is a mirror image to the ghosts—Siegel (1968), McMaster (1969); primal-scene trauma—Katan.

10. One reasonably simple way of talking about James's (successful) challenge to his readers in his late manner of characterization is to apply a cognitive theory of metaphor (such as Mac Cormac's 1985) and designate character as metaphor in a fuzzy set. Mac Cormac uses a declarative sentence—"John is tall and not tall"—based on a graded table for tallness as a fuzzy set in which the accident of falling at a median point would authorize the statement without mere controversion. What James does is to approach character creation by recording the character's impressions of sensory experience at the moment of registration. His practice shows consciousness on a preliterate plane in which a variety of impressionistic responses, some of which can even contradict others, are accurate ("real") reflections of the function of consciousness at the moment of reception of sense impression prior to the sorting functions of rational consciousness. Hence the penchant for interruption, for jumping, for jumbled and imperfect vocabulary, for involuted sentence structures, and for labyrinthine prose. As Sterne had shown, the appropriate metaphor for the conceiving mind is the labyrinth, complete with a monster at the core. James is, in a sense, down there at the core, perhaps with Theseus, observing the motions of the monster.

What James is doing is *not* stream-of-consciousness, but rather what happens the moment before thought as the beginning of the sorting process takes place—very much the beauty of inflection before the beauty of innuendo. In a clear set (for characterization this would be good guys and bad guys) the correlatives would be 0 and 1, all "0" or all "1"; in a fuzzy set, the correlations would be 0, 0.1, 0.2 and so forth to 1. James's characters are tall and not tall, moral and not moral, clever and not clever; they struggle with data that do not fall into equations cleared by perfect values for the exponents. James allows us to watch them initiate the process of sorting data, of making narrative out of the chaos of sensory experience. Of course we challenge them. But their struggle allows us to see the difference between truth-value and Truth; that is, the characters cannot lay claim to the completeness of organic wholeness (cannot, then, be judged according to the canons of truth-value while contributing to our knowledge of the Truth of minds making patterns out of experience). Ramras-Rauch says, "As I have tried to suggest, the tale is a metaphor—on many levels—for the problem of interpretation. But it goes beyond that, to take the problem of interpretation itself as a metaphor for the problem of understanding human existence" (1982, 95).

If we are to read, then we, too, must do some of the work of creating the narrative. It is art that makes life; it is narrative that vouches for art, for the necessary illusion of coherence; it is we who make narrative. Käte Hamburger understands this when she says that the nature of narrative is to dissolve the pastness of the preterit or the sequentiality of tenses (1973, 87–88). James's late narrators are "in it" in the same sense as we are, struggling, as James repeatedly says, for lucidity. No better example of the recording of sensory data occurs in literature than the governess's description of the first apparition of Quint. This is some of the new ground that James is breaking in the late fiction. The confrontation with chaos is the mechanism of horror fiction.

11. Elizabeth Sheppard follows Tuveson in this observation and collates the apparition seen only from the waist up with examples from PSPR. Once the recognition occurs it becomes a regular feature of the criticism, especially useful to the

psychological critics who emphasize its revelation of the governess's sexual suppressions. Nonetheless, as late as 1986 Linda Boren is prepared to proclaim that "with the third encounter, she sees Quint in full figure and loses her fear" (16). Beidler (1989) follows Sheppard in observing that the male ghost is seen only from the waist up.

12. As we have seen at the opening of this section, the Douglas-Miles equation starts early in the imaginative re-creation of the narrative. Carvel Collins (1955) was the first to suggest it; Louis Rubin (1963) Stanley Trachtenberg (1965), and Walter Stepp (1976) are among the others who join Collins and Thomson in this view. M. Karen Crowe (1982) argues that Douglas's relation to Miles is "a vital thread" (37) in the unfolding of the tale, but that Douglas "remains in the frame, both literally and spiritually" (38). Douglas is not Miles grown up.

13. Though if both Edel and Kaplan are to be credited, the acceptance of a male figure as the external narrator while not missing the sexual innuendo in this chain both of narrative transmission and the transmission of a sequence of affinities would not be out of bounds for James if he is viewed as an undisclosed homosexual. Here, too, the suggestion of the external narrator as female establishes a line of succession. Sheppard (1974) proposes it; A. R. Taylor (1981) considers it an essential to the tale; Kauffman (1981) assumes it.

14. Thus he joins the enlarging group who sees a kind of malevolence in the governess, not in a personal fury but as an agent of some cosmic force possibly as large as the Nemesis. We have seen that Van Doren (1942) had proposed that the helpless Cassandra was herself the agency through which the retributive will of the gods was enacted. In some sense both Lydenberg (1957) and Firebaugh (1957) saw a similar force, though with more personal responsibility for the menace on the part of the governess. Muriel West (1964a) also attributed a culpable malevolence to the governess. Variations on the theme of the governess as a malevolent force with or without divine agency or constraint can be found in McNaughton (1974), Houston (1977), Curtsinger (1980), McElroy (1981), Anne Taylor (1981), and Kaston (1984). Peter Dyson (1978) capitalizes on the progression of the images of the springing beast from chapter 3 to chapter 24 to suggest that the governess is the beast. Obuchowski (1978) says that the governess either scares Miles to death or accidentally murders him (381). Clark (1978) contributes a heart murmur to Miles's composition as the reason for his dismissal from school and says that the governess, unaware of the child's weakness, "squeezes him to death" (112). Glasser (1980) believes that the governess becomes entrapped in her own romance, has lost sight of ordinary cause-and-effect relationships, "while grasping Miles and squeezing the breath from his body" (231). Stanley Renner (1986) makes out her resemblance to the mother in a later story who destroys her son to keep him from growing up sexually.

15. It is only a small step from the heavy breathing that Bontly suggests here to the suggestion that the governess and Miles do indeed engage in sexual intercourse. Hill (1981) sees Miles believing that he and the governess are in a conspiracy to create ghosts so that all others at Bly will clear out and they can be alone together for sexual purposes. Hill sees the governess as betraying Miles's idea and insisting on the ghosts.

16. Once again this is a view that founds a line of succession. Timms (1976) suggests that she is a careful writer; that she writes long after the events at Bly and thus recollects in some tranquility; that she is careful to adorn her tale with stylistic devices that will enhance its value for its intended reader, Douglas. Fussell (1980) proposes that the governess is a writer of fiction and that the fiction is only her attempt to divert herself while she is engaged as governess for Douglas's sister either at Bly or at a location that she transforms into Bly. Marcella Holloway (1979) sees the narrative as a

confession on the part of the governess while still seeing it as essentially fiction. Linda Kauffman (1981) also suggests fictive intentions for the narrative. William Glasser (1980) sees the governess not only as a writer, but ideally as a romancer according to the dimensions of that worthy given by James in the preface to *The American*. Thus she is eager to "cut the rope" that holds the balloon of experience to earth and "carry us away" with her in the same fashion as the master and then Miles have carried her away. The governess perpetrates this romance upon herself. That is, she is attempting to pass off on the reader as well as on herself the liberation "from the conditions that we usually know," which is the "art of the romancer" (231). William Goetz (1981) sees the governess as an author whose text has the effect of trapping her. Authority has shifted from the master to her; she cannot return to the master (74). Kawin (1982) says that she is the author of a memoir; like Goetz, Kawin sees the frame tale as constricting, but rather as a fence than a prison and rather to find a place to contain the ghosts. The governess is thus "a partial site and a possible origin of the ghosts" (185). Mansell (1985) says, "*The Turn of the Screw* creates itself a text (the governess's manuscript) in the midst of the story's inner world, then takes away that world and leaves itself—a text" (55).

17. Here is another useful example of the difference between the British and American views of *The Turn of the Screw*. The most important difference will always have to do with class. We have seen Cranfill and Clark (1965a) and others disparage the governess for lording her exalted position over other members of the household at Bly. Though American fondness for both Jane Austen and Charlotte Brontë had shown clearly how little power the governess had, the American view finds her in a privileged position because of apparent rank. Austen showed her reader how little desirable the position appeared to be to Jane Fairfax, for example, in *Emma*; for Jane Eyre, the initial experience of being a governess is liberating. It is not long before she finds herself trapped. It is only a little later that she finds herself vulnerable to Blanche Ingraham's insults about the poisonous quality of governesses. Goode (1966) shows here a fairly clear sense of the governess's actual position, surely not one to be envied or coveted. The additional duties that she undertakes beyond those of the governess in a normal household are not added luxuries, but rather added burdens. The power of depersonalization was indeed a massive one. Gathorne-Hardy (1972) sees governesses as put upon to stand between civilization and chaos and as being successful, but as frequently becoming tense and soured through the years of vigilance. See Katharine West, *A Chapter of Governesses*, (1949, 81–86). Some of the essays in Scull (1981) suggest that one of the cultural streams that led into the madhouses was indeed the occupation of governess.

18. It is a phenomenon that recurrently in the critical history, areas of the textual geography of the tale that had received no prior commentary suddenly find simultaneous voice in a number of critics. In 1947–1949, for example the assault on Wilson's hypothesis of governess-hysteria by accenting the governess's identification of Quint was discovered by three critics simultaneously—that is, by Heilman, by Evans, and by Liddell. Though it is not impossible that one or another had seen the idea in the work of the others before claiming discovery, it is unlikely. The same is so for the group who discovers the mirrors at Bly and uses them to support a claim that James is developing the tale by making the ghosts a mirror image of the governess. Bernadine Brown (1974) takes Aswell and Siegel to task because they fail to prove out the mirror theme. Brown presses the idea that the mirror theme keeps reflecting through a series of character pairings representing ideal and demonic states for the governess (79–80). Though the group pressing Todorov's concept of the Fantastic into service for describing the seamless joint between the two tales was at least rooted in a single source,

they appeared without knowledge of one another; and in fact, Brooke-Rose, when she incorporates her three essays on *The Turn of the Screw* into *The Rhetoric of the Unreal*, goes back to praise Shoshana Felman's work of the identical moment as something with which she fully agrees. Kevin Murphy's "Unfixable Text" (1978) appeared at virtually the same time with no roots in either the Fantastics or in the others who were pressing the idea of the two simultaneous mutually incompatible readings of the tale. It is a fascinating exercise to watch a group of very skilled writers and theorists around the mid-1980s try to avoid falling into the trap of the tale by suggesting that the tale must not be solved.

The mirror theme is inevitable in the intensifying movements of the criticism. The mise-en-abyme or, as Meike Bal prefers, the mirror text, becomes an increasingly important configuration in the development of narrative theory and critics begin to find both the self-referentiality of *Screw* and its pursuit of Miles in one form or another into the abyss that awaits him according to the governess's metaphor— "With the stroke of the loss I was so proud of he uttered the cry of a creature hurled over an abyss" (k 88). Hana Wirth-Nesher (1979) sees the text disappearing into a well of silence in parallel with Conrad's *Heart of Darkness*: "Both nouvelles are about the terror of having to make moral choices on uncertain perceptions of evil; they are about false or exaggerated notions of innocence and the evil unleashed in trying to preserve what is only a fraud. And finally, they are structures of words acting as conspiracies of silence" (325). Millicent Bell (1982) speaks of this tendency of infinite reflection by the term "binary permutation" (41), in which it is crucial to see that "appearances are just what the governess will never trust, since all things may be replaced by their opposites" (42). Ramras-Rauch (1982) credits the structuralists (Rimmon and Brooke-Rose) with demystifying some of the tension in the reflexive character of the readings: "The overall effect of the structural approach has been to deflate the problem of ambiguity as a problem: In taking it as 'there,' we no longer suffer its effects, nor try to make the story 'work,' nor feel the need to explain what is inexplicable. We now see the parties—the protagonist/narrator and the commentator/reader—as standing on opposite sides of the mirror. Whether the mirror reflects back at us or allows a degree of through-vision is left open" (105). Siebers (1984) suggests that the mirror text occurs not in the governess's view of her person in the long glasses, but rather in a mutual reflection between the governess and the reader in which the reader adopts the governess's accusatory stance. Clews (1985), like Siebers, sees the reflexive problem unfolding in the strained relation between the narrator and the reader with an emphasis on the unseen and unstatable: "This emphasis is disturbing, in retrospect, to all but the most casual readers because it involves them in a struggle against, rather than with, the narrator; their acceptance of the narrator's authority can be accomplished only at the cost of abdicating their own responsibility as careful readers" (166). Wells (1985) simplifies the governess's metaphor: "There, Miles falls into an 'abyss,' a space shaped entirely by his 'loss'" (100). But she sees clearly into that abyss: "Gaining total possession of Miles, she abolishes him as an other; she absorbs him. But it is impossible to possess what one has already incorporated, so that the governess's account of Miles's fall wavers in its voice—he is a creature who is hurled; he is the boy she catches. But the hurler and the grasper are the same; the abyss and the governess's arms have become alternate expressions for the same vacant place" (100–101). Darrel Mansell (1985) sees a succession of rectangular surfaces—mirrors, windows, paintings. He comments that as the governess's tale moves on such surfaces, it moves to two dimensions in its internal orders from three, from the perspectival world to Flatland (63). The mirror text evolves as from a window to a mirror, with Mrs. Grose ("the governess gets 'the...reflection of [prodigious things]' in Mrs. Grose's face, so that Mrs. Grose is precisely her mirror").

And "by the story's final baffling scene there is next to nothing through or beyond the Bly-window to be seen or heard ... nothing but 'the quiet day'" (61). The reflex in the narrative transmission lies in such matters as the master's letter: "that final dimension beyond or outside of *The Turn of the Screw*, is merely a reference to a sealed text swallowed up into the self-referring text of the story itself—locked up in one of the drawers in the governess's room" (62); or "Flora's interrupted *0*'s turn into the 'nothing' Miles finds in the governess's unposted letter" (63).

19. Any close student of usage will know that it was not until well into the twentieth century that the term "intercourse" became exclusively the indicatory of sexual conjunction. Intercourse, Pennsylvania, could not have been so named if the word meant in earlier times what it means colloquially today, and the joke implicit in sending a sexually explicit men's magazine from that post office would have been lost on the founding fathers. A number of other discoverers press this point. Brooke-Rose is preeminent among those who set the record straight: "The stress in the second quotation for instance ["'... our perfect intercourse'"] is not on 'intercourse' but on the fact that Miles keeps such contacts secret. Of course the 'Freudian' interpreters would argue that contact with the ghosts does 'symbolise' sexual intercourse, as would contact with Miles. But it is only in the twentieth century that the legal term 'sexual intercourse' loses its adjective and becomes sufficient on its own for this meaning, so much so that today it is the adjective 'social' which has to be added" (144–45).

Chapter 6. Main Currents in Recent *Screw* Criticism

1. Armstrong wrestles hard with the dilemma of definitive readings, accuracy, and the quandaries of choice. He makes a good case that our knowledge of how we go about solving problems—the epistemology of hermeneutics—is inescapably linked to our selection of systems and their application to literary works. Thus the favored system slowly emerges as the foundation of interpretation and conflicting readings comes to seem more and more a matter of conflicting and often undisclosed epistemological assumptions. His study is a useful corrective to some critical excesses. The problem of close reading and careful reading, then, would be secondary to the problem of probing beneath the interpretation to discover its assumptions. Nonetheless, in his practice Armstrong shows some alarming evidences of inaccurate reading and thus shows once again how the interpretive process replicates the text. One example will have to do. Armstrong looks at two of the reviews and records the reviewers' aversion to the tale—those in *Outlook* and *Bookman*. Says Armstrong: "Early reviewers wondered about whether so harrowing a tale about such an abominable evil should ever have been written" (1988, 697), quoting the most intense objections of the two most unfavorable reviews. As we have seen, there were twenty-seven reviews at least, and it was more typical of them to praise James's genius than to assault his taste. Has Armstrong merely illustrated his argument by engaging in an act of choice here—and is the choice innocent, that is, unimportant to the reader's apprehension of how the novella was reviewed? The answer is yes and no—yes, he is exercising choice, and no, it is not innocent choice, because he leaves the reader to infer that he knows the critical tradition of the tale and that he has given enough of it to leave a fair impression of its content and import. In the same paragraph Armstrong recounts Virginia Woolf's review of her encounter with the tale: "Only twenty years later, however, the work's gruesome effects seem to have worn off, and Virginia Woolf finds James's ghosts too domestic and worldly to be frightening. 'What does it matter, then,' she asks, 'if we do pick up *The*

Turn of the Screw an hour or so before bedtime?'" (697; his reference is k 179). Again, is this a just, or accurate, representation of what Woolf has said? She continues by looking not at the inevitable loss of a ghost tale's emotional power, but at its shift from the world outside, where the old ghosts performed their terror, to the world inside where James's ghosts ravage: "'But it is not a man with red hair and a white face whom we fear. We are afraid of something unnamed, of something, perhaps in ourselves. In short, we turn on the light.... That courtly, worldly, sentimental old gentleman can still make us afraid of the dark'" (180). It is cogent to argue here that Armstrong forfeits his point that the tale had lost its terror in twenty years if he makes Virginia Woolf his evidential source. It would seem that Armstrong has not quite secured the argument that we can dispense with careful reading—of either artifact or critical text—by reducing hermeneutics to matters of readerly choice.

2. Felman is much given to the practice of underscoring; hence all italics in the following quotations will be understood as appearing in the original except where I designate supplied emphasis.

3. If the Labyrinth is the classical mythic emblem of mind with the monster at the center to designate the willful character of all that is human—the classical original sin, the theft of fire from the gods, and the presumption to judge among the gods—and if it is Sterne's image of mind with the generalized monster reduced to human sexuality, with Phutatorius's smug excursions into the sexual arcana as exemplary text—then it is also the perfect psychoanalytic emblem of the self with the monster now assuming the form of the id. Any distinctions in the progression are essentially without differences.

4. Brooke-Rose and Rimmon also recognize the letters. Once Felman has opened the subject, a number of later critics follow, some with appropriate acknowledgment of these propounders, some in the form of discoveries that they make themselves. Letters whose contents are not disclosed, or are not fully disclosed, or are not read into the record verbatim suggest very essentially the sense of narrative enigma, a dramatization of the sort of gap that the reader-response critics designate as the necessary result of narrative process and the necessary condition of reader response. Schleifer (1980), Kauffman (1981), Bell (1982), and Faulkner (1983) all treat the letters and the problem of failed communication in the text as an index to the unclosed gap in comprehension.

5. Felman uses Spilka's article on how not to do the Freudian thing as a pivot in relation to Wilson and the other earlier Freudians on the one hand and the needs of a Freudian or psychoanalytic criticism on the other. She proposes that Spilka's most forceful plea is his notion of what is now coming to be called a "generous critique." She advocates that we go back over the Freudian premises in the literary sense, being careful to cultivate in the literary context the ancient medical notion of the good bedside manner—that we approach the text once more with tact. She accuses Wilson of "wild psychoanalysis" in his approach to the text, to the author, and to the protagonist. She also raises the essential questions about what constitutes evidence in the relation between the analytic mind and the literary text: Just where should the emphasis fall? But her practice seems to me to be less kind and gentle than her theory. Nevertheless, her work tends to act as a corrective to those who have read it. Wild psychoanalysis, or free association of the (Freudian) senses, still occurs for some of those who have not read Felman's essay. Anne Taylor (1981) indicates early in her treatment of James that her position is that of Edel and those who "cracked" the tale—Goddard, Kenton, and Wilson (159). The governess is "the noble little governess," presumably in imitation of Kenton. James was a cowering and feminine figure: "To be active in the world as demanded of an American male frightened James deeply" (157); "it is obvious that this fear informs his fiction" (160). Linda Boren (1986) says that "we forget when her first-person confession begins that it is actually James assuming the persona of a woman"

(12); "those familiar with James's biography and his late story 'The Jolly Corner' will recognize in [the third Quint encounter] the routing of James's own fear when he turns to confront his pursuer, actually his alter ego, in a recurring nightmare of castration anxiety" (16).

6. And here one is forced to ask about the status of this essay in the critical tradition. Is it legitimate to expect that Felman should have read it in the process of formulating her own statement? If she can be excused it is because she is coming from another tradition. Clearly some of her energy has gone into her involvement with Lacan, with "the French Freud" and with the whole history of psychoanalysis, its association with European literature, and only as an afterthought, its association with American literature, as, for instance, with *The Turn of the Screw* and, because Lacan makes it a centerpiece for his arguments about the relation of literature and psychology, Poe's "Purloined Letter." If on the other hand she should be held accountable for an important source in her argument, especially when she is scolding others for inattention, the excuse falls away. Her footnote on the turns of the screw is distinctly enigmatic and is problematic in the context of her very solid insights into the problems of interpreting the frame of the tale. Norton's essay appears not in some obscure journal that is difficult to find at all and is not likely to be indexed in major bibliographical sources: rather it appears in *American Imago*, the American journal for the study of cultural psychoanalysis, some six years before Felman's Turning the Screw. It would be of some interest to know how she would react if the essay came to her attention.

7. Nonetheless, it has been a seminal one. The citation index on this one piece of work is substantial; and the citations are not merely comments in passing. As early as 1982, in an essay devoted to the perceived complexities of the relationship between psychoanalysis and literature, Gail Reed cited the important observations of Felman's opening of her volume, *The Question of Reading: Otherwise*. Reed finds that she must reject texts as clinical evidence, suggesting the problem of reification or imposing truth value as "wild analysis" (19, 20); but Felman suggests a way of using the criticism: "the kind of questions critics ask and avoid asking about a text, the kind of answers they offer or wish to receive, the language (especially metaphors) they use to describe a text, their interactions around a text, provide valuable clues to its latent but powerfully emotive content. Thus I suggest that critics may re-enact a fantasy which they do not consciously perceive, but which is nevertheless an integral part of the text's aesthetic power" (1977, 22). Reed seems very strongly to adopt the notion that if we are going to deal with reader response, we should watch (available) readers reading. Among the other respondents to Felman's ideas in *Turning the Screw* are Mieke Bal and others who join her in the special issue of *Style* (18, 1984) devoted to the development of a theory of psychopoetics. In the introduction to the issue she declares that "it is not yet a full, coherent theory but it consists of elements of a possible theory, from which a method, a taxonomy, an axiology, a hermeneutics and, indeed, a critical method can be drawn" (242). But she addresses "Felman's scornful metaphor" of literature as not a patient to be analyzed, but rather a master who outstrips analysis (241). Gilbert D. Chaitin, in the same issue, credits Felman with rediscovering "a theory of knowledge via Lacan's claim that the starting point of transference is the analysand's belief that the analyst possesses the knowledge of 'meaning as such.' ... At least in *The Turn of the Screw*, the storyteller relates to the listener as to a part of the story he is telling, just as an analysand, once transference has begun, weaves the analyst into the web of his associations. ... In this theory, narrative knowledge, whether in the storyteller or in the listener, turns out to be illusory; its only importance is to trigger the transference process" (1984, 291). Chaitin, then, finds that Felman's observations on James's tale restate the entire set of values in the relation between psychoanalysis and literature. Harly Sonne remarks: "all these

fundamental questions concerning problems of knowledge and the necessity of analytic construction still form the basis of most debates on interpretation, criticism [and] textual analysis.... Consequently, the analytical strategies employed in the reading of fiction, as well as texts in general, have turned the screws of interpretation a number of times (I am, of course, referring to the fascinating article ... by Shoshana Felman) (1984, 305). Jonathan Culler says, "A good example, drawn from a formidable discussion of literature and psychoanalysis which gives pride of place to transference, is Shoshana Felman's account of the relation between James's *The Turn of the Screw* and its critics. Among other things, Felman shows that when the critics claim to be interpreting the story, standing outside it and telling us its true meaning, they are in fact caught up in it, playing an interpretive role that is already dramatized in the story.... If transference is a structure of repetition linking analyst and the analysed discourse ... then we have something like that here, when in interpreting the governess the critic replays the role of the governess. That replaying emerges when a later critic—Felman—transferentially anticipating a transferential relation between critics and text, reads the text as dramatizing the activity of earlier critics" (1984, 371–72). Culler, while conceding Felman the power of a formidable critic and theorist—to the point of identifying here a significant theoretical particle of an emerging psychopoetics—nonetheless sees that Felman, too, must fall into the trap, must wish to possess the tale by becoming its exegete, even if at the metacritical rather than the critical stage. She proves her theory by unconsciously illustrating it, like all those who undertake an explication of *The Turn of the Screw*. Tobin Siebers in two pieces picks up some of the theoretical postulates at issue here. Though his main concern is with the flaws in Todorov's concept of the fantastic, he acknowledges Felman as a companion to Brooke-Rose in the attempt to understand the complex relationships between literature and its theoretical components on the one hand and literature and the character of mind on the other. He suggests that in fact one can both criticize the text and escape the trap: "The reader may choose to hesitate once more over the visitants, governess, or children; or he may choose to hesitate over hesitation and begin to interrogate the status of superstition in literature and society. If he chooses to hesitate over either the governess or the children, he affirms the founding oppositions of the story's underlying mythology and falls into James's well-laid trap. If he chooses to hesitate over hesitation and to recognize the occurrence of a radical discontinuity, he allows literature to teach him what literature is" (1983, 572). The implication is that he himself has chosen to hesitate over hesitation— as he explains, to avoid duplicating "the exclusionary logic of the governess," or that aspect of her own hermeneutics that must find the children guilty of conspiracy where the evidence is based on their unsoiled innocence (567). But he, too, falls. He says "That the governess apparently smothers the boy" (571). He gives up hesitation either over the governess or the children and chooses. He falls into the trap that Felman says Wilson has fallen into, and that Culler says Felman has fallen into: deciding the text from within. It is convenient for him to find that the governess "apparently" smothers the boy; and the subjunctivity of "apparently" might be argued to release him from reduction. But it doesn't. The text simply does not say how Miles dies beyond the fact of his heart stopping. And thus the presentation of the governess in the frame has as much authority as does the presented dispossession. It is important to remember, as Timms (1976) suggests, that in the textual determination of sequences, the actual written narrative very much postdates Douglas's discussions of Bly with the governess while she is his sister's governess. The indication is that she finally writes it shortly before she dies. Timms's suggestion that she writes it with a consciousness of possible effects, making it a conscious artifact, bears some thought.

8. The concept of frame becomes a focus of study after Brooke-Rose's treatment of it

here. The central piece is that of Jean-Jacques Weber in 1982, in which Weber suggests that James violates the laws of communication in the process of creating a frame that the fiction does not complete. He sees the prologue as a framing device, which implies completeness in both an artistic sense (closure) and in a formal or geometrical sense (the enclosed or completed rectangular frame). His contention is that the controversy over the tale arises from the intolerable gap that has been created by the broken or incomplete frame. William Goetz (1981) treats the frame tale as an imprisoning device. Bruce Kawin (1982) sees it as a device to fence in the unbearable ghosts. Michael Taylor (1982) focuses his comments on the frame tale with a different emphasis: the notion that the mystery surrounds the relationships between Douglas and the "first narrator" of the tale with the notion that the first narrator is possibly female and certainly androgynous. Anthony Mazzella (1980) also challenges the standard assumptions about the sex of the external narrator. Elizabeth Sheppard (1974) and Linda Kauffman (1981) also see the frame tale conditioned by the necessary femaleness of the external narrator.

9. The equations between James's governess and Brontë's are extensive, going back to the reviews in 1898 and 1899. Elizabeth A. Sheppard (1974) saw the obvious parallels and accepted the idea without finding it definitive. Claude Tournadre (1969) sees the analogy from the fact that the governess reads *Jane Eyre* while at Bly. I have already noted that Christine Brooke-Rose declares that James dates the action of the events at Bly precisely to 1847 so that the equation between *Jane Eyre* and the governess will make a part of the critical or apperceptive concept of the tale. Bernadine Brown (1974) comments upon a reading effect in which the characters fall into ideal pairs. Miles and Flora are the innocence of childhood with its rosy outlook on the future; Quint and Jessel are the dark version of this quest. The governess hopes to link herself with the absent master and to become the fulfillment of the future that lies before the children seen as innocents. Her Jane Eyre reference comes, then, in the form of a desire to marry her employer. Brown suggests that she unconsciously puts Quint in the uncle's place by virtue of the power of her unfulfilled wishes and thus destroys the idyll of Bly. Brown also acutely sees the children as emblem figures: Miles and Flora standing for "soldier and flower" and also M. and F. as Male and Female (with a nod to Heilman). As such they can be seen as function characters instead of merely the passive recipients, and Brown can at least point to these effects as embedded by James in the text (79–80). Linda Kauffman (1981) offers the interesting equation between the two books: Jane stands in relation to Bertha Mason as the governess stands to Miss Jessel, with the notion that in each case the shadow figures represent the dark personality of the protagonist. Kauffman suggests that because Jane accepts and to some extent identifies with her darker self, she can emerge from the subworld of infantile fantasy and secure her happiness in a world like our own; but that the governess, in rejecting and reviling Miss Jessel also refuses to acknowledge her own darker self and thus winds up entrapped in the subworld of fantasy (178). Kauffman, however, does not account for how the governess seems to emerge from Bly in the fashion that Douglas accords her. Alice Petry (1983) not only sees a point-by-point analogy between the two fictions but also suggests that this is a discovery of her own. Her version of the match is that the governess fails because she identifies herself with a fictional character (61).

10. It is notable that there is no technology in the tale to indicate absolute dating just as there is no topicality in political or social matters to do so. James was intensely aware of the sort of dating devices that Eliot used in *Middlemarch* to carry the time setting to very exact past times, including, of course dates. The fact that there are no comments on the Peterloo Massacre or the Corn Laws or the invention of the mower or other machines suggests to the reader how intensely James wished to keep the tale undatable. There are attractions to dating this tale to the time setting of *Middlemarch*—exactly

those advantages that Eliot herself derived—the sense of emerging from some dark ages into reform, of consolidating the constitutional monarchy into the modern state with the notion that the people ruled. One can see Eliot's use of Brooke standing for Parliament as a clear example of the movement. The governess is also a rebel: she knows what a fluttered young girl is not supposed to read—not only *Jane Eyre* but *Amelia* and *Pamela* as well. As others later point out, there is an attractive source in *Amelia* for Quint (see especially Renner 1988). But the dating back as far as Shelley's *Frankenstein* is also attractive, to some extent for reasons similar to those associated with *Middlemarch*. The salient reason for such a parallel would be the emphasis on the creation of monsters. After all, monsters are etymologically indeed apparitions. The reification of monsters, which is literalized in Mary Shelley's tale, replicates the manufacture of monsters as a characteristic of human consciousness. Or, perhaps one should suggest that there is as much ground to be gained by inquiring into the hypnotic power of *Frankenstein* as for that of *The Turn of the Screw*. Surely in each case, though for different reasons, the deep structure reflects that labyrinthine character of the mind identified by Sterne in *Tristram Shandy*.

11. We could carry this idea even further. James expected his stenographer to collapse with emotion when he was recording James's dictation of the story. The surrounding implication is that the emotion is powerful indeed. And James was justified in his assumption because the characteristic response to the story both in reviews and in the letters that reached him reflected that aroused emotion or, as James might put it, that "felt life." Thus it might be natural to expect that the governess, if highly neurotic, could be expected to falter in the recording of her tale. If, in fact, the writing is given in a beautiful and flowing hand, James could be construed as planting a clue that she has reached exactly the serenity that Douglas attributes to her. His voice, her hand, his sense of her infinite worth, her sense of the carrying of a heavy burden of knowledge, but sadly rather than neurotically—all these might be considered as analogues for her penmanship.

12. Schrero's reference is to Gordon N. Ray (1955), *Thackeray: The Uses of Adversity, 1811–1846* New York: McGraw-Hill. He also cites Frederic W. Farrar's *Eric; or, Little by Little: A Tale of Roslyn School*, in which a character named Bull plays bully with powerful homosexual overtones as "'he gradually dropped into their too willing ears the poison of his polluting acquirements'" (271). As Schrero indicates, it would have been possible for Bull (or Miles) to know the language of seduction only from adults.

13. Others who concern themselves with the social implications of the tale and find at least some ground for the governess's actions are John Fraser, Robert Slabey, and Graham McMaster. Slabey's accent is on the governess's creative activity in the composition of the narrative. But he sees the uncle in Harley Street "forcefully implicated in the guilt for the tragedy at Bly" (1965, 70). Fraser exonerates the governess from the complaint heard in American criticism of the tale that the governess is class-conscious to the point of dangerous and disaffecting snobbery. He declares that she is not (1965, 327). He claims that her behavior is more ethically motivated than the Freudians could possibly think, suggesting that she deserves a more generous critique (328). He sees her as admirably self-assured at the outset and entirely disinclined to call in the cavalry when the going gets tough: "she assumes the most awful spiritual responsibilities without a flicker of thought—in the face of appalling demonic threats to the souls of her precious charges—about God and the assistance of prayer." Perhaps Fraser is a bit easy on the governess, since he does not mention that the governess proceeds however blithely in order not to breach her compact with the gentleman in Harley Street, and therefore becomes at least potentially a co-conspirator in the breach

of authority at Bly. Nonetheless, Fraser does offer a stout defense for the governess, and has little enough company in the critical history in that mode. Wells (1985) tells us that the tragedy of Bly arises from a gong-tormented struggle over the unresolved and irresoluble tension between possession and ownership. She tries desperately to claim Bly and then Miles as "her own" and sinks under the burden of indeterminacy: "The governess's questions, delayed so long, have atrophied into gestures of possession. And in this question drained of meaning. I think, we can hear the sober echo of the governess's tragedy, of too long a labor at making sense of senseless social arrangements" (99). McMaster (1988) lays stress on the Anglo-Indian connection for the children, their parents and grandparents. The "underclasses" at Bly represent both the servants at home and the colonials abroad. He puts the principal accent on the children as symbols of empire; the death of Miles is tantamount to the death of empire (34).

14. This is again a guise of the breaching of the Cassandra dimension of the tale with the governess cast in the role of the especially endowed seer with the gift of incredibility who therefore becomes a vehicle through which the evil threatening the world first becomes articulated and, second, assumes efficient and direful forms—the precipitator first of the fall of Troy and then of the Oresteia. To hold her responsible or efficient cause in her own right would be an absurd reading of the myth. But to say that she is the necessary ground for the evil to express itself both as a form of words and as action bringing about a version of the fall seems an inescapable conclusion for those who raise the specter of the governess as the vehicle through which the evil at Bly materializes or manifests itself to the children. The prophet without honor is necessarily a prophet of doom.

15. Though Beidler comes to a conclusion almost identical to Rictor Norton's (1971), there is no citation of Norton's work either here or in the bibliography. Once again, the vexing subject of the critic's responsibility in the reading of the criticism must be asked. The Budd bibliography of comment on *Screw* between 1975 and 1981 alone contains over one hundred entries. And yet, Beidler, like others, claims to have read the criticism, and Beidler, like others, scolds those who have been remiss in this duty. Norton is central to the comment that Beidler makes here because he spends much of an extended essay on the practice of exorcism as he sees it enacted in the tale. Norton's conclusion is not a mere inference from the casual imagery of the tale, but a considered conclusion from the progression of imagery in the tale.

Coda

1. Henry Harland, for instance, a personal friend, a fellow author, and a neighbor, wrote one of the reviews, and if one were arguing from a logical force of circumstances, there is some sense in arguing that James would have seen this review. In fact, some of the internal evidence of the preface is consistent with the idea that James included Harland's review (1898) among the comments of the first readers, to which he was responding in that marvelous piece of tergiversation. Harland had, in his review, spoken of the children, "pursued to their destruction by two particularly hideous and evil ghosts," rather a stunning example of the reader thinking the evil for himself, as James had said so emphatically in the preface. The sense of the extratextual in Harland's comment is unmistakable.

2. Allan Lloyd Smith, in the introduction to the Dent edition of *The Turn of the Screw* (1993), puts it clearly: "In any case the story is a sadistic mechanism in which the children and the young governess are on display, exposed to, in James's words, 'the

very worst action small victims so conditioned might be subject to', for the delectation, amusement and even sexual frisson of those who are 'not easily caught'" (xxx). In the context, Smith cites the horror of the reviewer for the *Independent*, who had recoiled from the tale and charged James with infamy.

3. Eric Vogelin, the philosopher and theorist of symbolism, was in residence at Louisiana State University in 1947, and was thus a colleague of Robert Heilman's there at that time. Heilman had given him his essay attacking Wilson's reading of *The Turn of the Screw*, and Vogelin had responded with a long letter, based on a first reading of the tale and designating the master of Bly the symbolic god-figure in the tale. The letter was private and was not published at the time. In 1970, the editors of the *Southern Review* decided to publish the original essay, and Vogelin determined that he should add a postscript. The whole is listed in Scura under the heading "*The Turn of the Screw*," (1971), 3–48. Donald Stanford wrote a preface; Heilman wrote a foreword. In the postscript (25–48) Vogelin focused on "the deformed reality" of James's world and the incestual implications of the androgynic motif in the relations between the governess and Miles. The deformed reality of which he wrote was the world that had lost its sense of the divine and that had lost the authenticity of language in its attempt to describe and define its own conditions. At some points Vogelin seems to make James a perceptive student of the deformed reality; at others he seems to think of James as having only marginal control over the complexities of a world that has lost its sanctioning authority.

Works Cited

Reviews of *The Turn of the Screw*

Ackermann, Edward. 1899. Review of *The Two Magics*. *Book Notes* 2:48–49.

Books and Authors: Books of the Week. Review of *The Two Magics*. 1898. *Outlook* 60:537.

Books and Their Makers. 1899. *Ainslee's Magazine* 3:112.

Droch [Robert Bridges]. 1898. Bookishness: Henry James as Ghost Raiser. Life 10:368.

Harland, Henry. 1898. Academy Portraits: Mr. Henry James. 1898. *Academy* n. 1386 (November 26).

Huneker, James Gibbons. 1898. Mr. James. *M'lle New York* 2, Reprinted in *Musical Courier* 37 14 December (1898): 28. Both reprinted in Arnold T. Schwab, ed. *Americans in the Arts, 1890–1920: Critiques by James Gibbons Huneker*. 1985. New York: AMS Press.

Reviews of *In the Cage, The Two Magics, The Awkward Age*. 1899. *Bookman* 9:472–73.

Lanier, H. W. 1898. Two Volumes from Henry James. reviews of and *The Two Magics*. *American Monthly Review of Reviews* 18:732–33.

Mabie, H. W. *In the Cage, The Two Magics*. 1898. *Bookbuyer*, ser. 3:437–38.

Magic of Evil and Love: *The Two Magics*, Henry James. 1898. *Saturday Review of Books and Art, New York Times* 2:681–82.

Masterpiece, A, by Mr. Henry James. 1898. *New York Tribune*, 23 October, suppl.: 14.

McLean, M. D. 1899. Henry James's Latest, Review of *The Awkward Age*, including some comparisons with *In the Cage* and *The Turn of the Screw. Boston Sunday Post*, 21 May, sec. 2, 4.

More Novels. 1898. *Nation* 67:462.

On Books as Christmas Gifts. 1898. *Ainslee's Magazine* 2:516–19.

Sanborn, Annie. Review of *The Two Magics*. 1898. *Saint Paul Daily Pioneer Press, 15 November*: 19.

Talk About Books. 1899. *Chautauquan* 28:630.

The Recent Work of Henry James: *In the Cage ... The Two Magics*. 1898. *Critic* 33:523–24.

The Secret of Henry James's Style as Revealed by His Typist. 1916. *Current Opinion* 63:118.

The Two Magics (Review). *1898. Athenaeum* 3704: 564–65.

The Two Magics (Review). 1898. *Detroit Free Press*, 24 October:7.

The Two Magics (Review). *1898. Athenaeum* 3704: 564–65.
The Two Magics (Review). 1898. *Detroit Free Press*, 24 October:7.
The Two Magics. 1898. *Literature* 3:351.
The Two Magics. 1898. *Literary World* 19:367–68.
The Two Magics. 1898. *Overland Monthly* 32:493.
[*The Two Magics*]. 1898. *Portland Morning Oregonian*, 13 November:22.
[*The Two Magics*]. 1898. *Springfield (Massachusetts) Republican.* 30 October: 8.
[*The Two Magics*]. 1899. *Dixie* 1:59–60.
[*The Two Magics*]. 1899. *Current Literature* 25:213–14.
[*The Two Magics*]. 1899. *Independent* 51:73.
[*The Two Magics*]. 1899. *Sewanee Review* 7:124.

Other Works

Aldrich, C. Knight, M.D. 1967. Another Twist to *The Turn of the Screw. Modern Fiction Studies* 13:167–78.
Allara, Pamela Edwards. 1970. The Water-Color Illustrations of Charles Demuth. Ph.D. diss., Johns Hopkins University.
Archibald, William. 1950. *The Innocents, Based on "The Turn of the Screw," by Henry James.* New York: Coward-McCann.
Armstrong, Paul B. 1983. *The Phenomenology of Henry James.* Chapel Hill: University of North Carolina Press.
———. 1988. History and Epistemology: The Example of *The Turn of the Screw. New Literary History* 19:693–712.
Arvin, Newton. 1934. Henry James and the Almighty Dollar. *Hound & Horn* 7:434–43.
Aswell, E. Duncan. 1968. Reflections of a Governess: Image and Distortion in *The Turn of the Screw. Nineteenth Century Fiction* 23:49–63.
Austin-Smith, Brenda. 1992. The Man without Characteristics: The Rhetorical Narrator in the Late Novels of Henry James. Ph.D. diss., University of Manitoba.
Baffling Henry James. 1916. *Literary Digest* 52:714–15.
Bal, Meike. 1984. Psychopoetics: Theory/Introduction/Delimiting Psychopoetics. *Style* 18:241–45.
Banfield, Ann. 1978. The Formal Coherence of Represented Speech and Thought. *PTL: A Journal for Descriptive Poetics and Theory of Literature* 3:289–314.
Bannet, Eve Tavor. 1989. *Structuralism and the Logic of Dissent: Barthes Derrida Foucault Lacan.* Urbana and Chicago: University of Illinois Press.
Banta, Martha. 1972. *Henry James and the Occult: The Great Extension.* Bloomington: University of Indiana Press.
Barthes, Roland. 1972b. What Is Criticism? In Critical Essays. Translated by Richard Howard. Baltimore: Johns Hopkins University Press.
———. 1972a. *S/Z.* Translated by Richard Miller. New York: Hill and Wang.
Bates, Katharine Lee. 1898. *American Literature.* New York: Macmillan and Co.
[Battersby, H. F. P.]. 1903. The Novels of Henry James. *Edinburgh Review 197:59–85.*
Beer, Thomas. 1925. The Princess Far Away. review of Van Wyck Brooks's *Pilgrimage of Henry James. Saturday Review of Literature* 1:701–2, 707.
Beers, Henry A. 1915. Fifty Years of Hawthorne. *Yale Review,* n.s.,4: 300–15.

Beidler, Peter. 1989. *Ghosts, Demons and Henry James: "The Turn of the Screw" at the Turn of the Century*. Columbia: University of Missouri Press.

Bell, Millicent. 1966. *Edith Wharton and Henry James: The Story of Their Friendship*. New York: Braziller.

———. 1982. *The Turn of the Screw* and the *recherche de l'absolu*. *Delta* 15:33–48.

———. 1991. *Meaning in Henry James*. Cambridge: Harvard University Press.

Bengels, Barbara. 1978. The Term of the Screw: A Key to the Imagery in Henry James's *The Turn of the Screw*. *Studies in Short Fiction* 15:332–37.

Benson, E. F. 1930. *As We Were: A Victorian Peep Show*. London: Longmans, Green.

Berman, Lorna. 1968. The Marquis de Sade and His Critics. *Mosaic* 1:57–73.

Bethurum, Dorothy. 1923. Morality and Henry James. *Sewanee Review* 31:324–30.

Bewley, Marius. 1950a. James's Debt to Hawthorne. *Scrutiny* 17:14–37.

———. 1950b. Appearance and Reality in Henry James. *Scrutiny* 17:90–114.

———. 1950c. Maisie, Miles and Flora, The Jamesian Innocents. *Scrutiny* 17:255–63.

Blackmur, R. P. 1934a. The Critical Prefaces. *Hound & Horn* 7:444–77.

———. ed. 1934b. *The Art of the Novel: Critical Prefaces, by Henry James*. New York: Scribner's.

Boardman, Arthur. 1974. Mrs. Grose's Reading of *The Turn of the Screw*. *Studies in English Literature* 14:169–85.

Bonaparte, Marie, Princess of Greece. 1949. *The Life and Works of Edgar Allen Poe: A Psychoanalytic Interpretation*. Translated by John Rodker, foreword by Sigmund Freud, London: Imago Press.

Bontly, Thomas J. 1969. Henry James's General Vision of Evil, in *The Turn of the Screw*. *Studies in English Literature, 1500–1900* 9:721–39.

Books, Authors and Arts. 1899. *Springfield Republican*. 2 April, 19.

Booth, Wayne C. 1983. *The Rhetoric of Fiction, revised*. Chicago: University of Chicago Press.

Boren, Linda S. 1986. The Performing Self: Psychodrama in Austen, James and Woolf, *Centennial Review* 30:1–24.

Bosanquet, Theodora. 1917. Henry James. *Living Age* 294:346–57.

Bragdon, Claude. 1904. The Figure in Henry James's Carpet. *Critic*, 44:146–50.

Britten, Benjamin. 1954. *The Turn of the Screw, An Opera in Two Acts*. London: Boosey & Company.

Brooke-Rose, Christine. 1976. The Squirm of the True: An Essay in Non-Methodology. *Poetics and the Theory of Literature* 1:265–94.

———. 1976. A Structural Analysis of Henry James's *The Turn of the Screw*. *Poetics and the Theory of Literature* 1:513–46.

———. 1977. The Squirm of the True, III: Surface Structure in Narrative. *Poetics and the Theory of Literature* 2:217–62.

———. 1981. *The Rhetoric of the Unreal: Studies in Narrative and Structure, Especially of the Fantastic*. Cambridge University Press.

Brooks, Van Wyck. 1925. *The Pilgrimage of Henry James*. New York: E. P. Dutton.

Brown, Bernadine. 1974. *The Turn of the Screw*: A Case of Romantic Displacement. *Nassau Review* 2 no. 5:75–82.

[Brownell, William Crary]. 1880. James's *Hawthorne*. [review]. *Nation* 30:80–81.

———. 1905. Henry James. *Atlantic* 95:496–515. Included in Gard. 1968.

———. 1914. *Criticism*. New York: Scribner's.

———. 1909. *American Prose Masters* [revision of the above with inclusion of comment on the prefaces to the New York Edition]. New York: Scribner's.

Brownell, Gertrude Hall. 1929. *William Crary Brownell: An Anthology of His Writings*. New York: Scribners.

Byers, John. 1971. *The Turn of the Screw*: A Hellish Point of View. *Markham Review* 2:101–4.

Cairns, William B. 1916. Meditations of a Jacobite. *Dial.* 60, March 30:313–16.

Canby, Henry Seidel. 1909. The Deepening of the Short Story. Henry James. *The Short Story in English*. New York: Henry Holt: 60–3.

———. 1916. Henry James. *Harper's Weekly* 52:291.

Caramagno, Thomas C. and others. 1988. Virginia Woolf and Psychoanalytic Criticism. *PMLA* [Forum] 103:808–12.

Cargill, Oscar. 1956. Henry James as Freudian Pioneer. *Chicago Review*, 10. Reprinted in w 223–38.

———. 1963. *The Turn of the Screw* and Alice James. *PMLA* 78:238–49.

Cary, Elizabeth Luther. 1904. Henry James. *Scribners Magazine* 36:396–400.

Chaitin, Gilbert D. 1984. Psychoanalysis and Narrative Action: The Primal Scene of the French Novel. *Style* 18:289–96.

Chase, Dennis. 1986. The Ambiguity of Innocence: *The Turn of the Screw*. *Extrapolation* 27:197–202.

Chielens, Edward. 1986. *American Literary Magazines of the Eighteenth and Nineteenth Centuries*. Westport: Greenwood Press, 1986; Patricia Marks. *Life*: 213–217.

Christie, Agatha. 1926. *The Murder of Roger Ackroyd*. New York: Dodd Mead.

Clair, John. 1965. *The Ironic Dimension in the Fiction of Henry James*. Pittsburgh: Duquesne University Press.

Clark, Susan. 1978. A Note on *The Turn of the Screw*: Death from Natural Causes. *Studies in Short Fiction* 15:110–12.

Clews, Hetty. 1985. *The Only Teller: Readings in the Monologue Novel*. Victoria: Sono Nis Press.

Cohen, Paula Marantz. 1986. Freud's *Dora* and Henry James's *The Turn of the Screw*: Two Treatments of the Female 'Case.' *Criticism*, 28:73–87.

Cohn, Dorrit. 1978. *Transparent Minds: Narrative Modes for Presenting Consciousness in Fiction*. Princeton: Princeton University Press.

Collins, Carvel. 1955. James's 'The Turn of the Screw.' *Explicator* 13, no. 8, item 49.

Colby, Frank Moore. 1902a. In Darkest James (review of *The Wings of the Dove*). *The Bookman* 16: 259–60.

———. 1902b. The Queerness of Henry James. *The Bookman* 15:396–7.

Conrad, Joseph. 1905. Henry James: An Appreciation. *North American Review* 180:102–08.

Cook, David and Thomas J. Corrigan. 1980. Narrative Structure in *The Turn of the Screw*. *Studies in Short Fiction* 17:55–65.

Cooper, Frederick Taber. 1907. *The American Scene* (Review). *North American Review* 185:214–18.

Costello, Donald P. 1960. The Structure of *The Turn of the Screw*. *Modern Language Notes* 75: 313–21.

Coveney, Peter. 1957. Innocence in Henry James. In *The Image of Childhood*. Harmondsworth: Penguin.

Cranfill, Thomas M. and Robert L. Clark. 1963. Caste in James's *The Turn of the Screw*. *Texas Studies in Literature and Language* 5:189–98.

———. 1965a. *An Anatomy of The Turn of the Screw*. Austin: University of Texas Press.

———. 1965b. James's Revisions to *The Turn of the Screw*. *Nineteenth Century Fiction* 19:394–98.

————. 1970. The Provocativeness of *The Turn of the Screw*. *Texas Studies in Literature and Language*. 12:96–97.

Crowe, M. Karen. 1982. The Tapestry of Henry James's *The Turn of the Screw*. *Nassau Review* 4:37–48.

Crunden, Robert. 1993. *The American Salon: Encounters with European Modernism, 1885–1917*. New York: Oxford University Press.

Culler, Jonathan. 1984. Textual Self–Consciousness and the Textual Unconscious. *Style* 18:369–73.

Curtsinger, E. C. 1980. *The Turn of the Screw* as Writer's Parable. *Studies in the Novel* 12:344–58.

Daly, Mary. 1986. *Gyn/ecology: The Metaethics of Radical Feminism*. Boston: Beacon Press.

Davis, Douglas M. 1959. *The Turn of the Screw* Controversy: Its Implications for the Modern Critic and Teacher. *Graduate Student of English* 2:7–10.

De La Mare, Walter. 1916. Henry James. [*Westminster Review*] rpt. *Living Age*, 289:122–25.

Dillard, Annie. 1972. *Living by Fiction*. New York: Harper and Rowe.

Duthie, Enid. 1978. *The Turn of the Screw* and "The Old Nurse's Story." *Brontë Society Transactions*, 17:133–7.

Dwight, H. G. 1907. Henry James—'in his own country.' *Putnam's Monthly* 2:164–170 and 433–442. Included in Gard. 1968.

Dyson, A. E. 1972. Murderous Innocence: James's The Turn of the Screw. In *Between Two Worlds: Aspects of Literary Form*. London: Macmillan.

Dyson, Peter. 1978. James's *The Turn of the Screw*. *The Explicator* 36, no. 3, item 9.

Eaton, Marcia. 1983. James's Turn of the Speech Act. *British Journal of Aesthetics* 23:333–45.

Eaton, Marcia Muelder. 1989. *Aesthetics and the Good Life*. Rutherford et al., New Jersey: Fairleigh Dickinson Univ. Press.

Edel, Leon, ed. 1956b. *The American Essays of Henry James*. New York: Vintage.

————. 1969. *Henry James. The Treacherous Years: 1895–1901*. Philadelphia: Lippincott.

————. 1985. *Henry James: A Life*. New York: Harper and Rowe.

Edgar, Pelham. 1927. *Henry James: Man and Author*. Toronto: Macmillan and Co.

Egan, Maurice. 1920. The Revelation of an Artist in Literature. *The Catholic World*, 111:289–300.

Eliot, T. S. 1918. Henry James. *The Egoist*. 5:2.

Elton, Oliver. 1903. The Novels of Mr Henry James. *Quarterly Review* 198:1–14.

Evans, Oliver. 1949. James's Air of Evil: The Turn of the Screw. *Partisan Review*, 16: 175–87.

Fagin, Nathan Brillion. 1941. Another Reading of *The Turn of the Screw*. *Modern Language Notes* 56: 196–202; reprinted in w 154–159.

Falk, Robert P. 1955. The Literary Criticism of the Genteel Decades. Stovall 1955.

Faulkner, Howard. 1983. Text as Pretext in *The Turn of the Screw*. *Studies in Short Fiction* 20:87–94.

Felman, Shoshana. 1977. Turning the Screw of Interpretation. In *Psychoanalysis and Literature: The Question of Reading: Otherwise*. Edited by Shoshana Felman. *Yale French Studies* 55–56:94–207.

Feuerlicht, Ignace. 1959. "Erlkönig" and *The Turn of the Screw*. *Journal of English and Germanic Philology* 58:58–74. Reprinted in k 235–37.

Fiedler, Leslie. 1958. The Profanation of the Child. *New Leader* 41:26–29.

————. 1960. *No! In Thunder*. Boston:Beacon Press.

Firebaugh, Joseph. 1957. Inadequacy in Eden: Knowledge and *The Turn of the Screw*. *Modern Fiction Studies* 3:57–63. Reprinted in w 291–97.

Follett, Helen Thomas, and Wilson Follett. 1916. Henry James (1843–1916). *Atlantic Monthly* 117:801–11.

Fraser, John. 1965. *The Turn of the Screw* Again. *Midwest Quarterly* 7:327–36.

Freeman, John. 1917. Henry James. In *The Moderns: Essays in Literary Criticism*. New York: Thomas Y. Crowell.

Freundlieb, Dieter. 1984. Explaining Interpretation: The Case of Henry James's *Turn of the Screw*. *Poetics Today* 5:79–95.

Fullerton, Morton. 1910. The Art of Henry James. Review of the New York Edition. *Living Age* 265:643–52.

Fussell, Edwin. 1980. The Ontology of *The Turn of the Screw*. *Journal of Modern Literature* 8:118–28.

Gallatin, Albert E. 1927. *Charles Demuth*. New York: William Edwin Rudge.

Gard, Roger. 1968. *Henry James: The Critical Heritage*. New York: Barnes and Noble.

Gargano, James W. 1961. *The Turn of the Screw*. *Western Humanities Review* 15:173–79.

Gathorne-Hardy, Jonathan. 1972. *The Rise and Fall of the British Nanny*. London: Weidenfeld and Nicolson.

[Gilder, Joseph B.]. 1901. The Lounger. (re: the banning of *The Two Magics* by the Boston Public Library). *Critic* 38:403.

Glasser, William. 1980. The Turn Of The Screw. In *Essays in Honour of Erwin Stürzl on His Sixtieth Birthday*, edited by James Hogg, Salzburg: 212–231. Salzburg University Press.

Goddard, Harold C. 1957. A Pre-Freudian Reading of *The Turn of the Screw*. Edited by Leon Edel. *Nineteenth Century Fiction* 12:1–36. Reprinted in w 244–72

Goetz, William R. 1981. The "Frame" of *The Turn of the Screw*: Framing the Reader In. *Studies in Short Fiction* 18:71–74.

Goode, John. 1966. "Character" and Henry James. *New Left Review* 40:55–75.

Graham, Walter. [1930] 1966. *English Literary Periodicals*. New York: Octagon Books.

Green, Jack [pseud.]. 1992. *Fire the Bastards!* Normal, Ill.: Dalkey Archive Press.

Greene, Graham. 1936. Henry James: The Private Universe. In *The English Novelists*, Edited by Derek Verschoyle. London: Chatto and Windus.

Gretton, M. Sturge. 1912. Henry James and His Prefaces. *Living Age* 272:287–95.

Hackett, Francis. 1915. A Stylist on Tour. *New Republic* 2:320–21.

Hagemann, E. R. 1968. *Life* Buffets (and Comforts) Henry James. *Bibliographical Society of America*, 62:207–25.

Hale, Edward E., Jr. 1908. The Rejuvenation of Henry James. *Dial* 44:174–76.

———. 1916. Henry James. *Dial* 60:259–62.

Hallab, Mary Y. 1977. *The Turn of the Screw* Squared. *Southern Review* 13:492–504.

Halttunen, Karen. 1989. Through the Cracked and Fragmented Self: William James and *The Turn of the Screw*. *American Quarterly* 40:472–90.

Hamburger, Käte. 1973. *The Logic of Literature*. Translated by Marilynn J. Rose. Bloomington: Indiana University Press.

Hancher, Michael. 1978. Describing and Interpreting as Speech Acts. *Journal of Aesthetics and Art Criticism* 36:483–85.

Hapgood, Hutchins. 1939. *A Victorian in the Modern World*. New York: Harcourt, Brace.

Hapgood, Norman. 1898. Henry James. In *Literary Statesmen and Others*. London: Duckworth and Co.; Chicago and New York: Herbert S. Stone.

Hartman, Geoffrey. 1984. The Culture of Criticism and the Criticism of Culture. *PMLA* 99:371–97.

Haskell, Barbara. 1987. *Charles Demuth*. New York: Whitney Museum of American Art in Association with Harry N. Abrams, Inc.

Hawkes, Terrence. 1992. 'I Should Never Have Done It If I Had Had a Home for Him.' Paper presented in session 151 of the Modern Language Association Convention, New York.

Head, Ruth. [1916]. *Pictures and Other Passages From Henry James*. New York: Frederick A. Stokes.

Heilman, Robert B. 1947. The Freudian Reading of *The Turn of the Screw*. *Modern Language Notes* 62:433–45.

———. 1948. "*The Turn of the Screw*" as Poem. *University of Kansas City Review* 14. Reprinted in w 174–88.

Henry James as Literary Sphinx. 1907. *Current Literature* 42:634–36.

Hill, Robert W., jr. 1981. A Counterclockwise Turn in James's Turn of the Screw. *Twentieth Century Literature* 27:53–71.

Hocks, Richard A., and Paul Taylor. 1984. James Studies 1982: An Analytic Bibliographical Essay. *Henry James Review* 5:158–86.

Hoffman, Charles G. 1953. Innocence and Evil in James's *The Turn of the Screw*. *University of Kansas City Review* 29:95–107. Reprinted in w 212–22.

Holloway, Marcella M., CSJ. 1979. Another Turn to James' *The Turn of the Screw*. *CEA Critic* 41:9–17.

Houston, Neal. 1977. A Footnote to Miles's Death. *Re:Artes Liberales* 3:25–7.

Hoyt, Eleanor. 1903. What Manner of Man. *Lamp* 26:161–62.

Hueffer [Ford], Ford Madox. 1913. *Henry James*. London: Secker.

Iser, Wolfgang. 1971. Indeterminacy and the Reader's Response in Prose Fiction. In *Aspects of Narrative*, edited by J. Hillis Miller. New York: Columbia University Press.

———. 1974. *The Implied Reader: Patterns of Communication in Prose Fiction from Bunyan to Beckett*. Baltimore: Johns Hopkins University Press.

———. 1978. *The Act of Reading: A Theory of Aesthetic Response*. Baltimore: Johns Hopkins University Press.

———. 1989. *Prospecting*. Baltimore: Johns Hopkins University Press.

Ives, C. B. 1963. James's Ghosts in *The Turn of the Screw*. *Nineteenth Century Fiction* 18: 183–89.

Jackson, James C. 1862. *The Sexual Organism and its Healthful Management*. Boston: B. Leverett Emerson.

[James, Henry]. 1865. Arnold's Essays. Review. *Nation* 1:862.

James, Henry. 1879. *Hawthorne*. New York: Macmillan.

———. [1881.] 1977. *The Portrait of a Lady*. Edited by Leon Edel. Boston: Houghton-Mifflin.

———. [1893.] 1986. Criticism. In *The Art of Criticism: Henry James on the Theory and Practice of Fiction*, edited by William Veeder and Susan M. Griffin Chicago: University of Chicago Press.

———. [1898.] 1966. *The Turn of the Screw*. Edited by Robert Kimbrough. New York: W. W. Norton. Abbreviated in text as k.

———. 1898. *The Two Magics*. New York: Macmillan and Co.

———. 1902. George Sand: the New Life. *North American Review* 174:536–54.

———.1908. *The Ambassadors*. Vols. 21 and 22 of the New York Edition. New York: Scribners.

———. 1908. *The Turn of the Screw*. In vol. 12 of *The Novels and Tales of Henry James*. New York: Scribner's.

———. 1909. *The Golden Bowl*. Vols. 23 and 24 of the New York Edition. New York: Scribner's.

———. 1922. *Notes and Reviews*. Edited by Pierre de Chaignon La Rose. Cambridge, Mass,: Dunster House.

———. 1949. *The Turn of the Screw*, ed. Mark Van Doren; illus. Mariette Lydis. New York: The Heritage Press.

———. 1956. *The Future of the Novel*. Edited by Leon Edel. New York: Vantage.

———. 1987. *The Complete Notebooks*. Edited by Leon Edel and Lyall F. Powers. New York: Oxford University Press.

James, M. R. 1989. *A Warning to the Curious: The Ghost Stories of M. R. James*. Selected and introduced by Ruth Rendell. Boston: David R. Godine.

Jauß, Hans Robert. 1970. Literary History as a Challenge to Literary Theory. *New Literary History* 2:1–26.

———. 1982a. *Aesthetic Experience and Literary Hermeneutics*. Translated by Michael Shaw. Minneapolis: Univ of Minn Press.

———. 1982b. *Toward an Aesthetic of Reception*. Translated by Timothy Bahti. Minneapolis: University of Minnesota Press.

Jennings, Henry J. 1882 *Curiosities of Criticism*. London: Chatto and Windus.

Jones, Alexander E. 1959. Point of View in *The Turn of the Screw*. *PMLA* 74:298–318. Reprinted in w.298–318

Kaston, Carren O. 1984. *Imagination and Desire in the Novels of Henry James*. New Brunswick, N.J.: Rutgers University Press.

Katan, M., M.D. 1962. A Causerie on Henry James's *The Turn of the Screw*. *Psychoanalytic Study of the Child* 12:473–93.

Kauffman, Linda. 1981. "The Author of Our Woe": Virtue Recorded in *The Turn of the Screw*. *Nineteenth Century Fiction* 36:176–92.

Kawin, Bruce. 1982. *The Mind of the Novel*. Princeton: Princeton University Press.

Kenton, Edna. 1903. *What Manner of Man*. Indianapolis, Ind.: Bobbs, Merrill.

———. 1906. Love Laughs at Lions. *Century* 50:333–42.

———. 1924. Henry James to the Ruminant Reader: *The Turn of the Screw*, *Arts* 6:245–55. Reprinted in w 102–14

Kerfoot, J. B. 1903. *The Latest Books*. Review and commentary on Edna Kenton's *What Manner of Man*. *Life* 41:344.

Knight, Grant C. 1925. The Most Memorable Children in Literature. In *Superlatives*. New York: Alfred A. Knopf.

Knox, George. 1963. Incubi and Succubi in *The Turn of the Screw*. *Western Folklore* 22:122–23.

Krook, Dorothea. 1962. *The Ordeal of Consciousness in Henry James*. Cambridge: Cambride University Press.

Lacan, Jacques. 1977. *Ecrits*. Quoted in Desire and the Interpretation of Desire. Edited by Shoshana Felman. *Literature and Psychoanalysis: The Question of Reading: Otherwise*. *Yale French Studies*, 55–56.

———. 1981. *Le discours de Rome*. In *Speech and Language in Psychoanalysis*, edited by Anthony Wilden. Baltimore: Johns Hopkins University Press.

Lane, Margaret. 1967. The Disappearing Ghost-Story: Some Reflections on Ghost-Stories, in Particular on Henry James's *The Turn of the Screw*. *Cornhill Magazine* 1052:137–46.

Leach, Anna. 1916. Henry James: An Appreciation. *Forum* 55:551–64.

Leavis, F. R. 1950. James's "What Maisie Knew": A Dissent. *Scrutiny* 17: 115–27.

Lee, Sherman. 1942. Demuth's Illustrations of Henry James. *Art Quarterly* 5:158–75.

Levin, Harry. 1956. *Symbolism and Fiction*. Charlottesville: University of Virginia Press.

Levy, Leo Ben. 1956. *The Turn of the Screw* as Retaliation. *College English* 17:286–88.

Lewis, Clive Staples, with E. M. W. Tillyard. 1939. *The Personal Heresy: The Record of a Controversy*. Oxford: Oxford University Press.

———. Introduction. 1961. *The Poetical Works of John Milton*. New York: Oxford University Press.

Liddell, Robert. 1947. *A Treatise on the Novel*. London: Jonathan Cape.

Light on Darkest James. 1907. *Nation* 85:343–44

Literary Small Talk. 1904. *Advance* 47: 673.

Loomis, Charles Battell. 1905. An Attempt to Translate Henry James. *Bookman* 21:464–66.

Lubbock, Percy. 1916. Henry James. *Living Age* 290:733–42.

Ludwig, Sämi. 1994. Metaphors, Cognition and Behavior: The Reality of Sexual Puns in *The Turn of the Screw*. *Mosaic* 27:32–53.

Lydenberg, John. 1957. The Governess Turns the Screws. *Nineteenth Century Fiction* 12:37–58. Reprinted in w 273–90

———. 1964. Comment on Mr. Spilka's Paper. *Literature and Psychology* 14:6–8, 34.

Mac Cormac, Earl R. 1988. *A Cognitive Theory of Metaphor*. Cambridge and London: MIT Press.

Macy, John. 1913. *The Spirit of American Literature*. New York: Doubleday.

Mansell, Darrel. 1985. The Ghost of Language in *The Turn of the Screw*. *Modern Language Quarterly* 46:48–63.

Marks, Patricia. 1986. *Life*. In American Literary Magazines of the Eighteenth and Nineteenth Centuries. Edited by Edward Chielans, Wesport, Conn.: Greenwood Press.

Marsh, Edward Clark. 1909. Henry James, Autocritic. Review of the New York Edition. *Bookman* 30:138–143.

Maser, Edward A. See Ripa.

Matheson, Terence. 1982. Did the Governess Smother Miles? A Note on James's *The Turn of the Screw*. *Studies in Short Fiction* 19:72–75.

Matthews, Robert J. 1977. Describing and Interpreting a Work of Art. *Journal of Aesthetics and Art Criticism* 36:5–14.

Matthiessen, F. O. 1944. *Henry James: The Major Phase*. New York: Oxford University Press.

Matthiessen, F. O. and Kenneth B. Murdoch, eds. 1947. *The Notebooks of Henry James*. New York: Oxford University Press.

Mazzella, Anthony J. 1980. An Answer to the Mystery of *The Turn of the Screw*. *Studies in Short Fiction* 17:327–33.

———. 1981. A Selected Henry James Artsography. *Henry James Review* 3:44–58.

McElroy, John H. 1981. The Mysteries at Bly. *American Notes and Queries* 37:214–36.

McKay, Janet Holmgren. 1982. *Narration and Discourse in American Realistic Fiction*. Philadelphia: University of Pennsylvania Press.

McMaster, Graham. 1988. Henry James and India: A Historical Reading of *The Turn of the Screw*. *Clio* 18:23–40.

McMaster, Juliet. 1969. "The Full Image of a Repetition" in *The Turn of the Screw*. *Studies in Short Fiction* 6:377–82.

McNaughton, W. R. 1974. Turning the Screw of Ordinary Human Virtue: The Governess and the First-Person Narrators. *Canadian Review of American Studies* 5:18–25.

Messrs. Bigtype and Sharper Announce… (satire on James's style). 1901. *Life* 38:415.

Miner, Earl Roy. 1954. Henry James's Metaphysical Romances. *Nineteenth Century Fiction* 9:1–21.

Moon, Heath. 1982. More Royalist than the King: The Governess, the Telegraphist, and Mrs. Gracedew. *Criticism* 24:16–35.

Murphy, Brenda. 1979. Problems of Validity in the Critical Controversy Over *The Turn of the Screw*. *Research Studies* 47:191–201.

Murphy, Kevin. 1978. The Unfixable Text: Bewilderment of Vision in *The Turn of the Screw*. *Texas Studies in Literature and Language* 20:538–51.

Norton, Rictor. 1971. *The Turn of the Screw: Coincidentia Oppositorum*. *American Imago* 28:373–90.

The Novels of Henry James. 1903. *Harper's Weekly* 47:273. First published in the *Edinburgh Review* 197 (1903).

The Novels of Henry James. 1903. *Living Age* 236:577–95. First published in the *Edinburgh Review* 197 (1903).

O'Connor, William Van. 1952. *An Age of Criticism, 1900–1950*. Chicago: Henry Regnery.

Obuchowski, Peter A. 1978. Technique and Meaning in James's *The Turn of the Screw*. *CLA Journal* 21:380–89.

Panofsky, Erwin. 1952. *Meaning in the Visual Arts*. Chicago: University of Chicago Press.

Peck, H. T. 1901. Review of *The Sacred Fount*. *Bookman* 13:442.

Petry, Alice Hall. 1983. Jamesian Parody *Jane Eyre* and *The Turn of the Screw*. *Modern Language Studies* 13:61–78.

Phelps, William Lyon. 1916. Henry James. *Yale Review*, n.s., 5:783–97.

Piper, Myfanwy. 1955. *Libretto: Benjamin Britten's "The Turn of the Screw."* London: Hawkes and Son.

———. 1963. Some Thoughts on the Libretto of "The Turn of the Screw." In *Tribute to Benjamin Britten on his Fiftieth Birthday*, edited by Anthony Gishford. London: Faber and Faber.

Pitkin, Walter B. 1912. *The Art and Business of Story Writing*. New York: Macmillan.

Poets and Critics. 1903. *New York Times Saturday Review of Books* 8 February 7: 88.

Poor Literary Outlaws. 1901. *Washington Post* 22 February: 6.

Pound, Ezra. 1920. Henry James. In *Instigations*. New York: Boni and Liveright, 1920.

Pratt, Cornelia Atwood. 1899. The Evolution of Henry James. *Critic* 34:338–42.

———. 1901. Review of *The Sacred Fount*. *Critic* 36:368–70.

Preston, Harriet Waters. 1903. Review of *The Wings of the Dove*. *Atlantic* 91:77–82. Reprinted in Gard 1968.

Quinn, Arthur Hobson. 1910. Some Phases of the Supernatural in American Literature. *PMLA*, n.s., 25:114–133.

Raleigh, John Henry. 1955. Revolt and Revaluation in Criticism, 1900–1930. In Stovall 1955.

———. 1957. *Matthew Arnold and American Culture*. Berkeley and Los Angeles: University of California Press.

Ramras-Rauch, Gila. 1982. *The Protagonist in Transition: Studies in Modern Fiction*. Bern: Peter Lang.

Ramsay, Roger. 1971. The Available and Unavailable "I": Conrad and James. *English Literature in Transition*, 14:137–45.

Reed, Gail S. 1982. Toward a Methodology for Applying Psychoanalysis to Literature. *Psychoanalytic Quarterly* 51:19–23.

Reed, Glenn A. 1949. Another Turn of James's "The Turn of the Screw." *American Literature* 20:413–23. Reprinted in w 189–199.

Renner, Stanley. 1986. "Why Can't They Tell You Why?": A Clarifying Echo of *The Turn of the Screw*. *Studies in American Fiction* 14:205–13.

————. 1988. Sexual Hysteria, Physiognomical Bogeymen, and the "Ghosts" in *The Turn of the Screw*. *Nineteenth Century Fiction* 43:175–94.

The Return of the Native. 1904. *Outlook* 78:112–13.

Rimmon, Shlomith. 1977. *The Concept of Ambiguity: The Example of Henry James*. Chicago: University of Chicago Press.

Ripa, Cesare. 1971. *Baroque and Rococo Pictorial Imagery: The Augsburg 1758–1760 Hertel Edition of Ripa's "Iconologia."* Introduced and translated by Edward A. Maser. New York: Dover Press.

Roellinger, Francis X. 1949. Psychical Research and "The Turn of the Screw." *American Literature* 20:401–12. Reprinted in k 132–42.

Rorty, Richard. 1979. *Philosophy and the Mirror of Nature*. Princeton: Princeton University Press.

Rosenbaum, S. P. 1966. A Note on John LaFarge's Illustration for Henry James's *The Turn of the Screw*. James [1898] 1966. Reprinted in k 254–59.

Rowe, John Carlos. 1984. *The Theoretical Dimensions of Henry James*. Madison: University of Wisconsin Press.

Rubin, Louis D., Jr. 1963. One More Turn of the Screw. *Modern Fiction Studies* 9:314–28.

Russell, W. Clark. [1872]. *The Book of Authors: A Collection of Criticisms, Ana, Mots, Personal Descriptions, etc. Wholly Referring to English Men of Letters in Every Age of English Literature*. London: Frederick Warne and Company.

Said, Edward. 1972. *Abecedarium Culturae*. In *Modern French Criticism: From Proust and Valéry to Structuralism*, edited by John K. Simon. Chicago: University of Chicago Press.

Salmon, Rachel. 1980. A Marriage of Opposites: Henry James's "The Figure in the Carpet" and the Problem of Ambiguity. *ELH* 47:788–803.

Samuels, C. T. 1968. Giovanni and the Governess. *American Scholar* 37:655–78.

Schachter, Zalman. 1968. Eros in Homiletics and Literature. *Mosaic* 2:16–26.

Schleifer, Ronald. 1980. The Trap of the Imagination: The Gothic Tradition, Fiction and *The Turn of the Screw*. *Criticism* 22:297–317.

Schrero, Elliot. 1981. Exposure in *The Turn of the Screw*. *Modern Philology* 70:261–74.

Schuyler, Montgomery. 1903. Henry James's Short Stories. *Lamp* 26:231–35.

Scull, Andrew. 1981. *Madhouses, Mad-Doctors and Madmen: The Social History of Psychiatry in the Victorian Era*. Philadelphia: University of Pennsylvania Press.

Scura, Dorothy McInnis. 1979. *Henry James, 1960–1974: A Reference Guide*. Boston: C. K. Hall.

Shapira, Morris, ed. 1965. *Henry James: Selected Literary Criticism*. New York: McGraw-Hill.

Shaw, Harry. *A Complete Course in Freshman English*. 4th ed. New York: Harper, 1955.

Sheppard, Elizabeth A. 1974. *Henry James and "The Turn of the Screw."* Auckland: Auckland University Press.

Sherman, Stuart Pratt. 1917. The Aesthetic Idealism of Henry James. *Nation* 104:393–99.

Shine, Muriel. 1969. *The Fictional Children of Henry James*. Chapel Hill: University of North Carolina Press.

Slabey, Robert. 1965. *The Turn of the Screw*: Grammar and Optics. *College Language Association Journal* 9:68–72.

Smith, Allan Lloyd. 1993. Introduction to *The Turn of the Screw*, by Henry James. London and Rutland, Vt.: Dent.

Smith, Barbara Herrnstein. 1988. *Contingencies of Value*. Cambridge: Harvard University Press.

Solomon, Eric. 1964. The Return of the Screw. *University of Kansas City Review* 30:205–11. Reprinted in k 237–45.

Sonne, Harly. 1984. Problems of Knowledge in Fiction. *Style* 18:297–304.

Spilka, Mark. 1963. Turning the Freudian Screw: How Not to Do It. *Literature and Psychology* 13:105–11. Reprinted in k 245–253.

———. 1964. Mr. Spilka's Reply. *Literature and Psychology* 14:8, 34.

Stepp, Walter. 1976. *The Turn of the Screw*: If Douglas is Miles... *Nassau Review* 3:76–82.

Sterne, Laurence. 1964. *The Life and Opinions of Tristram Shandy, Gent*. New York: Holt, Rinehart and Winston.

Stevens, Wallace. 1972. *Collected Poems*. New York: Vintage.

Stierle, Karlheinz. The Reading of Fictional Texts. In Suleiman and Crossman 1980.

Stoll, E. E. 1948. Symbolism In Coleridge. *PMLA* 63:229–33.

Stone, Albert E. 1961. Henry James and Childhood: *"The Turn of the Screw."* Stetson *University Bulletin*, no. 61.

Stone, Edward. 1975. Edition Architecture and "The Turn of the Screw." *Studies in Short Fiction* 13:9–16.

Stovall, Floyd, ed. 1955. *The Development of American Criticism*. Chapel Hill: University of North Carolina Press.

Suleiman, Susan R., and Inge Crosman. 1980. *The Reader in the Text: Essays on Audience and Interpretation*. Princeton: Princeton University Press.

Sweeney, John. 1943. The Demuth Pictures. *Kenyon Review* 5:522–32.

Taylor, Anne Robinson. 1981. *Male Novelists and Their Female Voices: Literary Masquerades*. Troy, N.Y.: Whitston Publishing Co.

Taylor, Linda H. 1982. *Henry James, 1866–1917: A Reference Guide*. Boston: G. K. Hall, 1982.

Taylor, Michael J. H. 1982. A Note on the First Narrator of *The Turn of the Screw. American Literature* 53:717–22.

Thomson, A. W. 1965. *The Turn of the Screw*: Some Points on the Hallucination Theory. *Review of English Literature* 6:26–36.

Thorberg, Raymond. 1967. Terror Made Relevant: James's Ghost Stories. *Dalhousie Review* 47:185–91.

Tillyard, Eustace M. W. 1939. See C. S. Lewis 1939.

Timms, David. 1976. The Governess's Feelings and the Argument from Textual Revision of *The Turn of the Screw. Yearbook of English Studies* 6:194–201.

Tintner, Adeline R. 1979. An Illustrator's Literary Interpretations. *AB Bookman's Weekly* 63:2275, 2278, 2280, 2282.

Todorov, Tzvetan. 1973. *The Fantastic: A Structural Approach to a Literary Genre*. Translated by Richard Howard. Cleveland, Ohio: Case Western University Press.

———. 1977. *The Poetics of Prose*. Translated by Richard Howard. Ithaca: Cornell University Press.

———. 1981. *Introduction to Poetics*. Translated by Richard Howard, Vol. 1. of Theory and History of Literature. Minneapolis: University of Minnesota Press.

Tournadre, Claude. 1969. Propositions pour une psychologie sociale de *The Turn of the Screw. Etudes Anglaises* 22:259–69.

Tintner, Adeline R. 1979. An Illustrator's Literary Interpretations. *AB Bookman's Weekly* 63:2275, 2278, 2280, 2282.

Todorov, Tzvetan. 1973. *The Fantastic: A Structural Approach to a Literary Genre.* Translated by Richard Howard. Cleveland, Ohio: Case Western University Press.

———. 1977. *The Poetics of Prose.* Translated by Richard Howard. Ithaca: Cornell University Press.

———. 1981. *Introduction to Poetics.* Translated by Richard Howard, Vol. 1. of Theory and History of Literature. Minneapolis: University of Minnesota Press.

Tournadre, Claude. 1969. Propositions pour une psychologie sociale de *The Turn of the Screw. Etudes Anglaises* 22:259–69.

Trachtenberg, Stanley. 1965. The Return of the Screw. *Modern Fiction Studies* 11:180–83.

Turkle, Sherry. 1989. Why Are You Here? Review of books 1 and 2 of *The Papers of Jacques Lacan* (Cambridge, 1989). *London Review of Books* 11:3–4.

Tuveson, Ernest. 1972. *The Turn of the Screw:* A Palimpsest. *Studies in English Literature, 1500–1900* 12:783–800.

Twain, Mark. 1946. *The Viking Portable Mark Twain.* Edited by Bernard DeVoto. New York: Viking Press.

Vaid, Krishna Baldev. 1964. *Technique in the Tales of Henry James.* Cambridge: Harvard University Press.

Vampires. Review of *The Sacred Fount* and other titles). 1901. *New York Tribune* 8.

Van Doren, Mark, Katherine Anne Porter, and Allen Tate. 1944. Discussion (the radio panel on *The Turn of the Screw*, 1942). In *The New Invitation to Learning.* New York: New Home Library 1944, Reprinted in w 160–70.

Veeder, William, and Susan M. Griffin, eds. 1986. *The Art of Criticism: Henry James on the Theory and Practice of Fiction.* Chicago: University of Chicago Press.

Visnawanathan, Jacqueline. 1976. Innocent Bystander. *Hebrew University Studies in Literature* 4:27–47.

Vogelin, Eric. 1971. *The Turn of the Screw. Southern Review* 7:3–48.

Volume 12 of the New James. Review. 1908. *Louisville Courier Journal.* October 3:5.

Walcutt, Charles Child. 1956. Joyce's *Ulysses. Explicator* 14, no. 6, item 37.

Waldock, A. J. A. 1947. Mr. Edmund Wilson and *The Turn of the Screw. Modern Language Notes* 62:331–34. Reprinted in w 171–3.

Waley, Arthur. 1918. "The Turn of the Screw." *Egoist* 5:4.

Weber, Jean Jacques. 1982. Frame Construction and Frame Accommodation in a Gricean Analysis of Narrative. *Journal of Literary Semantics* 11:90–95.

Wellek, René. 1982. The Literary Criticism of W. C. Brownell. *Sewanee Review* 90:158–67.

Wells, Susan. 1985. *The Dialectics of Representation.* Baltimore: Johns Hopkins University Press.

West, Katharine. 1949. *A Chapter of Governesses: A Study of the Governess in English Fiction.* London: Martin Secker.

West, Muriel. 1964a. The Death of Miles in *The Turn of the Screw. PMLA* 79:283–88.

———. 1964b. *A Stormy Night with "The Turn of the Screw."* Phoenix: Frye and Smith.

Westcott, Glenway. 1934. A Sentimental Contribution. *Hound & Horn* 7:523–34.

Wilde, Oscar. 1983. *Two Society Comedies.* Edited by Ian Small. London: Ernest Benn.

Willen, Gerald. 1960. *A Casebook on Henry James's "The Turn of the Screw."* New York: Thomas Y. Crowell.

Wilson, Edmund. 1934. The Ambiguity of Henry James. *Hound & Horn* 7:385–406. Reprinted in w 115–53.

Wirth-Nesher, Hana. 1979. The Stranger Case of *The Turn of the Screw* and *Heart of Darkness. Studies in Short Fiction* 16:317–25.

Wolf, Christa. 1984. *Cassandra*. Translated by Jan van Huerck. New York: Farrar, Straus and Giroux.

Wolff, Robert Lee. 1941. The Genesis of *The Turn of the Screw. American Literature* 13:1–8. Reprinted in k 125–32

Woolf, Virginia. 1921. Henry James' Ghost Stories. *Times Literary Supplement.* New York: Harcourt, Brace and World.

———. 1958. The Ghost Stories. In *Granite and Rainbow.* New York: Harcourt, Brace and World.

Yeazell, Ruth Bernard. 1976. *Language and Knowledge in the Late Novels of Henry James.* Chicago: University of Chicago Press.

Young, Arlene. 1989. Hypothetical Discourse as Ficelle in *The Golden Bowl. American Literature* 74:382–97.

Zimmerman, Everett. 1970. Literary Tradition and "The Turn of the Screw." *Studies in Short Fiction* 7:634–37.

Index

DATE DUE MAY 08 1998

Demco, Inc. 38-293